THE HUMAN FACE OF LAW

The Human Face of Law

Essays in Honour of Donald Harris

KEITH HAWKINS

CLARENDON PRESS · OXFORD
1997

Oxford University Press, Great Clarendon Street, Oxford OX2 6DP

Oxford New York
Athens Auckland Bangkok Bogota Bombay
Buenos Aires Calcutta Cape Town Dar es Salaam
Delhi Florence Hong Kong Istanbul Karachi
Kuala Lumpur Madras Madrid Melbourne
Mexico City Nairobi Paris Singapore
Taipei Tokyo Toronto
and associated companies in
Berlin Ibadan

Oxford is a trade mark of Oxford University Press

Published in the United States
by Oxford University Press Inc., New York

10009-74443

British Library Cataloguing in Publication Data
Data available

Library of Congress Cataloging in Publication Data
Data available
ISBN 0–19–826247–7

1 3 5 7 9 10 8 6 4 2

Typeset by Hope Services (Abingdon) Ltd.
Printed in Great Britain
on acid-free paper by
Biddles Ltd., Guildford and King's Lynn

Preface

In the academic world those who build institutions and create the conditions in which scholarship can flourish tend to be taken for granted. Donald Harris is such a person, and one, it has to be said, who has never sought recognition of any kind. That he deserves recognition, however, is without question. This book is therefore intended to mark Don's retirement as Director of the Centre for Socio-Legal Studies at Oxford University and in some small way to recognize his various achievements: in contributing to the emergence of a new branch of learning, in founding and nurturing an academic institution, and in providing the opportunity for others to give of their best.

Don's academic work and career run parallel with and are part of the fundamental shift in the scope of legal scholarship that has occurred in Britain over the last twenty or thirty years in which traditional 'black-letter' approaches have been supplemented by a socio-legal perspective which recruits the insights of the social sciences. Don was a rarity among academic lawyers in the 1960s in recognizing the inadequacy of the existing tools of legal analysis in being able to say anything useful about the nature of law in its social context.

It is hard now to imagine how things were. Nearly thirty years ago there were few scholars, of whatever disciplinary persuasion, who were interested in law as a social phenomenon. By the late 1960s, criminology had been established long enough to be going through a period of internecine warfare (a sign of maturity in an academic endeavour?) with the attack on positivism. Indeed, many of the young lawyers of the 1960s who were dissatisfied with the state of academic study and research in law had gravitated into work in criminology and criminal justice. But lawyers who were interested in legal phenomena which lay beyond the usual—then rather tightly-drawn—boundaries of criminology and criminal justice were rare indeed. From small beginnings in the early 1970s, the nature of legal scholarship and of our conceptions of the law in general has been transformed. What once seemed daring, eccentric, or occasionally outlandish is now orthodox: socio-legal courses are now firmly established in the law-school curriculum; legal texts, including students' textbooks, bear the imprint of socio-legal thinking and research results, as any cursory study of law publishers' catalogues will indicate; social-science research into legal phenomena is now commonplace, often involving collaboration and dialogue between scholars at home and abroad; writing and empirical research about law are now much more sophisticated.

Donald Harris' career is inextricably bound up with the Centre for Socio-Legal Studies at Oxford University, an institution which he helped create, and which he directed for the first twenty-one years of its life. The Centre was founded in 1972 and for seven or eight years enjoyed a period of growth in what were, in retrospect, surprisingly optimistic times for the place. Then came a period of retrenchment and painful adjustment to rapidly reducing resources. The final period preceding Don's retirement was one of struggle following the decision of the Economic and Social Research Council in 1985 to end its core financial support for the Centre—despite constantly positive assessments of its work—with effect from 1993. Don spent his final years as Director fighting to keep the Centre alive. He worked to persuade the University to establish new posts in socio-legal studies at a time when its own resources were being significantly eroded; he strove to raise money for the Centre from other sources in Britain and the United States, and to have the Centre become an approved project for support by the Campaign for Oxford (the University's first fund-raising effort, launched in 1988). That the Centre has survived at all is an achievement.

*   *   *

Inviting people to contribute to such an enterprise as this is a pleasant task. But it is also an invidious one, for there are, without question, many others who would have welcomed the opportunity of joining in this tribute. In the end I invited contributions from those who were colleagues in the Centre at Don's retirement, together with a number of others who could be seen as representatives, as it were, of different groups of scholars who over the years have been associated with Don and the Centre, whether as members of staff, research students, or visitors. The papers are organized around themes that are either close to Don's own academic interests or drawn from major research programmes at the Centre for Socio-Legal Studies, thereby serving to illustrate the wide range of work that he has encouraged, supported, and conducted himself.

The book opens with a Prologue that is part biographical, part institutional history, and moves on to a paper which pursues some of the issues raised. This chapter is the work of two authors, Bridget Hutter and Sally Lloyd-Bostock, who were for many years colleagues of Don's in the Centre. They present a general essay which re-examines the relationship between law and social science and argues for the interdependence of theoretical and empirical research and social relevance in socio-legal studies.

Much of the material used by Hutter and Lloyd-Bostock is drawn from extensive research into social regulation conducted at the Centre, and this focus is taken up in the two papers which follow. The first of these also joins with another theme in the Centre's work, namely the historical analysis of law and its institutions. In the present volume this approach is represented in a paper by Peter Bartrip and R. M. Hartwell (respectively former Research Officer and Co-Director of the Centre). Their paper analyses nineteenth-century occupational-health legislation in the light of modern theories of economic regulation. The other paper, by Robert Baldwin, also a former member of the Centre's staff, is an assessment of command-and-control regulation. This essay reflects Don's interest in problems related to the efficiency and effectiveness of legal mechanisms, and the redesign of the legal apparatus where it is clearly not achieving its ostensible aims.

Don's strong support for economic analysis of law is represented by two papers. In the first, Anthony Ogus, a former Senior Research Fellow at the Centre, joins two of Don's major academic interests, economic analysis and tort law, in an analysis of exemplary damages. In the second, Paul Fenn and Neil Rickman, two of the economists formerly at the Centre, use the tools of economic analysis to revisit a favourite theme in Don's work, the behaviour of litigants in the pre-trial civil process.

Indeed, Don Harris was constantly interested in what lawyers (as well as litigants) do, and this is a central theme of a number of the papers that follow. Over the years the Centre has received countless academic visitors, the majority of whom have been from the United States: that is how Bill Felstiner's association with the Centre began. His contribution is both an essay and a proposal for research about the origins and consequences of professional neglect by lawyers. The work of the legal profession is further pursued by Philip Lewis, who was one of Don's first tutorial pupils at Oxford. Lewis' paper surveys current theory about lawyers' knowledge and goes on to explore empirically the nature of their knowledge in a specialized technological field. The focus on what lawyers do is extended in a paper by Doreen McBarnet, a senior member of the Centre's staff for many years, and Christopher Whelan, who is now at the Warwick Law School, having worked for several years as a Research Officer in the Centre. As the authors point out, their paper on 'creative compliance' is an example of the sort of socio-legal work in largely unresearched areas (in this case business, finance, and the law) that Donald Harris actively encouraged. Lawyers' activities in the business world is a theme also taken up by Ross Cranston, whose paper explores the nature of lawyers' involvement in commercial practice. Cranston, now the Cassel Professor of Commercial Law at London University, was the first research student to come to the Centre for Socio-Legal Studies, and wrote his doctoral dissertation under Don Harris' supervision.

Socio-legal research in family law has been a constant ingredient in the Centre's research programme from its inception, and is represented in this book by an essay by John Eekelaar and Mavis Maclean which deals with the property and financial consequences of divorce. Eekelaar is a long-serving member of the Oxford Law Faculty, and has been associated for many years with the Centre as a part-time member of its research staff. Much of his work at the Centre has been carried out (in precisely the sort of law and social science partnership that Donald Harris believed in) with Mavis Maclean, who was herself one of the first research staff to be appointed at the Centre.

The last essay is by Robert Stevens, an academic visitor to the Centre on a number of occasions and now Master of Pembroke College, Oxford. His paper returns to some of the themes taken up at the beginning of the book and considers the current tensions between judges and politicians. Most socio-legal research has shifted the focus of empirical research outside the courtroom, and Stevens' paper can be read as a plea for socio-legal scholars not to forsake the judiciary. Accordingly, he discusses some important and topical questions that deserve socio-legal analysis.

* * *

This book is an opportunity to reflect on what Donald Harris has achieved, as well as an occasion for some of us to mark his exceptional contribution as a scholar, an institution-builder, an academic administrator, and, perhaps especially, as a colleague who constantly looked on his dealings with others with a human face. We pay tribute to the research environment which Don created, in which the values of intellectual freedom, curiosity, and tolerance were emphasized, and to Don's open-mindedness, fortitude, and unquenchable optimism in the face of adversity. This volume is presented to him by its contributors, with admiration and affection.

KEITH HAWKINS
Oxford, April 1996

Editor's Acknowledgements

I am most grateful to Vanessa Spearman and Ann Hawes for helping me to prepare texts and disks for publication, and to Richard Hart at Oxford University Press for his advice and patience.

I would also like to thank Sally Lloyd-Bostock and Mavis Maclean for helpful comments on my own contributions to this book.

Notes on Contributors

ROBERT BALDWIN is Professor of Law at the London School of Economics and Political Science where he teaches Public Law, Regulation, and Criminal Law. He researches mainly in the fields of Administrative Law and Regulation, interests which first developed during his research officership at the Centre for Socio-Legal Studies from 1980 to 1983. He is the author of numerous articles and books, the most recent of which, *Rules and Government*, was published by Clarendon Press in 1995.

PETER BARTRIP is Senior Lecturer in History at Nene College, Northampton, and a Research Associate at the Centre for Socio-Legal Studies. He is author of *Mirror of Medicine: A History of the British Medical Journal* (Clarendon Press, 1990); *Themselves Writ Large; A History of the British Medical Association* (BMJ Publishing Group, 1996) and two monographs on workmen's compensation in nineteenth- and twentieth-century Britain. He has also published numerous papers on historical aspects of law and society issues.

ROSS CRANSTON is Cassel Professor of Commercial Law in the University of London, at the London School of Economics. He worked as a doctoral student under Don Harris from 1972 to 1976.

JOHN EEKELAAR is a Fellow of Pembroke College, Oxford, Reader in Law, University of Oxford, and Senior Research Fellow at the Centre for Socio-Legal Studies, Oxford. He has researched and published extensively in family law, his publications including *Family Law and Social Policy* (Weidenfeld and Nicolson, 1978 and 1984); *Regulating Divorce* (Clarendon Press, 1991); *The Protection of Children: State Intervention and Family Life* (Basil Blackwell, 1983) (with Robert Dingwall and Topsy Murray); and *Maintenance after Divorce* (Clarendon Press, 1986) (with Mavis Maclean).

W. L. F. FELSTINER is Professor, Law and Society Program, University of California, Santa Barbara, and Distinguished Research Professor of Law at the University of Wales, Cardiff. He is General Editor of the Onati International Series on Law and Society and President of the Working Group on the Comparative Study of Legal Professions. He is a former Director of the American Bar Foundation. His research has included studies of dispute processing, litigation costs, mass litigation, mediation, plea bargaining, and divorce lawyers.

PAUL FENN is the Norwich Union Professor of Insurance Studies in the School of Management and Finance at the University of Nottingham. He was appointed to the Chair in October 1993, prior to which he was Research Fellow in economics at the Centre for Socio-Legal Studies at Oxford. During his time at the Centre under the direction of Don Harris he was associated with the major research programmes undertaken there on compensation for personal injury, and on health-and-safety regulation. He has written or edited four books and numerous articles in peer-reviewed journals on the general themes of personal-injury litigation, liability insurance, health economics, and the economics of workplace risk. He has contributed to the public-policy debate relating to the proposals for no-fault compensation for medical injuries, and to the ongoing debate about the future of the welfare state and the role of the private insurance industry in this future.

MAX HARTWELL is an Australian. A graduate of the University of Sydney, he studied for his D.Phil at Oxford. From 1950–56 he was Dean of the Faculty of Humanities and Social Science in the University of New South Wales. From 1956–78 he was Reader in Recent Social and Economic History in the University of Oxford and Professorial Fellow of Nuffield College. Between 1978 and 1981 he was Co-Director (with Donald Harris) of the Centre for Socio-Legal Studies. He later held chairs in the University of Virginia and in the Graduate School of Business in the University of Chicago. His academic interests include the Early History of Australia, the Industrial Revolution in England, and the History of Modern Liberalism.

KEITH HAWKINS has worked at the Centre for Socio-Legal Studies since it opened in 1972. He is now Reader in Law and Society, Oxford University, and Fellow and Tutor of Oriel College, Oxford. His research interests are in legal decision-making, particularly in the area of governmental regulation, where his publications include *Environment and Enforcement* (Clarendon Press, 1984) and *The Uses of Discretion* (Clarendon Press, 1992). He serves as General Editor of *Oxford Socio-Legal Studies* (Clarendon Press) and as Co-Editor of *Law and Policy* (Basil Blackwell).

BRIDGET M. HUTTER is Lecturer in Sociology at the London School of Economics and Political Science, and was educated at the Universities of London and Oxford. She has been a Morris Ginsburg Fellow at the LSE, a British Academy Post-Doctoral Fellow, a Research Fellow at the Centre for Socio-Legal Studies, Oxford, and a Senior Research Fellow and Lecturer in Sociology at Jesus College, Oxford. She is author of *The Reasonable Arm of the Law?* (Clarendon Press, 1988) and a forthcoming book on *Compliance* (Clarendon Press, 1997). She has written numerous articles and reports on the subject of regulation. A further book on the impact of occupational health-and-safety regulation upon the railway industry is now being drafted.

PHILIP LEWIS is a Senior Research Fellow at the Oxford Centre for Socio-Legal Studies, a Senior Scholar at the Stanford Law School, and an Emeritus Fellow of All Souls College, Oxford. He was a Research Fellow in Law at All Souls from 1965–88. With Professor R. L. Abel he started the Working Group on Legal Professions of the Research Committee on the Sociology of Law, and edited *Lawyers in Society* (3 volumes, University of California Press, 1988–9). He has also edited *Law and Technology in the Pacific Community* (Westview Press, 1994). His current research is in the response of lawyers to technological change and their contributions to it.

SALLY LLOYD-BOSTOCK is a Senior Research Fellow in psychology and law at the Centre for Socio-Legal Studies. She joined the Centre in 1974, following her doctorate in psychology at Oxford, to which she has since added a BA in jurisprudence. She is a Fellow of The British Psychological Society and of Wolfson College, Oxford. During her time at the Centre she has conducted extensive research in psychological aspects of civil disputes and legal decision-making, principally within the Centre's research programmes on compensation and support for illness and injury, the regulation of health and safety, and law and health care. She has also actively pursued a long-standing interest in theoretical aspects of the relationship between psychology and law. Her current research is on complaints to hospitals and medical-negligence claims. Most recently she has been studying the effects of providing jurors with information about the defendant's previous convictions.

MAVIS MACLEAN has worked at the Centre for Socio-Legal Studies almost since its inception, studying the relationship between family law and family policy across Europe. She has written with John Eekelaar on the socio-economic aspects of divorce for women and children. She edited with Jacek Kurczewski a volume *Families, Politics and the Law* (Clarendon Press, 1994) bringing together material from Poland and the United Kingdom. She is currently President of the ISA Research Committee on the Sociology of Law.

DOREEN MCBARNET is Senior Research Fellow and University Research Lecturer at the Centre for Socio-Legal Studies. From an original research interest in criminal justice and the nature and ideology of law, published in a number of articles and notably in the book *Conviction: Law, the State and the Construction of Justice* (Macmillan, 1981), she has gone on to work in the area of business, finance, and the law. This has involved developing a programme of research encompassing the substantive areas of insolvency, tax evasion and avoidance, corporate finance, and the Single European Market.

ANTHONY OGUS was a Senior Research Fellow at the Oxford Centre for Socio-Legal Studies from 1975–78. He is currently Professor of Law at the University of Manchester. He is the author of *Regulation: Legal Form and Economic Theory* (Clarendon Press, 1994) and other publications on law and economics, and regulation.

NEIL RICKMAN has a BA in Economics from the University of Durham (1988) and a Ph.D in Economics from McGill University in Montreal (1995). From 1990–95 he was a Research Officer at the Centre for Socio-Legal Studies, and Lecturer in Economics at Pembroke College, Oxford. He is currently Foundation Fund Lecturer in Economics at the University of Surrey. His research interests are in applied microeconomic theory, with a number of interests in the regulation and delivery of legal services. In this area he has published articles and book chapters on contingent fees, legal aid, legal-expenses insurance, professional regulation, and civil procedure. He has also advised the Lord Chancellor's Department and Lord Woolf's Committee on the Reform of Civil Procedure.

ROBERT STEVENS, a Barrister, is Master of Pembroke College, Oxford, and also serves as Counsel to Covington and Burling, Washington, DC, and London. He was formerly Professor of Law at Yale (1959–76), Provost of Tulane University (1976–8), President of Haverford College (1978–87) and Chancellor, the University of California, Santa Cruz (1987–91).

CHRISTOPHER WHELAN spent nine years at the Centre for Socio-Legal Studies before joining the Law School at the University of Warwick where he is currently a Senior Lecturer. His work at the Centre involved participation in a major project on dispute resolution, informality, and justice. This led to a monograph which he edited on *Small Claims Courts: A Comparative Study* (Clarendon Press, 1990). He has collaborated with both economists and sociologists on a number of research projects. He now specializes in Commercial Law and Labour Law and his current research interests lie in the areas of business, finance, and insolvency.

Contents

Contents

Prologue: Donald Harris and the Early Years of the Oxford Centre

KEITH HAWKINS

I BEGINNINGS

Optimism is one of the first things you notice about Donald Harris. It is not surprising to learn, then, that at school and later as a university student law held a particular fascination for him, for here were rules that purported to organize society and to regulate human behaviour. Moreover, in contrast with other disciplines whose subject matter was determined by natural forces, law was a human artefact whose substance was entirely under human control and therefore perfectable. Don is quick now to acknowledge an irony in all of this in light of his subsequent scepticism about the capacity of rules to serve successfully as a mechanism for the attainment of social order. But in those days he clung to what he now regards as the idealistic view that, by changing the rules, you could change society for the better.

Don was born and grew up in New Zealand, the son of a schoolmaster and the third of five boys, all but one of whom have become involved in education in one way or another. At school an early interest in architecture was overtaken by an enthusiasm for law when, having discovered that architects had to take a law course, Don found the architecture of the legal system much more absorbing. He did not begin at university by reading law, however, but under the influence of an older brother who was a classics lecturer he took a degree in classics before turning to law as a graduate student. Don read for an undergraduate law degree and then completed his law studies in New Zealand with a Master's Degree. He took this part-time since, during the course of his graduate work, he was called to the New Zealand Bar and had to combine his LL.M with practice in a law firm. It was while reading for his LL.M degree that Don won a law scholarship designed to allow New Zealand students to spend time abroad. The award presented the opportunity of applying to Oxford and following in the footsteps of an older brother who had been a Rhodes Scholar at Balliol (though having already married, Don himself was ineligible for a Rhodes Scholarship). Don decided to take what was then the two-year Bachelor of Civil Law (BCL) graduate course at his brother's college.

Much of Don's enormous knowledge of substantive law was gained in his early years at Oxford, first as a student and subsequently as a law tutor. It was as a BCL student that he first developed some conception of the legal system as a whole, and of the interrelationship of its constituent parts. The BCL course was comprised entirely of traditional legal analysis in which the legal rules, their internal consistency (or otherwise), and their relationship to broader legal principles were examined. As a graduate law student Don was sent to other colleges for every one of his BCL subjects, where he was given a thorough grounding in a wide range of legal subjects by a number of distinguished tutors. Among those he recalls most readily were two Brasenose lawyers, Barry Nicholas (who taught Roman Law) and Ronald Maudsley (who taught Trusts); and there were also classes in Conflict of Laws from John Morris at Magdalen. One tutor for whom Don had a particular regard, and whose influence he readily acknowledges, was Peter Carter at Wadham, who taught Evidence and Conflict of Laws. Carter was evidently a formidable tutor whose rigorous approach to teaching Don still recalls vividly.

The picture that emerges of Donald Harris as student is of a young man, at once hard-working and thoroughly engrossed in the law, yet also a bit of a young turk who continually questioned the received wisdom. He recounts his persistence in debating matters with members of the Law Faculty in the BCL classes, concluding that he 'must have been a blessed nuisance'. Don also appreciated the often tough and combative character of the Oxford tutorial system—standing exposed at the other end of the wicket, as he puts it, unable to hide behind a larger group, as one might in a lecture, but instead having to bat back whatever the tutor bowls up. He unquestionably flourished in this testing environment and capped his student days by winning the Vinerian Scholarship, awarded annually to the person finishing top of the University's list in the BCL.

Having completed two years at Oxford, Don returned to New Zealand under a moral commitment to work in the law firm which had employed him while he was taking his LL.M. A major turning point arrived soon after his re-entry into law practice, however, when Balliol College offered Don a tutorial fellowship, though it took him some time, he says, to 'pluck up the courage to ask my partners to release me'. In October 1956, however, Don returned to Oxford take up his fellowship. Had Balliol not offered him the post, the story would have been different, and he would probably not have pursued an academic career at all.

Don's was a new tutorial fellowship, Balliol's second in law, and he was rapidly drawn into the life of a college tutor. His teaching burden at first was extremely heavy, because for his first three years he also served as a Lecturer in Law at Worcester College, with a stint of six hours a week at Worcester to add to his nine hours a week at Balliol. Don's teaching was, of course, accompanied by the other duties of the tutorial fellow: pastoral care of students, admissions, committees, College offices, and the like. Moreover, though his heart was in contract and tort teaching, Don had to develop a command of several other legal subjects because the senior law fellow at Balliol, Theodore Tyler, believed in College-teaching self-sufficiency and regarded it as a disgrace that his undergraduates should have to be sent outside the College for tuition. Don now recognizes that his fifteen-hour-a-week stint was a blessing in disguise, because it gave him an enormously broad knowledge of substantive law and a thorough understanding of law and its institutions. There was, of course, a cost: 'in that first year', he says, 'I just about killed myself.' But as his career as a tutor unfolded, he was able gradually to shed subjects and thereby reduce the burden by restricting the range of subjects he taught.

Other burdens, however, increased. Don became Senior Tutor of Balliol six years after being elected—'far too soon', he says now—and a few years later Estates Bursar. These College offices in fact proved to be extremely important, for they equipped Don not only with the political and administrative skills he was to deploy to great effect some years later but also with the essential knowledge of the arcane ways of the University: 'there's no doubt that having been a Senior Tutor and Estates Bursar, I knew quite a lot about how Oxford worked.'

It was during his time as a tutor that Don gradually formed an interest in socio-legal analysis. He felt uneasy about the way in which law was conventionally conceived of and studied, and, as a tort and contract specialist, was disturbed that there was in Britain in the 1960s virtually no interest in understanding the workings of the civil legal system. He sums up his views then as driven by 'dissatisfaction with library-based research, [and] the realization that . . . the gap between the rules in the books and the rules in action was enormous'. While this notion of the gap between legal word and legal deed has been much criticized as an organizing idea in recent years, there is no question that for many lawyers of the 1960s and 1970s it was a compelling conception, one responsible for encouraging them to think seriously about the socio-legal perspective.

Don's response to his personal intellectual dissatisfaction was the very practical one of exploring the 'gap' problem by conducting an empirical study of not only the legal, but also the social and economic, consequences of road accidents in Oxford. This pilot research project was funded by the Nuffield Foundation, and carried out in the late 1960s. Significantly, it was conducted in a multi-disciplinary way with a research assistant, and input from an economist and a statistician. Though the project was relatively modest in scale, it proved to be important for a number of reasons. It was to be the precursor of the major study of compensation and support for illness and injury that Don later directed at the Centre. Equally important, however, was the formative influence this project was to have on Don's approach to the conception and design of socio-legal research, for in this pilot study were the seeds of the basic ideas about the conduct of empirical research which Don was later able to put into practice at the Centre for Socio-Legal Studies. It was here, for example, that Don's belief in the value of collaborative, multi-disciplinary social scientific research on law began to take shape. The experience gained from the pilot study convinced Don that, in his words, 'a mere lawyer' could not hope to carry out research on the workings and impact of legal rules without the active collaboration of social scientists. 'After my initial experience [on the Oxford Pilot Survey]', he says, 'I was clearly of the opinion that unless lawyers could win over social scientists and get them to take this seriously as a new area of inter-disciplinary effort, lawyers on their own weren't going to make progress. That was the genesis of my belief about the Centre—we had to get genuine social scientists to make it their long-term commitment. . . . I was most concerned to carry respect on the social science side for any effort I was involved in. We couldn't give social scientists the impression that we were simple-minded lawyers playing around in the social sciences.'

There were not many law academics at that time who thought in the same way. In the late 1960s few wanted to redirect their scholarship to encompass empirical analysis of legal phenomena. But those who did were no longer content to analyse legislation or the latest judicial utterance, but began to be concerned to find out what the legal apparatus actually looked like in the real world. In reading unpublished papers produced in conjunction with early meetings of like-minded scholars, one becomes aware of an acute feeling among the participants of how little was known about what they called 'law in operation'. Their questions were, accordingly, not the sort of questions academic lawyers were much accustomed to thinking about. Instead they wanted to know how law actually worked. What difference did it make? How did it co-exist with other forms of social ordering and support? Some were prompted by a desire to devote to the civil legal arena the same sort of attention that the criminal law had been receiving from criminologists for some years. Lawyers (or, more precisely in some cases, those originally trained as lawyers) were, then, the driving force for social research on law and society in Britain—and still are, for the most part. Relatively few social scientists, then and now, have taken law and the legal system as a focus for their own work. Given the fundamentally social character of law and its powerful and pervasive presence in society, this apparent disinterest in law and legal institutions was, and remains, to legal eyes surprising in the extreme.

The academic interest in law in its social context was also driven primarily, but not exclusively, by questions of social policy. Civil law reform and social research seemed important in the late 1960s in light of the rapid increase in the number of law-reform proposals, many of which were based on assumptions that existing rules created hardship or anomalies. The case for socio-legal research to buttress informed ideas for change in the legal system seemed compelling: proposals were often appraised on totally inadequate evidence, and law reform was thought much too serious a matter to be left to guesswork; those making propos- als for reform had only limited personal experience or factual informa- tion on which to base their ideas; frequently, it seemed, little or no such information existed and reformers were therefore left to their own hunches as to what actually happened in the real world. Legal practi- tioners, meanwhile, saw only part of the working of legal rules, and then, for the most part, only the exceptional or unusual case: knowledge of the typical or the representative was almost always lacking. The position was exacerbated by the fact that the Law Commission had been unable to conduct its own research or to set up its own research unit. In these cir- cumstances it seemed essential to use social scientific approaches to put legal rules in their social context and enable an understanding to be developed of how legal rules worked, and the circumstances in which they failed to work, or to work as intended. The dominant view in all of this, not surprisingly, is the lawyer's.

II THE PREHISTORY OF THE CENTRE

Donald Harris was also one of the first people to begin thinking about the possibilities of creating an institutional focus in Britain for socio-legal work to give greater direction and purpose to the seemingly limited and fragmented academic interest and research in the field. There were few socio-legal initiatives in universities or in government departments in the late 1960s, and those that had been taken were modest.

The momentum in support of some sort of innovation built up slowly, as like-minded people began exchanging ideas. One of the moving spir- its, and a possible source of financial support, was the Joseph Rowntree Memorial Trust, under whose auspices a series of meetings were held to discuss the prospects of setting up some sort of centre for socio-legal research and to map out possible lines of research. It was in the course of various meetings held at that time that Don met O. R. (later Lord) McGregor (then Professor of Social Institutions at London University), who was to become the Centre's first Director. Other participants were K. W. Blyth of the Rowntree Memorial Trust and Professor L. C. B. Gower (at that time a Law Commissioner). A little later some more people became involved, including two Oxford academics, Otto Kahn-Freund,

Professor of Comparative Law (who turned out to be a major supporter of the Centre in its early days, serving as the first Chairman of its Standing Committee), and Mrs Jean Floud of Nuffield College.

It was decided to make an approach to the (then) Social Science Research Council (SSRC), which was still only a few years old, and understandably preoccupied with possible initiatives. According to Don, Andrew Shonfield, the Chairman of the SSRC, 'was incredibly receptive to the idea' of supporting some form of socio-legal activity, 'and I later learnt that it was because the SSRC was looking around for new initiatives to impress their governmental paymaster. And so the idea of taking on law . . . was very appealing.' In 1970 the SSRC set up an *ad hoc* 'Socio-Legal Panel', chaired by Mr Lewis Waddilove of the Joseph Rowntree Memorial Trust, to advise Council on how to deploy its financial resources to develop the field, with a membership that included Floud, Gower, Sir William Mansfield Cooper, Professor W. J. M. Mackenzie of Glasgow University, Shonfield, and Baroness Barbara Wootton.

It is instructive to look back at the thinking of the groups which met under the auspices of the Joseph Rowntree Memorial Trust and the SSRC. They appeared to have a common conception of the way forward. Once the principle of a funding initiative was accepted, the question then arose as to how financial support was to be deployed. Indeed, it is interesting in looking back to note how consequential the early reasoning which led to support for socio-legal studies and to the establishment of the Centre has proved to be.

The immediate dilemma was whether to concentrate resources on a new institution, or spread them around existing institutions. The primary disadvantage of a concentration of resources was thought to be that support for individual work might be drawn off and possible growth in the field stunted, that such a centre might, in other words, monopolize resources and personnel. The resources currently available for socio-legal work were slight and scattered, however, and it was concluded that a concentration of effort in the support of one centre, rather than its dispersal across different universities, was preferable for a number of reasons. It was believed that a centre would demonstrate the value and significance of the inter-disciplinary area more effectively and more quickly than fragmented work, however good it might be, in a number of institutions. Some sort of centre would make the best use of the small number of keen and competent people then available; it would more effectively build up knowledge of research methods and materials; it could help to stimulate developments elsewhere and to consolidate otherwise dispersed activities; it could offer excellent opportunities for training graduates, teachers, and researchers, and thereby support the wider establishment. Most importantly, a centre would offer the best environment in which to promote the continuous collaboration between lawyers and social scientists upon which the development of the research depended. One instructive example here was the Institute of Criminology at Cambridge, where a concentration of resources had been rapidly followed by the extension of teaching and research to universities which had previously had no provision for it. A centre might also allow for the development of valuable links with its host university. It was thought essential that close relations be maintained between the centre and its university, to provide assistance for teachers who wanted to do research in the field, and to provide facilities for graduate students researching for higher degrees. The SSRC was readily persuaded by the arguments in favour of a centre. This was in fact in line with its general thinking about institutional support at the time, as the Research Council's establishment of units for research into industrial relations and race relations was already under way.

So far as the question of what the support was to be for was concerned, it was agreed that the pre-eminent organizing idea was a commitment to research in the socio-legal field. This was because there was a strong sense that so little was known about the legal system, its processes, impact, and the like, that the primary effort should be to advance knowledge as quickly as possible. The research to be engaged in was intended to be long-term and, for the most part, large-scale. Once these decisions had been made, other important choices fell more easily into place.

First, it was felt that there was a strong case for research by staff on a full-time basis, so that they would not be burdened by the usual teaching and administrative responsibilities of university academics. A second important idea was that the socio-legal research to be carried out should for the most part be directly relevant to matters of public policy. While this was a reflection of the dominant concerns of legal scholars in the 1960s and 1970s, it was not regarded as an exclusive commitment, since it was also believed to be important to address more fundamental questions, as well as to develop research of a comparative kind since (as a paper prepared after one of the meetings put it) 'it would be intellectually restricting and distorting to limit investigation to the immediately utilitarian'. Though it was not long before much of the work at the Centre began to address questions that were less directly bound up with policy issues, the original approach was vindicated some years later in the pages of the Report into the future of the SSRC commissioned from Lord Rothschild. Writing of work which 'ought in any event to be undertaken at the public expense', Lord Rothschild cited the Centre's research into compensation for illness and injury. His Report also published a letter from the Chairman of the Law Commission which stressed the importance that body attached 'to making proper use of the social sciences in determining law reform'. Often, the letter continued, 'the main source of relevant data has been the SSRC and in particular the Oxford Centre for Socio-Legal Studies. Withdrawal of financial support for this socio-legal research could therefore have serious consequences for future law reform.'

Thirdly, and in consequence, research that was empirically-based and interdisciplinary was to be emphasized. Indeed, one of the major justifications for a centre of full-time research staff was that its members should be in a position to engage in time-consuming collaborative work in the field that university teachers might not be free to undertake. The hope was that the Centre staff would be able to undertake such projects unconstrained by the barriers to communication and contact that regularly arise in universities organized around the usual faculty and departmental structures. The interdisciplinary character of the research enterprise was intended, furthermore, to involve an equal commitment to law and to social science in the hope that effective relations between lawyers and social scientists would be created. While lawyers were not regarded as possessing the appropriate research and methodological skills, at the same time social scientists were thought to be in need of legal expertise in the conduct of any research enquiry about law. The key therefore was to undertake collaborative research which pooled the knowledge and skills of both. Equal partnership appealed not only because it seemed essential in the development of the sociology of law in the United Kingdom, but also because impetus could be given to initiating research in law and economics, which was already well-established in the USA. It followed from this that the Centre should be directed by both a lawyer and a social scientist in partnership, each reflecting the equal standing of the two major perspectives.

Fourthly, it was thought desirable that the research should explore those areas of legal life that seemed to be little known or understood, or otherwise to direct enquiry towards areas or approaches which seemed ripe for research and were being generally overlooked elsewhere. This argued for a certain amount of substantive demarcation, and in particular for, wherever possible, avoiding research that trespassed into territory already settled by criminology. Civil law and its processes therefore became the focus. Research on criminal law was not entirely abandoned in the event, however, as some of the Centre staff later began to embark on a series of analyses of the use of the criminal law in regulating business behaviour and organizational life, an important topic rather overlooked by criminologists. It also argued for the development of disciplinary perspectives on law that were neglected elsewhere, a rationale that was responsible for the Centre's early involvement in research in law and economics, law and psychology, and, a little later, law and language.

Fifthly, research at the Centre should be supplemented by a measure of teaching and training. It was part of the *raison d'etre* of the Centre to prepare a corps of researchers who would gain substantial experience, and could help develop the subject of socio-legal studies elsewhere. The aim of training a new generation of socio-legal scholars was to be met partly by the important expertise to be gained on the job by those appointed to research posts, but in particular by the election each year of a small number of research students who were to conduct research for Masters' and Doctors' degrees. It was a conscious decision to foster graduate research work, and not to get involved in undergraduate teaching, which would have been an unnecessary distraction: 'teaching is so important', in Don's view, 'you can't give it second place'. As time passed, research students became an important part of the life of the Centre, and their work was increasingly integrated into the Centre's projects. Over the years there has been a substantial dispersal, both at home and abroad, not only of members of the Centre's staff but also of large numbers of research students who have gone to other research institutions and universities, having had an opportunity to learn about and gain experience in the socio-legal field at the Centre. Indeed, Don takes particular pleasure in the number of former Centre staff and students who have been appointed to Chairs in British universities. Around the nucleus of research staff and students it was intended that there would be a number of academic visitors who would bring to the Centre their own expertise and experience which could contribute to the education of those at the Centre, whilst benefiting from close contact with the Centre's own staff and projects.

These, then, seemed to be the priorities. There remained the question of location. There were the beginnings of interest in socio-legal studies in a number of universities in the early 1970s, and it is quite conceivable that the Centre could have been located in two or three places. In the end, however, it was the facilities which the University of Oxford possessed, and, in particular, the support and enthusiasm for the socio-legal enterprise of some of its senior academics, who now included H. L. A. Hart, as well as Otto Kahn-Freund and Jean Floud, that persuaded the SSRC to locate the Centre in Oxford.

III EARLY YEARS

These broad outlines of its remit were settled before the Centre came into existence, and the remaining matters relating to the Centre's operation were worked out in an interpretation of its remit in the early years of its life by Don, McGregor, and the first research staff to be appointed. But while these early decisions left a deep imprint on the Centre's structure and work, the initial ideas about the nature of the research enterprise, powerfully moulded as they were by the interests of scholars of law and social policy, were later able to grow in different directions.

The way in which funding for the Centre and the accompanying arrangements for its accountability were organized proved to be highly influential in shaping the research programmes. The accountability of the Centre to its Research Council was real and direct. The jobs of the staff and the future of the Centre were dependent on the outcome of regular reviews conducted every few years by committees appointed for the purpose by SSRC (later the ESRC). Accordingly, in the early years of such an institution it was accepted that its senior staff could not be given security of tenure comparable with that enjoyed by equivalent teaching staff in universities, while it was recognized at the same time that academic status and tenure were vital in attracting and retaining staff. The Centre and its staff were not given an indefinite life, but rather an indeterminate one of up to ten years, subject to a satisfactory review of the Centre's work, to be conducted every five years or so by an independent panel of experts from other universities. This meant that staff could be assured of at least a five-year period of tenure for the completion of projects should a decision be made to close the Centre. These periods now seem generous, though in the 1970s, of course, university staff had expectations of jobs tenured to the retirement age and many of the Centre's researchers who were appointed felt that they were taking a risk ('they were very anxious days early on', as Don observed, 'because we knew we were going to be reviewed at least every five years'). The tenure arrangements, though not open-ended, were generous so as to attract staff who might otherwise prefer the security of tenured university appointments, but equally importantly, to enable long-term, large-scale research projects to be undertaken. The idea of career researchers based in universities working in parallel with university teachers was very important in the SSRC of the 1970s, as well as in the Centre, though it receded into the background in the 1980s, and was laid to rest, so far as the Centre was concerned, by the ESRC's decision in 1985 to end its financial support after another eight years (in 1993), subject to a further satisfactory review in 1989. Under both regimes (pre- and post-1985), staff had the freedom to do research, it is true, but at the cost of insecurity, and regular, and very time-consuming, reviews of their work.

In the event, the Centre was always reviewed favourably. It has to be said that for the Centre's staff the review process was extremely distracting, and seemingly interminable, and while they could appreciate the importance of accountability, the time and effort involved seemed excessively intrusive so far as their work was concerned. The first review, a preliminary one, took place in 1975, and was followed by full reviews in 1979, 1985, 1989, and 1993 by SSRC/ESRC panels. In 1990 the University of Oxford conducted its own review of the Centre (together with the University's Centre for Criminological Research), an enquiry whose findings contributed substantially to the Centre's survival in Oxford after the ending of ESRC support in 1993.

The open and relatively long-term structure of the Centre's funding had the great advantage of making certain kinds of large-scale, long-term collaborative research possible, as had been intended. For example, the programme of work on compensation and support for illness and injury, directed by Donald Harris, and the programme of interrelated studies of occupational health-and-safety regulation, both of which involved sizeable groups of the research staff, would have been very much more difficult (if not impossible) to bring off if the research staff had had to work within the constraints of normal university life. The funding structure was equally important because it allowed Don to give the staff space to read, think, and develop an intimate knowledge of new areas that called for research. As a result, staff were free to pursue their work less troubled by the constraints of time, which allowed very careful planning and preparation of their particular research projects. While funding for the Centre's work was structured in this relatively open way, it was possible to design research led by scholarly objectives (while the present shift to contract funding means that the aims, scope, and approach of research enquiries are increasingly at risk of being determined by others). The SSRC clearly regarded itself as the sole provider for the Centre in the 1970s. Indeed, the Research Council issued an instruction to the Centre not to seek outside funding for research from other bodies: if such funds were required, application should be made to SSRC (a prohibition not lifted until 1982).

The commitment to collaborative, interdisciplinary research was reflected from the start in a clear desire to hire and involve social scientists in the Centre as equal partners with lawyers, with fairly equal proportions of legally-trained staff and social scientists. Donald Harris always took a notion of 'parity of esteem' between social scientists and lawyers very seriously, both in the Centre's recruitment and in its management, by which Don meant giving the same degree of attention and intellectual respect to other disciplines as one would to one's own, while recognizing that lawyers could not be expected to match the specialist knowledge of economists, sociologists, and others. His hope was that sociologists and economists who worked on socio-legal projects would not feel that they were merely serving as a research tool for lawyers. The first social-science disciplines to be encouraged were intended to be sociology, social administration, and economics (which were, in fact, disciplines well represented in staff appointments in the early days). While sociology and economics have provided the majority of the appointments over the years, the Centre has also sought to foster research in psychology and law, and in social history of law. This has meant an inevitable neglect of other important perspectives. There have been, for example, only two anthropologists among the staff (both for relatively short periods), and no political scientists. It might be added that it remains a matter for regret for Don that social scientists continue to seem uninterested in researching into legal phenomena, and he is concerned for the future development of socio-legal studies if the subject is simply left in the hands of well-meaning lawyers who have acquired what may sometimes amount to only a modest knowledge of social science. 'All I could hope is that we could capture the interest of some younger, able social scientists', he says. 'That's what a full-time research Centre could do.' He is still keen to encourage those trained in social science, as well as those with dual law and social-science qualifications, to work on law, commenting that 'the interesting thing is that I've seen my own horizons widened immensely by social scientists. I am terribly privileged that I have had this opportunity to see more widely.'

When the Centre was set up, the SSRC was keen to build on existing knowledge and enthusiasms in the socio-legal field, and this has been another of the views to have pervaded the subsequent development of the Centre's research in various ways. It was expected, for instance, that McGregor would develop his research interests in family law (thereby starting a line of research which still flourishes), and Don would pursue his enquiries into compensation for misfortune. Since then, it has become a practice in the Centre that research programmes have gradually developed over the years in such a way as to take advantage of the staff's academic interests and expertise acquired in work on a particular project, hence the Centre's research programmes have tended to be confined to particular, but broad, areas though they have spawned substantial numbers of individual projects within those areas. Building on the staff's especial interests has, in Don's view, proved to be extremely productive for 'once we had invested our initial effort, there was a regular flow of material.' In fact it is fair to say that the Centre's output has been very large. Its most recently-compiled list of publications (produced in 1993), records nearly 100 books and more than 450 articles. Laying the foundation for this took time, but the eventual reward was substantial.

Another important early policy decision was one made about the Centre's external relations. Don recognized at the beginning that emerging socio-legal interest was by no means confined to Oxford and was very keen not to proselytize. The Centre staff were also very conscious of the fact that they, like others, were learning the ropes, and that it was inappropriate for the Centre to be seen as trying to occupy centre stage as socio-legal studies developed in the United Kingdom. It should be acknowledged, however, that Don was later very supportive, in his unobtrusive way, of efforts made in the early years to establish the Socio-Legal Studies Association in Britain, committing significant amounts of the Centre's resources and staff time to the venture.

This is not the place to chronicle the various comings and goings of staff and students, nor to rehearse the various programmes of research that have been undertaken at the Centre. It remains to observe that the Centre came into existence in October 1972, staffed by four part-time members, with O. R. McGregor as Director and Donald Harris as Associate Director. The Centre's research began in a modest way, but as soon as the first period of staff recruitment was over, work proceeded on a variety of fronts. McGregor, however, was heavily involved in a variety of national Committees from whose membership he could not extricate himself, and he was unable to devote the time that had originally been intended to the Centre's early development. Indeed, in every sense Don was from the Centre's beginning *de facto* Director. McGregor resigned in February 1975 when he was asked to take over the Chairmanship of the Royal Commission on the Press, following the death of Mr Justice Finer (with whom McGregor had worked as a member of the earlier Committee on One-Parent families), and Don was appointed Director in his own right.

In the early years the Centre was treated generously by the SSRC (which was itself treated much more generously by the government of the day) and it grew rapidly. By 1978–9 (the time of its first full review) it had a full-time staff of twenty-two, of whom there were three appointments at the Professorial level (the two Directors and Adam Podgorecki, who had arrived in Oxford from Poland via Holland, but who was to remain for only a short time before taking up a tenured position at Carleton University, Ottawa). Since the late 1970s, however, there has been a steady decline in the numbers of research staff as resources have shrunk. When McGregor left the Centre the SSRC adopted a model of joint Directors on the 'parity of esteem' principle, with a social scientist working in tandem with Don as the lawyer. Don worked for three years (1978–81) with Dr R. M. Hartwell, formerly the Reader in Recent Social and Economic History at Oxford, and then, from 1983–5, with Richard Markovits, an economist and lawyer, who was a Professor in the Law School of the University of Texas at Austin. When Markovits returned to the USA in 1985, Don took over as sole Director (a position he retained until his own retirement in the summer of 1993), and the dual-Director model was dropped in favour of one of a Director working with a Deputy Director. Among these unsettling changes in the social scientist

Directors Don remained a powerful force for continuity in the Centre's management.

A REFLECTION

Donald Harris' character and style were absolutely central to the nature of the Centre for Socio-Legal Studies, and to the people in it. It is surely significant that he was not from the conventional background nor trained in the conventional way that most of his law-teacher contemporaries were. He was from New Zealand, had first studied law as a graduate, and came to Oxford less intellectually constrained than the great majority of the academic lawyers of his generation, many of whom still seem to be disinterested in what they might learn about law from sociologists, economists, anthropologists, and others. Don has always had an open mind and a willingness to engage in thinking about law from different perspectives, an intellectual extraversion which he maintained throughout his time as Director of the Oxford Centre. Indeed, he has said frequently that one of the great privileges of working at the Centre was the opportunity he was given to learn from his social-scientist colleagues.

This intellectual modesty points to important personal qualities Don possessed as Director which led to the Centre being a congenial place in which to work, with few of the tensions or rivalries which often afflict academic institutions. He had a respect for his colleagues revealed in a readiness to consult them with an open mind, and to listen carefully to their views. He had enormous energy and capacity for hard work, allied with an infectious enthusiasm and, when necessary, great single-mindedness of purpose. He also retains a keen sense of humour and a great capacity for remembering funny stories (mostly about Balliol, only some of which the staff heard on more than one occasion). Don achieved what he did as Director with a gentle touch. He did not rule by fear, but led and inspired by the force of his personality and by example. He regarded people in the Centre as part of a family, and at the same time was enormously supportive of staff who had to combine research with the responsibilities of their own young families. As a result he was capable of inspiring great loyalty among his colleagues.

Don claims not to have consciously adopted any particular approach to research management, though certain of his core beliefs are clear. He acknowledges that he was imbued with a democratic idea from his experience in Balliol and this was transformed into a belief that you get the best out of people if you give them as much academic freedom as possible. 'I expected to know what was going on and I was in a position to show a red light if it needed to be shown. But normally if someone had a particular enthusiasm for the topic they happened to be working on, I was happy to say "Go ahead". And this was one of the advantages of having our core funding all these years: one didn't have to stick to a precise blueprint.' Thus projects were not imposed on staff, but emerged from their own interests. In developing the Centre's research strategy and designing particular projects possible relevance for future policy was only one of the criteria. And then it was often not the short-term or fashionable policy questions that now seem to be more attractive to those who fund social research. But if researchers wished to focus on some of the more fundamental research questions in the socio-legal field they would receive Don's support: 'People would make their best effort if they thought they would have a big say in where they wanted to go, and particularly if they thought they were going to get credit for their work.' This willingness to back his colleagues was coupled with a high degree of trust in them. As time went on, the management style became looser (even if that may have been somewhat unconventional) because Don could see that that was the way in which the best results were achieved: 'I don't think the Research Council would have been too happy if they had known this. They expected a much tighter degree of control.' This latter implied a management model much more familiar, of course, to natural and applied scientists in universities, in contrast with the strongly collegiate approach Don adopted.

Don did not, in fact, offer management, but leadership. Accordingly, he had a deep-seated belief in teamwork, though his faith in collaborative research was tempered by a realization that teamwork cannot be forced, that there are some people who are not team players. He not only arranged 'marriages' of Centre people, but also, where necessary, some divorces.

In a little over twenty years at the Oxford Centre Donald Harris was crucial to the creation and building of a multi-disciplinary academic research institution which became a vital and productive place. He built up a group of socio-legal staff and students, most of whom have now dispersed to take their knowledge and experience elsewhere. He has also contributed to the development of socio-legal studies more widely, since the Centre model has been adopted elsewhere, notably at The Ohio State University, which has set up its own Center for Socio-Legal Studies, and in whose establishment Don took an active part. Don also played a major role in developing in the Centre an international network of visitors and scholars, many of whom have had in turn a considerable influence on the Centre's work.

In all of this, Don continued to do his own research and to produce his own publications. Perhaps his best-known socio-legal contribution is the book he produced with others on *Compensation and Support for Illness and Injury*, the report of a large-scale, detailed, and exceptionally careful research undertaking he led that has since been used as a model by the American Federal government, which sponsored a replication by the RAND Corporation in the USA. But he has also published a book on *Remedies in Contract and Tort* (Weidenfeld and Nicholson, 1988) another on *Contract Law Today: Anglo-French Comparisons* (edited with Tallon, Clarendon Press, 1989), while continuing to act as Assistant Editor and contributor for a number of editions of Chitty on *Contracts* and Benjamin on *Sale of Goods*, the major works used by practitioners. There have been scholarly papers as well, of course, as well as considerable collaborative work on law and economics. Many of Don's publications appeared at a time when the Centre was under great pressure.

While Don retains his instinctive optimism about socio-legal studies, his view of the future is not untroubled. He remains enthusiastic about the idea of recruiting trained sociologists and economists and others who will take the law seriously as a subject worthy of academic study and research, but is anxious whether it will prove possible to recruit genuine social scientists and questions whether it is desirable for the development of the field that it be seen as very much a law-based effort from law-school staff. (It is noteworthy in this connection that most of the Centre's graduates and former staff are at work in law faculties.) In this respect the position has not changed markedly from the early 1970s, when very few social scientists were prepared to make law the central concern of their research enquiries. And it has to be said that, while the Oxford Law Faculty has been constantly supportive of research in and receptive to teaching in socio-legal studies, social scientists in Oxford have seemed much less interested. The 1980s and 1990s have brought problems of their own. The opportunity for lawyers to collaborate full-time with social scientists in future now seems reduced, much to Don's regret. The time available for collaborative work is now much less for many staff who continue to be burdened with teaching and administrative commitments, to which for some are now added research-proposal-writing and fund-raising responsibilities. Another threat is to the future of empirical socio-legal research: one of Don's concerns is that the new patterns of research forced upon universities by changes in funding and the reward structures within universities mean that, increasingly, senior staff will have to spend their time in libraries studying secondary sources, and that such first-hand data as may be collected will be thanks to the efforts of relatively inexperienced doctoral or post-doctoral students, working on short-term research projects that are inadequately funded.

Yet it is entirely characteristic of Don that he remains confident that the future of the socio-legal approach is now firmly established, and that the need for socio-legal scrutiny of the law and its life continues. Socio-legal research and scholarship remain essential for their capacity to advance our understanding of things legal and their power to change habits of thought. So far as the Oxford Centre is concerned, it has emerged from the dark days presaged by the ending of Research Council funding as an Oxford University research department. It now has three established University posts (including the Directorship that Don held, which now carries with it a Chair in Socio-Legal Studies—one of the first established Chairs in the subject in Britain). These posts thereby secure the future of the subject in the Oxford Law Faculty. These achievements are yet another reflection of Donald Harris' dedication, energy, and political skills.

1

Law's Relationship with Social Science: The Interdependence of Theory, Empirical Work, and Social Relevance in Socio-legal Studies[1]

BRIDGET M. HUTTER AND SALLY LLOYD-BOSTOCK

Contributing to this volume in honour of Don Harris gives us the opportunity to reflect on our work at the Centre for Socio-Legal Studies as part of an exciting period of innovation and development in socio-legal research. Socio-legal studies over the past twenty years has challenged traditional thinking about law and legal theory. Less obviously it has necessitated continuing re-examination of law's relationship with social science, and the development of new theory at all levels. Don Harris's style of directorship fostered innovative thinking and gave people the space to follow through their ideas in a genuinely interdisciplinary intellectual environment. Centre research has therefore built on a wide range of theoretical perspectives, disciplines and methodologies, in a variety of legal contexts.[2] In discussing socio-legal studies we shall refer principally to Centre work, but it is important to emphasize at the outset that it would be a mistake to attempt to define a Centre 'school' of socio-legal studies, or a common Centre view of the relationship between law and social science and the nature of socio-legal research. A consensus would not be found amongst those who have worked at the Centre, nor was the development of such a consensus ever a goal of the Centre.

Ours is therefore a personal view, but one that has both grown from and informed our socio-legal research over a number of years.[3] There are

[1] We would like to thank Nigel Dodd, Keith Hawkins, and Paul Rock for their helpful comments on an earlier draft.
[2] Theoretical perspectives and methods have included, e.g., such diverse approaches as participant observation, conversation analysis, economic analysis, social survey, and psychological experiment. Disciplines have included law, sociology, psychology, economics, social history, social policy, and anthropology. Contexts have included the field-level enforcement of governmental regulation, the processes of bringing and settling personal-injury claims; business, finance, and the law; aspects of family law; and many others.
[3] Sally Lloyd-Bostock, a psychologist, joined the Centre for Socio-Legal Studies in 1973 and has been engaged in socio-legal research since then. Bridget Hutter, a sociologist, has been engaged in socio-legal research at the Centre and elsewhere since 1978.

naturally differences between us (we are, for a start, from different disciplinary backgrounds); but we share certain core ideas about the nature
of socio-legal studies, and these form the basis of our paper. In particular we argue strongly against the contrast sometimes drawn between
empirical work and theoretical work, which underlies the early and still
persistent characterization of socio-legal studies as empirical (and therefore) not theoretical.[4] On the contrary, the interplay and interdependence of theory and empirical observation are at the heart of socio-legal
studies as we see it.

WHAT IS 'SOCIO-LEGAL STUDIES'?

Many incompatible views could be found on what constitutes 'socio-
legal studies',[5] and many different activities are now pursued under its
rubric. We do not wish to review attempts at definition or characterization of socio-legal studies.[6] Nor do we wish to become embroiled ourselves in the attempt to offer a definition. Indeed, Fitzpatrick (1995)
argues that it is in the nature of the social and the legal that the search for
an identity for socio-legal studies can never be successful. He writes, for
example, '[t]he uncertainty of identity in socio-legal studies . . . has not
been relieved by the constant search for some resolving presence, for
something that will enable us to at last say what it is' (105). Drawing on
Thomas (1994), he goes on:

Perhaps then a touch of ennui, even resignation, in recent assessments of the
field becomes understandable. . . . Some leading advocates of socio-legal studies
now employ a strategy of confession and avoidance: the field is there but its 'definition' is attended with unspecific and unrelieved 'problems', 'difficulty', and a
general absence of clarity in its 'lines of demarcation'.

Arguably we do not need unambiguously drawn boundaries to the
work we do. We are, however, concerned to reject some persistent features of the way socio-legal studies has been defined or viewed over the
life of the Centre for Socio-Legal Studies. Discussion of early work in
socio-legal studies was highly speculative and sometimes derogatory.
Since we wish to argue that socio-legal studies as developed at the Centre
is unrecognizable in characterizations such as that set out by Campbell
and Wiles (1976), we begin by referring to their paper and its continuing

---

[4] See, e.g., Campbell and Wiles (1976), quoted below. For some early contrary arguments
see Nelken (1981), and McBarnet (1978).
[5] There is not even agreement over whether 'socio-legal studies' is singular or plural—
we shall use the singular in this Chapter.
[6] See, e.g., Thomas (1994), Fitzpatrick (1995) for difficulties in the definition of socio-
legal studies.

influence. Campbell and Wiles, writing in 1976, examine what they perceive as a bifurcation in the field of law and society research at that time into two distinct approaches, adopted by two mutually hostile groups: socio-legal studies and sociology of law. They outline the two approaches (in deliberate caricature) as follows:

Behind the standard of the 'sociology of law' ranged those who denigrated the other side as antitheoretical, concerned with social engineering through the existing social order, and not with explaining that order or transcending it by critique. The word 'sociology' was emblazoned in gold on their banner because it signified a claim to greater theoretical sophistication. Under the ensign of 'socio-legal studies' encamped those who chastised the other side as abstract theoreticians, whose speculations were divorced from reality and lacked a practical relevance. Law, lawyers and the legal system were taken as they were found . . . [Campbell and Wiles, 1976, 548–9].

They go on to characterize the two approaches in some detail and to locate them in the context of wider developments and debates in the social sciences at the time.[7] The merits of 'sociology of law' over 'socio-legal studies' are emphasized throughout, and the paper can be read as a warning of the intellectual poverty and ultimate sterility of socio-legal studies as they saw it developing at that time.[8]

The view that opposes theoretical with empirical work tends also to align empirical work with pragmatic and policy-oriented concerns, so that socio-legal studies is portrayed as the atheoretical 'handmaiden of the law'. Instead of being seen as intimately bound up with theory, empirical research methodology comes to be seen solely as a technical matter. At its extreme this degenerates into the view that socio-legal studies merely involves lawyers acquiring some technical skills in gathering and describing some empirical data to back up their assumptions or reformist goals. Campbell and Wiles refer to this view when they write, for example: '[m]any law teachers, imbued with the notion of social scientists as data-gatherers, merely sought technical expertise and often gained it' (567) and '[s]ocio-legal studies may be entered with a few newly learned techniques, but sociology of law demands commitment and application' (573). To the extent that this view of socio-legal studies is correct, we share Campbell and Wiles' misgivings. It certainly does not describe socio-legal research at the Centre.

The discussion by Freeman in one of the most widely-used undergraduate texts on jurisprudence provides an illustration of the lasting

[7] Their paper is overwhelmingly concerned with sociology. They also refer briefly to debates in political science, economics and anthropology.

[8] It should be remembered that at the time Campbell and Wiles were writing grand theorizing was very much in vogue. Often it was marxist and typically it was very unsympathetic to alternatives.

legacy of Campbell and Wiles (Freeman, 1995). We think that most socio-legal scholars would broadly go along with the initial description of socio-legal studies offered by Freeman (1995): '[a]dvocates of socio-legal studies emphasize the importance of placing law in its social context, of using research methods, of recognising that many traditional jurisprudential questions are empirical in nature, not purely conceptual.' (538) However, we certainly do not recognize our work in the further definition offered:

A pervasive theme is the gap between the 'law in the books' and 'the law in action'. The gap is described, but it is rarely explained. . . . The researchers are reform-orientated: their concern is with making the system work as it should, that is in accordance with ideals such as the rule of law or justice. . . . [The work] is largely lacking in any theoretical underpinning. The law and the legal system are treated as discrete entities, as unproblematic [538–9]

In Freeman's discussion, the distinction between theory on the one hand, and pragmatic, policy-oriented empirical work on the other, becomes in effect the basis of a definition of socio-legal studies. Research in social sciences and law that falls outside his rather critical description is regarded as something other than socio-legal studies. Indeed, Freeman goes on to contrast socio-legal studies with sociology of law, of which he writes with more approval:

The approach of those who believe in the sociology of law is markedly different. According to Campbell and Wiles, 'the focus is no longer on the legal system, known and accepted, but on understanding the nature of social order through a study of law. . . . The goal is not primarily to improve the legal system but rather to construct a theoretical understanding of that legal system in terms of the wider social structure.' [541]

Such typifications of socio-legal studies are well beyond their sell-by date. The definition of socio-legal studies has become bound up to an unfortunate degree with its credentials and status as an academic enterprise. Early socio-legal work became caught in the crossfire of academic squabbles, notably a reaction in the 1970s by some sociologists against anything smacking of positivist approaches in sociology (described by Campbell and Wiles as 'an all-out onslaught on positivism' (561)). The debates continue, though protagonists and positions change. The current tension between 'positivistic' and 'interpretive' approaches to social sciences and law, for example, is made explicit in the series of open letters recently published in the *Law and Society Newsletter* for November 1995.[9] Indeed the law-and-society movement in the United States sees

[9] At 8–11. Letter from Carol Bohmer with responses from Allan Lind, Robert Kidder, Deborah Hensler, Jonathon Simon, Howard Erlanger, Sally Merry, John Conley, Susan Sterrett, and Carol Greenhouse.

itself in a time of crisis and self-criticism (Trubek and Esser, 1989). This need not be viewed negatively. Boaventura de Sousa Santos argues in his 1995 address to the Annual Meeting of the Law and Society Association that periods of 'paradigmatic transition' can be emancipatory (Santos, 1995).

In the next section we take up in more detail the question of how theory and empirical work are interrelated in socio-legal research, and why this relationship has been, we suggest, misunderstood. We return later to the question of policy orientation and pragmatism in socio-legal studies.

THEORY AND EMPIRICAL WORK

While we recognize that there are many different views about theory and many different types of theory, we have, for present purposes, taken the definitions offered by *The Concise Oxford Dictionary of Sociology* (Marshall, 1994) as our starting point. It defines a theory as follows: '[a] theory is an account of the world which goes beyond what we can see and measure. It embraces a set of interrelated definitions and relationships that organises our concepts of the empirical world in a systematic way.' (1994, 532) Beyond this distinctions have been drawn between different types of theory, notably grand theory and middle range theory. Grand theory refers to 'the form of highly abstract theorizing in which the formal organization and arrangements of concepts takes priority over understanding the social world' (*ibid.* 206). Middle-range theory was first defined (and advocated) by the American sociologist Robert Merton. Middle-range theories, he wrote, 'are theories that lie between the minor but necessary working hypotheses that evolve in abundance in day to day research and the all-inclusive systematic efforts to develop unified theory that will explain all observed uniformities of social behaviour, organization and social change' (quoted, *ibid.* 329).

Grand theorizing is in fact rather rare and its use and importance have been greatly over-estimated by critics of socio-legal studies. Middle-range theories are much more the stuff of socio-legal studies and it is at this level of theorizing that much socio-legal (and indeed other social scientific) research takes place. Indeed we would argue further that it is middle-range theory that has proven most useful and insightful in our understanding of society.

The term 'theoretical' is often contrasted with the term 'empirical'. To quote *The Oxford Dictionary of Sociology* again, the term empirical is defined thus:

As applied to statements, particularly research projects, the term 'empirical' implies a close relationship to sensory experience, observation, or experiment. Sometimes the term is contrasted with abstract or theoretical, sometimes with dogmatic, or sometimes with scholarly. In its derogatory uses, lack of attention to matters of principle or theory is implied. [*ibid.* 149]

We already see here how empirical work is sometimes seen as distinct from, lacking in, and indeed partly defined by its contrast with, theory; and the derogatory connotations of some uses of the term 'empirical'.

Our argument is that it is impossible to draw such a sharp distinction between the two. All research uses theory at some level, although the degree to which academic researchers are explicit about it differs. The attempt to oppose theory and empirical work has led to a thin view of what it is to do empirical socio-legal research. At the core of socio-legal studies is the belief that much of what has been treated non-empirically should be treated empirically. As Cotterrell expresses it, '[o]nly in the law in books can legal rules have a life of their own. Elsewhere their meaning and significance come from the way in which they are applied—if at all— to social situations and relationships.' (1992:vii)

There is very much more to this approach than naïvely adopting given legal frameworks and comparing what the law says with what the law actually does, in the manner Campbell and Wiles (1976) attribute to socio-legal studies. As Nelken (1981) and McBarnet (1978) argue, 'what the law says' is no less problematic than 'what the law does'. The law-in-action, empirical perspective that Cotterrell and others describe gives rise to questions new to both law and the social sciences, and with them to new theory—socio-legal theory. It expands our enquiry, not only beyond traditional approaches, but also beyond traditional arenas (such as the courts), traditional legal actors (such as the judiciary), and traditional sources of law (such as judicial decisions and the Law Reports) to study the use, enforcement, and workings of legal rules in out-of-court contexts by regulatory and other legal officials, the professions, and the general public. The Centre's research programmes in personal injury compensation,[10] regulation,[11] family law,[12] business law,[13] and law and health care,[14] are all examples. All these programmes necessitated the development of theory and the re-examination and refinement of a variety of concepts, such as discretion,[15] compliance,[16] common sense,[17]

[10] See, e.g., Harris *et al.* (1984); Genn (1987); Lloyd-Bostock (1979a, 1979b, 1991).
[11] E.g. Baldwin (1995); Brittan (1984); Cranston (1979); Genn (1993); Hawkins (1984, 1992); Hutter (1988, 1997); Lloyd-Bostock (1992); Richardson *et al.* (1983).
[12] e.g. Dingwall and Eekelaar (1988); Eekelaar and Maclean (1986); Maclean (1991).
[13] e.g. McBarnet (1978); Wheeler (1991).
[14] e.g. Lloyd-Bostock and Mulcahy (1994); Dingwall and Fenn (1992).
[15] Hawkins (1984); Lloyd-Bostock (1992).   [16] Hutter (1997).
[17] Lloyd-Bostock (1979a,b; 1981; 1986; 1991b).

enforcement,[18] dispute.[19] It is now difficult to realize that at the beginning of the Centre's life a focus on non-court settings represented a radical departure from accepted legal scholarship; and the extent to which the *conceptualization* of Centre research essentially started from scratch.

The conceptual and theoretical work necessary to, and growing from, the innovative empirical orientation of socio-legal studies has been greatly underestimated. For example, Campbell and Wiles gloomily express the expectation that the Centre's early research on compensation for illness and injury (then under way) will be another theoretically unsophisticated attempt to describe how law actually works, another in a line of examples illustrating 'a fascination with finding out how procedures work in reality and how they affect people' (571–2). As that relatively early project demonstrates, finding out how procedures work in reality and how they affect people is hardly a simple or intellectually uninteresting task. The research was ground-breaking and raised questions that could not be formulated in advance.[20] Nothing like it had ever been conceptualized before.

Paradigms and the Value of Diversity

A central part of our argument about the relationship between theory and empirical work is that it is impossible to conduct empirical work in a theoretical vacuum. Research questions do not arise out of thin air. Even if questions of theory and conceptual framework are not explicitly addressed, we select and formulate our research interests according to our intellectual preoccupations and the ways in which we study phenomena are equally informed by the epistemological traditions we find most fitting. Put another way, our work is created, formulated, and pursued according to the paradigms we adopt. Paradigms (Kuhn, 1970) set the direction of our research, inform what we regard as a legitimate and interesting topic of research and involve epistemological assumptions. They mould our ways of seeing the world, our ways of studying the world (including the questions we ask), and our ways of making sense of the world.

[18] Hawkins (1984); Hutter (1988); Lloyd-Bostock (1992).
[19] Lloyd-Bostock (1994, 1991a).
[20] Some of the work of one of us (Lloyd-Bostock) as part of the compensation project's research team provides one of many possible illustrations from the work of the Centre. Lloyd-Bostock related the social psychology of attributing causes and fault to questions in jurisprudence about the roots in common sense of legal definitions of fault and liability to compensate, as well as to policy questions about the workings of the compensation system and why only a minority of accident victims who might bring a damages claim in fact do so. These questions were not anticipated at the outset of the research, and had not been examined before, partly because they developed from empirical exploration of 'how procedures work in reality' which was itself part of the project; and also because even to raise them requires a depth of knowledge of both legal and psychological material.

Research design, data collection, data analysis, writing, and policy-making all overlap. They are not discrete activities. They all require conceptual thought, but the extent to which this is developed and systematized as theory is the point of controversy. Failure to address the importance of systematizing a conceptual framework and making theory explicit rightly attracts criticism. Ideally, empirical research is dependent on theory; and theory, we would argue, is dependent upon empirical research.[21] More than this, they feed into each other.

Socio-legal studies—like the disciplines it encompasses—draws upon a range and variety of theoretical perspectives within and across disciplinary boundaries. We regard this as a strength.[22] Different aspects of society demand different foci of study, and the multi-faceted aspect of the socio-legal world is arguably best researched from a variety of perspectives which may prove both complementary and contradictory (this reflecting the nature of the social worlds we live in). We do not argue for orthodoxies or a single style of working. Diversity is valuable, especially where work is genuinely innovatory in its exploration of new areas. We broadly agree with Silverman's observation, made with reference to sociology but equally valid for socio-legal studies, that we should beware two vices. The first is 'assuming that there are particular "right" and "wrong" models of society or methodologies' and the second 'taking sides on the many spurious polarities which still bedevil much of social science (e.g. quality *vs.* quantity, structure *vs.* meaning, macro *vs.* micro)' (1993, pp. viii–ix). We maintain that it is particularly important to avoid such pitfalls early in the history of a subject such as socio-legal studies. Clearly that is no easy endeavour, but at the very least it is important to be aware of the problems of being dogmatic about such matters. Being too prescriptive and blinkered can only damage the intellectual pursuits we are engaged in.

Preconceptions about Theory and the Social Sciences

Divergent paradigms are a rich source of misunderstanding. There is an understandable tendency to evaluate contributions to scholarship from within a particular framework of expectations and criteria of scholarship. The problems this can cause are naturally magnified in an interdisciplinary field. The incantation that socio-legal studies is lacking in theory may mean no more than 'socio-legal studies does not use the paradigms/do the kind of theory I am used to/I do'. In particular, it often

---

[21] Silverman (1993), discusses the dangers of grand theories which do not apply to the world but remain grounded in their own internal workings.

[22] Nelken made a similar point in his 1981 paper. A different view is expressed by G. Ritzer (1981).

seems that what is meant by 'lacking in theory' is 'not developing (or not clearly informed by) grand theories of law'.[23] Twining, for example, laments the lack of *general* theory guiding the research agenda in socio-legal studies in general and psychology and law in particular (Twining 1995. 42):[24] '[a]s with other areas of socio-legal studies there has been disappointingly little general theorizing which might guide research agendas or develop a general "psychology of law" in contradistinction to the much more fragmented "psychology in law".' But socio-legal studies draws on a complexity of social science perspectives, and involves varied kinds of theoretical development. Although concerned with the individual in society, psychology (to pursue Twining's example) does not offer, nor seek to offer, theories of law and society in the same sense that sociology or jurisprudence might do; but its focus at a more detailed level does not make psychological research atheoretical. Much of our own work has been concerned to develop sociological and/or psychological theory at the middle range—i.e. theory at a detailed level about what it is to make a legal decision and how such decisions very broadly defined are made (e.g. Lloyd-Bostock, 1992); how law and regulations translate into legal action (e.g. Hutter, 1988, 1997; Hutter and Lloyd-Bostock, 1992); how events and circumstances come to be perceived and defined in such a way that a particular legal response is perceived as appropriate (e.g. Lloyd-Bostock, 1991b); how law and 'common sense' interact (e.g. Lloyd-Bostock, 1979b, 1981, 1986); and so on. That does not mean that it is lacking in theory. In research on routine decision-making by factory inspectors, for example, Lloyd-Bostock draws on and develops psychological theory about the cognitive processes underlying these kinds of decisions, and attempts to integrate the psychology of routine decision-making into theory relating to routine decision making in the law and society literature. As we have already stressed, there is no particular 'level' at which all socio-legal research and theory ought to be focused. Research focused at a more detailed level is not thereby 'largely lacking in theory' any more than jurisprudence and grand theorizing about law and society are 'largely lacking in theory' because they do not give priority to developing a theoretical understanding of how law actually works at a micro level.

There is, however, an important point to be made here which may lie behind Twining's comment. Socio-legal research at a detailed level

[23] Although some comments of Campbell and Wiles (1976) indicate that when they describe socio-legal studies as atheoretical they mean totally lacking in theory, not only lacking in grand theory. As noted above, rather little attention is nowadays given to 'grand theorizing' by sociologists.

[24] Campbell and Wiles (1976) similarly write: '[u]nless socio-legal research can be part of an attempt to develop a more general theory of social order and law, then its contribution will remain piecemeal and ad hoc' (572).

needs to be set against a broader framework, or at least an awareness of broader questions. It is true that much research in psychology and law, especially in the 1970s and early 1980s, has lacked a sense of the wider intellectual picture. Sometimes it has implicitly taken for granted much that should arguably be treated as problematic (about, for example, the functions of legal rules and trials) in the way criticized by Campbell and Wiles because these are matters that do not obviously lend themselves to psychological study or debate. For a discipline such as psychology the interdisciplinary or multidisciplinary nature of socio-legal studies provides a framework that potentially transforms the relationship between psychology and law, applied or otherwise. For example, as Twining (1984) has argued, the 'problem' of identification and misidentification in legal processes takes a very different form if the courts are no longer viewed as occupying the centre of the stage, and attention is broadened from identification evidence that might be given in court. Because of its interdisciplinary environment, much of the Centre's output in psychology and law has been aimed at setting psychology and law in this wider context, examining and developing the theoretical relationship between law and psychology, and developing empirical research that is interdisciplinary rather than applied in the more traditional sense.[25]

Like the other social sciences, the character of psychology's relationship with law is a function of many things, including the questions that psychology addresses, the kinds of explanations and theories that it offers, and the changing culture of the discipline which affects the acceptability of particular approaches and the balance of its preoccupations. During the lifetime of the Centre for Socio-Legal Studies, psychologists working on legal topics have increasingly ventured into the multi-disciplinary law and society field.[26] Their work is therefore increasingly enriched by wider theoretical perspectives, approaches, and backgrounds, replacing a tendency to work on somewhat narrowly conceived topics within traditional legal models. While still applicable to much of psychology and law, Twining's comment that studies in psychology and law lack a general theory (as interpreted above) is perhaps losing some of its force. At the same time, advances within psychology itself have continued to expand and transform the relationship between psychology and law.

We acknowledge and endorse the need for all those engaged in socio-legal research to be uncomfortably aware of the many wider theoretical issues it raises, and the importance of avoiding naïve or unreflective assumptions about the nature of law. The general point of course applies to all social science research. However, that is not to say that socio-legal

[25] See e.g. Lloyd-Bostock (1984, 1988b, in press 1996).
[26] See e.g. the work of Neil Vidmar, Shari Diamond, Michael Saks.

studies in some sense *needs* a general theory before it can proceed—that general theory (or for that matter, sociological theory), rather than facilitative, is in some sense prior. We have already touched on the continual tensions within the social sciences arising from the adoption of different paradigms, and (by implication if not more explicitly) the rejection of others. Different paradigms predominate at different times and for different groups. A 'general theory guiding research agendas' could bring intellectual coherence in the short term. But, by the nature of theory, it would also be limiting and could only be provisional. In the long term it makes no more sense than the notion of a general theory guiding the research agenda in psychology, or sociology, or political science. Openness to new perspectives is fundamental to socio-legal studies, not least because of its interdisciplinary nature. Twining pinpoints as one of the Centre's key roles that:

it has been unique in providing a base for social research into law that is genuinely multi-disciplinary rather than just inter-disciplinary. This extends far beyond particular projects to its being the headquarters of a small, but very significant sub-culture that views almost everything through the multiple lenses of several disciplines [1995, 43]

Socio-legal studies is an ambitious attempt to tackle a highly complex subject matter from a range of social-science perspectives. Much of it is still exploratory. By its nature it involves investment in the exploration of what may turn out to be blind alleys. Friedman (1986, 766) struck a chord with many researchers when he wrote of the law and society movement: '[i]t uses scientific method; its theories are in principle scientific theories; but what it studies is a loose, wriggling changing subject matter, shot through and through with normative ideas.' Any general theory guiding the research agenda may not be compatible with the open-ended, interdisciplinary, and continually exploratory nature of socio-legal studies.

As well as preconceptions about theory, socio-legal studies has been denigrated on the basis of misunderstandings about the nature of research. For example, Freeman (1995) illustrates what he describes as the 'atheoretical, pragmatic orientation of socio-legal studies' with reference to some jury studies carried out in the 1970s and early 1980s, that take a particular approach (measuring jury performance against professional expectations of the 'right' verdict). These studies are taken to task for (amongst other things) not asking a whole range of additional questions that might be asked about juries. Rather than illustrating anything much about socio-legal studies, this kind of criticism illustrates a mismatch between the scale of social science researchers' aims in a particular piece of research and the scale of expectations among some commentators. A particular empirical study of jury decision-making (for example) can attempt to tackle only a small fraction of the questions one might wish to ask about juries. An individual study in psychology for the most part has quite limited aims, and inevitably proceeds on the basis of provisional assumptions. (Its methodological strength will often lie partly in the explicit statement of those aims and recognition of assumptions.) The theoretical rationale for a particular piece of empirical research is usually grounded in the existing body of research to which the new study contributes. Moreover, the nature of experimental research is easily misunderstood, and the reduction and control of a laboratory study easily taken for failure to appreciate the complexities of the questions (see Lloyd-Bostock, 1988a). It is a mistake to look for too much in a single empirical study, or to treat it in isolation from the stream of work to which it belongs. It is always dangerous to take a single publication, or even group of publications, in for example the psychological literature, as showing what psychology has to say on a question.

SOCIAL SCIENCE IN LAW AND SOCIAL SCIENCE OF LAW

As will already be apparent from the above, in rejecting the division between theoretical and empirical work we reject also the characterization of socio-legal studies as pragmatic *rather than* theoretical. A sharp distinction has sometimes been drawn between social science *in* law and social science *of* law. Friedman (1986) for example, views social science *in* law as peripheral to the law-and-society movement, just as forensic medicine is peripheral to the sociology of medicine. A similar distinction underlies Campbell and Wiles' (1976) contrast between socio-legal studies and the sociology of law in the 1970s. The distinction is implicitly evaluative. Social science *in* law works within a framework defined by law, serving legally defined ends. Social science *of* law is its own authority. Social science *of* law, it is implied, is less ethically dubious and theoretically more sophisticated than social science *in* law.

The 'applied' nature of socio-legal studies is seen by Fitzpatrick (1995) as offering an escape from the need to define socio-legal studies in order to justify it: '[t]here is . . . a kind of happy positivism. . . . Socio-legal studies is simply, and usually robustly, asserted to be an applied field and hence intrinsically valid and viable'. (105–6) His discussion again reproduces (without necessarily endorsing) the idea that socio-legal studies thus viewed somehow cannot do 'proper theory'; that the concepts of the legal and the social will be under-examined; that socio-legal studies has to take the integrity of law as given and ask questions about its effectiveness, about policy implementation, etc.; that it can be set in contrast to sociology (perhaps because socio-legal studies is seen as belonging to law), to which it must ultimately turn to provide a larger theoretical framework. As Fitzgerald puts it, '[s]ociologists should, after all, be on top as well as on tap' (106). This last idea echoes the suggestion we discussed and rejected above, that socio-legal studies needs a general theory to give it coherence, set its agenda, and rescue it from being piecemeal and *ad hoc*; and moreover, that this general theory must come from sociology.[27]

Fitzpatrick's comments draw attention to a widespread misconception about applied work—namely that being 'applied' somehow provides an escape from the need to confront theoretical questions. Nelken (1981) addresses the same false alignment between 'applied' and 'atheoretical': '[i]t is sometimes implied that the weakness of socio-legal studies lies in its commitment to practical, policy-making objectives. But the purpose behind an investigation is not itself a guide to its theoretical adequacy or inadequacy' (39).

Of course there is more to socio-legal research than an attempt to 'improve' the law, but the potential relevance of socio-legal research to the practice of law, and the responsibilities this brings, cannot be avoided. Socio-legal studies is almost by definition of social relevance. The importance of social scientific study and understanding of law in this respect is expressed by Cotterrell:

The major justification is that law is too important a phenomenon to be analyzed in a way that isolates it from other aspects of society and makes impossible an understanding of the complexity of its relations with other social phenomena, its 'reality' as a part of life and not merely as a technique of professional practice (1992, 1).

Those conducting research in social sciences and the law cannot simply dissociate themselves from policy concerns, and disclaim responsibility for any practical impact (intended or unintended) their work may have by insisting they are not in the business of evaluation, reform, or promoting justice.[28] The crucial point is that theory, research, and the subjects of research interplay and are interrelated. Just as theory feeds into empirical research, so empirical research feeds into theory: *and* in turn both may reflect back into the 'real world' and thus alter or influence the subjects of research.

Psychology and Law and the In law–Of law Distinction

Psychology has traditionally distinguished between pure and applied research in a way which superficially resembles the distinction between

[27] This presumably owes much to the fact that it is sociologists who have taken socio-legal studies seriously enough to develop a critique of it and examine how it can be embraced within their discipline.

[28] For discussion of this in the context of psychology research see Lloyd-Bostock (1988b).

socio-legal studies and sociology of law made by Campbell and Wiles, or between sociology of law and sociology in law made by Friedman. Those engaged in psychology and law research more readily view their work as applied than do researchers in sociology and the law. We therefore examine in more detail the 'in law–of law' distinction, and the idea of 'applied research' in relation to psychology and law.

In so far as the battles within sociology depicted by Campbell and Wiles were territorial, they appeared narrowly defined and largely irrelevant to psychology. But there were debates occurring within psychology during the 1970s (which have continued) that have some parallels with those they describe in the other social sciences, and which impinged on the developing field of psychology and law, particularly as a field of applied or 'real-world' study. Some psychologists—particularly social psychologists—wished to break away from positivist approaches, the laboratory and experimental methods, and develop 'new paradigms' and new models (see e.g. Harre and Secord, 1972). There was a growing belief that psychology should look beyond the laboratory and tackle the study of psychological processes in the 'real world'. The effect was particularly marked in cognitive psychology, with the growth of the 'ecological approach' (e.g. Gibson, 1950, 1966; Neisser, 1976, 1982, 1984; see Barsalou, 1992 for discussion). Proponents of the ecological approach argue that many laboratory paradigms are too artificial and simplified to be informative about important cognitive mechanisms; and that theories developed from such paradigms will only explain performance on laboratory tasks—tasks that humans did not evolve to perform. Human behaviour should be studied in the 'real world', messy though it is. A notable example is the growing study of 'practical memory'—i.e. memory as used in everyday life rather than memory for nonsense syllables in the laboratory (see e.g. Gruneberg *et al.*, 1978, 1988). Critics of the ecological approach worry about its supposed theoretical weakness, and that lack of theory may produce unorganized description (Potter, 1983). Over the same time period, psychologists have also been concerned about pressures from funding bodies to make their research at least appear 'useful'; and there has been much debate about the intellectual respectability, limitations, and ethics of applied research.[29]

Closer examination reveals deep ambiguities in the notion of applied research. Simply to characterize law and psychology as predominantly applied glosses over the multiplicity of approaches and facets to the relationship between psychology and law, often within a single piece of research. The label 'applied' tends to imply ground-level application of social science to a legally defined problem, within a given legal frame-

---

[29] e.g. Konecni and Ebbesen, 1979; King, 1979; McCloskey, Egeth, and McKenna, 1986.

work—the 'social-science-on-tap model'. But psychological research can 'apply' to law in a variety of ways, and at a variety of levels, some intended and some unintended, some explicit and some implicit. The questions or 'problems' tackled may or may not be defined by lawyers, and the products of the research may or may not be aimed at an audience beyond psychology itself.

Some of the most interesting aspects of the relationship between psychology and the law are at the more theoretical levels of law, where developments in psychology impinge on the premises of legal thinking and the terms of legal debate. Thus, psychological research on eyewitness memory can modify our understanding of the processes of memory, recall, and recognition in ways that recast rather than answer questions about evidence. Research on the psychology of confessions does not merely help to assess interrogation techniques and the reliability of confessions, but provides theoretical frameworks that render comprehensible why people questioned by the police confess to acts they did not perform. Psychological research and theory have been related to legal discussion and jurisprudence surrounding discretionary decision-making, obedience to law, fault and causation, the relationship between law and morality, and models of mental illness.[30]

On the other hand, what is presented as applied research is actually often concerned primarily with developing psychological theory and contributing to the psychological literature. What Twining, Friedman, and others might count as psychology *in* law has often been designed without reference to those who are *prima facie* intended to benefit, and published where those who might make use of it will not read it.[31] This paradoxical situation probably owes much to the longstanding pressure to portray psychology research in this and other fields as 'useful' in order to obtain funding. Discussing influences on the choice of research topics in law and psychology Lloyd-Bostock (1984) refers to what Baddeley calls the 'high speed serial exhaustive scanning in female black homosexual drug addicts' problem (Baddeley, 1979) which involves taking a laboratory technique one happens to be interested in and applying it in a way which will attract large amounts of research funds. Note that the result is a far cry from Campbell and Wiles' vision of socio-legal studies as based predominantly in law departments and carried out by lawyers with a smattering of social-science skills. On the contrary (but perhaps equally unfortunately) when research in psychology and law is generated in this way, lawyers are virtually excluded from all stages of the process.[32]

[30] See, e.g., Lloyd-Bostock, 1979a, 1979b, 1986; Tyler, 1990.
[31] See e.g. Broadbent, 1980; Lloyd-Bostock, 1984; Stringer, 1982.
[32] Demands from government and from funding bodies that research (not only social science research) should be policy-relevant and user-friendly are, if anything, increasing.

On analysis it becomes clear that the distinction between psychology *in* law and psychology *of* law does not work anywhere near as sharply as Friedman suggests. Throughout psychology, simple divisions into 'basic' and 'applied' work are increasingly being viewed as unhelpful. In so far as there is a difference of this kind it is more one of emphasis in the goals of research than a clear dichotomy. Nor (at least where psychology is concerned) does the distinction coincide with a distinction between more and less theoretically sophisticated, ethically sound, or politically committed research. The difficulty in drawing Friedman's distinction in relation to psychology points up ambiguities in the notion of socio-legal studies as social science 'applied to' law, and with it narrow conceptions of socio-legal studies as atheoretical, law-led pragmatism.

THE INTERPLAY OF THEORY AND EMPIRICAL OBSERVATION

In this final section we use an example from a major area of Centre research to show how a particular disciplinary perspective has influenced socio-legal research; how this led socio-legal researchers to break new ground; and how this forced us to reconsider existing concepts and theories. The disciplinary perspective we discuss is from sociology, namely the interactionist perspective; the new ground is that of the regulation of industry; the concepts we were forced to reconsider were those of enforcement and discretion; and the broader theories these relate to are social control theories.

The Interactionist Paradigm

Sociologists have been interested in the law from the inception of the discipline in the late nineteenth century. Durkheim, Marx, and Weber all recognized the importance of studying law and legal institutions in their endeavour to understand society, especially modern society. The rudiments of a sociology of law were thus associated with the beginnings of the discipline of sociology and involved laying the foundations for a variety of ways of approaching the study of law. The law has thus been seen

Indeed a Socio-Legal Research Users' Forum has been established comprising members of such 'user groups' as the Law Commission, CBI, EOC, CRE, Home Office, LCD, DTI, DOE, TUC, in addition to the ESRC and a representation of academics (*Socio-Legal Newsletter*, 17, 1995). Such a move is related to the ESRC's mission to enhance the competitiveness of the UK economy, promote the effectiveness of public services and public policy, and improve the quality of life. Clearly these developments increase the pressures on socio-legal researchers, medical researchers, and others subject to such funding policies, to act, ostensibly at least, in a service role, and to hold back from emphasizing theoretical development. This is especially so in an academic world which places value upon the number of publications one produces and the number of outside grants one raises.

as an instrument of the state and a dominant class structure (Marx), as an integrative mechanism (Durkheim), and as something which is not simply externally imposed but which is also given meaning and reality in social interaction (Weber). We focus here upon the interactionist perspective, and the contribution made by this sociological approach to socio-legal studies.

The interactionist tradition has proven particularly suited to the examination of the law in action.[33] This sociological tradition is specifically concerned with subjective meanings and experiences as constructed by participants in social situations (Burgess, 1984). Meidinger (1987, 356) regards the sociological approach as a cultural perspective which focuses on the understandings that are negotiated and enacted by actors in legal arenas. Following Becker (1982), Meidinger defines culture as 'a set of shared understandings which makes it possible for a group of people to act in concert with each other' (*ibid.*, 359). This cultural approach focuses attention upon the rules of the legal regulatory 'game'; conflicting interpretations of the social world; the political resolution of these conflicts; and social change and the social processes whereby change occurs. Such a definition is important because it draws attention to the impact of broader social pressures and structures upon the legal process and its participants. As Yeager (1991, 43) reminds us, the structural biases of the law are reproduced in the microsociology of interactions between inspectors and companies.

Socio-legal scholars at the Oxford Centre have used the interactionist paradigm to research regulatory control, such as Hutter's examination of the enforcement activities of field-level officials charged with applying the law in the areas of environmental health, occupational health and safety, and the control of environmental pollution (Hutter, 1988, 1997. See also Hawkins, 1984; Richardson *et al.*, 1983). The application of this paradigm to new areas of socio-legal (and sociological) research has proven especially illuminating. It is new to the extent that it has applied an interpretivist sociological paradigm to the study of areas of social control which are in many respects relatively recent and hidden from the public view. This is in spite of the fact that large areas of our economic life are now regulated by regulatory bureaucracies armed with delegated powers and high levels of administrative discretion. That their activities typically go unnoticed is particularly surprising given the extensive controls they have the potential to exercise (Hutter, 1988).

Kagan (1978) defined regulation as 'the control of economic activity by means of direct legal orders'. Economic or financial regulation is often

---

[33] e.g. Banton, 1964; Becker, 1963; Cain, 1973; Hawkins, 1984; Lemert, 1967; Manning, 1977; Richardson, 1983; Rock, 1973, 1986; Skolnick, 1975. See Rock, 1995 for a particularly good discussion of the role of interpretative sociology in socio-legal studies.

distinguished from social regulation. Economic or financial regulation refers to the regulation of financial markets, prices, and profits. Social regulation refers to the regulation of industrial processes which may cause harm to workforces, the public, and the environment (Hawkins and Hutter, 1993; Yeager, 1991). We would like to draw attention to two points here. First, regulation is concerned with the control of economic institutions, some of which may be regarded as being at the core of modern industrialized societies. The second, and related, point is that this often (but not always) involves the regulation of high-status offenders. Thus, this is an area of socio-legal studies which is concerned with the core of modern societies and economies and not with the marginal powerless groups which some commentators believed would be the focus of socio-legal work (Campbell and Wiles, 1976, 552).

Researchers in this area premised their work upon the assumption that legal mandates are inherently unclear. Lawmakers do not—and indeed cannot—categorically specify the meanings of words and phrases. Sometimes this is intentional, sometimes an oversight, and sometimes impossible, for what happens in the 'real world' is not reducible to the classificatory scheme of the law. The 'law in action' inevitably involves interpretation of the 'law in books' and in some systems, notably regulatory systems, enforcement officials are allocated a good deal of discretion in the form of broad and general legal standards. These officials are in the front line of regulatory enforcement, and it is they who have the discretion (perhaps even sometimes create the discretion) to determine how government regulation is ultimately translated into action—they are the 'gatekeepers' to the regulatory process. But they do not work in a vacuum or free from constraints—they operate within varying political, social, legal, and organizational parameters.

Given the social complexity of the regulatory process, the range of participants it involves, and the breadth of many legal definitions, there is considerable scope for variation in the definitions and in turn the achievement of compliance. But social activity is not random. It is patterned and structured, and part of the sociological enterprise is devoted to identifying and explaining the patterns of social interaction. Studies of regulation identified the adoption of common enforcement practices by regulatory officials from a variety of backgrounds, practices which directly challenge the view that enforcement of the law refers simply to legal action. Instead it encompasses a wide array of informal enforcement techniques including education, advice, persuasion, and negotiation. These are used by all law-enforcement officials, but come into particular prominence in the regulatory arena. Study of regulation has thus emphasized the negotiated and processual nature of much law.

The varying styles of enforcement are well encapsulated by Reiss

(1984), who takes two broad models of social control, the compliance and deterrence systems. His objective is to understand the conditions under which 'legal agents of control' opt for one system or the other. The compliance system is so called because its main objective is to secure compliance, through the remedy of existing problems and, above all, the prevention of others. The preferred methods to these ends are co-opera-tive and conciliatory with persuasion, negotiation, and education being primary enforcement techniques and legal action (especially prosecu-tion) a last resort. This model contrasts with the deterrence model, in which a penal style of enforcement accords prosecution and punish-ment an important role. Although the two models are analytically dis-tinct they are not mutually exclusive and enforcement officials typically draw on both models.

Reiss (1984) argues that systems of control will increasingly be built on compliance rather than deterrence. Similarly Rock (1995) has recently suggested that a negotiated style of social control may always have been the major pattern of formal social control in Western society. This refers both to the extent of regulatory control and the use of these methods by the police. There is now extensive evidence that regulatory officials in Australia, Britain, the Netherlands, Sweden, and the United States favour compliance-based methods in a variety of areas of social and financial regulation as well as certain areas of policing.[34]

Socio-legal research on regulation has therefore furthered our empir-ical and theoretical understanding of social control. This research has revealed alternative patterns of social control—patterns which force us to reconsider the concept of law enforcement and to acknowledge that much legal activity takes place 'in the shadow of the law' and in out-of-court contexts. This understanding has been reached by breaking boundaries and shifting the focus of theoretical thinking and empirical research to new areas. It shows how empirical research can develop the-oretical understanding and force us to develop concepts and explana-tions we might otherwise have taken for granted.

CONCLUSION

The central argument of this Chapter has been that theory and empirical work are inextricably related to each other and that it is a fundamental misunderstanding of the research process to suggest otherwise. This has

[34] On the subject of regulation see, e.g., Alders, 1993; Braithwaite, 1984; Clarke, 1986; Cranston, 1979; Dawson *et al.*, 1988; Gunningham, 1991; Johnstone, 1994; Kelman, 1981; Levi, 1997; Rees, 1988; Wilthagen, 1994; Yeager, 1991. On the subject of the police see Banton, 1964; Cain, 1973; Bittner, 1963; Waddington, 1994.

consequences for the way we view socio-legal studies and its policy rele-vance. In the course of the Chapter we have rejected the still-common caricature of socio-legal studies as atheoretical, pragmatic, and unques-tioningly policy-led. Behind this caricature we have identified a number of binary distinctions which we suggest are untenable—applied versus pure research; 'in law' versus 'of law'; theoretical versus pragmatic; the-oretical versus empirical. Further, we have argued that the caricature is based on a clustering of features that do not necessarily go together—for example, policy relevance has been associated with the definition of law as unproblematic; empirical work with theoretically unsophisticated pragmatism.

Socio-legal studies is not *necessarily* policy relevant. The primary goal of socio-legal research is often the development of socio-legal theory, and the particular empirical context is often a vehicle for pursuing theo-retical questions. Where empirical socio-legal research is designed to be applied, that fact does not obviate the need for theoretical adequacy. Overly simple assumptions about the nature of empirical work and narrow views of the nature of theory have too often drawn attention away from the most challenging task for socio-legal research, namely the development of *theory* in a new and complex field.

That is not to suggest that all socio-legal studies is or should aim to be theoretically sophisticated. Any research must focus on certain ques-tions, approaches, and priorities rather than others. We have argued that diversity in research is valuable, and that theoretical questions should not necessarily be treated as prior. Nonetheless, research will always be informed by intellectual preoccupations and epistemological assump-tions which may be implicit or explicit, and we believe that socio-legal scholars sometimes need to address them more explicitly. Attention con-stantly needs to be given to systematizing conceptual thinking and developing theory that facilitates our understanding of the social world. We have been arguing that the interplay of theory and empirical obser-vation is at the heart of this process.

Socio-legal studies is, in many respects, still in its infancy. We do not want to exaggerate what has been achieved nor make excessive claims for it. There is some truth in criticisms that have been made of socio-legal studies, and we have reservations about some of the work done under the socio-legal label. But socio-legal studies has successfully brought together a variety of scholars from different disciplines and created a focus for collaboration. Boundaries have been challenged and new ideas developed. It is vital that socio-legal scholars continue to advance and develop socio-legal studies, not only as a part of jurisprudence or an adjunct to legal policy, but also as a distinctive and theoretically power-ful intellectual approach to social scientific understanding of law.

REFERENCES

AALDERS, M. (1993), 'Regulation and in-Company Management in the Netherlands' *Law and Policy*, 15, 75–94.

BADDELEY, A. (1979), 'Applied Cognitive and Cognitive Applied Psychology: The Case of Face Recognition', in Lars-Goran Nilsson (ed.), *Perspectives on Memory Research* (Erlbaum, Hillsdale, N.J.).

BALDWIN, R. (1995), *Rules and Government* (Clarendon Press, Oxford).

BANTON, M. (1964), *The Policeman in the Community* (Tavistock, London).

BARSALOU, L. W. (1992), 'Frames, Concepts and Conceptual Fields' in E. Kittay and A. Lehrer (eds.), *Frames, Fields and Contrasts: New Essays in Semantic and Lexical Organisation* (Lawrence Erlbaum Associates, Hillsdaale, N.J.).

BECKER, H. S. (1963), *Outsiders* (The Free Press of Glencoe, New York).

—— (1982), 'Culture: A Sociological View', 71 *The Yale Review* 513–27.

BITTNER, E. (1967), 'The Police on Skid-Row: A Study of Peace Keeping', 32 *American Sociological Review* 699–715.

BRAITHWAITE, J. (1984), *Corporate Crime in the Pharmaceutical Industry* (Routledge & Kegan Paul, London).

BRITTAN, Y. (1984), *The Impact of Water Pollution Control on Industry* (Centre for Socio-Legal Studies, Oxford).

BROADBENT, D. E. (1980), 'The Minimization of Models' In E. J. Chapman and D. M. Jones (eds.), *Models of Man* (The British Psychological Society, Leicester).

BURGESS, R. G. (1984), *In the Field* (Routledge, London, 1991 Reprint).

CAIN, M. (1973), *Society and the Policeman's Role* (Routledge and Kegan Paul, London).

CAMPBELL, C. and WILES, P. 'The Study of Law in Society in Britain' *Law and Society Review* 10(4).

CLARKE, M. J. (1990), *Regulating the City: Competition, Scandal and Reform* (Open University Press, Milton Keynes).

COTTERRELL, R. (1992), *The Sociology of Law* (2nd edn., Butterworths, London).

CRANSTON, R. (1979), *Regulatory Business: Law and Consumer Agencies* (Macmillan, London).

DAWSON, S., WILLMAN, P., BAMFORD, M., and CLINTON, A. (1988), *Safety at Work: The Limits of Self-Regulation* (Cambridge University Press, Cambridge).

DINGWALL, R. and EEKELAAR, J. M. (1988), 'Families and the State: An Historical Perspective on the Public Regulation of Private Conduct', *Law and Policy* 10, 341–61.

—— and FENN, P. (eds.), (1992), *Quality and Regulation in Health Care* (Routledge, London).

EEKELAAR, J. M. and MACLEAN, M. (1986), *Maintenance After Divorce* (Clarendon Press, Oxford).

FITZPATRICK, P. (1995), 'Being Social in Socio-legal Studies' in D. J. Galligan (ed.), *Socio-Legal Studies in Context: The Oxford Centre Past and Future* (Blackwell, Oxford).

FREEMAN, M. D. A. (1995), *Lloyds Introduction to Jurisprudence* (6th edn., Stevens and Sons Ltd, London).

FRIEDMAN, L. M. (1986), 'The Law and Society Movement' 28 *Stanford Law Review* 766.

GENN, H. G. (1987), *Hard Bargaining: Out of Court Settlement in Personal Injury Actions* (Clarendon Press, Oxford).

—— (1993), 'Business Responses to the Regulation of Health and Safety in England', *Law and Policy*, 15, 219–34.

GIBSON, J. J. (1950), *The Perception of the Visual World* (Houghton Mifflin, Boston, Mass.).

—— (1966), *The Senses Considered as Perceptual Systems* (Houghton Mifflin, Boston, Mass.).

GRUNEBERG, M. M., MORRIS, P. E., and SYKES, R. N. (1978), *Practical Aspects of Memory* (Academic Press, London).

—— —— and —— (eds.) (1988), *Practical Aspects of Memory: Current Research and Issues* (Wiley, Chichester), i and ii.

GUNNINGHAM, N. (1991), 'Private Ordering, Self-regulation and Futures Markets: A Comparative Study of Informal Social Control', *Law and Policy*, 13, 297–326.

HARRE, R. and SECORD, P. F. (1972), *The Explanation of Social Behaviour* (Basil Blackwell, Oxford).

HARRIS, D., MACLEAN, M., GENN, H., LLOYD-BOSTOCK, S., FENN, P., CORFIELD, P., and BRITTAN, Y. (1984), *Compensation and Support for Illness and Injury* (Clarendon Press, Oxford).

HAWKINS, K. (1984), *Environment and Enforcement: Regulation and Social Definition of Pollution* (Clarendon Press, Oxford).

—— (1992), *The Regulation of Occupational Health and Safety: A Socio-Legal Perspective* (Report to the Health and Safety Executive).

—— and HUTTER, B. M. (1993), 'The Response of Business to Social Regulation in England and Wales: An Enforcement Perspective', *Law and Policy*, 15, 199–218.

HUTTER, B. M. (1988), *The Reasonable Arm of the Law?: The Law Enforcement Procedures of Environmental Health Officers* (Clarendon Press, Oxford).

—— (1997), *Compliance: Regulation and Environment* (Clarendon Press, Oxford).

—— and LLOYD-BOSTOCK, S. (1992), 'Field-level Perceptions of Risk in Regulatory Agencies', in J. F. Short, and L. Clarke (eds.), *Organizations, Uncertainties and Risk* (Westview Press, Boulder, Colo.).

JOHNSTONE, R. (ed.), (1994), *Occupational Health and Safety Prosecutions in Australia* (Centre for Employment and Labour Relations Law Occasional Monograph Series: University of Melbourne).

KAGAN, R. A. (1978), *Regulatory Justice* (Russell Sage Foundation, New York).

KELMAN, S. (1981), *Regulating America, Regulating Sweden: A Comparative Study of Occupational Safety and Health Policy* (MIT Press, Cambridge, Mass.).

KING, M. (1979), 'The Limits of Law and Psychology in Decisions Concerning the Welfare of Children' in S. Lloyd-Bostock (ed.), *Psychology in Legal Contexts: Applications and Limitations* (Macmillan, London).

KONECNI, V. J. and EBBESEN, E. B. (1979), 'External Validity of Research in Legal

Psychology', *Law and Human Behaviour*, 3 (special issue: Simulation research and the Law) 39–70.

KUHN, T. (1970), *The Structure of Scientific Revolutions* (2nd edn., University of Chicago Press, Chicago, Ill.).

LEMERT, E. (1967), *Human Deviance, Social Problems and Social Control* (Prentice Hall, Eaglewood Cliffs, NJ).

LEVI, M. (1987), *Regulating Fraud: White Collar Crime and the Criminal Process* (Tavistock, London).

LLOYD-BOSTOCK, S. (1979a), 'The Ordinary Man and the Psychology of Attributing Causes and Responsibility' (1939) 42 *Modern Law Review* 143–68.

—— (1979b), 'Common Sense Morality and Accident Compensation', in D. Farrington, K. Hawkins, and S. Lloyd-Bostock (eds.), *Psychology, Law and Legal Processes* (Macmillan, London, reprinted in *Insurance Law Journal*, 1980).

—— (1981), 'Do Lawyers' References to "Common Sense" have Anything to Do with What Ordinary People Think?', *British Journal of Social Psychology* 20: 161–3.

—— (1984), 'Legal Literature, Dialogue with Lawyers and Research on Practical Legal Questions: Some Gains and Pitfalls for Psychology' in G. M. Stephenson and J. H. Davis (eds.), *Progess in Applied Social Psychology* (Wiley, Chichester), ii.

—— (1986), 'Law and Psychiatry: Is the Conflict More Apparent than Real?' (1986) 49 *Modern Law Review* 389–95.

—— (1988a), *Law in Practice: Applications of Psychology to Legal Decision-Making and Legal Skills* (Routledge/British Psychological Society, London: US edn., Lyceum Press, Chicago, Ill.).

—— (1988b), 'Psychology and Law: From Understanding to Influencing Law in Practice', in P. J. van Koppen, D. Hessing, and G. van den Hoevel (eds.), *Lawyers on Psychologists and Psychologists on Law* (Swets & Zeitlinger, Amsterdam), 9–23.

—— (1991a), 'Propensity to Sue in England and the United States: The Role of Attribution Processes. A Comment on Kritzer', *Journal of Law and Society* 18, 4: 429–30.

—— (1991b), 'Interactions between Law and Everyday Thinking in the Social Categorization of Events', in R. Vermunt and R. Steensma (eds.), *Social Justice in Human Relations* (Plenum Press, New York), ii.

—— (1992), 'The Psychology of Routine Discretion: Accident Screening by British Factory Inspectors', *Law and Policy* 14, 45–76.

—— (in press, 1996), 'Psychology and the Law: Their Theoretical and Working Relationship', in P. A. Thomas (ed.), *Law and the Social Sciences* (Aldershot, Dartmouth).

—— and MULCAHY, L. (1994), 'The Social Psychology of Making and Responding to Complaints. An Account Model of Complaint Processes', *Law and Policy*, 16, 123–47.

MACLEAN, M. (1991), *Surviving Divorce: Women's Resources after Separation* (Macmillan, Women in Society Series, London; and New York University Press, New York).

MANNING, P. K. (1977), *Police Work: The Social Organisation of Policing* (MIT Press, Cambridge, Mass.).

MARSHALL, G. (ed.), (1994), *The Concise Oxford Dictionary of Sociology* (Oxford University Press, Oxford).

McBARNET, D. (1978), 'False Dichotomies in Criminal Justice Research', in John Baldwin and A. Keith Bottomley (eds.), *Criminal Justice. Selected Readings* (Martin Robertson, Oxford).

McCLOSKEY, M. E., EGETH, H. E. and McKENNA, J. (eds.) (1986), *The Ethics of Expert Testimony*, Special Issue of *Law and Human Behavior*, Vol 10, Nos 1 and 2.

MEIDINGER, E. (1987), 'Regulatory Culture: A Theoretical Outline', *Law and Policy*, 9, 355–87.

NEISSER, U. (1976), *Cognitive Psychology* (Freeman, New York).

—— (1982), *Memory Observed: Remembering in Natural Contexts* (Freeman, San Francisco, Cal.).

—— (1984), 'Toward an Ecologically Oriented Cognitive Science' in T. M. Schlechter and M. P. Toglia (eds.), *New Directions in Cognitive Science* (Ablex, Norwood NJ).

NELKEN, D. (1981), 'The "Gap Problem" in the Sociology of Law: A Theoretical Review', *Windsor Yearbook of Access to Justice*, 1, 35–61.

POTTER, M. C. (1983), 'Neisser's Challenge', *Contemporary Psychology*, 28, 272–4.

REES, J. (1988), *Reforming the Workplace: a Study of Self-Regulation in Occupational Safety* (University of Pennsylvania Press, Philadelphia, Penn.).

REISS, A. (1984), 'Selecting Strategies of Social Control over Organisational Life' in K. Hawkins and J. Thomas (eds.), *Enforcing Regulation* (Kluwer-Nijhoff, Boston).

RICHARDSON, G. M., OGUS, A. I., and BURROWS, P. (1983), *Policing Pollution: A Study of Regulation and Enforcement* (Oxford University Press, Oxford).

RITZER, G. (1981), *Toward an Integrated Sociological Paradigm* (Allyn and Bacon, Boston and London).

ROCK, P. (1973), *Making People Pay* (Routledge and Kegan Paul, London).

—— (1995), 'Sociology and the Stereotype of the Police', *Journal of Law and Society*, 22(1), 17–25.

SANTOS, B. DE SOUSA (1995), 'Three Metaphors for a New Conception of Law: The Frontier, the Baroque and the South', *Law and Society Review*, (Symposium: Charting a course for socio-legal scholarship) 29, 4, 569–84.

SILVERMAN, D. (1993), *Interpreting Qualitative Data* (Sage, London).

STRINGER, P. (1982), 'Introduction' in P. Stringer (ed.), *Confronting Social Issues: Applications of Social Psychology* (Academic Press, London), i.

SKOLNICK, J. (1975), *Justice Without Trial* (2nd edn., John Wiley & Sons, New York).

THOMAS, P. (1994), 'Socio-legal Studies in the United Kingdom' in F. Bruinsma (ed.), *Precaire Waarden* (Gouda Quint) 229–46.

TRUBEK, D. M. and ESSER, J. (1989), 'Critical Empiricism in American Legal Studies: Paradox, Program or Pandora's Box?' *Law and Social Enquiry*, 3–59.

TWINING, W. L. T. (1995), 'Remembering 1972. The Oxford Centre in the Context of Development in Higher Education and the Discipline of Law' in D. J. Galligan (ed.), *Socio-Legal Studies in Context: The Oxford Centre Past and Future*, (Blackwell Publishers, Oxford).

TYLER, T. (1990), *Why People Obey the Law* (Yale University Press, New Haven, Conn.).

WADDINGTON, P. A. J. (1994), *Liberty and Order: Public Order and Policing in the Capital City* (UCL Press, London).

WHEELER, S. (1991), *Retention of Title Clauses: Impact and Implications* (Clarendon Press, Oxford).

WILTHAGEN, T. (1994), 'Reflexive Rationality in the Regulation of Occupational Health and Safety' in T. Wilthagen and R. Rogowski (eds.), *Reflexive Labour Law: Studies in Industrial Relations and Employment Regulation* (Kluwer Law and Taxation Publishers, Deventer).

YEAGER, P. C. (1991), *The Limits of the Law: The Public Regulation of Private Pollution* (Cambridge University Press, Cambridge).

2

Profit and Virtue. Economic Theory and the Regulation of Occupational Health in Nineteenth and Early Twentieth Century Britain

PETER BARTRIP AND R. M. HARTWELL

I GOVERNMENT AND ECONOMY

As a scholar Donald Harris is perhaps best known for his work on compensation for illness and injury. However, as Director of the Centre for Socio-Legal Studies he not only did much to nurture the emerging law and economics tradition, but provided strong support for research in law and social history. It is therefore appropriate that this essay should embrace the disciplines of law, history, and economics. Its aim is to examine nineteenth-century regulation to safeguard the health of industrial workers in the light of modern theories of economic regulation. This brings together the interests of the two authors, Bartrip, who has worked extensively on the history of health and safety at work (Bartrip, 1979a, 1979b, 1988, 1996; Bartrip and Burman, 1983; Bartrip and Fenn, 1988, 1990), and Hartwell, who is interested in the growth of government since the industrial revolution (Hartwell, 1994). It brings together, also, two bodies of literature, the large historical literature on 'government and industry in Britain' (e.g. Grove, 1962; Checkland, 1983), which is of long standing, and the more recent literature on public regulation (e.g. Peacock, 1984; Tomlinson, 1994).

Government regulation of industry is not new: legislation to control the payment of wages in ready money dates back to 1464; Crown control of pollution was embodied in the Bill of Sewers of 1531; and Elizabeth I banned the burning of coal in London while Parliament was meeting (Peacock, 1984, 47, 51; Brimblecombe, 1987, 30). But the incidence and breadth of regulation increased with industrialization and urbanization. Much regulation before the industrial revolution was concerned with commerce and trade. As government relaxed its hold on trade during the industrial revolution, it increased its control of industry, but with a time-lag. Mercantilism gave way to *laissez-faire*, but *laissez-faire* gave way to what Dicey called 'collectivism'. By the end of the nineteenth century a welfare state was being established, and in the twentieth century it expanded as a consequence of two world wars and a great depression. At the same time, because of the Keynesian revolution in economics, the state increasingly took on the role of macro-economic manager, manipulating key economic variables and regulating widely. In the late twentieth century, however, there has been a swing away from government regulation and control towards economic liberalism, with privatization and regulatory reform. There had been already, in the nineteenth century, a general debate about the role of government in economy and society. The appropriate questions were posed authoritatively by John Stuart Mill in 1848: what are 'the proper limits of the functions and agencies of government?' 'How should governments be constituted, and according to what principles and rules should they exercise their authority?' And to what 'departments of human affairs' should that authority extend? (Mill, 1848, 795). To those questions Jevons later added another: 'the all-important question is to explain if possible why, in general we uphold the rule of laisser faire, and yet in large classes of cases invoke the interference of local or central authorities' (Jevons, 1883, v). Jevons' answer was emphatically utilitarian: 'I conceive that the State is justified in passing any law, or even doing any single act which, without ulterior consequences, adds to the sum total of human happiness' (Jevons, 1883, 12). Jevons was underlining the paradox of the existence of pressing social problems, which created a demand for government action, in the world's most successful economy whose remarkable growth was attributed to the liberal economic policy of *laissez-faire*. The need for action on social and economic problems such as public health and child labour was revealed particularly by public inquiries which led in turn to legislation in the 'public interest'. The argument was that industrialization in an unregulated economy, whatever its wealth-creating potential, generated social problems of such magnitude that, in a society in which the mass of the people was gradually being enfranchised, it was imperative to redress the problems by legislation and the creation of a bureaucracy of control, which included inspectorates. More radical interpretations of the existence of social problems included that of Polanyi, who argued that 'market economy was a threat to the social fabric', and that led naturally to moves for self-protection which took the form of defensive legislation (Polanyi, 1944). Essentially, this was a refinement of Marx's argument that exploitation and the declining standard of living of the working classes were the inevitable consequences of capitalism (i.e. of a free-market economy).

Modern historical analysis of what Victorian governments did, and why, centres in the 'nineteenth-century revolution in government' debate, which emphasized not only the legislative activities of government but the creation of a powerful bureaucracy with delegated executive authority (Hartwell, 1994, summarizes the debate). Together, the historians' explanations of government intervention in the nineteenth century have four related themes: the public-interest imperative, the self-growth of bureaucracies, electoral pressure from below in a reformed parliament, and intellectual changes in the theory of the state (in which belief in *laissez-faire* gave way to acceptance of government regulation and control). In a recent article Hartwell added an entrepreneurial theme, arguing that making legislation was an essentially political process which required political entrepreneurs and, initially, moral entrepreneurs. The role of the moral entrepreneur was to identify social problems and to publicize them until public conscience was roused and political entrepreneurs found it profitable to push for legislation (Hartwell, 1994). There is a large literature on the history of government intervention which includes histories of public finance and taxation, of particular industries and trades, of industrial relations, of the welfare state, of factory legislation, of local government, of public utilities, and of financial institutions. In general this literature shows that the need for intervention in the public interest was assumed, even though there were voices which questioned its necessity and some who questioned, not the need, but the effectiveness of particular legislation. By the 1890s the acceptance of intervention can be demonstrated by the publication of D. G. Ritchie's *The Principles of State Interference*, and by the beginning of the twentieth century there was almost unquestioning agreement on the need for government intervention in the economy.

In the first half of the twentieth century two world wars and the inter-war depression encouraged further government intervention—intervention rationalized by Keynes and Beveridge. Reaction, therefore, only came after the Second World War, when the now massive size of government, and the extent of government controls, produced an almost involuntary increase in interest by economists. This resulted in a new branch of economics—the economics of the public sector—which analysed the activities of governments and bureaucracies, and critically examined regulation and regulators (e.g. Buchanan and Tulloch, 1962; Buchanan, 1968; Stigler, 1971). The economists were particularly interested in evaluating regulation to determine its costs and benefits, not necessarily accepting the traditional 'public interest' justification. Indeed, much research was directed to determine whether regulation was economically desirable. This led to assessment of the economic importance of regulation, examining the behaviour of regulatory agencies and the motivation of regulators, and questioning the desirability of much regulation. The economists at first viewed regulations as attempts to correct market failures, to remedy situations where market prices did not

accurately reflect social costs. They identified causes of market imperfections in monopolistic behaviour, transactions costs arising from
imperfect information, and externalities not accounted for in market
prices. The publication in 1971 of Stigler's article, 'The Theory of
Economic Regulation', was particularly important in changing understanding of regulation (Stigler, 1971). Stigler argued for a 'capture theory
of regulation', claiming, at least for the USA, that well-organized interest
groups, usually of producers, were able to dominate the administration
of regulation for their own advantage. Bargaining from strength, the regulated influenced the regulators to impose regulations which strengthened their market position. Thus the regulators are 'captured' by the
industry they are regulating. This theory was further bolstered by the
new public-sector economics which showed that regulators are themselves economic agents in a complex political process and do not necessarily act 'in the public interest' (Niskanen: 1973). Recently Pelzman has
suggested that the outcome of any regulatory move involving various
interest groups depends on the costs and benefits of intervention for the
interested parties and on complex bargaining between them (Pelzman,
1981). Peacock, for Britain and Germany, has entitled a book *The
Regulation Game*, underlining the bargaining process in the making and
implementing of regulations (Peacock, 1984). This new approach
attempts to bring together the old public-interest view of regulation and
the increased understanding of political decision-making with self-
interested actors, politicians, and bureaucrats on the one hand, and, on
the other, the interest groups representing the producers and perhaps
the consumers. The new realism combines the detailed historical
account of the process of making regulations with the new analytical
insights derived from the capture theory and the economics of the public sector.

II REGULATION

Does the economic theory of regulation mean that the historians should
now revise their history? *Prima facie* there is a case for, if not revising,
then re-examining historical studies. Perhaps the most important lesson
to be learned from modern economic research is the need to examine
critically and sceptically the process of making regulation, the motivations and actions of interested parties, and the negotiations that finally
result in regulation and regulators. 'Public interest' there certainly was—
the evidence of revealed social ills, and the passion of reformers who
acted to redress them, cannot be ignored—but evidence and passion
were part of a political process in which producers almost invariably had

an important, and sometimes a determining, role in the outcomes. And with legislation there entered the bureaucrats—the inspectors who often enlarged and revised their responsibilities, in the public interest but, perhaps, also in the interest of a larger and more powerful bureau.[1] And in the enforcement of legislation there was often bargaining between inspector and producer in a compliance procedure depending on the strength and determination of the two parties, the costs of compliance to the producer and the cost of enforcement to the government (Bartrip and Fenn, 1983). Enforcement was not costless, and governments were unwilling spenders (Bartrip, 1982). To understand nineteenth-century regulation, then, it is necessary to combine the older normative paradigm of action in 'the public interest' with the modern economics of how political decisions are made, how regulatory agencies behave, and the incentives created in the process of regulation-making. Inspectorates were created and financed by Parliament, an elected body, so that the growth of regulation must be related to the changing electoral process, as many historians have pointed out. Finally, since much modern empirical literature on regulation is motivated by scepticism about the social and economic desirability of regulation, the historian should also ask whether the regulation was necessary or desirable in terms of solving problems and providing solutions even if it was politically acceptable.

It is impossible to subject the entire field of regulation to detailed scrutiny. Here our concern is with factory and workshop conditions. But this, too, is a vast subject, for there were as many as eighteen Acts of Parliament broadly concerned with factory and workshop conditions in the period 1802–91. Much of the remainder of this Chapter is concerned with a particular branch of regulation—industrial health—in a specific place and period—late nineteenth- and early twentieth-century Britain. Within this context we propose to examine the making of occupational-health regulations relating to industrial lead poisoning and to phosphorus poisoning in the match industry. In so doing we shall have in mind the following questions: how was the legislation 'justified'? Who was responsible for exposing the health hazards and what was their motivation? To what extent was parliament involved in this exposure? What were the stages and who were the actors in a process which finally resulted in legislation? How did producers react to the proposed legislation and how effective were they in modifying legislation in their own interest? To what extent was the final package of controls the result

---

[1] There are conflicting views about the role and influence of bureaucrats, particularly inspectors, in pressing for intervention as a means of enlarging their powers and responsibilities. Some historians (e.g. Roberts, 1960 and West, 1965) have emphasized bureaucratic importance in these respects. Bartrip (1982) argues that inspectors were often reluctant collectivists.

of a bargaining process? How did particular individuals influence outcomes?

III OCCUPATIONAL HEALTH IN HISTORY

For the purposes of this Chapter occupational ill-health is taken to mean
any disease, illness, or medical condition caused or exacerbated by contact with any process, product, or raw material encountered in the
course of and as a result of paid employment. In this sense, there is nothing new about occupational ill-health. Neither was its appearance a by-
product of the Industrial Revolution; indeed, it is probable that the first
cases date from about 7000 BC, in other words, from the time when man
first began to mine, smelt, and mould that highly toxic metal, lead. While
scholars are divided on the question of incidence, there is broad acceptance that occupational lead poisoning occurred in classical Greece and
Rome (Goldwater, 1936, 7–28; Teleky, 1948, 4; Nriagu, 1983, 309; Smith,
1986, 7–24). Extant medieval literature contains no reference to occupational illness, but in the sixteenth century both Paracelsus and Agricola
dealt with the subject (Rosen, 1943; Major, 1954, 387–8; Corn, 1992, 72).
The first comprehensive treatise on work and health was Bernardino
Ramazzini's *De Morbis Artificum* (*The Diseases of Workers*), which was
first published in 1700 (Wright, 1940).

English writers began to broach the subject in the mid-eighteenth century, mainly in connection with the diseases of soldiers and sailors
(Rosen, 1993, 751–8). Thereafter, a small but growing medical literature
dealt with the work-related ailments of chimney sweeps, needle point-
ers, cutlery grinders, stone masons, leather dressers, china makers, and
others. 'Britain's Ramazzini' made his appearance as late as 1831, the
year in which Charles Turner Thackrah published his path-breaking
*Effects of the Principal Arts, Trades and Professions, and of Civic States
and Habits of Living, on Health and Longevity; with Particular Reference
to the Trades and Manufactures of Leeds; with Suggestions for the
Removal of many of the Agents which Produce Disease and Shorten the
Duration of Life*. The *Lancet* immediately recognized the importance of a
volume which, since its first appearance, has been repeatedly and
deservedly acclaimed for its comprehensiveness, constructiveness, and
accuracy of observation (*Lancet*, 1831, 450; Raffle *et al.*, 1987, 125).
Thackrah's treatise, slim though it was, provided the foundations on
which such giants of British occupational medicine as Thomas Arlidge,
Thomas Oliver, and Thomas Legge built.

When Thackrah published his work the *Lancet* unfavourably contrasted English neglect of occupational health with Continental concern.

Yet the Factory Acts, the first of which had become law almost thirty years earlier, did deal with health and hygiene. The earliest of these measures, the Health and Morals of Apprentices Act, 1802 required cotton- and woollen-mill owners to ventilate their factories and regularly to limewash their interior walls in order to improve standards of sanitation and hygiene. However, this provision owed more to a desire to counter the spread of epidemic diseases, within and without the factory, than to any idea of improving occupational health. In any case, while limewashing requirements were re-enacted (albeit with reduced frequency of applications), in practice they were ignored. As for ventilation, after 1802 this was not mentioned in any subsequent Factory Act until 1864. The factory inspector, Alexander Redgrave, explained the inspectorate's approach to industrial health and hygiene in 1864: 'although the enactments of 1802 would be valid now in cotton and woollen factories the Inspectors have no special directions to enforce them and they have been treated as obsolete' (Parliamentary Papers, 1865, XX, 441–6). The reality is that the main thrust of the Factory Acts, at least until the 1840s, and arguably for considerably longer, was for reduced hours of work for children and young persons.

To be sure, in arguing the need for a shorter working day reformers pointed to physical as well as to moral, educational, and spiritual imperatives. Not only would reduced hours of work give time for religious and other instruction, they would lessen the incidence of bodily deformity caused by the imposition of excessive demands on immature frames and of accidental injury caused by tiredness. But while it is demonstrable that the Factory Acts had a health-and-safety agenda from the first, it was only in 1844 that specific measures for accident prevention in textile factories were enacted (Bartrip, 1979a, 1979b; Bartrip and Burman, 1983). The Factory Acts Extension Act, 1864, which initiated the process of bringing non-textile industries under regulation, included clauses for ventilation and sanitation, but it was not until 1883 and the passage of the Factory and Workshop Act, that occupational health came to be regulated in anything but a peripheral and incidental manner. The *Lancet* was therefore justified when, in 1831, it highlighted British neglect of the subject.

REGULATING OCCUPATIONAL DISEASE

Let us now consider the regulation of occupational disease with special reference to lead and phosphorus hazards in industrial processes. Lead is a metallic element which is widely distributed throughout the world. For centuries it has had numerous uses, including in the manufacture of piping, paint, ceramics, and a variety of important alloys. Phosphorus is a non-metallic element which, in minute quantities is essential to animal and plant life. In comparison with lead its commercial applications are limited. In the nineteenth century it was used as a rat poison and as medicine, especially in cases of nervous disease. It was also an ingredient of saccharin, distress flares, and luminous goods. Its greatest importance was in 'lucifer' match manufacture, an industry which began to 'take off' in the 1830s, following the invention of the friction match.[2]

The Factory and Workshop Act, 1883, which was the first attempt to suppress a specific industrial disease through legislation, came into being as a result of public concern over fatalities in the white-lead industry. This concern developed incrementally from the 1830s when Thackrah drew attention to the hazards of lead work. In the 1860s and 1870s a number of private and official inquiries, including investigations carried out by the factory inspector Alexander Redgrave and Charles Dickens' *All the Year Round*, initiated regulation of the white lead trade (Rowe, 1983; Bartrip, 1988; Harrison, 1989). However, by 1880 the degree of state intervention was limited to a prohibition of child labour and a ban on the consumption of meals except in rooms expressly provided for that purpose. In 1882 ill-health among white-lead workers became a matter of public scrutiny and controversy. This occurred when two working-class Liberal MPs, Henry Broadhurst and Thomas Burt, asked questions in Parliament about the death of a female white-lead worker from Shoreditch. Their interest was generated by press reports of the inquest on this worker. In the course of this inquest the medical officer of the Shoreditch infirmary had referred to numerous cases of poisoning and the need for precautions. Both MPs insisted that something had to be done (3 *Hansard* 268, 4 April 1882, cols. 666–7; *Daily News*, 3 April 1882). Following publication of these parliamentary proceedings Burt received two letters from the north-east which appeared to show that lead poisoning was a problem on Tyneside as well as in London. Burt forwarded these to the Home Office along with a covering letter in which he repeated his conviction that action was needed. The government, persuaded of the need to act, ordered the Chief Inspector of Factories to investigate (PRO HO 45/9620 A15330).

All of this is instructive, not least because of what it reveals about the ability of moral crusaders, especially if they were MPs, to influence government thinking. On the basis of a few parliamentary questions, a newspaper report, and a handful of letters the full machinery of government

---

[2] Matches are known to have existed in the 16th century but the first 'really practical' examples date either from 1827 England or 1831 France, depending on the source consulted. The first match factory was established in Wandsworth in 1832 (Heavisides, 1909; Dixon, 1925, 14–15, 19–21; Beaver, 1985, 18–19; Briggs, 1988, 188–9).

was unleashed against the white-lead trade. Yet dispassionate examination of the evidence provides little indication that there was a serious outbreak of industrial lead poisoning. On the basis of two established fatalities—one in London, one in Newcastle—and some astute questions, especially from Burt, the public-inquiry process swung into motion. Redgrave's report, when it came, amounted to a less than ringing endorsement of the need for regulation. In fact, he rejected state intervention. He agreed that action, in the form of 'excessive and enforced cleanliness' and the provision of protective clothing and appliances, for example, respirators, was needed, but he felt that it was for manufacturers and workers, rather than government to take the necessary steps (Parliamentary Papers, 1882, XVIII, 957–61). Seldom an advocate of an expanded role for the state, and never a zealot, if it had been left to Redgrave the regulatory process would have been stopped in its tracks. But it was not left to Redgrave. Burt's continuing pressure on the Home Office was supported by a string of letters from Poor Law Guardians. These highlighted poisoning cases, some of them fatal, called attention to the burden that victims were imposing on parochial funds, and called on the government to act (PRO HO45/9620 A15330).

By mid-1882 the Home Office, persuaded that action would have to be taken, instructed the unenthusiastic Redgrave to come up with a practical scheme. Reluctant to carry 'legislative regulations to too extreme a point', Redgrave rejected compulsory medical inspection (which at least one senior Home Office figure favoured), bans on female labour, and compulsory substitution of machines for people. What he recommended was a legal requirement that all white-lead manufacturers should observe six basic rules of hygiene. These involved the provision of protective clothing, washing and bathing facilities, a 'distinct and separate' dining room, and 'acidulated' drinks. Those who complied would receive an official certificate allowing them to remain in production.

A Bill based on Redgrave's proposals was soon drafted. In the House of Lords, where the Bill was introduced, there was intense criticism from the ultra-*laissez-faire* Lord Wemyss, founder of the Property and Liberty Defence Association (PLDA). He complained bitterly of 'grandmotherly legislation' and predicted the destruction of 'national liberty and self reliance' if the Bill became law. In contrast, the Duke of Argyll, who said he had given much thought to the 'legitimate province of legislation', supported it. He argued that it ought to be judged not by abstract principles but in the light of prevailing circumstances. The life and health of the population was one area where it was 'competent and desirable' for Parliament to legislate. Even Lord Granville, an avowed supporter of the PLDA agreed; the state needed to act because market forces did not produce the best working conditions and there would always be bad employers who fell below the standards of the best (3 *Hansard* 281, 19 July 1883, cols. 1865–8).

The measure, which was never debated in the House of Commons, became law at the beginning of 1884. Three factors were crucial to its acceptance. First, recognition that it would eradicate a terrible scourge; secondly, that it would relieve rate-payers of a financial burden by reducing the demands of the chronically ill on the parish; and thirdly, that it received no opposition from trade interests. The Act provided for Home Office certification of white-lead manufacturers. Anyone seeking a certificate had to demonstrate compliance with the six hygiene regulations proposed by Redgrave. Following certification employers were obliged to compile 'special rules' for the conduct of their works. These rules, to which workers were empowered to raise objections, were subject to approval by the Secretary of State (46 & 47 Vict. c. 53).[3]

It is not possible to quantify the impact of the 1883 Act upon the health of white-lead workers because the Act made no provision for the collection of morbidity or mortality statistics. All we have are conflicting opinions. In 1890 Redgrave, then on the verge of retirement, stated that the regulations were usually 'well observed' (Parliamentary Papers, 1890–91, XIX, 477). On the other hand, his successor, Frederick Whymper, spoke of their 'widespread' neglect and of the need for firmer measures to be taken (Parliamentary Papers, 1893–4, XVII, 67). A Home Office memorandum of 1892 emphasized the need for the rigorous enforcement of 'effectual and practicable precautions', adding that non-compliant employers should be shown 'no indulgence ' (PRO HO45/9620 A15330). However, by this time the terms of the Factory Act, 1891 had made it likely that, whatever the preferences of Home Office civil servants, a policy of tough rules rigorously applied would not be adopted. Instead, employers' occupational health obligations would remain within the bounds of what was 'reasonably practicable' (54 & 55 Vict. c. 75, section 58).[4]

The Factory Act, 1891, which a *Daily Chronicle* leader (24 November 1892) later termed 'cruelly inadequate', gave the Home Secretary power to certify particular industries or trades as dangerous or injurious to health. If he took this line he could proceed either to propose a set of special rules or to require the adoption of such special measures as appear

---

[3] Regulation by 'special rules' dated from the Factory Acts Extension Act, 1864. This provided for manufacturers to make such rules as a means of attaining the Act's hygiene and sanitation objectives.

[4] The act refers to 'such special measures as appear to the chief inspector to be reasonably practicable and to meet the necessities of the case' (in respect of dangerous and unhealthy occupations). The term 'reasonably practicable' which became a familiar feature of 20th-century factory legislation was used for the first time in the 1891 Act. It was not discussed in the course of any of the parliamentary debates on the Bill.

to the Chief Inspector of Factories to be appropriate and 'reasonably practicable' (54 & 55 Vict. c. 75, section 8). In relation to occupational health the Act was important in setting in motion the revision of the 1883 white-lead rules and in extending regulation to other unhealthy trades. In May 1892 the Home Secretary approved an order certifying white-lead manufacture, iron-plate enamelling, arsenic extraction, and the manufacture of paints and colours to be dangerous, thereby invoking the special-rule procedure. Subsequently, many other occupations were certified unhealthy and brought under special rules.

In some ways the 1891 Act was a significant step forward in the regulation of the dangerous trades. However, it gave employers a crucial role in the regulatory process while denying any formal role to workers, such as that which the Act of 1883 had allowed them in respect of white lead. It did this by withholding the right of objection conferred on workers under the terms of the 1883 Act, while conferring upon employers a power to object to any special rules which the Secretary of State or the factory inspectorate might compile. As a result employers could pressurize the Secretary of State either to accede to their views on how their industries should be regulated or to face the potentially expensive and time-consuming arbitration process which the Act allowed.[5] H. J. Tennant, a prominent figure in occupational-health issues, outlined the position in the *Fortnightly Review*: 'the matter in dispute is referred to two arbitrators. In the event of their disagreement they may appoint an umpire whose decision is final. Thus matters which ought to be settled by the Secretary of State with the guidance and control of Parliament, are taken out of his hands and placed either in those of a prejudiced or of an irresponsible power' (Tennant, 1899, 317). In practice, as Herbert Asquith pointed out, regulating occupational health by means of special rules meant that 'employers have these matters more or less in their own hands' (4 *Hansard* 63, 29 July 1898, cols. 475–6). Consequently, when the Home Office formulated special rules, it did so in the knowledge that a severe approach risked provoking an objection from employers. As a result, it tended either to compile a list of rules which employers would accept, or, if employers did not accept, to lower its standards in order to achieve agreement without recourse to arbitration. Tennant saw the latter scenario unfold in the case of special rules for lead poisoning in pottery and earthenware in 1894 (Tennant, 1899, 317).

[5] In matters of industrial safety a right of arbitration had been allowed to factory occupiers under the terms of the Factory Act 1856. This Act was passed in response to employers' complaints that factory inspectors were using their powers to compel the fencing of machinery and mill-gearing in an irresponsible and dictatorial fashion. In fencing questions employers' arbitration rights were restricted by the Factory and Workshops Act, 1878. They were rescinded in 1891, precisely at the time when they were introduced in the occupational-health context.

   A similar pattern developed in relation to lucifer-match manufacture (Satre, 1982; Harrison, 1995). The health hazards of lucifer-matchmaking were recognized as early as the 1840s. Exposure to oxidizing phosphorus created a risk of necrosis of the jaw or 'phossy jaw', as it became known. This disease, which particularly affected those with dental caries or gum disease, literally rotted living bone *in situ*, causing terrible pain, disfigurement, and death. Following numerous independent inquiries, chiefly by medical men, conditions in the match trade were officially investigated in the 1860s (Parliamentary Papers, 1863, XVIII; Parliamentary Papers, 1863, XXV). As a result the hygiene and sanitation provisions of the Factory Acts Extension Act, 1864, were applicable to match factories. Thereafter, for more than twenty-five years, the question virtually disappeared as a public-policy issue. As Redgrave told the Royal Commission on the Factory and Workshops Acts: 'that dreadful disease which used to be so fatal . . . has entirely ceased' (Parliamentary Papers, 1876, XXX, 6). In 1892, however, 'phossy jaw' became newsworthy because of revelations of disease and scandalous 'cover-ups'. These revelations were not the product of a public-inquiry process, but the outcome of investigations carried out by the *Star* newspaper into cases of death and disease from phosphorus poisoning at Bryant and May's East End works. In June the *Star*'s exposures prompted the Home Secretary, Henry Matthews, to certify lucifer-matchmaking as dangerous to health. In August special rules were agreed, without recourse to arbitration, but the continued occurrence of poisonings led to the compilation of revised special rules in 1894. Employer objections to a rule compelling monthly medical inspections of 'at risk' workers led the Home Office to drop this proposal rather than face arbitration. However, the promulgation and subsequent suspension of this rule had the effect not of encouraging match manufacturers to take occupational health more seriously, but, especially in the case of Bryant and May, of leading them to 'cover up' poisonings in the knowledge that the emergence of any new cases might lead to the rule's resurrection. This cover-up succeeded until 1898 when the *Star*, the *Daily Chronicle*, and other newspapers exposed Bryant and May's dishonesty and criminality (Satre, 1982, 20–5). The scandal which the newspapers revealed was a direct consequence of the special-rule process, for the Home Office, having 'flagged' its intentions, showed precisely how firms could sidestep them. In so doing it provided an open invitation for the unscrupulous to flout the law.

   The problem which faced regulators and others interested in occupational-health questions was how to improve standards without increasing costs to the extent that firms were driven out of business by making them unprofitable, thereby increasing unemployment, and 'exporting jobs'. A simple solution to the problem of lead poisoning in pottery manufacture or phosphorus necrosis in the match industry would have been to ban the toxic products which caused the problem, regardless of the availability of suitable alternative ingredients. Some parties favoured such an approach, with bans being placed on the manufacture of lucifer matches and lead-glazed pottery. John Burns, for example, was prepared to see businesses close. 'What the Home Secretary has got to do', he told the Commons,

is to send his nastiest but firmest inspector down to the Potteries, the man who has got a jaw of iron, and will take the worst employers, so to speak, by the scruff of the neck and run them before the magistrates. . . . If an industry can only be carried on by the destruction of the health of the potential mothers of many of our working classes, well, then, I say Germany can have that industry (4 *Hansard* 63, 29 July 1898, cols. 504–5)

But such views were not necessarily shared by the workers themselves. Thus in 1894, Herbert Burrows, treasurer to the Matchmakers' Union, told the Home Office of his concern that stricter regulation could mean job losses and that '[i]n the present state of society advantages [better health protection] have to be balanced against disadvantages [higher unemployment]' (PRO HO 45 9849/B12393). Furthermore, official documents provide evidence of a number of 'at-risk' workers who expressed a preference for taking a chance of contracting an occupational disease as against the certain loss of a job and all the hazards which that entailed. Such views accorded with those of the factory inspectorate and of senior Home Office officials who ruminated on the question of where a policy of prohibition, once introduced, might lead. Why not, they pondered, ban the use of each and every hazardous substance used in British factories? How were the seemingly conflicting priorities of economics versus health reconciled?

In the case of lucifer matches use of the toxic ingredient, white phosphorus, was banned under the terms of the White Phosphorus Matches Prohibition Act, 1908 (implemented in 1910). But this was less a case of the British Government suddenly opting for an uncompromising policy towards match manufacturers, more an example of legislative intervention recognizing changed technical and commercial circumstances. By 1908, following the International Labour Conferences of 1905 and 1906, there was not only widespread international agreement on the need for a ban, but acceptance by the British match industry that such a ban could have commercial benefits. This conversion of manufacturers was largely brought about by the development of a completely practical and totally harmless (sesqui-sulphide) safety match. Although this was the patented invention of a French company, Sevène et Cahen, in 1899–1900 Bryant and May acquired, at a cost of £8,000, options on the patent for all countries other than France and Russia. The timing of this acquisition was important, since it coincided precisely with Home Office proposals to revise existing special rules. Bryant and May thereupon abandoned its use of white phosphorus. At the same time it rigorously policed its patent rights—launching a successful action against a German company which infringed them in 1905—and 'bought off' its main British rival, the Gloucester firm of Moreland, by licensing it for sesqui-sulphide manufacture in 1906. (Bryant & May manuscripts, Directors' Minute Books XP 18/1; Bryant & May manuscripts, D/B/BRY/1/2/564–79; Satre, 1982, 29–30).[6]

All this meant that an international ban on white phosphorus would not only compel the regulators to cease their harassment of the British match industry (since the sesqui-sulphide match offered no health threat), it would go a long way towards freeing UK manufacturers from overseas competition and opening up foreign markets to British matches. Thus a ban on the manufacture and import of white phosphorus, far from threatening commercial interests, promised to give them a considerable fillip. It is not surprising, therefore, that such a ban was actively supported by the UK match industry. Indeed, in 1908 a deputation of match producers urged the Home Secretary to act 'at the earliest possible date' in the interests of worker health. The alternative of further Special Rules would mean, they argued, that 'several Factories would be put out of existence, and the rest would be very seriously handicapped' (Bryant & May manuscripts, D/B/BRY/1/2/564–79, Deputation to Home Secretary, 24 March 1908). While it is not necessary to accept that the late-Victorian and Edwardian match industry was preoccupied with profit at the expense of workers' health, there is abundant evidence to indicate that health priorities came second to commercial considerations. Burns' observation to the effect that Germany was welcome to any 'industry [which] can only be carried on by the destruction of the health of the potential mothers of many of our working classes' found little support in the board rooms of Britain's match companies.

Neither should we conclude that the matchmakers were simply a particularly 'hard-nosed' group of industrialists. In pottery and earthenware, where white lead was used as an ingredient of glazes, manufacturers vigorously resisted demands for the compound's prohibition. They did so on the grounds that there existed no suitable alternative to white lead (notwithstanding abolitionists' claims to the contrary). In this

---

[6] By 1900 the British match industry which, in the early-Victorian period, had had a very substantial 'cottage' element, was highly concentrated. In 1885, a year after it became a public company, Bryant and May took over its great rival, Bell & Black and its four associated companies. Thereafter, it expanded rapidly. Competition in the industry became intense with the opening of the American Diamond Match Company in Liverpool in 1895. However, Bryant & May and Diamond amalgamated in 1901.

industry the parallels with match manufacturers are obvious; the one difference was the absence of an agreed, commercially viable, and safe alternative to the toxic hazard. Commercial considerations again triumphed; the outcome being, in this case, no ban on the toxic substance at the centre of the dispute (Bartrip, 1996).

IV IMPACT

The existence, from 1896, of official statistics of poisoning in the lead and match industries enables us to compare workers' occupational-health experiences in these two trades with a view to determining the impact of the regulatory process. However, such an undertaking is highly problematic. In particular, there are difficulties in determining which factors were responsible, and in what degree, for the behaviour of statistical trends (Bartrip and Fenn, 1988, 1990). Detailed consideration of the impact of regulation on the incidence of reported poisoning cases is beyond the scope of this Chapter. It is worth noting, however, that between 1899 and 1914 the number of cases of lead and phosphorus poisoning fell significantly. A total of 1,278 cases of industrial lead poisoning was reported in 1898; in 1914 the figure was 445. After 1909 no further cases of phosphorus poisoning were reported (Parliamentary Papers, 1900, XI, 106; Parliamentary Papers, 1914–16, XXI, 485). The untested assumption of the factory inspectorate was that regulation was responsible. Although inspectors failed to consider the possible influence of factors such as changed reporting practice, technological change which rendered production safer, and reduced output and employment, there is little reason to suppose that any of these played a significant part. The regulation of occupational health in the late Victorian and Edwardian periods, for all its compromises, actually appears to have worked.[7]

V ECONOMIC THEORY AND OCCUPATIONAL HEALTH REGULATION

This account of the regulation of lead and phosphorus has purposively followed traditional historical lines, and it is not obvious that it would have been much changed by closer observance of modern regulatory theory. As in many histories of nineteenth-century regulation, it has traced the history of regulation through three stages: an exposure stage, a legislation stage, and, finally, a making and administering of

---

[7] Bartrip will consider these issues in detail in a future publication.

regulations stage. It has revealed the principal actors and has singled out the manufacturers as the most determined and self-interested group, and also the most successful, in keeping regulation largely under their control or influence. It concludes, however, that in the main aim of reducing mortality from industrial lead and phosphorus poisoning, the regulations appear to have been successful. Can we now sharpen the analysis by a closer attention to the theoretical insights of the modern theory of economic regulation? Perhaps the most important modern insights underline the complexity of the political process that produces regulation, and the self-interested actions and motivation of the principal actors. Although the notion of 'action in the public interest' does not disappear under critical scrutiny, its reality is less obvious and less important in determining regulatory action than was once thought. On the exposure of social ills, for example, the importance of investigative journalism in the burgeoning popular press was increasingly important, and the journalistic motivation was surely a compound of circulation-boosting by use of sensation, the ambition of particular journalists, and, one hopes, some desire to do good. But this type of exposure was different in kind from that caused by the moral fervour of a Wilberforce or Ashley. On the legislative stage the process was much the same as it had been earlier in the century. Parliamentary initiative required particular politicians to react to the exposure of problems and to promote legislative action. Thomas Burt emerges as an able political entrepreneur, achieving an effective parliamentary response on the basis of a small body of evidence. At the level of regulation making, there is more to be learnt from modern theory with its explicit recognition of the ability of the regulated to dominate the making of regulations, of the motivation of regulators who can be viewed like any other self-interested economic agents, and of a bargaining-negotiating process involving manufacturers, politicians, civil servants, and workers to determine the details of regulation. What is surprising in this particular case study is the absence of consumer interests and the minimal presence of workers. As regards the bureaucrats, it seems that they were employer-oriented, certainly in the case of Redgrave. At the same time, they were genuinely concerned about the cost of regulation, not only the direct costs, but also the possible cost in terms of loss of employment. For whatever reasons, the procedure of making the regulations gave the manufacturers residual powers of objection and arbitration. If the Home Secretary's role was crucial, in that he had the power to certify certain industries and trades as dangerous, the final say was given to the manufacturers by creating a process of bargaining for the regulations finally adopted.

Bargaining, however, did not get rid of regulation; it modified its incidence and intrusiveness. Manufacturers recognized the need for the control of toxic substances—the evidence was too strong not to—as a result their policy was to bargain for a level of control that was politically and commercially acceptable, given the certainty of continued exposure. Stronger regulation may have reduced mortality more quickly, but, given the politics of making regulations and the economic interests involved, the bargained outcome was socially beneficial. To an important extent, then, this case study gives support to 'the capture theory' as well as to 'the bargaining process' in the final determination of regulations. And it confirms the necessity of seeing regulation making as the final outcome of a complex political process involving many personalities and many interest groups in their reactions to the exposure of a social problem.

REFERENCES

BARTRIP, P. W. J. (1979a), 'Safety at Work: The Factory Inspectorate in the Fencing Controversy, 1833–57', *Centre for Socio-Legal Studies Working Paper no. 4* (SSRC Centre for Socio-Legal Studies, Oxford).

—— (1979b), '*Household Words* and the Factory Accident Controversy', *Dickensian* 75, 17–29.

—— (1982), 'British Government Inspection, 1832–1875: Some Observations', *Historical Journal* 25, 605–26.

—— (1988), 'Expertise and the Dangerous Trades, 1875–1900' in MacLeod, R. M. (ed.), *Government and Expertise in Britain, 1815–1919* (Cambridge University Press, Cambridge).

—— (1996), ' "Petticoat Pestering": The Women's Trade Union League and Lead Poisoning in the Staffordshire Potteries, 1890–1914', *Historical Studies in Industrial Relations*, 2, 3–25.

—— and BURMAN, S. B. (1983), *The Wounded Soldiers of Industry. Industrial Compensation Policy, 1830–1897* (Clarendon Press, Oxford).

—— and FENN, P. T. (1983), 'The Evolution of Regulatory Style in the Nineteenth Century British Factory Inspectorate', *Journal of Law and Society* 10, 201–22.

—— and —— (1988), 'Factory Fatalities and Regulation in Great Britain, 1878–1913', *Explorations in Economic History* 25, 60–74.

—— and —— (1990), 'The Measurement of Safety: Factory Accident Statistics in Victorian and Edwardian Britain', *Historical Research* 63, 58–72.

BEAVER, P. (1985), *The Match Makers* (Henry Melland, London).

BRIGGS, A. (1988), *Victorian Things* (Batsford, London).

BRIMBLECOMBE, P.(1987), *The Big Smoke* (Routledge, London).

BRYANT AND MAY manuscripts. Hackney Archives, London.

BUCHANAN, J. M. (1968), *The Demand and Supply of Public Goods* (Rand McNally, Chicago, Ill.).

—— and TULLOCH, G. (1962), *The Calculus of Consent: Logical Foundations of Constitutional Democracy* (University of Michigan Press, Ann Arbor, Mich.).

CHECKLAND, S. G. (1983), *British Public Policy, 1776–1939* (Cambridge University Press, Cambridge).

CORN, J. K. (1992), *Response to Occupational Health Hazards. A Historical Perspective* (Van Nostrand Reinhold, New York).

Daily News, 3 April 1882.

DIXON, W. H. (1925), *The Match Industry. Its Origin and Development* (Pitman, London).

GOLDWATER, L. J. (1936), 'From Hippocrates to Ramazzini: Early History of Industrial Medicine', *Annals of Medical History* new ser. 8, 27–35.

GROVE, J. W. (1962), *Government and Industry in Britain* (Longmans, London).

Hansard's Parliamentary Debates.

HARRISON, B. (1989), ' "Some of them Gets Lead Poisoned": Occupational Lead Exposure in Women, 1880–1914' *Social History of Medicine* 2, 171–95.

—— (1995), 'The Politics of Occupational Ill-Health in late Nineteenth Century Britain: The Case of the Match Making Industry' *Sociology of Health and Illness* 17, 20–41.

HARTWELL, R. M. (1994), 'Entrepreneurship and Public Inquiry: The Growth of Government in Nineteenth-Century Britain' in F. M. L. Thompson (ed.), *Landowners, Capitalists and Entrepreneurs* (Clarendon Press, Oxford).

HEAVISIDES, M. (ed.) (1909), *The True History of the Invention of the Lucifer Match by John Walker of Stockton-on-Tees in 1827; With an Account of the Ancient Modes of Procuring Light and Fire* (Heavisides, Stockton-on-Tees).

JEVONS, W. S. (1882), *The State in Relation to Labour* (Macmillan, London).

Lancet, 9 July 1831, 449–57.

MAJOR, R. H. (1954), *A History of Medicine* (Blackwell, Oxford).

NISKANEN, W. A. (1973), *Bureaucracy: Servant or Master. Lessons from America* (Institute of Economic Affairs, London).

MILL, J. S. (1848), *The Principles of Political Economy* (Longman, London).

NRIAGU, J. N. (1983), *Lead and Lead Poisoning in Antiquity* (Wiley, New York).

PEACOCK, A. (ed.) (1984), *The Regulation Game* (Blackwell, Oxford).

PELZMAN, S. (1981), 'General Developments in the Economics of Regulation' in G. Fromm (ed.), *Studies in Public Regulation* (MIT Press, Cambridge, Mass.).

POLANYI, K. (1944), *The Great Transformation* (Gollancz, London).

PARLIAMENTARY PAPERS 1863, XXV, 'Fifth Report of the Medical Officer of the Privy Council' (1862).

—— 1863, XVIII, Children's Employment Commission, First Report.

—— 1865, XX, Report of Factory Inspectors.

—— 1882, XVIII, Report by Alexander Redgrave . . . upon the Precautions which can be Enforced under the Factory Act.

—— 1890–91, XIX, Report of Chief Inspector of Factories.

—— 1893–4, XVII, Report of Chief Inspector of Factories.

—— 1900, XI, Report of Chief Inspector of Factories.

—— 1914–16, XXI, Report of Chief Inspector of Factories.

PUBLIC RECORD OFFICE (PRO), Home Office Files (HO45/9620 A15330) (HO45/9849/B12393).

RAFFLE, P. A. B., LEE, W. R., McCALLUM, R. I., and MURRAY, R. (eds.) (1987), *Hunter's Diseases of Occupations* (Hodder and Stoughton, London).

RITCHIE, D. G. (1891), *The Principles of State Interference* (Sonnenschein, London).

ROBERTS, D. (1960), *Victorian Origins of the British Welfare State* (Yale University Press, New Haven, Conn.).

ROSEN, G. (1943), *The History of Miners' Diseases* (Schuman, New York).

ROWE, D. J. (1983), *Lead Manufacturing in Great Britain. A History* (Croom Helm, Beckenham).

SATRE, L. (1982), 'After the Match Girls' Strike: Bryant and May in the 1890s', *Victorian Studies* 26, 7–31.

SMITH, MARJORIE (1986), 'Lead in History' in R. Lansdowne and W. Yule, *The Lead Debate: The Environment, Toxicology, and Child Health* (Croom Helm, London).

STIGLER, G. (1971), 'The Theory of Economic Regulation' *Bell Journal of Economics and Management Science* 2, 3–21.

TELEKY, L. (1948), *History of Factory and Mine Hygiene* (Columbia University Press, New York).

TENNANT, H. J. (1899), 'Dangerous Trades. A Case for Legislation' *Fortnightly Review* 71, 316–25.

THACKRAH, C. T. (1832), *Effects of the Principal Arts, Trades and Professions, and of Civic States and Habits of Living, on Health and Longevity; With Particular Reference to the Trades and Manufactures of Leeds; with Suggestions for the Removal of many of the Agents which Produce Disease and Shorten the Duration of Life* (Longman, London).

TOMLINSON, J. (1994), *Government and Enterprise. The Changing Problem of Efficiency* (Clarendon Press, Oxford).

WEST, E. G. (1965), *Education and the State: A Study in Political Economy* (Institute of Economic Affairs, London).

WRIGHT, W. CAVE (1940), *De Morbis Artificum. Bernardino Ramazzini. Diseases of Workers. The Latin Text of 1713 Revised with Translation and Notes* (Chicago University of Chicago Press, Chicago, Ill.).

3

Regulation: After 'Command and Control'

ROBERT BALDWIN

Just one of Don Harris' contributions to the development of socio-legal studies has been his work on different methods of providing compensation and support for illness and injury (see Harris *et al.*, 1984). Such research has manifested a concern that administrative and legal mechanisms should be tested for their appropriateness to particular tasks and a belief that the way such mechanisms operate on the ground should be a focus of attention. Echoing such interests, this chapter looks at different methods of controlling industrial or social activities and looks, in particular, at the potential of new regulatory techniques—techniques that can be contrasted with what might be called 'old-fashioned command-and-control' regulation. I begin by outlining the command-and-control method and its supposed problems. The alternatives to command and control are then reviewed and questions are asked about the limitations of such methods and their capacity to overcome familiar regulatory difficulties. Finally, comments are offered on how choices of control device can be made.

COMMAND AND CONTROL AND ITS LIMITS

Governments possess a number of basic capacities or resources (see e.g. Hood, 1983, 5; Daintith, 1994) and particular regulatory strategies build on these. Such resources are:

- To command—where legal authority and the command of law is used to pursue policy objectives.
- To deploy wealth—where contracts, grants, loans, economic subsidies, or other incentives are used to influence conduct.
- To harness markets—where governments channel competitive forces to particular ends.
- To inform—where information is deployed strategically.
- To act directly—where the state takes physical action itself.
- To confer protected rights—where liability rules are structured to create desired incentives and constraints.

The essence of command-and-control (C and C) regulation is the exercise of influence by imposing standards backed by criminal sanctions.

Thus, the Health and Safety Executive may bring criminal prosecutions against occupiers who breach health and safety regulations. The force of law is used to prohibit certain forms of conduct or to demand some positive actions or to lay down conditions for entry into a sector.

Regulators who operate C and C techniques by enforcing standards are sometimes equipped with rule-making powers (as is often the case in the United States). In the United Kingdom, however, it is common for regulatory standards to be set by government departments through primary or secondary legislation and then enforced by regulatory bureaucracies. The strengths of C and C regulation (as compared to techniques based, say, on the use of economic incentives) are that the force of law can be used to impose fixed standards with immediacy and to prohibit activity not conforming to such standards. Entry to a sector or activity can, accordingly, be screened or restricted in accordance with the public interest. Some forms of behaviour can be outlawed completely and the ill-qualified can be stopped from practising. The public, as a result, can rest assured that the might of the law is being used as a protective device. C and C also has symbolic significance in that it legally declares some forms of behaviour to be unacceptable. C and C techniques might thus be said to be best suited to sectors where there are needs for enforced minimal standards and legal prohibitions rather than incentives.

A number of problems allegedly afflicts C and C regulation and, during the 1980s in particular, a number of North American socio-legal scholars pointed to these weaknesses (see e.g. Breyer, 1982; Stewart, 1988; Bardach and Kagan, 1982). Such concerns were echoed by many politicians on both sides of the Atlantic—at least those predisposed to doubt the value of governmental rather than market-based methods of influence.

A first worry was that in C and C regulation the relationship between the regulators and the regulated might tend to become too close and lead to capture—the pursuit of the regulated enterprises' interests rather than those of the public at large. A number of versions of capture theory have been put forward (for reviews see Mitnick, 1980; Quirk, 1981; Wilson, 1984): 'life-cycle' accounts suggest that agencies progress through various stages until, lonely, frightened, and old, they become the protectors of the regulated industry rather than of the public interest (see Bernstein, 1955); 'interest-group' explanations stress the extent to which regulators can be influenced by the claims and political influence of different groups; and 'private interest' or economic analyses see regulation as a commodity liable to fall under (or be established under) the sway of the economically powerful (see Posner, 1974; Stigler, 1971). The proximity of regulator to regulatee relationships that is associated with C and C techniques might be thought to be particularly conducive to capture in so far as agencies, when drawing up and enforcing rules, must rely to some extent on the co-operation of the regulated firms. It should be noted, however, that many examples of the above capture theories would put capture down to factors other than the regulatory technique to be put into effect—for instance, to political, institutional, or economic considerations.

Secondly, C and C has been said to produce unnecessarily complex and inflexible rules and, indeed, a proliferation of rules that leads to over-regulation, legalism, delay, and the strangling of enterprise.[1] Thirdly, setting appropriate standards has been argued to pose major difficulties for regulators (see Breyer, 1982, 109–19; Ogus, 1994) because the informational requirements are so severe. Thus, anti-competitive effects must be addressed; the appropriate type of standard selected (see Ogus, 1994, ch. 8) (be this an *output* standard specifying a level of performance or an *input* standard calling for a particular design or specification of operation or machinery), and the level of exposure to judicial review may be high. Setting the appropriate level of performance is, moreover, technically difficult and liable to be contentious.

A final matter sometimes said to be a particular problem in C and C regimes is that of enforcement. In the socio-legal literature considerable attention has been focused on the way in which sanctions and other inducements have been used to secure compliance with prescribed standards and on whether compliance will achieve desired results.[2] On the one hand, certain commentators have argued that prosecution is often an inefficient method of enforcement compared to negotiated compliance-seeking—where negotiation, education, and warnings are used and prosecution reserved as a weapon of last resort (see Fenn and Veljanovski, 1988). On the other, advocates of prosecution-led enforcement have seen negotiated compliance-seeking as offering evidence of capture (see Pearce and Tombs, 1990; Hawkins, 1990). A further school has, again, stressed the benefits of co-operative relationships between regulators and regulated and has pointed to the dangers of allowing a culture of resistance to regulation to develop (see Ayres and Braithwaite, 1992).

As for securing compliance, socio-legal researchers (including, again, a number working with Don Harris) have argued that success on this front may not always produce the 'right' results. The rules being complied with may be too narrow or too broad. They, accordingly, may fail to

---

[1] See Stewart (1988); Bardach and Kagan (1982). On whether C and C *necessarily* operates in a highly restrictive fashion see the text with n. 11 below.

[2] Work conducted at the Centre for Socio-Legal Studies during Don Harris' directorship has contributed not insignificantly to studies of this issue: see e.g. Hawkins, 1984; Hutter, 1988; Fenn and Veljanovski, 1988; Baldwin, 1990.

encompass conduct that should be controlled or else may constrain conduct that should be unrestrained (see generally Baldwin, 1995, ch. 6). In addition, there may be problems of 'creative compliance' (see McBarnet and Whelan, 1991). These occur when those regulated avoid the intentions of rules by circumventing rather than breaking them. An example would be the response of a large superstore to a rule restricting Sunday trading to x hours for retail outlets with a floor area of y square metres or more. The superstore, which has an area of y square metres, divides itself into two 'separate' units of ½ square metres each. In doing so it complies with the law yet defeats the core objective behind the law.

Regulators employing C and C techniques thus face substantial difficulties of rule use (see Baldwin, 1995, chs. 9 and 10). Not only must the rules employed be capable of enforcement and be accessible to regulated firms and individuals (see Baldwin, 1990) but the appropriate types and levels of standards must be fixed, problems of scope (or inclusiveness: see Diver, 1983) must be overcome, and the propensity of affected parties to indulge in creative compliance must be taken on board. Such problems, moreover, must often be faced in political environments that are hostile to rules that impose compliance costs on industry, are unlikely to produce the resources necessary for effective enforcement and are quick to point to the excessive 'legalization' (see Teubner, 1987)[3] produced by C and C methods.

In the light of such difficulties, some commentators have advocated a move away from command strategies and towards 'constitutive', 'less-restrictive' or 'incentive-based' styles of control (see Stewart, 1988; Breyer, 1982; Teubner, 1984).[4] It is to the potential of such styles that I now turn.

IN THE PLACE OF COMMAND AND CONTROL

The alternatives to C and C regulation are numerous and subdivisions might be made to give a highly complex picture. What follows, however, will categorize fairly broadly and deal with seven main types of alternative strategy.

---

[3] By 'legalization' is meant the tendency increasingly to subject a sector to control by means of detailed and rigidly enforced rules. For discussion and alternatives see Teubner, 1987.

[4] On incentive-based regulation see Ogus, 1994, ch. 11. For a European view of the limits of command law see Teubner, 1984.

1. Enforced Self-regulation

A variation of C and C that can be termed an alternative might be described as self-administered C and C or as enforced self-regulation.[5] In this system, the Government requires the firm or trade association to write its own rules and a regulatory agency is given the power to approve these or demand amendment. Enforcement functions are also delegated to firms with oversight by regulators. Advantages claimed for such regimes include:

- Their potential for rapid adjustment of rules and for regulatory innovation.
- The greater comprehensiveness of rules.
- The high commitment of firms to their own rules.
- Low costs to government.
- A closer fit between regulation and the firm's realities.
- Greater effectiveness in detecting violations and in securing convictions where prosecution is necessary.
- More effective complaints procedures.

The method is not, however, problem-free. The costs to the public purse of approving rules may be considerable. The rules written by self-regulators many prove self-serving or in other ways unsatisfactory. Compliance units within firms may not retain their independence, and those regulated may not always behave in a rational or predictable manner.

British experience of such a regulatory technique is limited but elements of the approach are encountered. The Health and Safety Executive, for instance, has experimented with self-regulation under supervision and employs self-assessment procedures. Fair-trading legislation has relied, particularly in the 1970s, upon trade-association codes of practice while financial-services regulation involves a degree of monitored self-regulation.

2. Incentive-based Regimes

Regulating by means of economic incentives (see Ogus, 1994, ch. 11; Daintith, 1994; Breyer, 1982; Stewart, 1985) might be thought to offer an escape from rule-bound C and C regimes. The posited advantages of incentive systems are that they involve low levels of regulators' discretions (and, consequently, supposedly low dangers of regulatory capture); they leave managers free to take managerial decisions; they involve light burdens of information collection and costs, yet they produce results by

---

[5] See Ayres and Braithwaite, 1992, ch. 4; Braithwaite, 1992, 1982; Black, 1996. On varieties of self-regulation see Ogus, 1995.

creating economic pressures to behave in socially desirable ways. Thus, taxes, subsidies, and government contracts can be used as regulatory tools and bring an additional benefit: they encourage regulated firms to reduce harmful conduct as much as possible, not merely down to the level that is demanded by the standard stipulated in a C and C regime. (An example of such an incentives strategy is the differential between the tax on leaded and unleaded petrol, introduced in Britain in 1987.)

The advantages of incentive regimes can, however, be exaggerated (see, for evaluation, Ogus, 1994, and Breyer, 1982). Such systems often have to be put into effect by highly complex systems of rules (see e.g. Markovits, 1987) and, in order to prevent regulatees evading their liabilities (e.g. to taxes), a variety of inspection and enforcement mechanisms may have to be employed. As a result, many of the difficulties associated with C and C regulation can arise (see Bardach and Kagan, 1982, chs. 8–10; Braithwaite, 1982). Whether, moreover, incentive regimes will act to prevent undesirable behaviour in the manner and to the extent assumed is also open to doubt. Enthusiasts of incentive systems tend to assume that those regulated operate generally in an economically rational manner but, in practice, many problems (e.g hazards in the workplace) arise out of irrational, accidental, or negligent behaviour.

In C and C regulation, standard setting gives rise, as noted, to a number of problems, but in incentive regimes it may be extremely difficult for the regulator to predict the outcome of a given incentive. Fixing incentive levels will thus make severe informational demands. C and C regimes, moreover, can be enforced in a flexible manner so as to maximize the achievement of desired results and to limit the imposition, for example, of unnecessary restrictions on particular firms or individuals. In contrast, in so far as incentive regimes operate in a mechanical manner (a supposed advantage in reducing tendencies to capture), a disadvantage is the lack of such flexibility as allows constraints to be tempered or tailored to individual circumstances. Regulatory lag may also prove a significant problem with incentive regimes, given their indirect mode of operation. Incentives may thus be poor regulatory tools where crises are liable to occur, when catastrophic thresholds (e.g. levels of pollution killing all the fish) are involved or where the sector is subject to rapid economic changes.

Presentationally, a move from C and C towards incentive regimes may prove popular with firms regulated but it may give rise to public concern on the grounds that it fails to stigmatize socially harmful activity and indeed offers a 'licence' for socially undesirable behaviour (see Ogus, 1994, 255). Positive incentives, in the form of subsidies, may be condemned as making payments from the public purse to those acting undesirably, while negative incentives, or taxes, may be criticized for taking away from industry the very resources that might have been spent on measures for avoiding the undesirable consequences of their activities.

3. Market-harnessing Controls

The most direct method of regulating by channelling market forces is to control competition within a sector. Thus, a body such as OFTEL can regulate not only the amount of competition that a major firm faces but also the kind of market behaviour it will deem to be consistent with desired competition (on OFTEL and competition, see OFTEL, 1995). Competition laws can thus be used instead of, or in conjunction with, regulation in order to sustain sufficient competition to allow the market to provide adequate services to consumers and the public.

Franchising is a system of control that can be employed in naturally monopolistic sectors to replace competition *in* the market with competition *for* the market (see generally Williamson, 1985; Domberger, 1986). It has been employed notably in the independent television, radio, and rail sectors. Franchising authorities may seek to achieve advantages for consumers or the public by inviting applicants to bid against each other for fixed-period franchises and to compete on a number of possible bases. These bases include: price per unit to be charged to the customer; quality of service offered; or the size of lump sum offered to (or demanded from) the Government for the privilege of serving the market. (Channel 3 television franchising by the Independent Television Commission is an example of lump sum auctioning.)

The idea behind franchising is that, in making bids competitively, applicants are driven to adopt assumptions (and make promises) of efficient operation. After the award of the franchise, the promises as to the price and other aspects of performance that were made in bidding are enforced and consumers and public benefit accordingly.

For franchising to work, however, it must be possible to specify the service to be performed; the bidding process has to be competitive and effective enforcement of franchise promises must take place. Adequate service specification is important, first, as a basis for generating competition in the bidding process and, secondly, in order to establish benchmarks for evaluating bids. If specification is unclear, bidders will face uncertainties, and not only will costs of bidding be increased but the costs of uncertainties will be passed on through the system to consumers. Particular problems may arise in a sector such as rail, where there are a number of interdependent operations making up the service, since uncertainties can arise in specifying how risks will be allocated between different parties and in outlining the potential exposure of the franchise holder to competition. Again, such uncertainties may lead franchise bidders to demand excessive subsidies or to charge consumers excessive prices.[6] Specifications may require value judgements to be made and discretions to be exercised (for example in defining what is a good or acceptable television service). If this is the case, however, a supposed advantage of franchising over C and C regulation is undermined—namely that in franchising it is not the bureaucrats who judge and cost market preferences, as with C and C, but firms operating in and familiar with the sector. When franchising authorities have to compare bids qualitatively using discretion it is the staff of such authorities who, ultimately, select the appropriate service.

Defining, with precision, the service to be offered may be useful in terms of the bidding process, but a difficulty in franchising is that there is tension between such precision and allowing franchisees enough flexibility to develop services innovatively and to be responsive to changes in demands and preferences.

Competitive bidding calls for sufficient numbers of well-informed applicants. A particular worry in utilities and television franchising is that the number of bidders available may be so small as to rule out real competition (see Glaister and Beesley, 1990). The more uncertain the franchising arrangements and the higher the franchise application costs, the smaller the expected number of bidders will be.

Enforcement is a substantial issue in C and C regulation but, as noted, franchising also depends for its success on effective enforcement of promises given in making applications. The effectiveness of enforcement depends to a large degree on the ease with which franchise authorities can replace poorly-performing incumbents. Ease of replacement varies from sector to sector, and will depend, for example, on the availability of new entrants and the disruption likely to be occasioned by a handover. In sectors such as Channel 3 TV that are organized regionally, services may be transferable to some extent from one area to another and thus may help to fill gaps. The term of the franchise will also affect replaceability. Short terms enhance enforcement and allow replacements to be made before consumers suffer lengthy periods of poor service, but longer terms may be required in order to encourage applications, continuity, and investments in infrastructure.

Franchising, in summary, does offer an alternative to C and C regulation but the degree to which it produces hands-off, non-interventionist regimes can be exaggerated. Substantial difficulties have been encountered in applying the technique in such sectors as television and rail, where judgements on services and uncertainties loom large, but fran-

---

[6] For discussion see the Rail Regulators' Consultation Document, *Competition for Railway Passenger Services* (Office of the Rail Regulator, London, 1994).

chising has a more readily identifiable role in fields where products are relatively homogeneous and specification is comparatively simple; where there will be healthy competition to enter the market, where uncertainties are manageable (e.g. because cost and revenue risks can be allocated explicitly); and where monitoring and enforcement can be carried out effectively.

A further regulatory technique coming under the market-harnessing heading is the use of *tradeable permits* to engage in the activity to be controlled (e.g. discharging pollutants into the river). This, like franchising, controls both entry to the market and behaviour within the market. (Since 1991 the US Environmental Protection Agency (EPA) has sought to control sulphur dioxide emissions by allocating tradeable emission permits to coal-burning electric-power plants.) In such regimes the public agency issues a given number of permits, and each of these allows a specified discharge. After the initial allocation, permits are tradeable, and this allows, say, a generating company to switch to cleaner fuels and sell its excess allowances to other firms. The initial distribution of permits may be carried out by auction or according to public-interest criteria.

Such systems thus create incentives to reduce discharges and, whereas C and C techniques demand reductions down to the level fixed in a standard (often a standard that relatively poor-performers can achieve), tradeable permit systems create incentives to reduce right down to zero—they thus reach the parts that C and C strategies cannot and impinge on the best, as well as the worst, performers.

Further claimed advantages of permits are that: permissions are allocated by the market to those who will generate most wealth per unit of pollution; the regulator can control total harm by restricting numbers and values of permits; managers are not subjected to highly interventionist regulation; and regulatory costs and discretions are low.

Tradeable permit systems are not, however, problem free (see Ogus, 1994, ch. 7; Breyer, 1982, ch. 8). Enforcement still has to be practised, otherwise non-permit-holders may pollute or holders may exceed the terms of their permits. Such a method of regulation may involve a degree of regulatory lag, so that if, for example, permits are used to control river pollution, it may be difficult to adjust pollution levels rapidly to cope with sudden drops in the river's capacity to absorb pollution, as might occur in a heatwave or drought. Total costs imposed on industry under such a system are also difficult to predict.

The political costs of giving licences to pollute may, furthermore, be considerable and permit systems may fail to reassure potential victims, in so far as they do not provide resources to compensate such victims.

Much depends, in tradeable permit regimes, on there being healthy markets in permits. This demands that there are numbers of potential buyers with good information. If the market is weak due, say, to uncertainties or lack of information, the value of permits may be low, and so the incentive to reduce harms may be less than optimal. This, it has been suggested, has been a problem in the EPA's scheme of control for carbon dioxide (see Lapper and Morse, 1995; Van Dyke, 1992). The hoarding of permits by certain firms may prove a further problem where this leads to anti-competitive effects, such as the creation of barriers to market entry. Finally, some types of emission or pollution may have to be prohibited absolutely—in such situations the permit system would be inappropriate.

4. Disclosure Regulation

Controlling the disclosure of information may constitute a useful mode of regulation that is not heavily interventionist, since it will not regulate the production process, the level of output allowed, prices charged, or the allocation of products. Disclosure rules tend to involve either mandatory disclosure—which obliges suppliers to provide information on price, identity, composition, quantity, or quality (familiar in the food and drinks sectors)—or the control of false or misleading information.

Information regulation carries the drawback that citizens may make mistakes, fail to use or understand disclosed information, or misassess risks and so may come to harm. Consumers, moreover, may not respond in anticipated ways to the supply of information. When purchasing, the citizen may choose according to price and not respond to information suggesting that dangers or externalities may be involved in consuming the particular product. The costs of processing information may also be excessive. Thus, if, instead of C and C regulations on food safety, information-disclosure rules were employed, a visit to the supermarket would be a very lengthy process. It might, in many circumstances, be far more efficient for consumers to rely on the expertise and work of public regulators rather than all make their own individualized assessments of risks.

Dangers may be so great in some sectors that it is felt inappropriate merely to inform, and C and C methods may be deemed necessary (see Ramsay, 1989). Information regulation, it should be borne in mind, tends to assist parties who are well-resourced, expert, and able to protect themselves rather than weaker, less well-resourced, and less expert individuals or groups.

As with other alternatives to C and C regulation, enforcement tends not to be an issue that can easily be disposed of in disclosure regulation. Mechanisms will have to be put into force to monitor the accuracy of information given and claims made. This increases the costs of information-based regimes. The strongest case for information regulation appears to be where the following circumstances obtain:

- The hazard involved is not potentially catastrophic (e.g. the importance of the difference between high- and low-quality products or processes is not major).
- The relevant information can be processed at reasonable cost.
- Risks can be assessed accurately by affected parties.
- Affected parties are likely to give proper consideration to the information given.
- Monitoring the accuracy of information is feasible and can be carried out at acceptable cost.

5. Direct Action

Governments, rather than regulate, may take direct action short of full public ownership in order to control conduct in an area. Thus, rather than set and enforce standards on dust-extraction levels in factories, central government (or a local authority) might build properly ventilated premised and lease these to private manufacturers. Public ownership of infrastructure can also be combined with vertical separation and the franchising out of a sector's operational aspects. Long-term capital investments, accordingly, may be planned by government and, at the same time, the substitutability of franchise holders may be enhanced. Thus, in the period to 1991, the public regulator in the independent-television sector, the Independent Broadcasting Authority, owned and operated the transmission infrastructure and franchised out programme-making.

A further advantage of direct action is that public money may be used to ensure protections in circumstances where firms, particularly small ones, might not invest in the required measures. A degree of subsidization may, by such means, be effected and the public purse spent in a manner that actively assists firms rather than funds C and C enforcement regimes. The fairness of access to subsidized premises may raise distributional issues but there is no reason why the pricing policies attending leases cannot be adapted to cope with criticisms. A more substantial problem may, however, be that the public funding of one aspect of an industrial or economic process may encourage firms to build operations around the funded element and, as a result, innovations may not be driven by the market and may lack responsiveness.

6. Rights and Liabilities

The allocation of rights and liabilities can be used to provide incentives to encourage socially desirable behaviour (see generally Breyer,

1982,174–7; Calabresi and Melamed, 1972). Thus, the argument runs, the prospective polluter of the river will be deterred by his or her potential liability to pay damages to the riparian owner or angling club (the deterrent effect being the quantum of the likely damages multiplied by the probability of those damages being inflicted). The precise effects of liability rules are, however, difficult to predict and liability rules may fail to deter efficiently for a number of reasons, notably:

- Many instances of undesirable conduct or effects result from accidents, random events and irrational behaviour and even 'efficient' levels of deterrence may operate randomly (see Harris *et al.*, 1984).[7]
- Enforcement costs for individuals may prove daunting and co-ordination between victims may prove non-feasible or subject to high transaction costs.
- Evidential difficulties may reduce the probabilities of proving causation to low levels.
- Legal uncertainties may undermine the force of rights and liability rules.
- Many victims in the pool of victims may lack the resolve to proceed against the harm causer and so deterrent effects will be sub-optimal.
- The harm causer will often be able to settle out of court for compromise sums and so will reduce deterrence levels.
- The courts would face substantial informational hurdles in fixing damages at levels that create appropriate deterrence even if they were willing to look beyond victim compensation and towards deterrence.
- Insurance may limit the deterrent effects of liability rules.

On the last point, liability rules, combined with insurance, may have effects that are difficult to manage or predict.[8] Insurance may, under certain conditions, spread risks very widely, and this may undermine deterrence. On the other hand, excessive levels of deterrence and, for firms severe financial difficulties, may be caused if insurance is subject to restrictions, withdrawals, and crises so that there is non-availability of effective cover at affordable prices. Thus, in the tort sector, what has been described as a crisis was experienced in the mid 1980s in the United States and Canada (see, e.g., Priest, 1987; Stewart, 1987; Trebilcock, 1987) and it has been the unpredictability of the liability-insurance market that has urged a number of North American critics to look to regulatory devices as alternatives to the tort system (see e.g. Stewart, 1987).

---

[7] On the deficiencies of liability rules in providing compensation see Harris *et al.*, 1984, ch. 12.

[8] See Finch, 1994, 880, at 915 ('[r]eliance upon insured personal liability represents a movement from design to accident').

Contractually-based remedies and liabilities can be seen as one alternative to tortious rules. Thus, within the philosophy associated with the Citizen's Charter,[9] public services can be supplied by single operators or internal markets involving networks of contracts (as in the National Health Service: see Harden, 1992) and, in parallel, the rights of individuals can be seen in consumerist terms—as rights to choice and quality in services. A central notion in such schemes of provision and control is that policy-making can be separated off from service delivery—that accountability involves not so much allowing citizens a say on the nature of the service at issue and its mode of delivery as giving citizens consumers' remedies to be exercised in the event that the service (as defined with little consumer involvement) fails to be delivered according to promises given. What is involved is a faith in managers as trusted experts—they are seen as capable of defining the public's desires and preferences with little assistance from the public. In return for exercising such expertise they are held to account only for failing to deliver on the promises that *they* have formulated (see Barron and Scott, 1992; Lacey, 1994).

In such systems built on 'expert', 'managerial' modes of delivery and organized in contractual frameworks, discretions are exercised quite freely and operators evaluated according to results (rather than questioned as to policies pursued) (see Baldwin, 1995, 31). Accountability, accordingly, tends to operate not so much through the application of rules but through devices attuned to the contractual context—for example, systems of inspection and valuation, audit mechanisms; performance targets and indicators; quality controls; complaints mechanisms; and the capital markets as sources of scrutiny and discipline.

The strongest case for charterist regimes and modes of control can be made when the importance of efficient service delivery is at its highest and when there is little concern to debate the policy issues involved in defining what appropriate service-definition and delivery is. In the real world the divorce of service-definition from policy-making is possible only in the rarest of contexts.

7. Public Compensation/Social Insurance Schemes

Economic incentives to avoid undesirable behaviour can be created not merely by systems of taxation and subsidy but also by schemes of compensation or insurance that link premiums to performance records. One field in which a good deal of research into insurance-based incentives has been conducted is that of the working environment. It is worth

---

[9] On the Citizen's Charter and citizens as consumers see: Lewis, 1993; Drewry, 1993; Barron and Scott, 1992; Lacey, 1994.

noting briefly the research of the European Foundation for the Improvement of Living and Working Conditions (the 'European Foundation').[10] In its 1994 review, the European Foundation found a number of insurance-based schemes impinging on workplace safety and health around the world. These were all no-fault liability schemes linked to workers' compensation payments.

National schemes were encountered in several EU countries, the United States, Canada, Japan, and New Zealand with strategies under development in Denmark, Poland, and elsewhere. Many were essentially compensatory, but some also provided means of funding improvements in conditions—as in the French, Swedish, and Albertan systems.

In the typical scheme workers surrender their rights to sue employers for damages in return for statutory compensation, often amounting to full payment of lost earnings plus costs. The employers' premiums depend on the organization's past claims experience (see Bailey, 1995).

Could private insurance firms provide such incentives to improve working conditions? The answer appears to be 'no'. The concern of private insurers is not to reduce hazards but to generate profits. Distinguishing good from bad risks demands resources and, although a competitive insurance market will to some extent drive insurers to bear such resource costs, such discrimination between good and bad risks will tend to be confined to sectors in which statistical guidance on the quantum of risks is readily available. Thus, in motor insurance, with a wealth of accidents, and as a result useful data available, discrimination might be high, whereas in relation to workplace safety, where accidents are infrequent but often serious, weak statistics might be expected to lead to low risk-discrimination and the linking of premiums to very broad categories. The tension between the basic functions of insurance (to spread risks) and risk-discrimination (notably to isolate poor risks) also imposes limits on the willingness of private insurers to identify poor risks and apply localized economic incentives.

For such reasons, the European Foundation has proposed a scheme which is publicly administered and which links payments into the fund not to statistics on accident records (which were said 'not [to] make any sense' for firms with under 100 employees (see EFILWC, 1994, 19)) but to the factors that can be measured properly: the conditions of the working environment, the state of the machinery, etc. Such a linkage also encourages accurate reporting of injuries—a contrast with reliance on past accident records which encourages firms to bring pressure on employees not

---

[10] The EFILWC (Loughlinstown House, Shankill, Co. Dublin, Ireland) is a European Community institution and has published, on the topic at issue: *Catalogue of Economic Incentive Systems for the Improvement of the Working Environment* (1994) and S. Bailey (ed.) *Economic Incentives to Improve the Working Environment* (EFILWC, Shankill, 1994).

to report accidents (e.g. by offering bonuses to accident-free teams of workers and creating peer pressures not to report). It would be possible in such schemes to offer incentives to use e.g. low-noise machines or low-emission materials, either on a relative or absolute basis by allowing premium reductions to companies taking preventative measures.

The case for such schemes can be based on the following points (EFILWC, 1994, 24–5):

- They make employers aware of the costs of their actions (e.g. of increasing pressures on workers to take risks to increase production).
- Whereas C and C strategies are so expensive to enforce that they are patchily and ill-implemented, insurance-based incentives offer financial motivations to all employers.
- C and C techniques offer incentives to comply with set standards but no further; incentive schemes can aim to achieve continuing incentives beyond such standards.
- Employers will respond to the emergence of new hazards automatically—without the need for fresh legislation.
- Prevention will be given a newly high priority because it will impinge on profits in a way not experienced with C and C regulation.
- Incentives can be a positive benefit to companies unlike the burden of more legislation.

Certain difficulties should also be anticipated in relation to insurance-based schemes. If compensation is over-generous or seen as an easy option, this may encourage some individuals to accept partial disability in return for cash.

The European Foundation strategy suggests that all employers will be inspected and given ratings for the purposes of calculating their premiums. (Such inspections would have to be repeated periodically unless stable conditions are to be assumed.) This would not be possible using, for instance, the present staffing of the UK Health and Safety Executive whose scheme of inspection involves, in the case of an average medium-sized firm, several years between inspection visits. Something in the order of a tenfold increase in inspection resources would not seem an outlandish precondition for the proper implementation of the European Foundation regime in the UK health and safety sector. It might be argued, indeed, that the important difference between the proposed regime and the present C and C system lies in the assumption concerning resources: that, with a tenfold increase in resources (and a commensurate increase in enforcement activity) C and C regulation might achieve similar results; that the proposed regime, furthermore, is not that different from C and C in so far as inspectors would check compliance with rules designed to limit risks and would penalize non-compliance not with a fine or administrative order but with an adjusted premium. What the insurance-based method amounts to, it could be contended, is a C and C regime with a variation in the sanctioning device. Fines, after all, might be described as disincentives. Such a point emphasizes, again, that once enforcement realities are taken into account, the extent to which the alternatives to C and C are able to escape from the difficulties attending C and C may be less than would first appear.

CONCLUSIONS: CHOOSING REGULATORY METHODS

What are the bases for criticizing C and C techniques? How can appropriate regimes of control or influence be identified?

The above account has outlined a number of objections to C and C regimes, considered the main alternative control devices, and reviewed the potential flaws in those alternatives. This is not to urge that, for certain situations and to achieve certain purposes, it will not be advisable to operate by 'alternative' mechanisms. It is, above all, to caution that comparing C and C, with all of its problems of application and enforcement, to a series of devices, assumed to be enforceable in a problem-free manner, is not to offer a balanced perspective. Enforcement is not a difficulty confined to C and C regimes (see Ogus, 1994; Breyer, 1982; Smith, 1974; Burrows, 1979). Nor, indeed, are the *positive* aspects of enforcement to be denied to C and C regulation. It is arguable that many of the objections that US commentators make in relation to C and C regulation are not compelling when applied to C and C regulation as encountered in Britain because British enforcement practices are more flexible, more administrative, and less prosecutorial than those encountered in the United States and because C and C techniques do not operate on the ground in such a restrictive or legalistic fashion on this side of the Atlantic.[11] The objections, it could be said, relate to a *style of applying* C and C regulation, one that is not the norm in Britain.

As for the bases for criticizing or for identifying appropriate regimes, it is worthwhile (as has been argued elsewhere: see Baldwin, 1995, ch. 3; Baldwin and McCrudden, 1987, ch. 3) assessing the extent to which the different strategies can, in the given context, be said to be liable to achieve legitimate objectives efficiently, expertly, accountably, and fairly. In reviewing the various strategies above and the criticisms most commonly made of them, it is easy to be drawn into a heavy focus on the efficient achievement of objectives. In looking more fully at, say, the

---

[11] On contrasting styles of regulatory enforcement see Vogel, 1986.

potential of liability rules or marketable permits as control devices, questions should, nevertheless, also be asked about such issues as the accountability of those who devise and apply such rules or permits and the fairness and openness to representation (accessibility) of the procedures involved—again in both devising and applying the schemes.

It is necessary also, as discussion of the contractual/charterist approach made clear, to take on board such issues as the *extent* of the accountability that a scheme of control offers—does it, for instance, cover matters relating to the definition of the operation and its objectives or is it confined to mere issues of delivery? Similarly, when looking at questions of fairness and openness, the extent and significance of access should not be left out of account. In the case, for instance, of marketable permits is public access to the process of establishing how permits work undermined by the strong role of the market in dictating such matters?

More generally, the extent to which schemes require application through rules should be borne in mind. A criticism of C and C regulation, as seen, has related to problems of rule-making and standard-setting—for instance in finding the appropriate level of precision and inclusiveness in rules; in using formulations of rules that cope with potential creative compliers; in incorporating the right kinds of standards within rules (whether, for instance, these be target, permission, specification (design) types: see Richardson, Ogus, and Burrows, 1983, 35–8; Ogus, 1994, ch. 8). As already indicated, however, 'alternative' regulatory methods may require implementation by means of rules, for instance, on: *when* incentives will apply; the *conditions* under which franchises will be held or marketable permits transferred; the *kinds* of information to be disclosed; the *use* of publicly-supplied premises; the *extent and form* of liabilities; or the *nature* of premium variations in a social-insurance system. Just as enforcement issues cannot be assumed away when moving to 'alternative' methods, neither, it should be repeated, can those problems attending rulemaking processes (see Markovits, 1987). Such difficulties, moreover, may go not merely to the efficiency and expertise with which legitimate objectives can be achieved but also to the accountability and fairness issues.

It should further be cautioned that an historical association between certain regulatory methods (e.g. C and C and the use of highly restrictive administrative rules) should not be taken as a demonstration of inevitable or exclusive linkage. The North American enthusiasm for alternative methods of regulation was to a degree fuelled by concerns that C and C methods had led to a 'crisis of legalization' (see Stewart, 1988), but other possible causes of over-proliferation and complexity in rules can be pointed to—thus, to instance a few: the particular demands made by judges of regulators in seeking to protect quality, rationality, fairness, and accessibility of rules or rule-making processes; the prevalence of certain conditions leading to litigiousness; the operation of certain statutory rule-making procedures; the political forces surrounding particular types of regulatory institutions (see e.g. Bardach and Kagan, 1982); or the internal politics and disciplinary divisions within regulatory bodies (see e.g. Nonet, 1969). In the face of such other factors, it is difficult to conclude with confidence that a move from C and C to alternative strategies constitutes even a start in combating excessive legalization.

Two final cautionary messages to be drawn from a review of regulatory alternatives are, first, that C and C strategies often combine with and supplement other techniques and, accordingly, a temptation, in advocating 'alternative' strategies, is to hive-off their unattractive features and dub these 'C and C intrusions'. Secondly, the distinction between C and C and the alternatives may be less stark than first appears. It is certainly less stark when desiderata other than effectiveness are taken on board and when romanticism concerning alternative strategies is dispensed with.

REFERENCES

AYRES, I., and BRAITHWAITE, J. (1992), *Responsive Regulation—Transcending the Deregulation Debate* (Oxford University Press, New York).

BAILEY, S. R., 'Economic Incentives for Employers to Improve the Management of Workplace Risk', paper to W. G. Hart Legal Workshop, 4 July (on file, Institute for Advanced Legal Studies, London).

BALDWIN, R. (1995), *Rules and Government* (Clarendon Press, Oxford).

BARDACH, E., and KAGAN, R. A. (1982), *Going by the Book: The Problem of Regulatory Unreasonableness* (Temple University Press, Philadelphia, Penn.).

BERNSTEIN, M. (1955), *Regulating Business by Independent Commission* (Princeton University Press, Princeton, NJ).

BRAITHWAITE, J. (1982), 'The Limits of Economism in Controlling Harmful Corporate Conduct, 16 *Law and Society Review* 481.

BREYER, S. (1982), *Regulation and Its Reform* (Harvard University Press, Cambridge, Mass.).

BURROWS, P. (1979), *The Economic Theory of Pollution Control* (Martin Robertson, Oxford).

CALABRESI, G., and MELAMED, A. (1972), 'Property Rules, Liability Rules and Inalienability: One view of the Cathedral', 85 *Harvard Law Review* 1089.

DAINTITH, T. C. (1994), 'The Techniques of Government' in J. Jowell and D. Oliver (eds.), *The Changing Constitution* (3rd edn, Clarendon Press, Oxford).

DIVER, C. S. (1983), 'The Optimal Precision of Administrative Rules', 93 *Yale Law Journal* 65.

DOMBERGER, S. (1986), 'Regulation Through Franchise Contracts' in J. Kay *et al.* (1986), *Privatisation and Regulation: The UK Experience* (Clarendon Press, Oxford).

European Foundation for the Improvement of Living and Working Conditions (1994), *Economic Incentives to Improve the Working Environment* (EFILWC, Shankill, Ireland).

Fenn, P., and Veljanovski, C. (1988), 'A Positive Theory of Regulatory Enforcement', 98 *Economics Journal* 1055.

Glaister, S., and Beesley, M. (1990), *Bidding for Tendered Bus Routes in London* (Mimeo).

Harden, I. (1992), *The Contracting State* (Open University Press, Buckingham).

Harris, D. *et al.* (1984), *Compensation and Support for Illness and Injury* (Clarendon Press, Oxford).

Hawkins, K. (1990), 'Compliance Strategy, Prosecution Policy and Aunt Sally—A Comment on Pearce and Tombs', 30 *British Journal of Criminology* 444.

Hood, C. (1983), *The Tools of Government* (Macmillan, London).

Lapper, R., and Morse, L. (1995), 'Market Makers in CO^2 Permits', *Financial Times*, 1 March.

Markovits, R. S. (1987), 'Antitrust: Alternatives to Delegalization', in G. Teubner (ed.), *Juridification of Social Spheres* (Walter de Gruyter, Berlin).

McBarnet, D., and Whelan, C. (1991), 'The Elusive Spirit of the Law: Formalism and the Struggle for Legal Control' (1991) 54 *Modern Law Review* 848.

Mitnick, B. (1980), *The Political Economy of Regulation* (Columbia University Press, New York).

Nonet, P. (1969), *Administrative Justice* (Russell Sage Foundation, New York).

OFTEL, (1995), *Effective Competition: Framework for Action* (OFTEL, London).

Ogus, A. I. (1994), *Regulation: Legal Form and Economic Theory* (Clarendon Press, Oxford).

Pearce, F., and Tombs, S. (1990), 'Ideology, Hegemony and Empiricism', 30 *British Journal of Criminology* 423.

Posner, R. (1974), 'Theories of Economic Regulation', 5 *Bell J.Econ.* 335–58.

Priest, G. (1987), 'The Current Insurance Crisis in Modern Tort Law', 96 *Yale Law Journal* 1521.

Quirk, P. J. (1981), *Industry Influence in Federal Regulatory Agencies* (Princeton University Press, Princeton, NJ).

Ramsay, I. (1989), *Consumer Protection* (Weidenfeld and Nicolson, London).

Richardson, G., Ogus, A. J., and Burrows, P. (1983), *Policing Pollution* (Clarendon Press, Oxford).

Smith, R. (1974), 'The Feasibility of an Injury Tax Approach to Occupational Safety, 38 *Law and Contemporary Problems* 730–44.

Stewart, R. B. (1985), 'The Discontents of Legalism: Interest Group Relations in Administrative Regulation' [1985] *Wisconsin Law Review* 685–86.

—— (1987), 'Crisis in Tort Law? The Institutional Perspective', 54 *Univ.of Chicago Law Review* 184.

—— (1988), 'Regulation and the Crisis of Legalism in the United States' in T. Daintith (ed.), *Law as an Instrument of Economic Policy* (Walter de Gruyter, Berlin).

Stigler, G. (1971), 'The Theory of Economic Regulation', 2 *Bell J.Econ.* 3–21.

Trebilcock, M. (1987), 'The Social Insurance–Deterrence Dilemma of Modern

North American Tort Law: A Canadian Perspective on the Liability Insurance Crisis', 24 *San Diego Law Review* 929.

Van Dyke, B. (1992), 'Emissions Trading to Reduce Acid Depositions', 100 *Yale Law Journal* 2707.

Williamson, O. E. (1985), *The Economic Institutions of Capitalism* (Free Press, New York).

Wilson, G. (1984), 'Social Regulation and Explanations of Regulatory Failure', 32 *Political Studies* 203.

4

Exemplary Damages and Economic Analysis

ANTHONY OGUS[1]

Don Harris has played a leading role in establishing socio-legal studies both as a necessary complement to doctrinal analysis of law and as a major input to policymaking. He has been an inspiration to those of us at the Centre who came from a more or less 'straight' legal background and were eager to explore the exciting, but also forbidding, territory of the social sciences. He once expressed to me his conviction that, among those sciences, economics had perhaps the greatest potential to illuminate legal concepts and principles (see also Harris and Veljanovski, 1986a); and his collaborative work with economists explores some of that potential (Harris *et al.*, 1979; Harris and Veljanovski, 1983, 1986b).

His major, scholarly text on *Remedies in Tort and Contract* (Harris, 1988) nevertheless reveals a cautious approach to economic analysis. He remained, perhaps wisely, sceptical of the far-reaching explanatory and normative conclusions of many law-and-economics exponents in relation to tort law, particularly where they did not match his intuitions or the empirical evidence (*ibid.* 306–8). I cannot know why his account of exemplary damages in that book (*ibid.* 228–33) eschews the economic approach, but I would hope that what follows will not unduly disturb his intuitions. As we shall see, on one interpretation, the current English law on the subject explicitly adopts a deterrence goal, which is the basis for the economic framework for analysing tort law. In any event, the topic is of considerable contemporary relevance, given its recent review by the Law Commission (Law Commission, 1993[2]), and the economic literature provides some rich insights which should assist in designing appropriate reforms.

THE AVAILABILITY OF EXEMPLARY DAMAGES IN ENGLAND AND ELSEWHERE

Since the landmark decision of *Rookes* v. *Barnard* (1964), English law has adopted a restrictive approach to exemplary damages (see also *Broome* v. *Cassell*, (1972) and *A.B.* v. *South West Water Services Ltd*, (1993)). For

---

[1] I should like to thank Neil Duxbury for comments on an earlier draft.
[2] It is anticipated that its Report on the subject will be published in 1997.

the purposes of this Chapter, the following summary should prove sufficient (for a detailed account, see Burrows, 1994, 270–86). In general, tort
damages are intended only to compensate, and thus successful plaintiffs
should be awarded no more than the amount of their losses. Exemplary,
or punitive, damages which exceed those losses may nevertheless be
awarded in the three exceptional categories of case identified by Lord
Devlin in *Rookes* v. *Barnard* (1221–5):

(1) 'oppressive, arbitrary or unconstitutional action by the servants of
    the government';
(2) 'wrongful conduct which has been calculated by the defendant to
    make a profit for himself which may well exceed the compensation
    payable to the plaintiff'.

In either case, exemplary damages may be recovered only for certain
causes of action (*A.B.* v. *South West Water Services Ltd* (1993)) notably
defamation, private nuisance, trespass torts, and the economic torts; and
not, for example, for negligence claims. In addition, they may be
awarded where they

(3) 'are expressly authorised by statute'.

No statutory provision currently in force unambiguously permits such
an award, but the view is generally held that it is available for infringe-
ments of copyright and design right under the Copyright, Designs and
Patents Act 1988[3] (Law Commission, 1993, 64–6).

In other common law jurisdictions, the availability of exemplary damages has not been so narrowly constrained (Law Commission, 1993,
95–103). So, for example, in Australia, they may be awarded in cases of
wanton conduct showing a 'contumelious disregard of the plaintiff's
rights' (*Uren* v. *John Fairfax* (1966), 132, *per* Taylor J) and, in Canada, in
cases of 'extreme' conduct 'deserving of condemnation and punishment, because of its harsh, vindictive, reprehensible and malicious
nature' (*Vorvis* v. *Insurance Corporation of British Columbia* (1989), 208,
per Mr Justice McIntyre; see also Chapman and Trebilcock, 1989, 750–8);
and in neither country is there a cause-of-action test. In the United
States, there has been a tendency to allow punitive damages in a broad
range of cases involving deliberate tortious conduct, not the least for professional malpractice and products liability (Owen, 1982).

THE DETERRENCE FUNCTION OF EXEMPLARY DAMAGES

There has been extensive discussion of the possible justifications for the
award of exemplary damages (Ellis, 1982; Chapman and Trebilcock,

_____
[3] Ss. 97(2) and 229(3), respectively.

1989; Law Commission, 1993, 114–27). Here I shall be concerned only with its alleged deterrence function, that in appropriate circumstances damages exceeding the loss sustained by the plaintiff are necessary to discourage undesirable behaviour. That proposition gives rise to four important questions. (1) What, for this purpose, is to be characterized as undesirable behaviour? (2) In what circumstances will compensatory damages fail to provide an adequate deterrent for undesirable behaviour (so defined)? (3) Is the current English law on the availability of exemplary damages consistent with the answer to (2)? (4) If not, what alternative principles should be adopted?

The Characterisation of Socially Undesirable Behaviour

Tort law deals with frictions arising from social interaction. The behaviour of an actor (A) may harm, or create the risk of harm to, another (B). Normative economics provide us with two alternative tests for determining when such behaviour should be regarded as undesirable (Harris, 1988, 6–8). On the Pareto test, we should permit activity only to the extent that it does not generate losses to the welfare of others. Applying this criterion, A's behaviour is undesirable unless B recovers perfect compensation for the harm which, in this context, implies that B is indifferent between (i) not being harmed, and (ii) being harmed and receiving the stipulated amount of compensation. On the more frequently adopted Kaldor–Hicks test, the behaviour should be permitted if it confers sufficient benefits on those who gain, such that potentially they can compensate fully all the losers and still remain better off. The fact that under this test the gainers are not required to compensate the losers means that in practice it is satisfied when the gains (to whomsoever) exceed the losses (to whomsoever). Applying this criterion, we should regard A's conduct as undesirable only if the costs to B (and others) exceed the benefits to A (and others).

The cost-benefit test implicit in the Kaldor–Hicks approach is of course not always easy to apply. Where the conduct creates only a risk of harm, the cost should be calculated by discounting the amount of harm by the probability of the harm occurring.[4] If the harm involves personal injury or death, the high degree of subjectivity involved in the valuation creates major problems of assessment, although economists have striven to devise techniques of dealing with these (Jones-Lee, 1989).

---

[4] e.g. if there is a 10% probability of a loss to B of £1,000, the cost of the risk to B is £1,000 × 0.1 = £100.

The Adequacy of Compensatory Damages as Deterrence

Let us take first a tort regime in which A is strictly liable to B. If liability is automatic and the damages payable to B constitute perfect compensation for all the harm caused, then the regime constitutes an adequate deterrent of undesirable behaviour, judged by the Pareto test, and therefore also necessarily by the Kaldor–Hicks test. The problem is rather one of potential over-deterrence. If B can avoid the harm more cheaply than A, subject to defences such as that of contributory negligence, B will have no incentive to do so; and A will be deterred from engaging in conduct which, on the Kaldor–Hicks test, would generate net benefits (Shavell, 1987, 37–40).

Under a negligence regime, A will be liable to pay compensation to B only if A fails to take reasonable care. If, in this context, reasonable care means the socially optimal level of care (i.e. where the costs of taking care are roughly equal to the benefits generated in terms of a reduction in the risk-discounted damage costs) and if, when payable, there is perfect compensation for all harm caused, the damages constitute adequate deterrence. Two respects in which the negligence regime differs from strict liability should be noted. First, there should be no problem with incentives for victim care since, if A takes care, the damage costs fall entirely on B. Secondly, the very fact that A is not liable if she takes care, at least in some cases (see, further, below, 91) sharpens the deterrent effect of damages (Cooter, 1982, 82–5). If (say) the optimal level of care requires an expenditure of £100, and A is planning to spend £90 on care, she should realize that spending the additional £10 will reduce her liability for damages costs from (perhaps) a substantial sum to zero.

The analysis has, to this point, adopted some key assumptions on the workings of the tort system. In many circumstances those assumptions are not justified and by relaxing them we can identify cases where compensatory damages may constitute sub-optimal deterrence.

Situation (a): Loss of Ability to Trade Assets

We begin by considering situations in which the system does not provide perfect compensation to B. The first such situation arises if the Pareto test is adopted. As we have seen, that test requires perfect compensation, in the sense that B is indifferent between being harmed and receiving the assessed compensation. To determine what level of compensation will render him indifferent, we need to know for what sum of money he would have voluntarily agreed to suffer the harm. The inquiry can be facilitated by hypothesizing that B's right not to be injured can be enforced by an injunction,[5] and predicting what price B would agree with A to release A from the injunction. If the benefit A derives from the activity exceeds the minimum which B is prepared to accept, there is a surplus to be gained from such an agreement. How that surplus is divided between A and B will depend on the bargaining strategy of each party, but it is clear that B can hold out for more than the minimum price he is prepared to accept. On a strict application of the Pareto test, it can thus be argued that, for compensation to be an adequate deterrence, it should be assessed by reference to what B would have been paid as a result of the hypothesized bargain (Haddock *et al.*, 1990). The argument does not apply, it should be noted, to cases where there is a substitute for the damaged asset readily available to B in the market, since here the cost of obtaining the substitute constitutes adequate compensation to B (*ibid.* 21–4; Harris *et al.*, 1979, 582–6).

The argument for adopting the Pareto test in cases where no substitute is available in the market is, however, unlikely to be widely supported. The fact that injunctions are never mandatory and in practice are rarely imposed except for continuing and threatened interferences with property (Burrows, 1994, 391–9) suggests that judges and other decision-makers consider the test to be too restrictive, inhibiting activity which on the looser Kaldor–Hicks test is regarded as socially beneficial. Given that attitude, it would surely be inconsistent to aim at a level of deterrence equivalent to that which would operate if all harm, or all risks of harm, were to be subject to injunctive relief.

A narrower version of the argument which calls for this level of deterrence where A could have bargained with B but deliberately avoided doing so (Landes and Posner, 1981; Biggar, 1995) is more compelling, but it gives rise to the problem of identifying cases for which such characterization is appropriate. Would it apply to situations where bargaining was theoretically possible but in practice very costly? Would it apply to non-intentional, as well as intentional torts?

Situation (b): Harm Not Fully Covered by Compensatory Damages

The compensation payable by A to B may not cover all the harm generated by A's activity. Several possibilities must be considered. First, not all harms give rise to tort liability. Judges are, for example, cautious in allowing claims by persons other than the immediate victims of accidents (e.g. *Alcock* v. *Chief Constable of South Yorkshire* (1992)). Although, for the purpose of private legal rights, such claims may be treated as too 'remote', the harm is a genuine cost which should be taken into account in assessing the amount of deterrence required. Secondly, in multiple-

---

[5] What Calabresi and Melamed, 1972, refer to as a 'property rule', and thus distinguishable from a 'liability rule', which allows for enforcement only by means of damages.

victim cases, the amount of harm suffered by some or all of those injured may be too low to justify bringing a tort claim, and yet the aggregate harm may be extensive. Thirdly, the damages awarded for a particular claim may be substantially lower than the harm caused. Fatal-accident (or wrongful death) actions constitute the classic example, since here the award is designed largely to compensate dependants of the deceased for their loss, rather than to reflect the value of life to the deceased himself. Fourthly, although the damages awarded may purport to provide compensation for the harm suffered, they may not represent B's own evaluation of the loss. The problem arises most frequently where there is no market, and therefore no objectively determinable value, for the asset damaged or destroyed. Damages in personal-injury claims for loss of amenities and pain and suffering constitute the obvious example. The courts conventionally assess the amounts to be awarded under these heads by reference to a 'tariff' (e.g. £4,500 in 1994 for loss of hair: *Turner* v. *N.S. Hair Treatment Clinic* (1994)) which may provide consistency between comparable cases but which is arbitrary, bearing little relation to what B would have been prepared to pay to avoid the loss (Ogus, 1972). The same can apply where there is a market value for the relevant asset but B's own evaluation is significantly higher.[6] As we have already seen, these problems of under-compensation may in some cases be met by protecting B's right with an injunction: if A has to purchase the right to inflict the harm, B's subjective value should be revealed in the process of bargaining (Calabresi and Melamed, 1972, 1092). But in the case of accidental harm, B's right is rarely, if ever, protected by an injunction, and compensatory damages may therefore give rise to sub-optimal deterrence.

Situation (c): Probability of Harm Higher than Probability of Liability

For compensatory damages to be an adequate deterrent, A must, at the time of contemplating the activity, perceive that the costs (including the damages) will outweigh the benefits. This means, in particular, that the *ex ante* perceived probability of harm occurring must not be significantly higher than the *ex ante* perceived probability of liability. Suppose that A's activity creates a 10 per cent risk of causing £1,000 damage to B. It is then (Kaldor–Hicks) efficient for A to invest in a safety measure which will avoid the risk if it costs less than £100. If there is a 100 per cent certainty that B, on sustaining the injury, will successfully sue A for £1,000, A rationally will make the desirable investment (e.g. of £99, since $99 < 1 \times (0.1 \times 1,000)$). If, on the other hand, there is only a 50 per cent probability that B will successfully sue, A will not have the appropriate incentive unless

---

[6] The difference between the market value and the victim's subjective value is often referred to as the 'consumer surplus': Harris *et al.*, 1979.

the safety investment costs less than £50. For example, A will not spend £51 since $51 > 0.5 \times (0.1 \times 1,000)$.[7]

A singular feature of intentional torts is that the *ex ante* probability of A harming B is very high, approaching certainty, but the *ex ante* probability of A being held liable to B, for e.g. assault, battery, or conversion, may remain low (Landes and Posner, 1981). As regards unintentional torts, it is not possible to give a comprehensive list of all the circumstances in which the probability of liability will be driven significantly lower than the probability of harm, but it would include the following: (i) where the necessary causal link between the harm and A's activity is difficult for B to prove (e.g. medical malpractice); (ii) where B brings a claim in negligence and evidence relating to A's fault is difficult to obtain (e.g. professional or manufacturer negligence); (iii) where A deliberately attempts to conceal the wrongdoing activity; (iv) where B has financial difficulties in suing A.

Situation (d): Negligence, Uncertainty and Judicial Errors

It has been powerfully argued that the problems identified in situations (b) and (c), where the amount payable by, or the probability of liability of, A is too low should not be of serious concern if the liability regime is that of negligence (Cooter, 1982, 82–5). Here, as we have seen, a relatively small sanction might be sufficient to induce A, at the margin, to take additional care since at the point of optimal care, A's liability costs suddenly leap from zero to a substantial amount, representing B's recoverable losses.

But this argument must be treated with caution (Grady, 1983, 1988). It assumes that the courts, in determining negligence liability, seek to identify what constitutes optimal care on a continuum of incremental standards (e.g. the speed at which a vehicle should be driven). It does not obviously apply where the alleged negligence is the failure to take a single, desirable precaution (e.g. fitting a safety device).

Further, even where liability is determined by reference to incremental standards, there is still a problem arising from uncertainty regarding the outcome of litigation and the possibility of judicial error. Such errors are prevalent in the adjudication of negligence claims because courts typically have imperfect information as to the relevant damage and avoidance costs. If there is a possibility that A will be held liable notwithstanding that she has taken optimal care (false positive) or, conversely, that she will not be held liable where she fails to take optimal care (false negative), then there is no longer such a sharp break in the liability costs at the point of optimal care (Png, 1986; Johnston, 1987). In the context of

---

[7] This arithmetical example assumes risk-neutrality. If A is risk-averse, the right-hand side of the inequality will be raised and the deterrent effect will be greater.

this uncertainty, the compensatory damages award will constitute an imperfect sanction: in relation to a false positive, it will over-deter; in relation to a false negative, it will under-deter.

A novel liability regime has been proposed to deal with the problem (Johnston, 1987). A higher burden of proof on the plaintiff (requiring clear and convincing evidence, rather than simply on the balance of probabilities), combined with a lower standard of care (e.g. gross negligence) would combat false positives; and imposing a sanction significantly higher than compensatory damages, when liability on this basis is established, would eliminate false negatives.

This is an ingenious suggestion, but one which is open to serious objections. In the first place, the problem may be overstated. Uncertainty *per se* does not necessarily lead to inappropriate incentives: if, having regard to the distribution of probabilities, there is an approximately equal chance of a false positive and a false negative, the error costs will be cancelled out. Secondly, the proposed solution would pose considerable problems for the court (Chapman and Trebilcock, 1989, 816–17) and one type of uncertainty might replace another. How would judges decide when to apply the regime? How would the lower standard of care be defined? What level of damages would constitute an appropriate sanction?

Situation (e): 'Illicit' Benefits for the Injurer

In general, the deterrence goal is best served by basing damages on the harm suffered by B, rather than the benefit accruing to A (Polinsky and Shavell, 1994). If, for example, the benefit from A's act exceeds the cost to B, then, on the Kaldor–Hicks test, it should not be deterred as it generates a net gain in social utility. Making A disgorge the benefit will deter her from the act; if she is liable only for the harm caused, she will undertake it. The situation may, however, be different where the benefit accruing to A is not one which, on some moral ground, can be characterized as adding to social utility. Most people would consider that the satisfaction derived by a rapist or by a sadistic injurer is an 'illicit' benefit which should not be included in the utility calculus. If that is the case, to achieve the necessary deterrence, A's liability should encompass the benefits which are regarded as illicit[8] (Cooter, 1982, 89; Ellis, 1982, 32).

There is, of course, a major problem in distinguishing between 'licit' and 'illicit' benefits, and this has led some economists to adopt an amoral calculus in which all benefits are considered (Haddock *et al.*, 1990; Biggar, 1995). Alternatively, it may be argued that the moral constraint is more appropriately exerted in the context of the criminal law

---

[8] Or, as Ellis (1982, 31) puts it, where the subjective cost of avoidance is greater than the cost recognized by the law.

which typically penalizes conduct of the kind described. The desirability of using tort law for this purpose then depends on whether optimal enforcement of the law is best achieved by vesting exclusive rights of prosecution in public officials or extending such rights to victims—a complex issue (Landes and Posner, 1975; Polinsky, 1980; Chapman and Trebilcock, 1989, 786–97) which cannot be discussed here.

SUB-OPTIMAL DETERRENCE AND THE ENGLISH LAW ON EXEMPLARY DAMAGES

To what extent can the principles of English law determining the availability of exemplary damages be reconciled with the identified situations in which compensatory damages constitute sub-optimal deterrence?

Deterrence may not be the primary objective of Lord Devlin's first category ('oppressive, arbitrary or unconstitutional action by servants of the government'). The latter may rather reflect the long-established judicial sensitivity to abuse of power by the executive (Ogus, 1973, 35) and serve the symbolic function of marking disapproval of such conduct (Law Commission, 1993, 59). In so far as deterrence is envisaged, the category can perhaps be best justified in terms of situation (c). The cloak of secrecy which surrounds much civil-service decision-making may make it particularly difficult for the victim to obtain evidence of the wrongdoing and thus result in the probability of harm being significantly higher than the probability of liability.

In contrast, Lord Devlin's second category ('wrongful conduct which has been calculated by the defendant to make a profit for himself which may well exceed the compensation payable to the plaintiff') appears to adopt a deterrence function. The impression is confirmed by the judge's subsequent observation, elaborating the second category, that '[e]xemplary damages can properly be awarded whenever it is necessary to teach a wrongdoer that tort does not pay' (*Rookes* v. *Barnard*, at 1227); and by subsequent judicial interpretation, notably: '[s]ome deterrent, over and above compensatory damages, may in these circumstances be called for'.[9]

It is, however, not so easy to reconcile the principle with the situations which, on the analysis above, are appropriate for exemplary damages. Where A calculates that (say) she will make a gross profit of £1,000 from committing a tort which inflicts £500 loss on B, the principle enables the court to award £500 exemplary damages in addition to £500 compensatory damages; thereby A is deterred from committing the tort. Judged

---

[9] Lord Kilbrandon in *Broome* v. *Cassell & Co.* [1972].

by the Kaldor–Hicks test,[10] this outcome is economically undesirable: an act which would have generated a net addition to social utility of £500 no longer takes place.[11]

Can the principle be otherwise interpreted, so as to accord with economic normative reasoning? The key to such an interpretation is the fact that English law circumscribes the causes of action for which exemplary damages may be awarded. These are mainly intentional torts, requiring that the defendant either desires to harm the plaintiff or deliberately does an act in the knowledge that such harm is a probable consequence of the act. Although exemplary damages may be awarded for other torts, such as defamation, private nuisance, and breach of copyright (Lord Devlin's third category), it would seem that the defendant must at least know that the act is wrongful.[12] Intentional or advertent wrongdoing of this kind correlates well, if not perfectly, with two of the situations for which compensatory damages constitute sub-optimal deterrence: that in which A deliberately avoids the possibility of negotiating a purchase of A's right not to be injured (situation (a)); and that in which the probability of harm is significantly higher than the probability of liability (situation (c)). In cases where the harm is to an individual's person or reputation, it is also possible to argue that the 'profit' derived from the act should be characterized as an 'illicit' benefit, and thus not be included in the utility calculus (situation (e)).

REFORMING THE LAW: ENTITLEMENT TO EXEMPLARY DAMAGES

The above analysis suggests that there is only a partial correlation between the principles of English law governing the availability of exemplary damages and the situations where, on the basis of economic analysis, compensatory damages may constitute sub-optimal deterrence. That is, however, not sufficient by itself to lead us to the conclusion that the law should necessarily be remodelled, the better to reflect those situations. The imposition of exemplary damages may sharpen the disincentives for conduct which, on the Kaldor–Hicks test, is allocatively inefficient but at the same time generate other costs. The net effect on aggregate social welfare may, then, be unclear or even negative (Ellis, 1982, 43–53).

We must therefore take account of possible, second-order conse-

---

[10] If £500 constitutes perfect compensation for B, it is also undesirable judged by the Pareto test.

[11] For criticism of the famous Ford Pinto case (*Grimshaw* v. *Ford Motor Co.* (1981)), which resembled this simple arithmetical example, see Ellis, 1982, 48–50.

[12] *Broome* v. *Cassell & Co.*, n. 9 above, 1079, *per* Lord Hailsham.

quences of broadening the availability of exemplary damages. Perhaps the most important of these is an increase to the cost of settling disputes. If reform of the law creates greater uncertainty regarding either entitlement to exemplary damages or the amount to be awarded, there is likely to be a wider divergence in the parties' predictions of the outcome of litigation, and therefore a smaller proportion of claims which are settled without formal adjudication (Bebchuk, 1984; Priest and Klein, 1984). Secondly, a combination of increased liability costs and uncertainty concerning their incidence and amount may induce actors, particularly if they are risk-averse, to engage in costly risk-reducing measures or avoid the activity altogether, neither of which may be justified by the cost-benefit calculus. Thirdly, the prospect of receiving a sum which is larger than that necessary to compensate the loss may entice the plaintiff not only to behave litigiously but also, and perversely, to encourage defendant behaviour which potentially may give rise to exemplary damages (Clarkson *et al.*, 1978).[13]

It would also be wrong to ignore the interaction between tort law and other legal regimes designed to achieve similar ends (Law Commission, 1993, 79). If, for example, the gap between optimal deterrence and compensatory damages is effectively filled by the threat of a criminal sanction, imposing exemplary damages may at best give rise to unnecessary administrative costs and, at worst, over-deter socially valuable behaviour. Indeed, in some areas traditionally deemed appropriate for exemplary damages, the criminal law is likely to be a more effective deterrent. An impecunious individual contemplating the consequences of committing a theft or an assault will find the prospect of a criminal sanction, including imprisonment, more constraining than the possibility of being sued for damages, however large the award.

With these considerations in mind, we may return to the situations identified as giving rise to sub-optimal deterrence.

Situation (a): Loss of Ability to Trade Assets

We have already expressed doubts on the wider definition of this situation, which—based on the Pareto test of efficiency—would imply an additional sanction wherever B is deprived of an asset for which no substitute is available on the market. The narrower definition, focusing on cases where A deliberately avoids bargaining with B, proved to be more appealing. One possibility of dealing with this problem of sub-optimal deterrence, not far removed from existing judicial principles, may be suggested. Some assets are protected against continuing tortious interference by an injunction, therefore effectively forcing A to trade with B, if

---

[13] Behaviour of this kind by the plaintiff may nevertheless be a ground for denying exemplary damages: *Holden* v. *Chief Constable of Lancashire* (1987).

she wishes to persist in the invasion. In lieu of an injunction, the court
sometimes awards 'equitable' damages, based on what it regards as a
reasonable price for which B would have sold the asset to A, if trading had
taken place (Harris, 1988, 331–3). This jurisdiction could be extended
beyond cases where injunctions may be imposed to the protection of
assets more generally. If A's act, continuing or not, was done with knowledge that it interfered with B's right and in such a manner (e.g. 'in contumelious disregard of the plaintiff's rights': *Uren* v. *John Fairfax* (1966))
as to reveal deliberate avoidance of the trading possibility, damages
equivalent to those which would have been awarded under the equitable
jurisdiction could be imposed. The principles governing quantum would
be the same as those already applied under that jurisdiction. Whether
the circumstances governing entitlement to the special award could be
sufficiently clearly defined so as to avoid an escalation of litigation costs
remains nevertheless doubtful.

Situation (b): Harm Not Fully Covered by Compensatory Damages

More radical reform would be necessary to meet the deterrence deficit
identified in this situation. In particular, exemplary damages would have
to be available for unintentional torts, including negligence, as well as
intentional torts. Given a wider jurisdiction to impose the sanction, it
becomes all the more important that the principles of entitlement are
well-targeted and sufficiently certain.

One possibility would be to confer a general discretion on judges,
permitting them to make the award where the aggregate harm suffered is
substantially larger than the compensatory damages payable. This
would provide a comprehensive solution to the problem, but would be
difficult for the courts to apply in practice. In a multiple-victim case, for
example, how would they know how many of the potential claims would
be brought? Errors are likely to abound and, as we have seen, the costs of
such errors may well be substantial.

The main alternative is to identify categories of claims which are noto-
riously subject to the deterrence deficit problem. There are two prime
candidates. The first is a claim for fatal accidents, since here the compensatory award by definition (since it is payable to dependants) does
not reflect the value of life to the victim. The second comprises what the
Law Commission refers to as a 'serious violation of personality interests',
actionable by such torts as false imprisonment, malicious prosecution,
and defamation and 'harassment' trespass (Law Commission, 1993,
20–9). The asset in question (freedom, dignity, reputation) is one which
defies measurement on any objective scale, and unlike personal injuries,
which is subject to the same problem, typically gives rise to no tangible
losses. It is a reasonable assumption that compensatory awards fall well

short of what the victim would exact as the price of the harm. The case for awarding exemplary damages in both categories is enhanced by the fact that neither may be the subject of criminal sanctions.

Situation (c): Probability of Harm Higher than Probability of Liability

Similar considerations apply to this situation, but here the difficulties of targeting exemplary damages awards to appropriate cases become even more acute. A general principle to the effect that judges could make the award where the probability of harm was substantially higher than the probability of liability would be subject to two major objections. First, *ex hypothesi*, cases giving rise to the widest divergence between the two probabilities would be the least likely to reach the court. Secondly, it is not clear how judges would be able to determine *ex post* what the relevant probabilities were *ex ante*, thus posing intractable problems as to both the appropriateness of an exemplary award and the determination of quantum.

Nor would it be easy to formulate more specific rules, tailored to the variety of identified circumstances (e.g. problems in obtaining evidence, proving the causal link, or financing claims) in which the probability of liability is likely to be driven significantly lower than the probability of harm. Intentional torts constitute an important exception but these are largely covered by existing principles governing the award of exemplary damages.

Situation (d): Negligence, Uncertainty, and Judicial Errors

Johnston's suggestion for exemplary damages in this situation (Johnston, 1987) is part of a more general proposal, including also modifications to the onus of proof and the required standard of care, to deal with problems of both inadequate and excessive deterrence. The view has already been advanced (above, 92) that the proposed solutions would generate as much uncertainty as the unreformed law and thus would not generate net benefits to social welfare.

What if we were to focus only on those judicial errors which led to sub-optimal deterrence? For this, it must be shown that the preponderance of such errors falls asymmetrically on the side of false negatives (wrong decisions relieving the defendant of liability), rather than false positives (wrong decisions imposing liability). Where this occurs, the case is, in essence, an example of situation (c), the probability of harm exceeding the probability of liability. Seeking a solution to the problem by means of exemplary damages is clearly not viable: it would require the judges to identify situations in which they were themselves prone to make errors in favour of the defendant!

Situation (e): 'Illicit' Benefits for the Injurer

Economic analysis can provide no guidance on whether or not to discount benefits which are 'illicit', for the purposes of assessing the aggregate utility of the defendant's act; nor can it help in distinguishing between 'licit' and 'illicit'. The matter thus remains one for moral judgement. If the law adopts a moral stance—in my view, it should—then the existence of an 'illicit' benefit may tip the scales in favour of exemplary damages in other situations (notably (b) where the case for such a sanction is only marginal). Where the moral repugnance created by the defendant's desired benefit is large,[14] this by itself may justify an exemplary award, if the moral benefit of deterring the act is deemed to outweigh the costs, particularly those incurred in enforcing the claim.

The moral perspective suggests that only intentional torts should give rise to exemplary damages in this category, but beyond that it would not seem possible to circumscribe judicial discretion by anything other than general principles which referred to, for example, the moral abhorrence of the defendant's aims. At the same time, since conduct so characterized may also fall within the ambit of the criminal law, judges would have to take account of any penal sanction which had been, or was likely to be, imposed (Law Commission, 1993, 79).

REFORMING THE LAW: SECONDARY ISSUES

The Law Commission Consultation Paper raises several secondary issues, consequential on recognizing entitlement to exemplary damages. Comments on these can be kept relatively brief.

Windfall to the Plaintiff?

The deterrence goal may imply that the defendant should pay a sum larger than the plaintiff's loss, but why, in contrast to the criminal law, should that be paid to the plaintiff (Law Commission, 1993, 146)? Where the additional sum represents an 'illicit' benefit, this may be justified by invoking principles of corrective or restitutionary justice (Coleman, 1992, 369–71): the benefit derived by the tortfeasor in a moral sense 'belongs' to the plaintiff. From an economic perspective, the issue can be addressed by reference to the effects which the 'windfall' may have on plaintiff enforcement behaviour. On the one hand, it may encourage plaintiffs to litigate vexatiously or prolong proceedings, thus adding to

[14] Cf. 'conduct involving some element of outrage similar to that usually found in crime': US *Restatement (Second) of Torts* (1977), § 908, comment b.

dispute-resolution costs. On the other hand, it may motivate them to take proceedings in situations where otherwise they would not have sufficient resources to do this, or where, in cases of overlap with the criminal law, there is sub-optimal enforcement by public officials. Which effect is more likely, and with what welfare implications, is a complex empirical question. Intuitively, one might expect the benefits to outweigh the costs.[15]

Vicarious Liability

Where an employee commits a tort for which an employer may be vicariously liable and in circumstances in which, on the above analysis, exemplary damages are justifiable, the case for imposing the additional sanction on the employer is supported by economic analysis (Chapman and Trebilcock, 1989, 819–21). Employees often do not have the resources to satisfy judgments, thus diluting the deterrent effect of liability. Imposing the equivalent degree of liability on the employer should create an incentive for the latter to constrain the behaviour of the employee (Sykes, 1984), thus preserving the degree of deterrence for which exemplary damages against the employee would have been deemed desirable.

Insurance

Should the law prohibit exemplary damages being covered by insurance contracts (Law Commission, 1993, 146–8)? This is a difficult question which does not receive uniform answers in the law and economics literature (Ellis, 1982, 71–6; Chapman and Trebilcock, 1989, 821–2; Priest, 1989). The balance of arguments does not, however, support a prohibition of insurance coverage. The situation may be different from that envisaged in relation to vicarious liability, in that a firm may seek to transfer to insurers a liability which it has the resources to meet. Nevertheless, insurers, like employers, may be in a good position to exert influence on the insured's behaviour and thus deter what is economically undesirable. Further, if insurance coverage were to be prohibited for exemplary damages consequent on negligence liability, this might lead to over-deterrence. This could occur if a risk-averse firm were to be discouraged from engaging in an activity which gave rise to a small risk of a swingeing damages award, but which on objective cost-benefit grounds was socially desirable. In any event, the question may largely be pre-empted by consideration of what forms of coverage the insurance

---

[15] The availability of triple damages in US antitrust suits is usually justified on this basis (Besanko and Spulber, 1990).

market is likely to offer. On grounds of moral hazard and/or adverse selection, insurers are unlikely to provide protection against intentional torts.

I have not attempted, in this Chapter, to investigate the full range of justifications which might exist for exemplary damages. Although some reference to moral values proved to be unavoidable, my primary concern has been to deal with the issue within the narrower framework of economic analysis.

Pursuit of the economic goal requires us to identify situations in which compensatory damages lead to sub-optimal deterrence. Filling the deterrence gap by exemplary damages is, however, justified only if the benefits derived therefrom are not outweighed by additional costs, notably those arising from increasing the uncertainty of the law.

On this basis it would seem that a good case can be made out for awarding exemplary damages where: (a) the defendant's act interfered with an asset, normally protected by an injunction, intending to avoid the possibility of trading with the plaintiff to purchase the asset; or (b) an intentional or unintentional tort gives rise to a fatal-accident claim or involves a serious violation of a personality interest; or (c) an intentional tort generates for the defendant a benefit which, on grounds of moral repugnance, should be disgorged.

If one of these conditions is met, it seems on balance preferable to impose an exemplary award on an employer according to general principles of vicarious liability, to allow insurance coverage of the increased sanction, and to permit the plaintiff to retain the entire proceeds of a successful claim.

CASES

A.B. v. South West Water Services Ltd [1993] QB 507.
Alcock v. Chief Constable of South Yorkshire [1992] AC 310.
Broome v. Cassell [1972] AC 1027.
Grimshaw v. Ford Motor Co., 174 Cal. Rptr. (1981)
Holden v. Chief Constable of Lancashire [1987] 1 QB 380.
Rookes v. Barnard [1964] AC 1129.
Turner v. N.S. Hair Treatment Clinic [1994] CLY 1591.
Uren v. John Fairfax (1966) 40 ALJR 124.
Vorvis v. Insurance Corporation of British Columbia (1989) 58 DLR (4th) 193.

REFERENCES

BEBCHUK, L. (1984), 'Litigation and Settlement Under Imperfect Information', *Rand Journal of Economics* 15, 404–15.

BESANKO, D. A. and SPULBER, D. F. (1990), 'Are Treble Damages Neutral? Sequential Equilibrium and Private Antitrust Enforcement', *American Economic Review* 80, 870–87.

BIGGAR, D. R. (1995), 'A Model of Punitive Damages in Tort', *International Review of Law and Economics* 15, 1–24.

BURROWS, A. S. (1994), *Remedies for Tort and Breach of Contract*, (2nd edn., Butterworths: London).

CALABRESI, G. and MELAMED, A. D. (1972), 'Property Rules, Liability Rules and Inalienability: One View of the Cathedral', 85 *Harvard Law Review* 1089–128.

CLARKSON, K. W., MILLER, R. L. and MURIS, T. (1978), 'Liquidated Damages v. Penalties: Sense or Nonsense?' [1978] *Wisconsin Law Review*: 351–90.

CHAPMAN, B. and TREBILCOCK, M. (1989), 'Punitive Damages: Divergence in Search of a Rationale', 40 *Alabama Law Review* 741–829.

COLEMAN, J. J. (1992), *Risks and Wrongs* (Cambridge University Press, Cambridge).

COOTER, R. (1982), 'Economic Analysis of Punitive Damages', 56 *Southern California Law Review* 79–101.

ELLIS, D. D. (1982), 'Fairness and Efficiency in the Law of Punitive Damages', 56 *Southern California Law Review* 1–78.

GRADY, M. (1983), 'A New Positive Economic Theory of Negligence', 92 *Yale Law Journal* 799–829.

—— (1988), 'Discontinuities and Information Burdens: A Review of the Economic Structure of Tort Law', 56 *George Washington Law Review* 658–78.

HADDOCK, D., MCCHESNEY, F. and SPIEGEL, M. (1990), 'An Extraordinary Rationale for Extraordinary Legal Sanctions', 78 *California Law Review* 1–51.

HARRIS, D. R. (1988), *Remedies in Contract and Tort* (Weidenfeld and Nicolson, London).

—— OGUS, A., and PHILLIPS, J. (1979), 'Contract Remedies and Consumer Surplus', 95 *Law Quarterly Review* 581–610.

—— and VELJANOVSKI, C. (1983), 'Remedies for Breach Under Contract Law: Designing Rules to Facilitate Out-of-Court Settlements', 5 *Law and Policy Quarterly* 97–127.

—— and —— (1986a), 'The Use of Economics to Elucidate Legal Concepts: The Law of Contract' in T. C. Daintith and G. Teubner (eds.), *Contract and Legal Organisation: Legal Analyses in the Light of Economic and Social Theory* (Walter de Gruyter, Berlin and New York).

—— and —— (1986b), 'Liability for Economic Loss in Tort' in M. Furmston (ed.), *The Law of Tort: Policies and Trends in Liability for Damage to Property and Economic Loss* (Duckworth, London).

JOHNSTON, J. S. (1987), 'Punitive Liability: A New Paradigm of Efficiency in Tort Law', 87 *Columbia Law Review* 1385–446.

JONES-LEE, M. (1989), *The Economics of Safety and Physical Risk* (Blackwell, Oxford).

LANDES, W. and POSNER, R. (1975), 'The Private Enforcement of Law', *Journal of Legal Studies* 4, 1–46.

—— and —— (1981), 'An Economic Theory of Intentional Torts', *International Review of Law and Economics* 1, 127–54.

LAW COMMISSION (1993), Consultation Paper No. 132, *Aggravated, Exemplary and Restitutionary Damages* (HMSO, London).

OGUS, A. I. (1972), 'Damages for Lost Amenities: For a Foot, a Feeling or a Function?', 35 *Modern Law Review* 1–17.

—— (1973), *The Law of Damages* (Butterworths, London).

OWEN, D. (1982), 'Problems in Assessing Punitive Damages Against Manufacturers of Defective Products', 49 *University of Chicago Law Review* 1–60.

PNG, I. P. L. (1986), 'Optimal Subsidies and Damages in the Presence of Judicial Error', *International Review of Law and Economics* 6, 101–5.

POLINSKY, A. M. (1980), 'Private Versus Public Enforcement of Fines', *Journal of Legal Studies* 9, 105–27.

—— and SHAVELL, S. (1994), 'Should Liability Be Based on the Harm to the Victim or the Gain to the Injurer?', *Journal of Law, Economics and Organization* 10, 427–37.

PRIEST, G. L. (1989), 'Insurability and Punitive Damages', 40 *Alabama Law Review* 1009–35.

—— and KLEIN, B. (1984), 'The Selection of Disputes for Litigation', *Journal of Legal Studies* 13, 1–55.

SHAVELL, S. (1987), *Economic Analysis of Accident Law* (Harvard University Press, Cambridge, Mass).

SYKES, A. O. (1984), 'The Economics of Vicarious Liability', 93 *Yale Law Journal* 1231–80.

5

Four Offers and a Trial: The Economics of Out-of-court Settlement

PAUL FENN AND NEIL RICKMAN

I. INTRODUCTION

Long before it became fashionable for economists to utilize powerful theoretical and empirical techniques to investigate bargaining behaviour in a litigation context, Don Harris appreciated the importance of adopting an analytical perspective to the problem of delay in the courts. The chapter in *Compensation and Support for Injury and Illness* devoted to offers and delay was mainly his responsibility, and those of us who worked with him on this project were swept along with his infectious enthusiasm for using the dataset to reveal more about the 'black box' of personal-injury litigation. Although he was prone to use a rather more idiosyncratic style of diagram than economists are used to, it was clear to us that the data emerging from the study were unique in their detail on the *process* of settlement as well as its *outcome*. While some of those data have been explored subsequently (Fenn and Vlachonikolis, 1990), the theoretical literature on pre-trial bargaining has progressed significantly since then.

The importance of this area of law and economics lies partially in its relevance to the continuing policy debate concerning the efficiency of the civil justice system. In England, this debate has been most recently embodied in Lord Woolf's proposals for reforming civil procedure. His draft report highlighted cost, complexity, and delay as being the 'key problems' faced by our civil justice system (Woolf, 1995), an observation for which ample evidence has been collected over recent years. The causes of such cost, complexity and delay, are not, however, well understood. Instead, they are the focus of a growing body of research across a number of disciplines, looking at the way parties involved in litigation behave during the process of their case. The aim of this Chapter is to contribute to this work using economic analysis. We do this by first reviewing the theoretical literature available on the economics of out-of-court settlement and demonstrating some of the factors which this highlights as important determinants of settlement behaviour. Following this, we examine some of the predictions arising from a recent contribution to this work (Spier, 1992) with the aid of the Oxford compensation data which Don Harris did so much to realize. As we shall see, Spier's paper is particularly appropriate in the context of settlement delay because it focuses on the way litigants bargain over the duration of their case, from filing of the writ to a possible trial.

We divide our survey of the theoretical contributions in this area into three sections, which present the material in chronological order. In this way it is possible to see how economists' modelling of the settlement process has developed over the past twenty-five years. Our aim is not to provide a comprehensive survey of this literature but, rather, to highlight its main themes and set the model upon which we focus in section III in context.[1]

1. Non-Strategic Analyses

Early papers on pre-trial settlement (Friedman, 1969; Gould, 1973; Posner, 1973, in the civil context; Landes, 1971, in the criminal) focus on the decision to settle or go to trial. They ask the question: what factors are *necessary* for a case to be settled out of court? They answer this in the simplest possible framework, abstracting from the process of settlement negotiation itself and the potential this creates for information transfer between the parties. In this sense, they are 'non-strategic'; both parties assess their expected gain from trial on the basis of their knowledge, and these assessments determine whether, and what, scope for settlement exists. Neither takes account of the other's actions.

All four papers argue, as Posner (1973, 417) does: '[t]he necessary condition for settlement is that the plaintiff's minimum offer—the least amount he will take in settlement of his claim—be smaller than the defendant's maximum offer.' In other words, there must be a surplus available from settling which can be split between the parties in order to make both better off than if trial had occurred. We can examine the determinants of this surplus in a Posner-type model. Define x_i, $i = P,D$, as the recovery the plaintiff (P) and the defendant (D) expect the former to receive at trial, p_i as their subjective probability estimates of the plaintiff's chances of prevailing at trial, c_i as their settlement costs and k_i as

---

[1] Cooter and Rubinfeld (1989) and Rickman (1995, Ch. 2) provide more complete surveys. For example, the former also deals with the effects of settlement behaviour on accident levels and the overall volume of litigation, while the latter considers work on the role of lawyer–client relationships in settlement outcomes.

their court costs. (All monetary amounts are present values.) We also assume that both are risk-neutral, and that their expenditures on the case are independent of x_i and p_i and each other's. The plaintiff's minimum acceptable offer is his expected gain from trial which, assuming that the losing party bears all the trial costs (as in the United Kingdom), is $p_P x_P - (1-p_P)(k_P+k_D)$ plus his settlement costs, while the defendant's maximum offer is his expected trial payout, $p_D(x_D+k_D+k_P)$, minus his settlement costs. Thus, the necessary condition for settlement is

$$p_P x_P - (1-p_P)(k_P+k_D) + c_P < p_P(x_D+k_P+k_D) - c_D$$

or

$$p_P x_P - p_D x_D < (1-p_P+p_D)(k_P+k_D) - (c_P+c_D) \tag{1}$$

Looking at Inequality (1), we see that a necessary condition for settlement is that the expected costs involved in gaining a trial judgment must outweigh the expected benefits (in terms of the damages expected to be transferred between the parties). This is the surplus referred to above. Note that it is the parties' *expected* trial costs which appear as the first term on the right-hand side because the UK rule makes liability for these costs a function of the uncertain trial outcome. This is different from the situation under US cost-allocation rules where, because each party pays its own costs for certain, only (k_P+k_D) appears on the right-hand side, the expression involving probabilities $(1-p_P+p_D)$ disappearing. Clearly, from the inequality, anything which raises costs, or lowers stakes and probabilities, will make the necessary condition easier to fulfil, and we might interpret this as raising the prospects of settlement.[2]

Inequality (1) is not a sufficient condition for settlement to take place, e.g., parties may fail to agree on a settlement amount. However, as Salant (1984, 1) and Schweizer (1989, 164) note, without private information and a bargaining framework, it is difficult to explain why and how two rational agents disagree when they know that gains from trade exist. Also, within this context, it is impossible to specify a settlement amount. Instead this will be determined by the two sides' relative bargaining strengths. We shall return to these issues in the next section.

The analysis can be made more general by introducing risk aversion. One way to think about this is in terms of certainty equivalents. Define the plaintiff's certainty equivalent to trial as v_P, i.e.:

---

[2] In particular, as the two parties become more optimistic about their chances at trial (p_P increases and p_D falls), inequality (1) becomes harder to satisfy. This is often referred to as Posner's 'mutual optimism' condition.

$$U^P(v_P) = p_P U^P(x_P) + (1-p_P)U^P(-k_P-k_D),$$

where $U^P(\cdot)$ is his von Neumann–Morgenstern utility function. Similarly, the defendant's certainty equivalent, v_D, is given: by

$$U^D(-v_D) = p_D U^D(-x_D-k_D-k_P) + (1-p_D)U^D(0).$$

We can now define the parties' risk premiums, i.e., the maximum they are willing to pay to avoid trial. For the plaintiff, this is defined by

$$v_P{}^* \equiv p_P x_P - (1-p_P)k_P - v_P > 0$$

and for the defendant, it is

$$v_D{}^* \equiv v_D - (p_D x_D + k_D + k_P) > 0.$$

Clearly, the plaintiff's minimum demand is now $v_P + c_P$, while his opponent's maximum offer is $v_D - c_D$. We can use the definitions of $v_P{}^*$ and $v_D{}^*$ to rewrite these minimum demands and offers, and obtain the necessary condition for settlement as:

$$p_P x_P - (1-p_P)k_P + c_P - v_P{}^* < p_D(x_D+k_D+k_P) - c_D + v_D{}^*.$$

Rearranging yields

$$p_P x_P - p_D x_D < (1-p_P+p_D)(k_P+k_D) + (v_P{}^*+v_D{}^*) - (c_P+c_D).$$

Comparing this with inequality (1), we can see that risk aversion makes the necessary condition for settlement easier to satisfy. Accordingly, the range of parameters for which settlement can occur increases. Note also that, as either party becomes more risk-averse, an increase in $v_i{}^*$ is implied, making the 'settlement range' still wider. Gravelle (1989) shows that, in the context of imperfect information, an increase in one party's risk-aversion makes the settlement terms more favourable to the other party: effectively, the widening of the settlement range is accomplished by a weakening in the risk averter's bargaining position. (This confirms earlier results in Phillips *et al.*, 1975; Phillips and Hawkins, 1976.)

Thus, the non-strategic models isolate expectations and the financial and psychological costs of litigation as the main influences on whether there are mutual gains from out-of-court settlement. The simple framework within which these results are derived has both advantages and disadvantages. Certainly, the framework generates testable hypotheses about a complicated process which may not have been so easily derived elsewhere.[3] Further, the model is easily adapted to consider more complicated problems, such as the effects of changing the rule by which litigation costs are allocated (see Shavell, 1982), or the effects of cost rules on the effort expended by the parties on their litigation (Hause, 1989; Hersch, 1990). Nevertheless, the framework's simplicity prevents it from addressing a number of important issues. In particular, the failure to specify who has what information removes strategic considerations from the analysis, while the lack of a bargaining structure and time dimension to the settlement negotiations makes the size of the settlement amount and issues of settlement delay intractable. Also, the role of lawyers and clients in the process is ignored. The following sections generalize the model in order to overcome these shortcomings, beginning with the introduction of information asymmetries between the litigants and a bargaining structure in which settlement negotiations can take place.

2. Strategic Analyses

P'ng (1983, 539) argues that, by sidestepping the strategic element in the decision to file suit, and to settle or go to trial, the above models are unable to address a number of issues relevant to these decisions. These issues include 'nuisance suits', the non-co-operative nature of legal disputes (recall that, in the above models, the parties evaluate their positions without being able to react to their opponents' actions) and the role of private information in the outcome of settlement negotiations. The solution is to model the settlement process as a game in which the players (i.e. the litigants) have private information about their cases and in which they are able to react to each other's decisions.

Two early models which do this, following P'ng, are Bebchuk, 1984, and Reinganum and Wilde, 1986. In each case, the bargaining structure allows one, 'take-it-or-leave-it', settlement offer to be made. This is either accepted or rejected, with the latter leading to trial. The difference between the two models lies in which of the plaintiff or defendant has private information about the strength of his case. In Bebchuk's model, the defendant has private information concerning his liability: he knows how liable he is for the accident. The plaintiff, who is assumed to make the single settlement offer (or, in this case, demand) therefore does so whilst being uncertain as to his opponent's type; he must make the demand based on his expectations about the type of defendant he faces. In contrast, Reinganum and Wilde assume the plaintiff to have the private information, this time about the extent of his losses. Again, he is also assumed to make the settlement demand. The difference between the

---

[3] For examples of such tests see Coursey and Stanley, 1988; Thomason, 1991; Snyder and Hughes, 1990, 1995.

two models therefore is in whether an informed or uninformed party makes a settlement offer. From an economic perspective this is interesting because settlement offers (or reactions to them) can convey information if they are from informed parties in a take-it-or-leave-it game.

In both models, the presence of asymmetric information prevents the case from being certain to settle. Unlike in Posner *et al.*, this is so despite the existence of mutual gains from trade (i.e. a surplus). The results confirm Salant and Schweizer's observation (105 above) that the satisfaction of a necessary condition for settlement is not sufficient to guarantee that trial is avoided. It is this which illustrates how the introduction of private information generates departures from the non-strategic models.

Interestingly, the intuition behind cases going to trial differs between Bebchuk and Reinganum and Wilde's models. For Bebchuk, the uninformed plaintiff is simply unable to make an accurate settlement demand on all occasions: because he cannot tell his opponent's type, he is unable to tailor a settlement demand that cannot be refused. In Reinganum and Wilde, the plaintiff is able to signal to the defendant via his settlement demand. The plaintiff has an incentive to inflate his settlement demand since his opponent does not know true damages. Accordingly, the latter must retain a positive probability of rejecting the demand. Further, this probability must increase with the demand to prevent less damaged plaintiffs from emulating more heavily damaged ones. The outcome is that asymmetric information again creates a non-zero equilibrium probability of trial. Unlike Bebchuk, however, where this is because the offerer was too ill-informed to make an accurate enough offer, it is now because the offerer must be prevented from exploiting his informational advantage.

A variety of extensions to these basic models is available. For example, Nalebuff (1987) adapts Bebchuk's model by assuming that the plaintiff may be unwilling to take the case to trial if no settlement is reached: he has brought the suit in the hope of capitalizing on its nuisance value. The effect of this is to make settlement more likely when the level of damages is high (*contra*, Bebchuk). This is because high damages make the plaintiff's threat to go to trial more credible, thereby allowing him to relax his bargaining stance. In other extensions, Schweizer (1989) allows for the possibility that both litigants have private information, while Rubinfeld and Sappington (1987) and Katz (1988) allow parties' bargaining efforts to affect their litigation costs as well as their prospects of success.

All of the models in this section have utilized a 'take-it-or-leave-it' framework to capture the litigation context. Given the modelling complexities that can be introduced by explicitly considering asymmetric information, this is an understandable (and acceptable) simplification in the pursuit of added realism. The particular benefits derived from such models have been an enhanced understanding of why cases go to trial and several insights into the complexities of comparing jurisdiction-specific rules (especially cost rules) when assessing reform proposals. Clearly, however, the 'take-it-or-leave-it' assumption is restrictive. Not only does it fail to capture the richness of the litigation process (in terms of its potential for strategic behaviour and information transfer), it is also unamenable to a number of policy questions that are increasingly being asked of legal systems. Thus, we might be interested in the effects of different bargaining environments (say, the number of periods[4]) on settlement amounts or in the reasons for delay often observed in civil disputes. We finally turn therefore to recent models, whose distinguishing features include a bargaining framework of potentially many periods, i.e. dynamics.

3. Introducing Dynamics

It is only since Rubinstein's paper in 1982 that economists have been able satisfactorily to analyse situations where parties bargain for (potentially) many periods. It is not surprising therefore that only a small number of multi-period bargaining models have been developed to analyse the settlement–trial decision. However, as Kennan and Wilson's (1993) recent survey of bargaining theory demonstrates, litigation is becoming an accepted setting for such models.

Bargaining models have traditionally focused on situations where a buyer and seller are haggling over the price of a product (Fudenberg and Tirole, 1983; Sobel and Takahashi, 1983; Cramton, 1984). Private information can be incorporated by allowing either or both of the players to keep their true valuations of the good from the other. One can reinterpret this environment as a settlement negotiation by (for example) supposing that the defendant is the seller with the plaintiff acting as the buyer. In this context, what would have been selling-price offers in the buyer–seller game become settlement offers from the defendant, with the plaintiff deciding whether to buy the good (settle the case) at the requested amount.

Perhaps the most important issue in litigation addressed by dynamic bargaining models concerns explaining delay in settlement. Two types of model have emerged (so far) to offer explanations for this. Again, asymmetric information is used to prevent instant settlement being guaranteed (as Cheung, 1988, shows will otherwise be the case).[5] The models in

---

[4] A 'period' is defined here as the amount of time needed for an offer of settlement to be made by either party.

[5] In fact, complete information is not sufficient to prevent instant resolution of a bargaining dispute (Fernandez and Glazer, 1992).

question explain delay in one of two ways: (i) as the result of a war of attrition between the litigants (Ordover and Rubinstein, 1986); (ii) as the result of litigation costs (Spier, 1992).

In Ordover and Rubinstein's (1986) war of attrition model, bargaining takes place over a finite horizon, and there are two possible outcomes, (α) and (β), preferred differently by the litigants. One party has information about which of these will occur should agreement not take place by the end of the game; for example, the plaintiff might have private information about the extent of his injuries so that, if these are high, he receives (β), and if low, then (α). The defendant perpetually offers (α) but if he concedes, he settles at (β). (Similarly, the plaintiff concedes by accepting (α).) Thus, the game is decided when the first player 'drops out'. It is this which gives the game its 'war-of-attrition' quality. Ordover and Rubinstein show that the unique equilibrium outcome depends on whether the defendant is initially optimistic or pessimistic about which type of opponent he faces. One awkward feature of this model as applied to settlement bargaining is the lack of compromise on either side. Such 'holding out' might be more normally observed in situations where one, or both, of the parties has a reputation at stake/to make. Genn (1987) demonstrates that this will often be the case in personal-injury litigation when an insurance company is involved, and Swanson (1988) presents an economic model to show how such a strategy can be profitable in this case. However, we would generally expect to see at least one of the parties changing settlement offers/demands over the course of negotiations, and there is evidence to confirm this (Fenn and Vlachonikolos, 1990; Harris, 1984; Kritzer, 1990). Thus, although the war of attrition might explain some settlement delay, it does not explain the negotiation patterns we observe in much of the available evidence.

In a version of Spier's model, the plaintiff has private information concerning the case and his opponent makes settlement offers (Rickman, 1995). Notice that, in contrast with Bebchuk's 'take-it-or-leave' model where the uninformed party moved first and learned nothing, Spier's dynamic environment changes this. Now, the prospect of several chances to make offers allows the defendant to learn something about his opponent from the latter's response to settlement offers. Thus, the defendant's settlement offers rise as negotiations progress, because rejection of previous ones indicates that the plaintiff is ever more badly damaged.

From an empirical perspective, Spier's most interesting result concerns her discovery of a 'deadline effect' in the timing of settlement. In other words, her model predicts that the probability distribution of settlement over time is often 'U-shaped'. This means that there is a relatively large chance that settlement will take place in the last period of bargaining before trial. Since 'doors-of-the-court' settlement behaviour is often said to characterize the pre-trial process, the model might provide a valuable insight into its explanation.

The deadline effect in Spier's model is due to strategic behaviour and the costs of litigation faced by the informed party. In every period of bargaining, the plaintiff decides whether to accept the defendant's demand or reject it in the expectation of a higher one next period. He must thus trade off the gains here with the extra cost incurred by forcing negotiations to another period. When the last period before trial is reached, the parameters of the defendant's decision may change: rejection of a settlement demand now implies incurring trial costs. To the extent that these are larger than the per-period costs that have entered his calculations until now, such costs will prompt a larger likelihood of settlement in this period than in the previous ones. Therefore, the probability of settlement is higher just before trial; this is the deadline effect.

The preceding survey has described how the economic analysis of pre-trial behaviour has evolved over the last two decades. The development of new theoretical techniques in microeconomics has enabled us to address the modelling of the settlement process with increasingly realistic assumptions. In particular, analysis of the role of private information and sequential bargaining behaviour has significantly improved modelling in this area. However, these theoretical developments have rarely, as yet, been subject to empirical testing. In the following section, we attempt to use the Oxford Compensation data to make a contribution in this area.

III. EVIDENCE ON SETTLEMENT DELAY

The result from Spier's paper discussed above, relate to the probability distribution of settlements over time. The central concept used in this section is that of the *conditional probability* of an event taking place. On entry to any given state, there exists a given probability that the individual will leave that state on the following day. More generally, for any individual who has been in a particular state for t(>0) days, there exists a probability that he/she will exit that state on day t+1. The empirical version of the conditional probability of exit is often referred to as the *hazard rate*, where the latter is estimated by the number of exits observed at time t, divided by the number of people at risk of exit at time t. This concept is important in the context of this Chapter in so far as it helps focus attention on the process of settlement over time rather than the outcome in terms of settlement delay. For example, a delay of twenty weeks is the product of a sequence of conditional settlement probabilities in each of the preceding nineteen weeks. Our focus therefore is on the individual decisions underlying settlement delay rather than on the overall delay itself.

1. Simulation Analysis

In this section we use simulation techniques in order to illustrate results obtained by Spier (1992) with respect to the settlement process. In particular, we choose some specific assumptions and graphically examine the resulting settlement offers and their associated acceptance probabilities over time as calculated from Spier's model. In making our assumptions, we are concerned to reflect certain known facts in relation to personal injury litigation, referring in particular to the work of Harris *et al.* (1984). First, very few cases get to trial, and most are settled well before the trial date. Secondly, there are typically only a few offers made over the duration of any one case, with as many as 63 per cent of plaintiffs accepting the first offer made to them (Harris *et al.*, Table 3.3). With these observed facts in mind, we choose to set the number of offers available to the defendant prior to trial at four, and the following values for the other parameters: delay cost = £40 per period; litigation cost = £50; plaintiff's losses distributed uniformly between £200 and £500; and a discount rate of 0.9 for both parties.

The predicted settlement paths resulting from these assumptions are given in Figure 1:

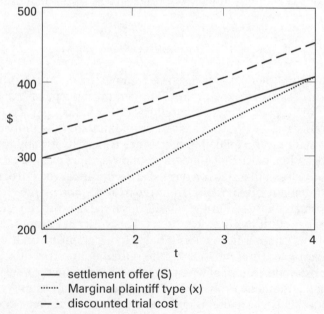

Fig. 1: Equilibrium settlement path

The discounted trial cost in the figure is included in order to show that the necessary condition for negotiating over settlement is met. The settlement offers are gradually increased, resulting in most plaintiffs settling prior to trial. The 'marginal plaintiff type' (x) is a measure of the severity of the remaining plaintiffs' losses after a given offer has been made. The larger is x, the more severe are the remaining losses.

The conditional probability of settling after an offer given that the previous offer was rejected can be derived from the computed values of x. The effect on this of varying the baseline assumptions can be shown in Figure 2 below. Here, we have assumed that actual damages fall between 150 and 550, rather than 200 and 500. This constitutes an increase in the uncertainty faced by the defendant.

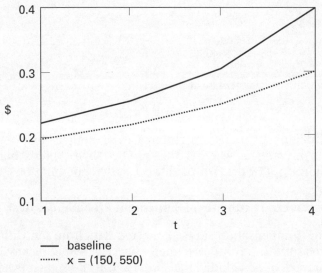

Fig. 2: Settlement hazard rates

For the baseline assumptions we see that the hazard rate is rising over time with each successive offer. The effect of an increase in uncertainty about the plaintiff's losses is to reduce the hazard of settlement, with the strength of this effect also increasing over time. Given our objective to discover whether this predicted pattern of behaviour is consistent with observed data on settlement durations, it is useful to represent the above diagram in terms of the cumulative hazard over time (otherwise known as the 'integrated hazard'). The following figure does this (see Fig. 3):

It can be seen from Figure 3 that we would expect the integrated hazard to be reduced with increasing uncertainty over the expected damages, and for this effect to get proportionately larger over time: the

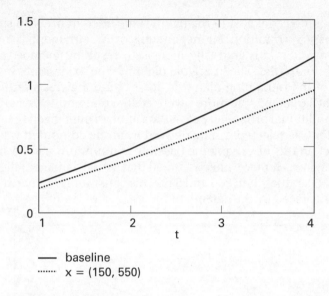

Fig. 3: Cumulative settlement hazard

increased defendant uncertainty increases settlement delay. We now proceed to investigate whether this prediction of Spier's bargaining model is borne out by the Oxford data on settlement durations.

2. Non-parametric Estimates of Settlement Probabilities over Time

The Oxford Compensation survey collected data from individuals who experienced some interruption of their normal activities due to illness or injury. A sample of 2,142 individuals were asked about their experiences in claiming compensation for their losses and the effects of their illness/injury. Some 224 cases reported that they had pursued a claim for compensation against an individual held responsible for their loss. These data were further supplemented by a follow-up survey of plaintiff's solicitors, at which point detailed information about the settlement process was obtained, including the amount and dates of offers, and whether or not there was any dispute between the parties about liability, prognosis, or quantum.

In order to examine whether the pattern of delay was consistent with bargaining models such as Spier's, we estimate integrated hazard functions for the duration to settlement in the Oxford sample, stratified by various factors relating to the uncertainty surrounding the expected outcome in court. The following three figures show our results:

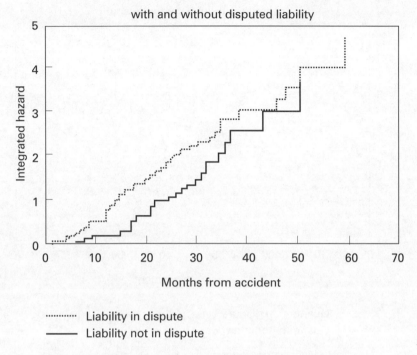

Fig. 4: Settlement hazard rates, with and without disputed liability

It is clear from Figures 4–6 that the settlement behaviour observed in the Oxford survey is not entirely consistent with the predictions of Spier's bargaining model. It is true to say that increased uncertainty about liability, quantum, and prognosis all initially reduce the conditional probability of settlement (and thereby contribute to increasing delay); however, this effect in all cases appears to wear off over time, and indeed seems to be reversed beyond some eighteen to twenty months after the accident. That is, after this time, the presence of initial uncertainty actually *increases* the conditional probability of settlement. This phenomenon is most pronounced when prognosis and liability are disputed, and least pronounced when quantum is in dispute. What this appears to indicate is that there is usually a progressive reduction in uncertainty over time: disclosure of relevant information and the healing process itself both contribute to a clearer picture about both the chance of success in court and the likely damages. What we see measured in the Oxford survey is initial uncertainty; we have no information on the way in which the uncertainty was resolved over time, but we can infer from the data that such a process did take place.

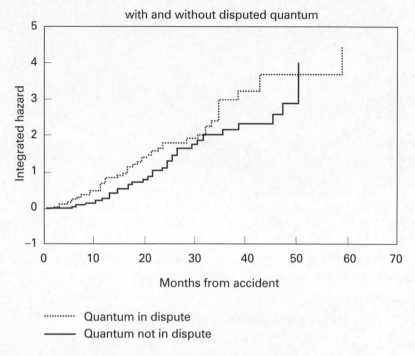

Fig. 5: Settlement hazard rates, with and without disputed quantum

IV. CONCLUSION

We have argued in this Chapter that the law and economics of out-of-court settlements provide a valuable perspective when considering the causes of settlement delay and policy responses such as those emphasized by Lord Woolf's report on civil procedure. In particular, as we have shown, recent developments in bargaining theory as applied to litigation have considerable potential for explaining the existence of delayed settlements. However, we believe that our findings are also sufficient to cast doubt on the realism of some of the assumptions underlying recent work on pre-trial bargaining, and therefore suggest that it may have limited predictive power in this context. The settlement process appears to be one in which information which is held privately by both parties is gradually revealed over time, thereby reducing uncertainty. In contrast, Spier's model assumes that only one party has private information, and this is revealed to the other party only by means of the offers which are accepted. If the private information held by one party changes over time, there is nothing in Spier's model which suggests why this should be revealed to the uninformed party.

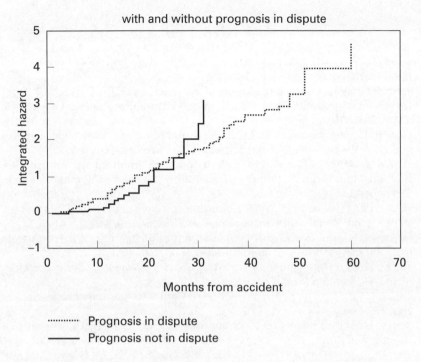

Fig. 6: Settlement hazard rates, with and without prognosis in dispute

This is not to denigrate the contribution of Spier's paper. As we have maintained in section II above, the earlier theoretical approaches to the settlement process would have been explicitly less equipped even to confront the issue of delay. Bargaining theory has now moved on from the time when P'ng, driven to defend a take-it-or-leave-it assumption in a model of settlement, said: '[w]e recognise that this is a very restrictive assumption: our justification is that a realistic model of the process of settlement must rely on a theory of bargaining. Such a theory is still in gestation' (P'ng, 1983).

The gestation period is now over, but bargaining theory as applied to pre-trial contexts is still far from being sufficiently mature to offer a plausible model of that process. We believe that the evolving literature on bargaining will ultimately be capable of explaining some of the complexities of litigation as revealed by Don Harris's Compensation Survey. Whether such a rich source of data will again be collected is more doubtful.

REFERENCES

Bebchuk, L. A. (1984), 'Litigation and Settlement Under Imperfect Information', *Rand Journal of Economics* 15(3), 404–15.

Cheung, R. (1988), 'A Bargaining Model of Pre-Trial Negotiation', Working Paper No. 49, John M. Olin Programme in Law and Economics, Stanford Law School, Cal. 94305–8610.

Cooter, R. D., and Rubinfeld, D. L. (1989), 'Economic Analysis of Legal Disputes and Their Resolution', *Journal of Economic Literature* 27(3), 1067–97.

Cramton, P. (1984), 'Bargaining with Incomplete Information: An Infinite-Horizon Model with Continuous Uncertainty', *Review of Economic Studies* 51(4), 579–93.

Fenn, P., and Vlachonikolis, I. (1990), 'Bargaining Behaviour of Defendant Insurers: an Economic Model', *The Geneva Papers on Risk and Insurance*, 14, 41–52

Fudenberg, D., and Tirole, J. (1983), 'Sequential Bargaining with Incomplete Information', *Review of Economic Studies* 50(2), 221–47.

Genn, H. (1987), *Hard Bargaining: Out of Court Settlement in Personal Injury Actions* (Clarendon Press, Oxford).

Gould, J. P. (1973), 'The Economics of Legal Conflicts', *Journal of Legal Studies* 2(2), 279–300.

Gravelle, H. S. E. (1989), 'Accidents and the Allocation of Legal Costs with an Uninformed Court', *Geneva Papers on Risk and Insurance* 14(50), 11–26.

Harris, D. R., Maclean, M., Genn, H., Lloyd-Bostock, S., Fenn, P., Corfield, P., and Brittan, Y. (1984), *Compensation and Support for Illness and Injury* (Clarendon Press, Oxford).

Hause, J. C. (1989), 'Indemnity, Settlement, and Litigation, or I'll Be Suing You', 18 *Journal of Legal Studies* (1), 157–79.

Hersch, P. L. (1990), 'Indemnity, Settlement, and Litigation: Comment and Extension', *Journal of Legal Studies* 19(1), 235–41.

Kennan, J., and Wilson, R. B. (1993), 'Bargaining with Private Information', *Journal of Economic Literature* 31(1), 45–104.

Landes, W. M. (1971), 'An Economic Analysis of the Courts', *Journal of Law and Economics* 14(1), 61–107.

Nalebuff, B. (1987), 'Credible Pretrial Negotiation', *Rand Journal of Economics* 18(2), 198–210.

Ordover, J. A., and Rubinstein, A. (1986), 'A Sequential Concession Game with Asymmetric Information', *Quarterly Journal of Economics* 101(4), 879–88.

Phillips, J., and Hawkins, K. (1976), 'Some Economic Aspects of the Settlement Process' 39 *Modern Law Review* 497–513.

—— —— and Flemming, J. (1975), 'Compensation for Personal Injuries', *Economic Journal* 85(1), 129–34.

P'ng, I. P. L. (1983), 'Strategic Behaviour in Suit, Settlement and Trial', *Bell Journal of Economics* 14(2), 539–50.

Posner, R. A. (1973), 'An Economic Approach to Legal Procedure and Judicial Administration', *Journal of Legal Studies* 2(2), 399–458.

REINGANUM, J. F., and WILDE, L. L. (1986), 'Settlement, Litigation, and the Allocation of Litigation Costs', *Rand Journal of Economics* 17(4), 557–66.

RICKMAN, N. (1995), 'The Effects of Contingent and Hourly Fees on Litigation Outcomes', Unpublished PhD dissertation, McGill University

RUBINFELD, D. L., and SAPPINGTON, D. E. M. (1987), 'Efficient Awards and Standards of Proof in Judicial Proceedings', *Rand Journal of Economics* 18(2), 308–15.

RUBINSTEIN, A. (1982), 'Perfect Equilibrium in a Bargaining Model', *Econometrica* 50(1), 97–109.

SALANT, S. W. (1984), 'Litigation of Settlement Demands Questioned by Bayesian Defendants', Social Science Working Paper No. 516, California Institute of Technology, Pasadena, Cal., 91125.

SCHWEIZER, U. (1989), 'Litigation and Settlement Under Two-Sided Incomplete Information', *Review of Economic Studies* 56(2), 163–78.

SHAVELL, S. (1982), 'Suit, Settlement, and Trial: A Theoretical Analysis Under Alternative Methods for the Allocation of Legal Costs', *Journal of Legal Studies* 11(1), 55–81.

SOBEL, J., and TAKAHASHI, I. (1983), 'A Multi-Stage Model of Bargaining', *Review of Economic Studies* 50(3), 411–26.

SPIER, K. E. (1992), 'The Dynamics of Pretrial Negotiation', *Review of Economic Studies* 59(1), 93–108.

THOMASON, T. (1991), 'Are Attorneys Paid What They Are Worth? Contingent Fees and the Settlement Process', *Journal of Legal Studies* 20(1), 187–223.

6

Professional Inattention: Origins and Consequences

W. L. F. FELSTINER

'Those are my wishes, and I made this very plain to you, from day one. You, on the other hand, as the lawyer have ignored my wishes and gone about your merry business doing whatever the hell you wanted.'

John Grisham, *The Chamber*, 392 .

FOREWORD

I spent a year at Oxford in the 1980s. Originally it was a matter of living out a youthful dream that had been interrupted by the Korean War. But half-way through that wonderful year, I agreed to become the Director of the American Bar Foundation, the closest equivalent in the United States to the Centre for Socio-Legal Studies. For my remaining time at Oxford I was smart enough to pay attention to the way Don Harris directed activities at the Centre. It was from him that I learned some of the most important obligations and opportunities that are encountered by the directors of research institutions. I found out the importance of maintaining absolutely rigorous standards in recruitment and then devoting one's energies to providing the support and protection that able researchers require to get on with their work. I could see that a director who was flat-out dedicated to the welfare of the institution, and turned his back on any opportunities to promote his own affairs at its expense, would in return secure for the institution the loyalty of its scholars. And I saw how the morale of the staff was maintained as much by the personal attention that the director paid to their individual welfare and the collective ambience of the institution as by the objective conditions of work. This contribution to Don's volume is an inadequate and belated thank-you note.

Lawyer–client interactions are simultaneously concerned with the substantive content of clients' legal problems and with the ordinary interpersonal dimensions of human communications. This chapter concerns
the latter: the non-substantive side of lawyer–client interactions in the
United States. Although it is primarily about the situation in the United
States, there is good reason to believe that professional behavior and the
interpersonal problems it engenders is similar in the United Kingdom
(see The Law Society, 1992) and, in fact, I will make that point with reference to asbestos litigation in Britain. Extensive survey research conducted over many years, frequently on behalf of the organized profession
itself, indicates that interpersonally the lawyer–client relationship is
deeply troubled (ABA Leadership Forum, 1994: 1; see, Scottsdale II, 1988,
2, 12; Abel, 1989, 164; Curran, 1977, 229–30). All too often lawyers are
thought to be inattentive, unresponsive, insensitive, non-empathetic,
uncooperative, and arrogant.

Yet there is no reason to believe that lawyers in the main are incompetent, lazy, callous or greedy. Law may attract disproportionate numbers
of certain kinds of people and fail to attract other kinds (see Nelson and
Trubek, 1992a, 183), but the guiding assumption of my research is that
for the most part the criticized behavior has structural origins, origins
that are rooted in the training and socialization of lawyers and in the
structure, organization, and economics of law practice. The central goal
of this Chapter is to provide a map, a working guide as it were, to these
structural origins.

Until recently, the organized bar believed that the public's low opinion
of lawyers was a public-relations rather than a substantive problem. The
public did not value lawyers correctly because it misunderstood their
role in the adversary dimensions of the American legal system rather
than because lawyers behaved inappropriately. There has been a total
switch of attitude and the organized bar today frequently and roundly
blames lawyers for the profession's low public esteem (Hengstler, 1993,
61; Vogel, 1989, 1). But the bar may now be as naïve about the source of
such behavior and the steps that would have to be taken to cure it as it
once was about the existence of the problem itself. The cure is a form of
professional Boy Scout pledge (see Appendix A) to be delivered to new
clients and hung on office walls coupled to a program of instructional
videotapes (see Commission on Partnership Programs, 1993, 2–3). The
thesis of this Chapter, on the other hand, is that lawyer behavior has
complicated structural origins and that any change in that behavior is
likely to be slow, uncertain, and grudging. The bar, on the other hand,

believes that the only difference between good and bad practice is the level of self-awareness; that the substitution of good for bad practice is cost-free.

Before I embark on the discussion of the origins of lawyer inattention to clients, I want to consider the impact of such objectionable behavior. Law may impose various kinds of untoward consequences on those subject to its operations, ranging from grievous harm in a large number of cases (laws enforcing slavery or the subjugation of women) to serious mistakes in a small number of cases (executing the innocent) to minor indignities inflicted on many people (loss of time, money and dignity described by Feeley (1979) as 'process as punishment'). Where along this scale do client reactions to inappropriate lawyer behavior fall? Are clients merely annoyed by the bad manners and consultative postures of lawyers or do these behaviors inflict serious social or psychological traumas on them?

Procedural-justice theorists have found in a wide range of contexts that people are remarkably sensitive to the process that they experience in encounters with authority figures like lawyers (Lind and Tyler, 1988, ch. 4). This sensitivity to process has been found to outweigh outcome concerns in politics and in organizations as well as in a wide variety of legal settings, including those of misdemeanor and felony defendants and citizens in their encounters with the police and when involved with divorce, mediation, and small-claims courts (see Casper *et al.*, 1988, 483–4).

Before procedural-justice researchers turned their attention to tort litigation (see Lind *et al.*, 1990), litigant satisfaction was assumed to reflect only considerations of outcome, cost, and delay. Economic analyses of procedures, and the proposals for reform to which they lead, assume that litigants are primarily concerned with recoveries and payouts and with how much it costs and how long it takes to bring a case to closure. Lind and his colleagues (Lind, 1994; Tyler and Lind, 1992; Lind *et al.*, 1990), on the other hand, have found that what they call 'dignitary process' issues are even more important than objective outcomes because respectful and dignified treatment implies that the recipient is a full-fledged, valued member of society, a belief that goes to the core of the way that we define our self-identity.

When applied to the question of the level of attention that lawyers give to clients, the procedural-justice argument goes like this. People learn about how they stand in the world, they search out and learn about their status, from the quality of their treatment by people in positions of authority, by people who have power over them (see Freeman and Weihope, 1972, 30). When a client, for instance, is treated politely and with dignity and when respect is shown for and attention is paid to her needs and opinions, her feelings of positive social status are enhanced. On the other hand, when a lawyer treats a client disrespectfully or impolitely, when he ignores her needs or her existence, the client's self-definition is affected and her self-respect is threatened.

If this theory of status-definition is correct, then we can see that a lot of ordinary behavior in the lawyer–client context is charged with much greater significance than lawyers either realize or intend. Not answering a telephone call, or worse ignoring a string of telephone calls, not answering the mail, not sharing plans and developments with clients, not pushing a client's affairs on to closure, are no longer just bad manners or the inescapable social abrasions inflicted by busy people on those who have hired and depend on them. Instead such behavior may inflict serious psychological trauma. In other words, there are sound theoretical reasons to believe that lawyer neglect of clients is a serious social problem.

In the remainder of this Chapter I summarize the relevant portions of the literature on lawyer–client relations, present evidence of lawyer misbehavior, and describe what I believe may be the origins of such behavior. These origins include the roles of legal education, socialization into practice norms, work habits, workload, financial considerations, and occupational stress and substance abuse.

THE LITERATURE ON LAWYER–CLIENT RELATIONS

The literature on lawyer–client relations is vast. In this section I concentrate on that segment of it that is most directly concerned with the interpersonal dimensions of those relations: that is, analyses of the distribution of power between lawyers and clients. I expect that lawyers, like the great bulk of humanity, pay more attention to the powerful people in their professional lives and less to those who are not able to inflict penalties on inattentive or inconsiderate behavior. Thus the distribution of power between lawyer and client can be expected to affect the nature of their interactions.

In the socio-legal literature there are five conventional views of this distribution of power and one idiosyncratic perspective. The conventional views are, in the main, structural. The work on legal services (Hosticka, 1979; Alfieri, 1991; Cunningham, 1992; see Menkel-Meadow, 1994, note 66 (collecting references)) and personal-injury lawyers (Hunting and Neuwirth, 1962; Rosenthal, 1974) portrays professional dominance and lay passivity to be rooted in the bureaucratic dimensions of mass legal services. Other scholars see the locus of power to vary by area of practice (Heinz and Laumann, 1982), task (Nelson, 1988;

Spangler, 1986), social status (Abel, 1989; see Olson, 1984, collecting references), or resources (Flood, 1987; O'Gorman, 1963).

On the other hand, Austin Sarat and I (1992) believe that power, although conditioned by position and habit, is continually created and resisted as it is exercised in the ordinary routines that comprise most social interactions. Power between lawyer and client, in our view, is enacted in the stream of negotiations that constitute their relationship and shifts back and forth as they contest their competing agendas. Although this view is based on research on divorce cases only, we believe that it has more general applicability (see White, 1990; Sarat and Felstiner, 1995, 151–3). It is not that resources such as status, experience, and money are irrelevant, but that they condition the exercise of power, rather than dictate its unidirectional flow.

Other research that I have conducted in both the United States and the United Kingdom suggests a difficulty in our approach in the case of mass tort litigation. An empirical assumption necessary to the performance of power that Sarat and I envisage is that the relationship be constituted through a 'stream of negotiations'. In mass torts, however, the relationship between lawyers and clients may be so attenuated that the negotiations assumed to occur in our theory of power are, in fact, rare events. For instance, we (Hensler *et al.*, 1985) concluded that asbestos litigation in the United States involves sets of powerful actors (lawyers on both sides, defendants, insurance companies, and judges) each going about its own affairs with relatively little regard for the condition of and consequences to the injured victims.

These agendas unconnected to the interests of plaintiffs lead to the question why, as clients, they do not through their lawyers do more to promote their own affairs. The picture of client powerlessness in mass tort begins with the demographic characteristics of asbestos plaintiffs— blue-collar, frequently laborers who have worked at many sites, middle-aged or older, and often ill. These plaintiffs are inexperienced in dealing with lawyers and the legal system and frequently become clients *en masse* through union referrals or, on some occasions, through direct solicitation. They have often had little contact with their lawyer. What contact they had with the firm was more likely to be with the paralegals widely used in the bureaucratic processing of large numbers of asbestos cases. Finally, asbestos plaintiffs are not the employers of their lawyers in the sense that they have paid for their services. They are more likely to be in debt to their lawyers, who have advanced money for filing fees, medical examinations, and discovery costs. Thus, when inaction and inattention ought to alert the plaintiffs to spur their lawyers to get on with their cases, they are unlikely to act because of their inexperience, their debtor position, their lack of a personal relationship with their lawyers, and the social distance between them and their lawyers. In this setting, they are not socially, psychologically, or experientially equipped to promote their own interests.

Robert Dingwall, Tom Durkin, and I found the relationship between lawyers and clients in asbestos litigation in the United Kingdom to be similar.[1] Plaintiffs' solicitors decide when to bring the action, how much case preparation will be completed before the claim is initiated, when to set the case for trial where the typical decision is whether to finish case-preparation first, as the rules contemplate, or to complete preparations as the time to trial passes, as horse sense suggests. They judge when an employment history is sufficient to pass defense muster and when additional time must be spent gathering data from co-workers and ancillary records. Most important, they control the pace at which their own labor is applied to particular cases. They cannot force the pace at which cases proceed through the barriers imposed by doctors, sponsors, and government, but they can determine the extent to which dead time is attributable to lack of attention on their part.

We observed these lawyers structuring their relationships with clients in two different ways. In the predominant model, the lawyer organized an extensive, initial interview with the client, tried to secure all of the information required to file and organize the claim at that time and minimized client contact thereafter. To quote one of these solicitors: 'I don't believe in getting clients in and out every couple of months in drips and drabs. Sometimes I don't see the client from day one until the day of trial, or a week before trial. I get the whole lot done on the first day.' In the minority model, very much the minority, the lawyer's time is organized to make continuing access possible. The client becomes a partner in case development.

We have better information about the significance of pace to the plaintiffs in Britain than in the United States because we were able to interview a relatively large number of them (see Durkin, 1994). Of course, the pace of litigation dictates when victims are compensated. As sick people they are particularly sensitive to the opportunity costs of receiving money sooner rather than later. However, the victims experience time in more than material terms in their encounters with lawyers, doctors, and courts. These encounters have a distressing similarity. Victim experiences are episodic, confusing, repetitive, and pathetic. Victim responses to processing time vary from impatient to deferential. Some expect immediate payment. For them two years is an outrageous amount of time to settle a claim. The vast majority defer to their solicitor, showing

---

[1] The next several paragraphs are from an unpublished paper that Dingwall, Durkin, and I jointly wrote and are reproduced here with their permission.

CARDIFF UNIVERSITY INFORMATION SERVICES   EA00018
****
          Law Resource Centre

                                          15 MAR 2002

Hawkins, Keith:
The human face of law: essays in honour
of Donald Harris
1997
New York: OUP

DUE BACK TO INTER-LIBRARY LOANS: 19 APR 2002

If recalled before the above date, it must be returned immediately.
Failure to return the item promptly may cause the supplying Library
to charge the reader.
This item must not be lent to another person. Responsibility for the
return rests with the signatory of the loan.

   ** This item MUST be returned to the ILL DEPARTMENT **
   **   before leaving Cardiff for vacations.   **

PLEASE DO NOT REMOVE THIS SLIP

little impatience unless the actual time differs greatly from their solicitor's estimate.

The pattern behind the sequence in which events occur in litigation is opaque to victims, who respond to what seems to them to be random commands. Repeated physical examinations appear to be unrelated to case progress. The medical establishment appears to be incoherent. Victims are told by their own doctors that they have asbestosis and are then cured by a visit to the Department of Social Services pulmonary disease panel where no sickness is identified.

In their search for medical information, all sources appear trustworthy: '[w]atching this (BBC) program I got the impression that . . . you last two years from when you get the cancer . . . so every morning I wake up, I think "any pain" and I say to myself, well, I've got two years from today at least.'

Many questions that victims asked us concerned these comparisons. How long do victims last? How do I look in relation to other victims? How old was the oldest victim that you interviewed? How was he doing? What was his life like?

Experienced solicitors know how long a case is likely to take, and act to make it a self-fulfilling prophecy. Since little more than this end-point is told to victims, since they have little power to affect others' timetables and there is little organizational need for them to become more deeply involved, they perceive the pace of litigation as immutable, rather than the constructed matter that it actually is. Victims are acutely sensitive to the deterioration of their health and the stages that it goes through. On the other hand they have little awareness of the progress of their legal claim or the stages that it must go through. They are unable to connect the two processes and often conclude, with reason to do so, that the litigation is drifting, is stalled, or is being conducted in a way indifferent to their needs.

The lesson to be learned from the 'power' literature and the research on divorce and mass tort litigation is that power over and attention to clients in the broad sense are likely to be highly correlated and may also be different ways of defining the same behavior. Lawyers are unlikely to treat run-of-the-mill clients with small contingent fee cases in the same way that they treat CEOs of powerful corporations with millions to spend on legal fees. The more powerful the client, the more we would expect the lawyer to heed his or her needs and vice versa. But not necessarily. There may be many lawyers who are uniformly attentive to their clients whatever their relative social strengths; there may be arrogant lawyers who maltreat even their most affluent clients.

THE EVIDENCE OF LAWYER INATTENTION

The data suggesting that the lawyer–client relationship is troubled appear in several different forms. These are:

(1) Interviews by socio-legal researchers with specific segments of the profession.
(2) Public opinion polls, both third-party and commissioned by the organized bar.
(3) Reform programs of academics and the organized bar.
(4) Published statements by leaders of the organized bar.
(5) Reports of lawyer disciplinary bodies.
(6) ABA membership polls.
(7) ABA and state/city bar association reports.
(8) ABA organized lawyer and client focus groups.
(9) New York state rules governing matrimonial lawyers.

These sources complain, or report, that lawyers:

(1) *Fail to treat clients with respect.* Clients frequently experience lawyers as condescending (see Abel, 1989, 247). Legal Aid clients are particularly prone to being treated as instances of categories of legal problems rather than full-fledged persons (Hosticka, 1979; Cunningham, 1991). Clients become exasperated when lawyers try to overwhelm them with jargon (Levine, 1992, 60). Even an ABA Commission chaired by Hillary Rodham Clinton describes lawyers as becoming dehumanized, unable to relate to clients with compassion (Commission on Women in the Profession, 1988, 16). Other researchers assert that lawyers, convinced that clients are so involved in their problems that they cannot know their own best interests, fail to treat them with the respect that they deserve (see Wasserstrom, 1975, 16–17). The literature is full of assertions that lawyers are arrogant (Hengstler, 1993, 62; see Menkel-Meadow, 1994, 595 (criticizing the MacCrate Report for not paying enough attention to the human aspects of lawyering)) and paternalistic (see Guttman, 1993, 1769; Wasserstrom, 1975, 1).

(2) *Do not consider the nature of interpersonal relations with clients to be an important aspect of law practice.* Although clients evaluate lawyers' services on more than technical merit (Podgers, 1994, 92; Seron, 1994, 8–268; The Beyond the Breaking Point Task Force, 1992, 3), lawyers may think of the interpersonal dimensions of their relationships with clients as unwanted inefficiencies that impose unnecessary costs on clients and require capacities in which lawyers have no background or training (see Sarat and Felstiner, 1988, 766; but see Campbell, 1976, 34). The problem does not just arise from inclination: interpersonal skills to meet client needs for responsive, intelligible counsel are required of lawyers whose

professional education and socialization have been skewed in the direction of technical efforts (Seron, 1994, 2–43; Schon, 1984; see Brill, 1994). The organized bar pushes the perspective that lawyers are indifferent, rather than ignorant, about good client relations (see Partnership Programs Client Relations Program, 1993, 15), but the effect is the same whether the cause is lack of care or of skill.

(3) *Are motivated more by financial returns than professional values.* This is the familiar litany that law practice has been transformed from a profession into a business. This refrain has been heard for many decades (Solomon, 1992, 145, 173; Nelson and Trubek, 1992, 12), but the self-flagellation by the profession seems to have more force and is more generally endorsed in the last ten years than in the past (see Galanter, 1994, note 154 (collecting references); Commission on Professionalism, 1986; Scottsdale II, 1988, 3). An extreme example of such behavior, quoted in Flood's (1994, 400) recent review of two books about large law firms, is Kumble of Finley, Kumble etc., instructing junior lawyers that they should 'praise the adversary. He is the catalyst by which you bill your client. Damn the client. He is your true enemy.' Sarat and I (1995), in a study of lawyer–client interactions, encountered several divorce lawyers who refused to take further steps in cases until their retainers had been replenished even if their clients were put at a disadvantage by this inaction. Other researchers have found that divorce clients feel excluded by their lawyers from important activities such as settlement negotiations (McEwen *et al.*, 1994, 165). Blumberg's (1967) famous Mr Green, the fictional witness who was a signal to judges that defense counsel had not been paid, reappears in Phillips' (1978) autobiographical account of a famous murder trial in the South Bronx. That the socio-legal community believes that tort lawyers routinely subordinate their clients' financial interests to their own is reflected in the voluminous literature on conflicts of interest in contingency fees (see Johnson, 1981, 569; Kritzer *et al.*, 1985, 252–3; on lawyers' conflicts of interest generally, see Shapiro, 1995). Finally, the conventional understanding of the 'courtroom workgroup' is that criminal defense lawyers are more interested in their relationships with other court regulars than they are with pleasing their clients (Eisenstein and Jacob, 1977, 50).

(4) *Are inaccessible and unresponsive.* Clients complain that lawyers are uncooperative, uncommunicative (Curran, 1977, 230; Harris *et al.*, 1984, 68; Abel, 1985, 584), lack empathy (Hengstler, 1993, 62; compare Seron, 1994, 8–273–4, 278, 300), are rude, unresponsive, and evasive (Rosenthal, 1974, 52) and are tardy in providing services (Levine, 1992, 62). Studies of lawyer–client relations often report client files that were forgotten or lost (see Rosenthal, 1974, 48; Felstiner and Sarat, 1992, 1475–6). The most common client complaint about lawyers is that they

do not respond to telephone calls and letters (Seron, 1994, 6–216; Stevens, 1994; Sussman, 1993; see Samborn, 1993; Scottsdale II, 1988, 13; Abel, 1985, 585).[2] And, communications specialists allege, 'nothing says as much to people that I don't care about you as unanswered phone calls' (CLE videotape 'One Client at a Time').

(5) *Are poor communicators.* Lawyers fail both to listen (Seron, 1994, 8–270) and to explain legal matters adequately in lay terms (Vogel, 1989, 23): both are matters of capacity (Jaquish and Ware, 1993) and of disposition (Guttman, 1993, 1759). Rosenthal (1974, 19) quotes advice given to lawyers by the Wisconsin Bar Association: '[g]et at the client's problem immediately and stick to it. Don't bother to explain the reasoning process by which you arrived at your advice. . . . This not only prolongs the interview, but generally confuses the client.' Lawyers and clients tend to be involved in the following kinds of miss-communication:

Lawyer—Clients have unreasonable expectations.

Client— The lawyer makes me feel dumb.

Lawyer—Clients do not appreciate my work.

Client— Why can't the work get done? Why does the lawyer take on too much work? Why doesn't the lawyer tell me about her schedule?

Lawyer—Clients blame me for their problems.

Client— I'm just another case; the lawyer doesn't care about me.

Problems in communications with clients exist despite the high importance training in such skills is accorded by both law students and their prospective employers (see Garth and Martin, 1993).

(6) *Do not know how to deal with clients effectively* (Scottsdale II, 1988, 14). Lawyers fail to realize that nonlegal concerns and their consequences may outweigh legal issues in structuring solutions to client problems (Binder *et al.*, 1991).[3] People who make their living by studying or giving advice to law firms about management matters agree that clients are more frequently lost through poor communications than through poor legal work (ABA Leadership Forum, 1994, 1).

(7) *Are indifferent to client feelings.* The irrelevance, if not contaminating effect, of client feelings is axiomatic in traditional definitions of the lawyer's role (Binder *et al.*, 1991).[4] Sarat and Felstiner (1995, 128–33) pro-

---

[2] Poor communications appears to be a concern of clients in other parts of the Anglo-American legal world (see Tomasic, 1978).

[3] Criticism of the client-centered approach on grounds that it generates excessive self-revelation and client dependence, makes unreasonable demands on lawyers untrained to deal with many non-legal dimensions of client problems, and overemphasizes the importance of the lawyer–client relationship for its own sake has itself been discounted by Dinerstein (1990).

[4] This attitude is not just characteristic of the lawyer–client relationship, but pervades the legal system. 'Neglect of the real-life experiences and feelings of the people whose fate

vide extensive accounts of lawyers both refusing to engage with their clients' emotions and schooling clients about the need to separate their emotions from their objectives (see also Cunningham, 1992, 1300–1 on literature in poverty and civil-rights practice to the effect that lawyers routinely silence their clients even while 'purporting to tell their "stories" '). Clients whose feelings are ignored or discounted have difficulty in responding to the legal counsel that the lawyer provides as well as to the lawyer herself (see Sarat and Felstiner, 1986, 123–4).

(8) *Are frequently indifferent to the pace of clients' legal affairs.* A common complaint of clients is that no action is taken in their cases over long periods of time (see Sarat and Felstiner, 1995, 59–62; Mansnerus, 1995, 8). Lawyers may or may not have good reason to delay attending to their clients' affairs, but in either case the clients' frustration is exacerbated by the lawyers' frequent failure to explain the sources of delay.

THE ORIGINS OF LAWYER MISBEHAVIOR

A. Legal Education

The experience of most students in law school, particularly in the first year, is intense and distressing. Pedagogic techniques provoke anxiety. Assignments are long, difficult, confusing, and couched in an unfamiliar vocabulary. Competition in the sense of the comparative quality of fellow students is stiff. The stakes appear high: grades influence first job opportunities and first jobs have a significant effect on career possibilities. Expenses are high and usually lead to relatively high debt burdens.[5] These unfamiliar conditions and formidable concerns make students unsure of themselves and vulnerable to the professional suggestions of the faculty, the only guides that they have over this difficult intellectual and emotional terrain (Watson, 1975, 250).[6] What, then, are the explicit

is decided by law is characteristic of a wide range of legal decisions' (Sarat and Kearns, 1991, 213; see Noonan, 1976).

[5] Almost 40 years of research documents the high levels of stress under which law students labor. In 1957 Eton and Redmount noted that law students scored higher on a scale of general anxiety than medical students throughout their graduate education. In the 1970s, studies reflected the prominence of alienation (Carrington and Conley, 1977, 1978) and depression (Beck and Burns, 1979) in distressed law students (see, also, Taylor, 1975). In the 1980s, Heins and her colleagues (1983) and Shanfield and Benjamin (1985, 69) reaffirmed that law students were subject to more stress than either medical students or a contrasting normalized population. All these findings have been echoed in the 1990s, particularly with respect to women students (see Guinier *et al.*, 1994; see also Weiss and Melling, 1988).

[6] Abel (1989, 213) collects materials indicating that many students experience compulsion, anxiety, depression, or hostility during law school. But because personal contact with faculty is rare, students are mature on arrival, the student body is diverse in gender, social

faculty agendas and the implicit faculty messages embedded in the work of the classroom?

Legal education is a professionalized experience. This means that the focus of legal education is on professional resources, such as rules, their origins, and interpretations, professional actors such as lawyers, judges, administrators, and legislators, and professional results such as legal regimes and their connection to social policies and consequences. Left out or trivialized in this professionalized education is concern for individual people, for the very clients whose cases are hyper-analyzed in the classroom dance around precedents, issues, consistency, efficiency, balances, and policies.[7]

Law professors assume that the habits of analysis, the intuitions, and the values of beginning law students require adjustment. They assume that their students are entering the boot camp[8] of the mind with an inclination toward particularistic values that give priority to the fates of the actual people whose legal difficulties they are asked to analyze. They assume that, if undirected and uncorrected, law students will view case situations in terms of the life effects of the participants in those cases, will respond to the emotional pull that various actors in the case dramas will evoke, and will put into play their first-order inclinations toward fairness, justice, and fair dealing (Granfield, 1992, 74).

To counter these tendencies, law professors try to habituate students to value the rational response over the emotional,[9] the general effect over the particular, the efficient solution over the seemingly just result, and the unpalatable outcome in preference to the awkward exception (see Harris and Shultz, 1993, 1773–6; Guinier *et al.*, 1994: 54–5). As Menkel-Meadow (1992,305) notes, students learn 'to block feelings, analyze intellectually, and deal with abstractions'.[10] In the words of a Penn student

origins, and experience, and the bar examination influences course selection, he believes that there is reason to doubt the effect of law school as a socializing agent (1989, 212–14). As the text indicates, I believe that while he may be right with respect to politics and many moral values, he may be wrong in those matters of value and style that affect the way that lawyers interact with clients.

[7] Translated into the medical situation this would mean that medical school is concerned with bodies and diseases, but not with patients, which would involve a deprofessionalized (or even unprofessional) focus on people. In actuality, medical schools are ahead of law schools in required concentration on communications and other people treating skills (see Gutman, 1993, 1770).

[8] There is evidence that students perceive law school in this way. See Guinier *et al.*, 1994, 43 (quoting a student: '[t]he first year is like basic training. They need to mold you'.).

[9] Law teachers ignore at their student' peril Watson's warning that: 'while it is true that emotions can grossly disrupt rationality, it is also a fundamental fact of psychological life that to ignore the existence of emotions is itself irrational' (1975, 252).

[10] It is quite possible that this experience is generally more distressing for women than men students. Weiss and Melling (1988, 1299) report that the women they consulted at Yale Law School experienced alienation from self, law school, the classroom, and the content of legal education. See also Guinier *et al.*, 1994, 43; Homer and Schwartz, 1989.

quoted in Guinier *et al.* (1994, 50), it is the difference between talking about 'how a woman feels having to have a baby' and talking about a constitutional right to privacy. This effort to separate personal values from legal issues is part of what Nelson and Trubek (1992, 186) call the '"hidden" curriculum that is embodied in the way schools are organized, classes conducted and values transmitted in informal ways'.[11] In this law-school indoctrination the actual parties to the cases get left out in two senses. They are slighted in the classroom interaction as, the students soon learn, their interests are subordinated to general categories of people like tenants or bondholders or abstract concepts such as efficiency or due process. Moreover, the general practice of demanding that students argue both sides of a case, or be prepared on a moment's notice to jump from one side to the other, reduces the client to a token piece representing the side the student happens to be arguing at that moment (Shalleck, 1993, 173; Rowe, 1992, 40). In other words, the client becomes an unimportant part of the legal process, the occasion for a legal controversy, but not powerfully connected to it (Shalleck, 1993, 1731).[12] Just as students are tutored to quash their own emotional reaction to reported cases, they are rewarded in the classroom when they strip the parties of those dimensions of their humanity that are not directly connected to the resolution of 'legal' issues and are punished by their instructors and classmates when they seek to include the full scope of the parties' humanity in the analysis (Granfield, 1992, 75–81).[13] Lawyers, as follows from this socialization, are seen to do the same thing: 'they reify the boundaries of legal relevance, legitimating some parts of human

[11] Wonderfully captured in the old aphorism 'hard cases make bad law'. Harris and Shultz (1994, 1781) allege that students who break the rules of the classroom by responding emotionally are considered 'out of place' and irrational. In the classroom domain of rationality, students risk experiencing a withdrawal of the self from the educational process. This alienation prepares them for a more 'significant withdrawal of their selves from their professional identity as lawyers'.

Although there is little doubt that students are quickly indoctrinated not to raise concerns about cases based on their intuitive or emotional reactions, there is also substantial evidence that their basic moral values are generally unaffected by the law school experience. See Granfield, 1992, 229 (collecting references). However, these studies are more focused on abstract moral values or political ideologies than they are with concerns about the relevance of various dimensions of the positions of parties in cases.

[12] The irrelevance of the client to the law-school classroom has provoked critical comment since the heyday of the legal realists. See Shalleck, 1993, fn. 2 (collecting references).

[13] As Gilkerson (1992, 871) observes, law works through narratives that 'have the power to close off dialogue by locating certain substantive inquiries outside of [it]. By restricting ways of framing questions and arguments, . . . the law constrains and limits possible stories a lawyer can tell.'

A striking exception to this pedagogical scheme appears to be the Legal Theory and Practice program at the University of Maryland Law School (see the discussion entitled 'Students and Lawyers, Doctrine and Responsibility: A Pedagogical Colloquy' (1992), and particularly La Rue, 1992; see also Lesnick, 1992).

experience and denying the relevance of others' (Sarat and Felstiner, 1995, 147). Moreover, law professors are either preaching to the converted or quickly do a good job of conversion. Shaffer and Redmount (1977), for example, found that law students were somewhat more 'tough-minded' than people in general and themselves gave law a low rating for humanism (see also Miller, 1967 (students who dropped out of law school more concerned with people than those who stayed); Solkoff and Markowitz, 1967 (law students less sensitive to others' needs than medical students)).

Parties in reported cases are also left out of the classroom as they are *clients* of lawyers (see Gutman, 1993, 1759, 1770–1). That is, the classroom discussion will rarely pay any attention to them as clients, to their predicaments, limitations, reactions, and needs as lay people in the hands of powerful professionals with their own affiliations and agendas and operating on their own turf.[14] Issues are abstracted from the problems in which they are embedded, and there is little attention paid to what Menkel-Meadow (1994, 620) calls 'empathy training'. As an example of the disjuncture between the way law is practiced and taught, Sarat and Felstiner (1995) illustrate the extent to which negotiations *between* lawyer and client are frequently as time-consuming and consequential as those between opposing parties in litigation: yet the appellate reports, and thus the classroom discussion, are absolutely silent about this dimension of professional tension and practice. Sarat and I (1995, 133) also found that lawyers frequently turn off their clients' expressive communications and prefer to concentrate hard instead on property issues. Most clients have a place to live, a job, possessions, career prospects, and the like and to the lawyers we studied these are accessible, familiar, and more or less fungible factors in legal problems. However, people do not understand themselves as much in these terms as in those relating to their loves, anxieties, compulsions, dislikes, and dreams. If to know a person is to know the latter dimensions, then to refuse to listen to their expression is to deny the importance of the personality of the client, a lesson learned in spades in law school.

How might the parties be attended to as clients in the law school classroom; what alternatives do law teachers have; what is not going on in class that might sensitize students to the choices that lawyers have in the way that they interact with their clients?[15] The case reports are not much

[14] This capacity is another illustration of Auerbach's (1978, 42) wonderful description of the legal mind as one that 'can think of something that is inextricably connected to something else without thinking about what it is connected to'.
[15] Both Menkel-Meadow (1994, 606) and Kronman (1993, 66) believe that the affective dimensions of lawyering can be taught. Menkel-Meadow provides some rather cryptic hints about how it might be done (1994, 610–11, 618).

help by way of stimulus. They might identify the time line of events in the past which could raise questions about whose interests are being served by various periods of apparent inaction. But beyond the question of responsibility for case progress (see Felstiner and Sarat, 1992, 1466–72), the appellate reports rarely provide any material for discussion of the roles, conflicts, and interactions of lawyers and clients.[16]

In other words, outside the reach of any clinical instruction, the lesson from the law-school classroom is that clients do not matter, that they simply provide the setting in which the people who do matter, that is judges and lawyers, are able to carry on their professional task of analysis and argument.[17] If this is an accurate picture, then law students leave school and become lawyers imprinted with a set of priorities in which the only client concerns that are valued are those closely tied to their narrow legal posture and everything else about the clients' lives is subordinated to the lawyers' technocratic function (Condlin, 1983, 379).[18]

In principle, there ought to be two exceptions to the pedagogical trivialization of clients—courses in professional responsibility and instruction and experience in clinical programs. Since most ethical problems concern the temptations and threats that lawyers and clients pose for each other, one would think that clients would play a major role in classes on professional responsibility. However, Shalleck (1993, 1737–9) suggests that the clients that are constructed in these courses are once again stick figures in a decontextualized posture. They are, she alleges, assumed to have no goals other than wealth or freedom, their subjective interests are generally constituted prior to their interaction with a lawyer, and the process of discovering their motives is straightforward and transparent. As a result 'students have no sense of how hard it often is to identify what a client wants, nor do they develop any insight into how they themselves can participate in shaping clients' understanding of the client's goals. Students do not attend to the ways power operates within their client relationships, nor are they taught the role that it can play in the definition of client interests' (1993, 1739).

On the other hand, so-called 'live-client' clinics may, for those students who engage in them, counter the conventional classroom marginalization of clients. These clinics certainly create the opportunity for students to attend to a fully contextualized version of clients' law-related

[16] Except for comment about their intractability with respect to the humanity of the actual litigants.

[17] Of course, this picture of a rule of law in which the humanity of the individuals subject to it *ought* not to count may be the conventional understanding about the way that the legal system should operate. That such a view is not monolithic, see Henderson, 1987.

[18] See Watson (1975, 150–1) for a description of the circumstances under which the behavior of law teachers reinforces student beliefs 'that issues about lawyer–client relationships are unimportant and of secondary consequence'.

problems. Depending upon the objectives and skill of their supervisors, students in these relationships may learn to treat clients with respect, act with compassion, pay attention to client feelings, learn not to be arrogant or paternalistic, listen carefully, and behave responsively. The ABA Task Force on Law Schools and the Profession reports on the content of courses in communication and counseling (MacCrate, 1992, 256–7) in terms that could provide, but do not necessarily require, instruction in such values (see Binder *et al.*, 1991, ch. 2). Or clinical courses may not do the job. Shalleck (1993, 1741), for one, believes that as 'lawyers in their daily practice often replicate the construction of the client within legal education', students in the clinical setting may reproduce the version of the client in which they are schooled in the rest of the curriculum.

Shalleck is even concerned with the actuality of the famous 'client-centered' approach of Binder, Bergman, and Price (1977, 1991). Their orientation, which requires laser-like attention to client emotions and accounts and legal solutions that are cooperatively constructed, obviously puts the client at stage center. Nevertheless, Shalleck (1993, 1743–8) is concerned that Binder, Bergman, and Price provide a program that obscures differences in clients, uses a single model (chronological) for gathering information, provides a closed list of factors that are to be considered in decision-making, is inattentive to the dynamics of power in the lawyer–client relationship, and, by confining clients to the nonlegal world, provides no basis on which to criticize the legal world, which is then dominated by lawyers. It is thus an open question whether clinical opportunities in law school actually train students to interact constructively with clients, can overcome the influence of the rest of the curriculum, and stick with students as they confront the realities of practice (see MacCrate, 1992, 7 (employers unconcerned with whether students have undertaken clinical courses)).

In addition to this picture of the effects of the classroom to teach students 'to think like lawyers', Benjamin *et al.* (1986) suggest an interesting psycho-structural analysis of the hidden agenda of legal education. They begin with the finding that while pre-law students score within the normative range on nine scales of psychological distress, the levels they report increase significantly within their first year of law school. These high levels of distress and the symptoms that accompany them such as substance abuse and excessive anger were found not to decrease within the first few years of law practice. Thus psychological disorders that follow students into practice seem to be a product of legal education.

Benjamin and his colleagues believe that the causes of this distress are the intense competition of the law-school environment coupled to classroom pressure to remain unemotional and neutral in the face of issues that in other contexts would evoke feelings and partisanship. They find that the interesting question is not *whether* law schools cause high levels of distress in students, but *why* they continue to maintain those pedagogical practices that cause such distress. They suggest that legal educators may encourage students to relate to law and their roles as future professionals in a manner that results in significant levels of psychological distress because they view such distress as a beneficial and adaptive aspect of being a lawyer (see Guinier *et al.*, 1994, 63). For instance, they raise the questions whether the jobs that lawyers must perform require qualities that accompany phobic anxiety or paranoid ideation or whether the clients for whom they will work are assumed to require qualities that are found in psychologically distressed people.[19]

Thus the question is whether an indoctrination regime that produces people who are capable of becoming simultaneously angry and unemotional, who are hyper-aggressive, highly stressed, sleep-deprived, work excessively long hours, and have little social support is doing what their professional tasks require and their clients are perceived to want. To legal educators who consciously or not see reality in such a professional world, the psychological distress that is produced in law school is not a cost, but a responsibility, and the students themselves are not victims, but rather are volunteers who have assumed these burdens in order to achieve the goals of high status and liberal compensation. Hagan and Kay (1995, 200) seem to confirm this picture: they quote a Toronto lawyer who said: '[t]oo many young lawyers are stressed out and have lost a sense of perspective. But senior lawyers have cultivated this paranoia. They look at juniors as "revenue generating units" and do not put enough efforts into cultivating character, self-confidence and integrity.' If litigation is warfare, then these are its front-line troops, the Delta Force of Heinz and Laumann's corporate hemisphere of practice.[20]

B. Socialization

It is axiomatic that lawyers learn how to practice law in their early years in the profession rather than in school (Abel, 1989, 221; Seron, 1994, 2–53). This proposition generally refers to the technical and practical knowledge that a practitioner needs in order to meet the day-to-day, down-to-earth, requirements of serving client interests (Carlin, 1962, 9, 225; Seron, 1994, 2–35; see Granfield, 1992, 160 ('students at Harvard often feel ill-equipped to practice law.')). It is conventionally contrasted

---

[19] In this respect art parallels science. 'Stress was the air he had been breathing since day one of law school. Stress separated warriors from boys and girls . . . and law school stress was kindergarten' (Dooling, 1994, 72).

[20] Benjamin *et al.* (1986) believe that this view badly misinterprets client needs and objectives. See also Resnick, 1993.

to the theoretical and substantive knowledge of legal doctrine that the lawyer has learned in school. It can be thought of as exposure to knowledge of the ropes rather than of the rules. However, although it is acknowledged that many lawyers are confused about the behaviors that are appropriate to 'professionalism' (Hagan and Kay, 1995, 330) and that ideas about professional behavior are emulated by young lawyers 'even when such practices border on unethical behavior' (Watson, 1975, 251), the literature on the profession (to my knowledge) never addresses the parallel experience of being socialized into a set of habits for dealing with clients.[21] Even the theoretics of practice literature (see, e.g., *Hastings Law Journal* 1992; *Cornell Law Review* 1992) which concentrates in great, even excessive, detail on how lawyers for the disadvantaged are led to (mal)treat clients, never discusses the influences through which lawyers learn how to behave in such a fashion.

We can, however, develop an *a priori* common-sense understanding of how most lawyers learn how to interact with clients. One would expect that neophyte lawyers begin practice with reasonably good manners. Presumably they realize that private clients both have some choice of lawyer and pay the bills. However, especially if they are working for a firm, as most are, they soon are presented with more work than they can handle, client demands that are difficult or impossible to meet or unrelated to their legal affairs, and clients who are on occasion ill-mannered, evasive, abusive, and blame them for difficulties in their cases that predate the lawyer's involvement. There is virtually nothing in lawyers' previous training that prepares them for such predicaments. As a consequence, we would expect that they would either seek counsel from more experienced lawyers or follow the lead of those they are able to observe (Seron, 1994, 2–54). They then, of course, are at risk of advice or a model, or both, that reflect the negative attitudes and behaviors outlined above—inadequate respect for clients, inadequate attention to interpersonal relations, putting financial considerations ahead of professional values, poor communications, and indifference to client feelings.

---

[21] The Task Force on Law Schools and the Profession (MacCrate, 1992, 295–301) documents the low level of 'transition education' in the US and the general inattention to lawyer–client interaction in the efforts that do exist. It does note the growing number of in-house training programs for new lawyers (1992, 299–301), none of which appears to have received any scholarly attention.

Hagan and Kay (1995, 200) make the same point about gender relations; that lawyers do not know what gender-related behaviors are 'truly appropriate and supportive of unbiased professionalism'.

C. The Organization of Practice

Law practice is highly conditioned by financial considerations. From solo practice (see Carlin, 1962, ch. 3) to very large multi-national firms (see Galanter and Palay, 1991, 52, 117), lawyers are preoccupied with two dimensions of the financial challenge —producing returns from the work that is under way and maintaining a backlog of work. We may think of them as the problems of *rate* and *inventory*.

The contours of the rate problem are determined by the fee arrangement and the employment relationship. I will consider contingent fees and fees by the hour one after the other. The lawyer's incentives in a contingent-fee relationship are obvious. Her financial aim is to maximize the recovery while minimizing the time spent on the case. Any efforts that the lawyer must make, any periods of time that the lawyer must expend, that do not advance the case toward closure, that are designed instead to please or appease the client, are likely to be perceived as uneconomic by the lawyer.[22] If such efforts are uneconomic, they are a luxury, they are not necessary to produce the 'outcome' that the lawyer believes the client wants, or should want, and they do not have to be made. The incoming telephone call or letter that is out of sequence, that arrives when the file is 'inactive' or when the lawyer is preoccupied with other business, need not be answered. When the appropriate time to take up the client's cause arrives, the lawyer will do it. Until then a response would constitute an unnecessary diversion.[23] Since employed lawyers who work in a contingent-fee environment are frequently compensated in part by the level of settlements they achieve and are evaluated for retention and promotion on the same basis, their priorities are similar to those of the lawyers for whom they work.

Whether they are litigators or not, lawyers are drilled from their first days in law school to be acutely sensitive to the issue of relevance. One of the distinguishing marks of thinking like a lawyer is the ability to distinguish matters that are legally relevant from those that are not. Lawyers believe that if clients seek to push dimensions of their lives that are not directly connected to their legal problems onto lawyers' agendas (see Sarat and Felstiner, 1995, 113), they are sitting in the wrong offices, and ought instead to consult some other kind of counsel, whether they be

[22] This stance may be short-sighted, in that it focusses on the case at hand and disregards the long-term returns that may result from satisfied clients. But since I believe that lawyers do not believe that client satisfaction is as much a product of feelings about process as about outcomes (see Pierce, 1995, 122), I do not think that they are concerned that their 'manners' will affect their economic well-being.

[23] Abel (1989, 247) alleges that common sources of dissatisfaction with the profession such as 'discourtesy and delay' are the result of what he calls 'market imperfections' and might respond to more open competition.

accountants, investment advisers, therapists, doctors, or clergy. For a lawyer to engage with issues that are not germane to the client's legal problems wastes the lawyer's time even if a client believes otherwise. In the contingent-fee situation, the lawyer's time is the lawyer's money, and as such will be jealously guarded.

Where lawyers are paid more or less in relation to the time they spend on clients' affairs, one would think that these factors would be reversed (Johnson, 1981, 575–7); that lawyers would be tempted to indulge any client inquiry at all and to be willing to respond to any client communication promptly and at length. There are, I believe, two reasons why the opposite behavior, behavior that conforms to that of the contingent-fee model, is common. One is connected to the inventory problem and will be discussed later. The other may be labeled the implicit-fee factor. The implicit-fee consideration is suggested by unreported observations in the divorce cases that Sarat and I followed (Sarat and Felstiner, 1995). Lawyers in divorce cases generally are paid by the hour. Clients are uncomfortable with this arrangement. They press lawyers for estimates of the amount of the total fee. Lawyers resist, citing all the uncertainties that can affect the amount of time that they might be required to spend on the case. Clients persist, demanding that at least the lawyers provide them with a possible range of fees. Lawyers eventually capitulate; they express all kinds of caveats and reservations, but in the end they provide a rough figure or range of figures as an estimate.

But then the estimate takes on a life of its own. The lawyer behaves as if she were committed to bringing the case to closure in such a way that the estimated fee will not be exceeded, or not exceeded by much. We do not know whether the motivation is a matter of pride in being able to transform the estimate into reality, worry about the client's displeasure if the estimate proves inadequate, or simply concern for the client's pocketbook, but the lawyers we observed seemed as parsimonious with their time and as acutely sensitive to questions of legal relevance as the most profit-oriented contingent-fee lawyer.

The inventory problem is probably more important than the rate factor in producing lawyer neglect. I start with a simple proposition. Almost all lawyers want to be overcommitted, and a large proportion of them actually are (see Hensler *et al.*, 1985, 90–1; Sarat and Felstiner, 1995, 61).[24] The incentive structure pushes in that direction. Lawyers generally cannot assure future business by contract. Many do not have clients who know that they will require legal services of any particular volume in the

[24] One of the lawyers that Seron (1994, 9–308) studied reported that: 'no lawyer feels financially secure. I believe that and I think that's one of the rules of law. That's why lawyers are the way they are; I think they are very insecure. And, I that they're insecure because their client-base is not secure.'

future, and those that have them frequently find that those clients are unwilling to *commit* that future business to their current lawyers (Galanter and Palay, 1991, 50; Nelson and Trubek, 1992b, 14). The typical lawyer and law-firm response is to take on all the work that they can get. Their only insurance for the future is the backlog of the present (see Carlin, 1962, 73). No amount of history seems to cure this habit; the lawyer's drive to assure that the clients required to pay the overhead and profits in the future will be on tap seems more to reflect some deep prudential urge than it does reasonable management planning.

I have in another context analogized the lawyer's backlog to a form of inventory of raw materials.[25] Before the inventory can be sold (the client's business brought to closure), it must be processed (the lawyer must do that which is legally required, e.g., prepare cases for trial). But there is a limited amount of processing machinery (the lawyers).

If the supply of raw materials is large, the limits of processing machinery mean that much of the raw material will either sit on the shelf for long periods before it can enter the production line, or move through the production phase more slowly than it would if more machinery were available. It is here that the analogy between [legal business] and ordinary production breaks down. In the ordinary case, the manufacturer would not permit a large supply of raw materials to build up: it is improvident to invest money in resources that cannot be put to ready use. [But in law practice], a large stock of raw materials is an asset to the lawyer, and an asset for which the lawyer does not initially pay much. Cases are a scarce resource, rather than one generally available, and thus represent future profits rather than current expenses [Hensler *et al.*, 1985, 90–1].

The same risk-aversion that moves lawyers to taking on more business than they can handle often precludes them from hiring the assistance that they require to process the existing inventory. The concern, of course, is that a decrease in future business will saddle them with unnecessary overheads.

The connections between lawyer overload and their inattention to clients are obvious.[26] Even if they follow a killing regime, lawyers can do just so much. The clients either do not understand that their affairs are, for the time at least, in cold storage or refuse to accept that posture, and so they make overtures of various kinds that would require the lawyers' attention. But matters that do not absolutely require immediate attention, may receive either no, or a glancing, response. Clients who are on the receiving end of such behavior experience neglect, rejection, and disrespect. The lawyers whom Carol Seron (1994, 8–275) studied say that

[25] The other context was a discussion of plaintiffs' lawyers in asbestos cases. See Hensler, 1985, 90.
[26] Abel (1985: 617) calls our attention to the link between caseload and 'bedside manner'.

they are aware that 'an entrepreneurial concern to be fast and cheap must in fact be balanced by the demands to be responsive and caring', but the general report from clients indicates that the responsive and caring side of the balance is slighted.[27]

We have considered rate and inventory problems one at a time, although, of course, they act in tandem. Overloaded, harassed lawyers with their eyes directed to the returns from their work are all too likely to be short-tempered, impatient, highly focused on the instrumental dimensions of their work, and little inclined toward caring, empathy, responsiveness, cooperation, sharing, and patience.

D. Stress, Distress and Substance Abuse

Several studies over the past ten years document unusually high levels of distress and substance abuse among American lawyers (see Beck, 1993; Benjamin *et al.*, 1990; Kozich, 1988; McPeak, 1987). As measured by reports from Washington, Wisconsin, and Florida, the incidence of depression is three to five times that of the general population, while alcohol abuse is more than double that of Americans generally (Benjamin *et al.*, 1992, 114–15). Beck's (1993, 31–2) recent cross-sectional study found that over 20 per cent of Arizona and Washington male lawyers at all career stages scored above the 98th percentile on standard tests for anxiety, social isolation and alienation, depression, and obsessive-compulsiveness, while the scores of female lawyers were nearly as high. Both male and female lawyers scored significantly higher than the normal population mean for seven of nine items in the Brief Symptom Inventory subscales (Beck, 1993, 32).[28] Easton and his colleagues (1990, 1081–6) found that lawyers ranked fifth in major depressive disorders among the 104 occupations studied; when the rates were adjusted for socio-demographic factors, lawyers topped the list.[29]

Another reflection of the ubiquity of distress in the legal profession is the elevated level of substance abuse among lawyers, particularly the

[27] There is some indication in the legal services area that the nature of practice affects lawyer responsiveness. Abel (1985, 584) notes that private lawyers apparently do a better job of maintaining contact with their clients than salaried lawyers. They may also have a smaller caseload.

[28] The test subscales are for somatization, obsessive compulsive behavior, interpersonal sensitivity, depression, anxiety, hostility, phobic anxiety, paranoid ideation, and psychoticism (Beck, 1993, 20–1). The subscales on which lawyers are not significantly above the population mean are somatization and phobic anxiety.

[29] Thomas and her colleagues (1994) compared burnout (emotional exhaustion, depersonalization, and dissatisfaction with personal accomplishments) rates between women lawyers and travel agents. The lawyers exhibited higher degrees of burnout which the researchers attributed to their greater commitment to producing work within narrow time limits.

abuse of alcohol. Drogin's (1991) conservative estimate is that 15 per cent of American lawyers suffer from alcoholism, a number that today would exceed 100,000 lawyers. Although Carroll's (1992) estimate of lawyers who drink 'alcoholically' is a few percentage points less than Drogin's, he concludes that, for every six lawyers who abuse alcohol, another one is addicted to either tranquilizers, sleeping or diet pills, heroin, cocaine, methamphetamines, or marijuana. These conditions are very much on the agenda of the organized bar, particularly since there is a high correlation between alcohol abuse and client complaints that lead to disciplinary proceedings (Benjamin *et al.*, 1992, 118). In 1988 the ABA established a Commission on Impaired Attorneys which has developed an active intervention program. State bar associations have organized lawyer-assistance programs in all fifty states, double the number that existed in 1980 (Blodgett, 1988, 144).

It is generally assumed that if there is one root-cause of the *elevated* levels of psychological distress and substance abuse among lawyers it is the conditions under which they work. It does not seem to matter whether they are employed by large multi-national firms or are in solo or small-firm practice: the story all too often is one of alienated labor, overwork, anxiety over status, concern about financial returns and layoffs, intense competition, difficult relations with clients, technological changes that have transformed the pace of practice from deliberate to hectic, the strain of balancing career and family responsibilities, gender bias, moral ambiguity, truncated career ladders, and the accentuation of hierarchy (see, generally, Epstein, 1994; Horne, 1994; Galanter and Palay, 1991; Abel, 1989; Spangler, 1986; Carlin, 1962).

My assumption is that these conditions frequently lead to what we may think of as a kind of psychological disconnection from professional responsibility (see Drogin, 1991, 158). Under such pressures the lawyer may become depressed, bored, apathetic, distracted, overwhelmed, or lose motivation and initiative. The consequence to clients is a lawyer who is unapproachable, uncommunicative, abrupt, or impolitic; a lawyer who shuns contact with the client, neglects the client's work, and treats the client as an object rather than a person.

AFTERWORD

This is the state of my consideration of the matter of lawyer neglect. This material was gathered and organized as a preliminary step to seeking funding to get at these connections empirically. It is going to this next stage that differentiates academic lawyers and their speculation from the kind of scholar that Don Harris represents. I began this essay with some of the lessons that I learned from Don. Here is another. One of the many things in life to be suspicious of is the conventional wisdom. We only begin to approach what we know by going out in the field and looking at the questions as hard and systematically as we can. This Chapter reports what I found out in the library about professional neglect of clients by American lawyers. The real work is still ahead. In the Harris tradition, I am, as you read these words, out there somewhere talking to lawyers and watching them work.

APPENDIX A

My Declaration of Commitment to Clients

To treat you with respect and courtesy.

To handle your legal matter competently and diligently, in accordance with the highest standards of the profession.

To exercise independent professional judgment on your behalf.

To charge a reasonable fee and to explain in advance how that fee will be computed and billed.

To return telephone calls promptly.

To keep you informed and provide you with copies of important papers.

To respect your decisions on the objectives to be pursued in your case, as permitted by law and the rules of professional conduct, including whether or not to settle your case.

To work with other participants in the legal system to make our legal system more accessible and responsive.

To preserve the client confidences learned during our lawyer–client relationship.

To exhibit the highest degree of ethical conduct in accordance with the Code of Professional Responsibility/Model Rules of Professional Conduct.

REFERENCES

ABA Leadership Forum (1994), *Report and Plan for Follow-Up to the Summit on the Profession* (ABA, Chicago, Ill.).

Abel, Richard L. (1985), 'Legal Aid', 32 *UCLA Law Review* 474.

—— (1985), 'Law Without Politics: Legal Aid under Advanced Capitalism', 32 *UCLA Law Review* 474.

—— (1989), *American Lawyers* (Oxford University Press, New York).

—— and Lewis, Philip S. (1989), 'Putting Law Back into the Sociology of Lawyers' in Richard L. Abel and Philip S. Lewis (eds.), *Lawyers in Society: Comparative Theories* (University of California Press, Berkeley, Cal.).

ALFIERI, ANTHONY (1991), 'Reconciling Poverty Law Practice: Learning Lessons of Client Narrative', 100 *Yale Law Journal* 2107.

AUERBACH, JEROLD S. (1978), 'What Has the Teaching of Law to Do With Justice', 53 *New York University Law Review* 457.

BECK, CONNIE J. (1993), *A Model of Lawyer Distress* (unpublished MA thesis, University of Arizona).

BECK, PHYLLIS W. and BURNS, DAVID (1979), 'Anxiety and Depression in Law Students: Cognitive Intervention', 30 *Journal of Legal Education* 270.

BENJAMIN, G. ANDREW H., and KASZNIAK, ALFRED, SALES, BRUCE, and SHANFIELD, STEPHEN B. (1986), 'The Role of Legal Education in Producing Psychological Distress Among Law Students and Lawyers', 1986 *American Bar Foundation Research Journal* 225.

—— ANDREW H. and SALES, BRUCE D., and DARLING, ELAINE (1992), 'Comprehensive Lawyer Assistance Programs: Justification and Model', 16 *Law and Psychology Review* 113.

BEYOND THE BREAKING POINT TASK FORCE (1992), *Beyond the Breaking Point* (ABA, Chicago, Ill.).

BINDER, DAVID, BERGMAN, PAUL, and PRICE, SUSAN (1991), *Lawyers as Counselors: A Client-centered Approach* (West Publishing Co., St. Paul, Minn.).

BLODGETT, NANCY (1988), 'Substance Abuse: New Commission Will Aid Impaired Lawyers', 74 *ABA Journal* 74.

BLUMBERG, ABRAHAM (1967), 'The Practice of Law as a Confidence Game', 1 *Law and Society Review* 15.

BRILL, JAMES E. (1994), 'Frequent Flyer: A "Simple Matter" for an Attorney Can Often be Traumatic for a Client', 80 *ABA Journal* 85.

CAMPBELL, COLIN (1976), 'Lawyers and Their Public', XX *Juridical Review* 20.

CARLIN, JEROME E. (1962), *Lawyers on Their Own* (Rutgers University Press, New Brunswick, Canada).

CARRINGTON, PAUL D., and CONLEY, JAMES J. (1977), 'Alienation of Law Students', 75 *Michigan Law Review* 887.

—— and —— (1978), 'Negative Attitudes of Law Students: A Replication of the Alienation and Dissatisfaction Factors', 76 *Michigan Law Review* 1036.

CARROLL, JOHN R. (1992), 'When Your Colleague is Hooked', 55 *Texas Bar Journal* 268.

CASPER, JONATHAN D., TYLER, TOM, and FISHER, BONNIE (1988), 'Procedural Justice in Felony Cases', 22 *Law and Society Review* 483.

COMMISSION ON PARTNERSHIP PROGRAMS (1993), *Report to Board of Governors* (ABA, Chicago, Ill.).

COMMISSION ON PROFESSIONALISM (1986), *In the Spirit of Public Service: A Blueprint for the Rekindling of Lawyer Professionalism* (ABA, Chicago, Ill.).

COMMISSION ON WOMEN IN THE PROFESSION (1988), *Report* (ABA, Chicago, Ill.).

CONDLIN, ROBERT (1983), 'The Moral Failure of Clinical Legal Education', in David Luban (ed.), *The Good Lawyer* (Rowman & Allenheld, Totowa, NJ).

CORNELL LAW REVIEW (1992), 'Symposium on The Emperor's Old Prose: Reexamining the Language of Law', no. 6.

CUNNINGHAM, CLARK (1992), 'The Lawyer as Translator: Towards an Ethnography of Legal Discourse', 77 *Cornell Law Review* 1298.

CURRAN, BARBARA (1977), *The Legal Needs of the Public: The Final Report of a National Survey* (American Bar Foundation, Chicago, Ill.).

DINERSTEIN, ROBERT D. (1990), 'Client-centered Counseling: Reappraisal and Refinement', 32 *Arizona Law Review* 501.

DROGIN, E. (1991), 'Alcoholism in the Legal Profession: Psychological and Legal Perspectives and Interventions', 15 *Law and Psychology Review* 117.

DOOLING, RICHARD (1994), *White Man's Grave* (Farrar, Straus and Giroux, New York).

DURKIN, TOM (1994), *Constructed Law: Comparing Legal Activity in the U.S. and U.K.* (unpublished diss., University of Chicago, Ill.).

EASTON, WILLIAM W., ANTHONY, JAMES C., MANDEL, WALLACE, and GARRISON, ROBERTA (1990), 'Occupations and the Prevalence of Major Depressive Disorder', 32 *Journal of Occupational Medicine* 1079.

EISENSTEIN, JAMES S., and JACOB, HERBERT (1977), *Felony Justice* (Little Brown, Boston, Mass.).

EPSTEIN, CYNTHIA F. (1994), 'Mixed Messages: Structured Ambiguity in the Career Lines of Wall Street Lawyers' (Paper delivered at the meeting of the Law and Society Association, Phoenix, Ariz., June, 1994).

ETON, LEONARD D., and REDMOUNT, ROBERT S. (1957), 'The Effect of Legal Education on Attitudes', 7 *Journal of Legal Education* 431.

FEELEY, MALCOLM (1979), *The Process is the Punishment* (Russell Sage, New York).

FELSTINER, WILLIAM L. F., and SARAT, AUSTIN (1992), 'Enactments of Power: Negotiating Reality and Responsibility in Lawyer–Client Interactions', 77 *Cornell Law Review* 1447.

FLOOD, JOHN (1987), *Anatomy of Lawyering: An Ethnography of a Corporate Law Firm* (unpublished diss., Northwestern University).

—— (1994), 'Shark Tanks, Sweatshops, and the Lawyer as Hero? Fact as Fiction', 21 *Journal of Law and Society* 396.

FREEMAN, HARROP, and WEIHOPE, HENRY (1972), *Clinical Law Training: Interviewing and Counseling* (West Publishing Co., St. Paul, Minn.).

GALANTER, MARC (1994), 'Predators and Parasites: Lawyer-Bashing and Civil Justice', 28 *Georgia Law Review* 633.

—— and PALAY, THOMAS (1991), *Tournament of Lawyers: The Transformation of the Big Law Firm.* (Chicago University Press, Chicago).

GARTH, BRYANT G., and MARTIN, JOANNE (1993), 'Law Schools and the Construction of Competence', 43 *Journal of Legal Education* 469.

GRANFIELD, ROBERT (1992), *Making Elite Lawyers* (Routledge, New York).

GUINIER, LANI, FINE, MICHELLE, and BALIN, JANE (1994), 'Becoming Gentleman: Women's Experience at One Ivy League Law School', 143 *Pennsylvania Law Review* 1.

GUTMANN, AMY (1993), 'Can Virtue Be Taught to Lawyers?', 45 *Stanford Law Review* 1759.

HAGAN, JOHN, and KAY, FIONA (1995), *Gender in Practice: A Study of Lawyers' Lives* (Oxford University Press, New York).

HARRIS, ANGELA P., and SHULTZ, MARJORIE M. (1993), ' "A(nother) Critique of Pure

Reason": Toward Civic Virtue in Legal Education', 45 *Stanford Law Review* 1773.

HARRIS, DONALD, and MACLEAN, MAVIS, GENN, HAZEL, LLOYD-BOSTOCK, SALLY, FENN, PAUL, CORFIELD, PETER, and BRITTAN, YVONNE (1984), *Compensation and Support for Injury and Illness* (Oxford University Press, Oxford).

HASTINGS LAW JOURNAL (1992), 'Theoretics of Practice: The Integration of Progressive Thought and Action', number 4.

HENDERSON, LYNNE N. (1987), 'Legality and Empathy', 85 *Michigan Law Review* 1574.

HENGSTLER, GARY A. (1993), 'Vox Populi: The Public Perception of Lawyers', 79 *ABA Journal* 60.

HENSLER, DEBORAH R., FELSTINER, WILLIAM L. F., SELVIN, MOLLY, and EBENER, PATRICIA A. (1985), *Asbestos in the Courts: The Challenge of Mass Toxic Torts* (Rand Corporation, Santa Monica, Cal.).

HEINS, MARILYN, FAHEY, SHIRLEY N., and HENDERSON, ROGER C. (1983), 'Law Students and Medical Students: A Comparison of Perceived Stress', 33 *Journal of Legal Education* 511.

HOMER, SUZANNE, and SCHWARTZ, LOIS (1989), 'Admitted But Not Accepted: Outsiders Take an Insiders Look at Law School', 5 *Berkeley Women's Law Journal* 1.

HORNE, CHRISTINE (1994), 'Responses to Economic Decline: A Look at Associate Attorney Dissatisfaction' (paper delivered at the meeting of the Law and Society Association, Phoenix, Ariz., June, 1994).

HOSTICKA, CARL (1979), 'We Don't Care What Happened, We Only Care What Is Going to Happen', 26 *Social Problems* 599.

JAQUISH, GAIL A., and WARE, JAMES (1993), 'Adopting an Educator Habit of Mind: Modifying What It Means to "Think Like a Lawyer"', 45 *Stanford Law Review* 1713.

JOHNSON, EARL, JR. (1981), 'Lawyers' Choice: A Theoretical Appraisal of Litigation Investment Decisions', 15 *Law and Society Review* 567.

KOZICH, DENNIS W. (1988), *An Analysis of Stress Levels and Stress Management Choices of Attorneys in the State of Wisconsin* (unpublished diss., University of Wisconsin).

KRITZER, HERBERT M., FELSTINER, WILLIAM L. F., SARAT, AUSTIN, and TRUBEK, DAVID M. (1985), 'The Impact of Fee Arrangement on Lawyer Effort', 19 *Law and Society Review* 251.

KRONMAN, ANTHONY T. (1993), *The Lost Lawyer* (Harvard University Press, Cambridge, Mass.).

LA RUE, HOMER C. (1992), 'Developing an Identity of Responsible Lawyering Through Experiential Learning', 43 *Hastings Law Journal* 1147.

LAW SOCIETY (1992), *Quality, A Briefing for Solicitors* (Legal Practice Directorate, London).

LESNICK, HOWARD (1992), 'Being a Teacher, of Lawyers: Discerning the Theory of My Practice', 43 *Hastings Law Review* 1095.

LEVINE, ALAN P. (1992), 'Looking for Mr. Goodlawyer', 78 *ABA Journal* 60.

LIND, E. ALLAN (1994), 'Procedural Justice and Culture: Evidence for Ubiquitous Process Concerns', 15 *Zeitschift für Rechtssoziologie* 24.

LIND, E. ALLAN, MACCOUN, ROBERT J., EBENER, PATRICIA A., FELSTINER, WILLIAM L.F., HENSLER, DEBORAH R., RESNICK, JUDITH, and TYLER, TOM (1990), 'In the Eye of the Beholder: Tort Litigants' Evaluations of Their Experiences in the Civil Justice System', 24 *Law and Society Review* 953.

—— and TYLER, TOM R. (1988), *The Social Psychological Psychology of Procedural Justice* (Plenum, New York).

MANSNERUS, LAURA (1995), 'Looking for an Attorney? Here's Counsel,' *New York Times*, 11 June 1995, sect. 3, 1.

MACCRATE, ROBERT (chairman) (1992), *American Bar Association Section of Legal Education and Admissions to the Bar, Task Force on Law Schools and the Profession: Narrowing the Gap* (ABA, Chicago, Ill.).

MCEWEN, CRAIG, MATHER, LYNN, and MAIMAN, RICHARD (1994), 'Lawyers, Mediation and the Management of Divorce Practice', 28 *Law and Society Review* 149.

MCPEAK, ALLAN (1987), *Lawyer Occupational Stress* (unpublished diss., Florida State University).

MENKEL-MEADOW, CARRIE (1992), 'The Power of Narrative in Empathetic Learning: Post-Modernism and the Stories of Law', 2 *UCLA Women's Law Journal* 287.

—— (1994), 'Narrowing the Gap by Narrowing the Field: What's Missing from the MacCrate Report-Of Skills, Legal Science and Being a Human Being', 69 *Washington Law Review* 593.

MILLER, PAUL VAN R. (1967), 'Personality Differences and Student Survival', 19 *Journal of Legal Education* 460.

NELSON, ROBERT L., and TRUBEK, DAVID M., (1992a), 'Arenas of Professionalism: The Professional Ideologies of Lawyers in Context' in Robert L. Nelson, David Trubek, and Rayman L. Solomon, *Lawyers' Ideals/Lawyers Practices: Transformations in the American Legal Profession* (Cornell University Press, Ithaca, N.Y.).

—— and —— (1992b), 'New Problems and New Paradigms in Studies of the Legal Profession' in Robert L. Nelson, David Trubek, and Rayman L. Solomon, *Lawyers' Ideals/Lawyers Practices: Transformations in the American Legal Profession* (Cornell University Press, Ithaca, N.Y.).

O'GORMAN, HUBERT (1963), *Lawyers in Matrimonial Cases* (Free Press, Glencoe, Ill.).

OLSON, SUSAN (1984), *Clients and Lawyers: Securing the Rights of Disabled Persons* (Greenwood Press, Westport, Conn.).

PARTNERSHIP PROGRAMS CLIENT RELATIONS PROGRAM (1993), *Attorney Focus Group* (ABA, Chicago, Ill.).

PIECE, JENNIFER L. (1995), *Gender Trials: Emotional Lives in Contemporary Law Firms* (University of California Press, Berkeley, Cal.).

PODGERS, JAMES (1994), 'Client Matters: Closing the Gap Between Lawyers and Their Clients', 98 *ABA Journal* 92.

RESNICK, JUDITH (1993), 'Ambivalence: The Resiliency of Legal Culture in the United States', 45 *Stanford Law Review* 1525.

ROSENTHAL, DOUGLAS (1974), *Lawyer and Client: Who's In Charge* (Russell Sage Foundation, New York).

ROWE, JONATHAN (1992), 'Loot Court: How Harvard Devours its Young', 24 *Washington Monthly* 39.

Samborn, Randall (1993), 'Anti-Lawyer Attitude Up', 15 *National Law Journal* no. 49, 1.

Sarat, Austin, and Felstiner, William L. F., (1986), 'Law and Strategy in the Divorce Lawyer's Office', 20 *Law and Society Review* 93.

—— and —— (1995), *Divorce Lawyers and Their Clients: Power and Meaning in the Legal Process* (Oxford University Press, New York).

—— and Kearns, Thomas R. (1991), 'A Journey Through Forgetting: Toward a Jurisprudence of Violence', in Austin Sarat and Thomas R. Kearns, *The Fate of Law* (University of Michigan Press, Ann Arbor, Mich.).

Seron, Carroll (1994), *When Lawyers Go to Market: The Restructuring of Private Legal Practice* (unpublished manuscript).

Schon, Donald (1984), *The Reflective Practitioner: How Professionals Think in Action* (Basic Books, New York).

Scottsdale II, Long Range Planning Committee, Section on Communications and Public Relations (1978), *An Updated Communications Agenda for the Legal Profession* (National Association of Bar Examiners, Chicago, Ill.).

Shaffer, Thomas L., and Redmount, Robert S. (1977), *Lawyers, Law Students and People* (Sheperd's Inc., Colorado Springs, Colo.).

Shalleck, Ann (1993), 'Constructions of the Client Within Legal Education', 45 *Stanford Law Review* 1731.

Shanfield, Stephen B., and Benjamin, G. Andrew H. (1985), 'Psychiatric Distress in Law Students', 35 *Journal of Legal Education* 65.

Shapiro, Susan P. (1995), 'Conflicting Responsibilities: Maneuvering Through the Minefield of Fiduciary Obligations' (paper presented at the Law and Society Association meeting, Toronto, June, 1995).

Solkoff, Norman, and Markowitz, Joan (1967), 'Personality Characteristics of First-Year Medical and Law Students', 42 *Journal of Medical Education* 195.

Solomon, Rayman L. (1992), 'Five Crises or One: The Concept of Legal Professionalism, 1925–60' in Robert L. Nelson, David Trubek, and Rayman L. Solomon, *Lawyers' Ideals/Lawyers Practices: Transformations in the American Legal Profession* (Cornell University Press, Ithaca, N.Y.).

Spangler, Eve (1986), *Lawyers for Hire: Salaried Professionals at Work* (Yale University Press, New Haven, Conn.).

Stevens, Amy (1994), 'Lawyers' Annoying Misdeeds Targeted', *Wall Street Journal*, 9 September, sect. B, 1, cols. 1–3.

'Students and Lawyers, Doctrine and Responsibility: A Pedagogical Colloquy' (1992), *Hastings Law Journal*, no. 4.

Sussman, Fern S. (1993), 'Lawyers Have to Take the Complaints of Clients More Seriously', *New York Times* 26 November, 1993, sect. 18, cols. 3–5.

Thomas, Kecia M., Ringenbach, Kathleen, Kohler, Stacey, and Landy, Frank J. (1994), 'Time Urgency and Burnout among Working Women in Traditional and Non-Traditional Careers' (paper presented at the American Psychological Association's National Conference on Psychosocial and Behavioral Factors in Women's Health, Washington, DC, May 1994).

Tomasic, Roman (1978), *Law, Lawyers and the Community* (The Law Foundation of New South Wales, St. Leonards).

TYLER, TOM, and LIND, E. ALLAN (1992). 'A Relational Model of Authority in Groups', 25 *Advances in Experimental Social Psychology* 115.

VOGEL, HOWARD H. (1989), *Report of ABA Task Force on Outreach to the Public* (ABA, Chicago, Ill.).

WASSERSTROM, RICHARD (1975), 'Lawyers as Professionals: Some Moral Issues', 5 *Human Rights* 1.

WATSON, ANDREW (1975), 'Lawyers and Professionalism: A Further Psychiatric Perspective on Legal Education', 8 *Journal of Law Reform* 248.

WEISS, CATHERINE, and MELLING, LOUISE (1988), 'The Legal Education of Twenty Women', 40 *Stanford Law Review* 1299.

WHITE, LUCIE (1990), 'Subordination, Rhetorical Skills and Sunday Shoes: Notes on the Hearing of Mrs G.', 38 *Buffalo Law Review* 1.

7

Knowing the Buzzwords and Clapping for Tinker Bell: The Context, Content and Qualities of Lawyers' Knowledge in a Specialized Industrial Field

PHILIP LEWIS

It was quite a shock for me, after a tutor with settled views on black-letter law that he wanted to impart, to go to a young New Zealander with an inquiring and penetrating mind. Ever since 1957 Don has been a model for me and those others who have wondered how things work out in practice. It is hard now to remember how little sense there was of the world outside the books when the Centre for Socio-Legal Studies was started, and it is an honour to be one of those who can pay direct tribute to Don for his part in the change, as well as thank him publicly for the support he has given me personally.[1]

Before rules can be used, whether in extra-judicial contexts—the focus of this book—or in courts, someone has to know them. If we are thinking of private persons or corporations in the late twentieth century, the relevant knowledge is likely to be that of a lawyer, someone professionally qualified to advise on the law after study, examination, and often further training; even if those not legally qualified are involved in advising, a lawyer is likely to have established or approved the system by which they do so. If there is a gap in that knowledge, those rules do not exist, for practical purposes, as Stewart Macaulay found to be the case for certain consumer protections in Wisconsin (Macaulay, 1979). This essay is on the knowledge that lawyers have in one area of practice in one country. It cuts across a focus on the use of rules, but I hope that it may incidentally illustrate some of the processes by which rules come into being, and in particular how rules may be not just altered or modified but also constituted in their application.

[1] The research reported in this essay was carried out under an ESRC grant R–000–23–3849, which is gratefully acknowledged. Don kindly allowed me to use the facilities of the Centre for the research which led to the application for the grant, and for the research itself, and without the assistance of the Centre and its staff, particularly Jenny Dix and Jeanette Price, neither the application nor the research would have been possible. My thanks are also due to Denis Galligan for his continuing hospitality while this essay was being written.

The literature on lawyers' knowledge was sketched by Abel and Lewis (1989, 501–13), who concentrated on the values implicit in the assessment of lawyers' skills and knowledge. Their survey antedated recent work which originates from a concern with professional training (Stebbings, 1994). This literature is expressed in terms of skills rather than knowledge, a distinction to which I return. Stebbings, in particular, draws on literature which makes helpful distinctions between lawyers' task skills and the wider skills involved in deploying them. It is not intended to go into this literature here, but merely to note the point that skills (and knowledge) can be conceptualized either as a flat list of separate items, or as hierarchical, in which one skill is knowing in what circumstances to use another, or as clustered or networked, in which skills go together and interact.

This Chapter revisits the sociological literature.[2] Whereas the training and management literatures emphasize skills, sociological literature emphasizes knowledge, for reasons which seem historical. The literature of the professions, in particular, tends to concentrate on conceptions of knowledge which carry the connotations of method, discovery, authority, and truth associated with scientific knowledge. But knowing how to perform certain tasks has also been part of the story of knowledge, and it is this part of the story which is often now conceptualized as skills. The terminology of skills is better adapted to the classification of the elements of lawyers' training and to the assessment of their progress in it. The terminology of knowledge provides a bridge to the structure of the outside world with which lawyers interact, and I therefore prefer it as a general descriptive term. The word 'expertise' is also used in cases where the knowledge is sufficient and sufficiently relevant to be marketable or to confer authority, where, that is, the social implications of the knowledge as well as its content come into play.

What follows cuts across the tangled debate in the sociology of the professions about whether there is actually a problem about the social control of occupations with expert knowledge. Instead two strands of recent discussion are identified, not necessarily totally distinct. In one, professions are seen as occupations which have successfully claimed certain privileges, notably of monopoly and autonomy, by appeal, *inter alia*, to the possession of special expertise. In the other, certain occupations have defined fields as their own by constructing common ways of seeing and communication, fields which acquire prestige by the social capital which participants bring to them from outside, and also by characteristics of their social interactions. Within the first strand there is an important distinction between those authors who accept the reality of some, at

---

[2] For a different viewpoint see McCahery and Picciotto (1995).

least, of the claim to knowledge and those who either deny it or see its reality as socially immaterial, pointing rather to the role of university validation and credentialism in underpinning the profession's claims.

In his *Profession of Medicine* (1970) Eliot Freidson gave substantial arguments for some of the prevailing distrust of professions' claims to authority, but yet, in the case of medicine, conceded the existence of an area of scientific knowledge through which the medical profession could claim authority. The subtitle 'A Study of the Sociology of Applied Knowledge' is illuminating. He considers the argument that knowledge should be equated with what professionals do, and rejects it on the ground that this would come to defining knowledge as 'what knowledgeable people do'. He then restricts the term 'knowledge' for his purposes (see, for instance, 338–9) to what is systematic, reliable, and objective (in the case of medicine the scientific system and discoveries on which practical medicine is based); practice then becomes, in the words of his subtitle, 'applied knowledge', incapable because of its lack of system and validation, and its susceptibility to bias and idiosyncrasy, of giving rise to the exclusive authority over the conditions and exercise of practical judgement which the medical profession has claimed.[3] The elegant analysis and differentiation in this book have not always been matched in other critical literature. In a later work (1986) he generalized the discussion of practical knowledge to all professional occupations, placing the responsibility for producing the formalized knowledge they needed in a class of researchers often associated with universities, while the practitioners used that knowledge in modified form (1986, 211; questioned by Abel and Lewis, 1989, 506 ff.).

We may set against this account the work of Larson (1977) and Abel (1979, 1989), for whom professional knowledge is at best tangential and at worst non-existent. Since the services professionals render are intangible, so the argument goes, there is no objective way by which practitioners can assure the quality of their work or distinguish themselves from competitors. They thus resort to various devices of closure to limit competition, externally by enlisting the help of the state in restricting the number of those who produce such services, and internally by restricting the services which practitioners may perform and the conditions under which they perform them.

In the present context the relevant aspect of this process is the limitation of the provision of services to those who have gone through various forms of educational and occupational qualification. The argument that it is closure which is the important aim rather than the improvement in

---

[3] Statistical studies of the efficacy of treatments may well have grown in sophistication and power since the time he wrote.

services is supported by the frequent obvious irrelevance of qualifications to job performance (Latin, for instance, for nineteenth-century English solicitors) or a prevalent tolerance of inadequate skills and incompetent performance. In this context, academic and professional discussions of the nature of law and legal knowledge are seen as efforts to ally the occupation seeking closure with currently influential intellectual approaches, rather than as casting any genuine light on realities.

Halliday (1987) grappled with the central thesis exemplified by Larson and Abel, and concluded that in fact modern professions (he was particularly concerned with the legal profession) were so firmly entrenched in society that their actions could no longer be explained in terms of seeking to maintain a monopoly for their services. On this basis professional efforts relating to expertise have to be taken seriously, and Halliday does not question the reality of professional expertise. In fact, he uses the experience of the legal profession to argue that the collective action of a profession may, in certain circumstances, put its expertise at the service of a weakened state to solve problems with which the state itself does not have the resources to cope (ch. 12).

The literature so far discussed is oriented towards the role of claims of special knowledge towards the state, which establishes and defines the scope of the professional monopoly. Most recent sociological discussions, however, concern the position of professions in the market, so that there is a shift of focus, and we might expect proportionately more attention to practical knowledge. Yet the divisions cannot be clear-cut. Claims for state assistance could not ordinarily be successfully deployed unless they had some general social appeal, and obviously if a profession is to achieve some moral authority the same must be true. The weakness of justice as a general warrant for a profession was long ago noted by Rueschemeyer (1964). Law is man-made rather than natural, and is applied in the interests of particular parties, rather than universal.

The work of Abbott (1988) helps to bridge the gap between state and market theories. For the specific claims to monopoly and autonomy he substitutes the concept of jurisdiction, the link between a profession and its work (1988, 20), and the establishment of claims to jurisdiction in the arenas of public opinion, the law, and the workplace. In this context two points are important. One is that claims in the different arenas may be variously founded; while in the public and legal arenas the claim is likely to be a broad cultural claim, based on university-based abstraction and formal knowledge (see 1988, 47, 53 ff.), and formulated in wide terms, for instance, assuming a homogeneous profession and abstractly defined tasks, in the workplace arena (1988, 64 ff.) the claim will be more oriented to the particular tasks involved and the professional segments which perform or compete for them.[4]

More importantly, Abbott argues that professions do not exist and make their claims in isolation; they seek to establish their jurisdictions as against other professions and in competition with them, not just in markets, but in all the arenas he describes.[5] As he argues (1988, 102), 'knowledge is the currency of competition', though abstract knowledge is central; nevertheless, he emphasizes the need for professions, if they are to succeed in the competition, to achieve 'an optimum level of abstraction that lies between the extremely general and the extremely concrete' (104). Their claims to jurisdiction have to be founded on some combination of a cultural warrant and a plausible claim for the efficacy of their practice. Thus he too accepts the reality of professional knowledge. His account of academic knowledge is more nuanced than Freidson's: he argues that in its abstraction from practical knowledge it supports the profession's cultural claims, but that the abstraction from particular practical situations means that it is only available in a 'peculiarly disassembled state that prevents its use' (1988, 53).

I turn now to the second strand of sociological thought, associated with Bourdieu, in which the profession and the knowledge it uses on which to base its claims are not conceptually separate; instead there is a social field where participants share a *habitus*, a common way of looking at the world and understandings of how to behave in it. He suggests, for instance (1987, 820), that it is a 'universalizing attitude' which 'constitutes the entry ticket into the juridical field—accompanied, to be sure, by a minimal mastery of the legal resources amassed by successive generations, that is, the canon of texts and modes of thinking, of expression, and action in which such a canon is reproduced and which reproduce it'.

Even if 'texts' refers to legal texts, which is by no means certain (see translator's comment at 808–9), the emphasis is rather on shared modes of thinking, which define the class of permissible participants, serve to exclude lay or ethical thinking, and mark off the autonomy of the field from political and social influences. The relation of thinking in terms of a community to jurisprudence was illustrated by Simpson (1973), who argued that rules (his particular topic was precedent) did not arise until judges and lawyers ceased to be a small group, a small community in constant contact with each other, who shared understandings of proper

---

[4] He argues that in the workplace arena '[t]here is usually little debate about what the tasks are or how to construct them'(1988, 64), but as we shall see in some forms of competition this debate is central.

[5] He does not emphasize market competition in his general account, though he describes examples of it (e.g. 1988, 64–5, ch. 9). The identification of the workplace as an arena and a recognition of the degree to which professional work now takes place in organizations seem to limit his discussion of market competition.

behaviour which it was unnecessary and perhaps impossible to articulate.

What has proved to be the most fruitful insight in Bourdieu's work is the role played in the construction of the juridical field (he has shown the same for other social fields) by a competition between groups with particular interests which nevertheless has the effect of strengthening the social authority of the field as a whole. He says:

The juridical field is the site of a competition for monopoly of the right to determine the law. Within this field there occurs a confrontation among actors possessing a technical competence which is inevitably social and which consists essentially in the socially recognized capacity to *interpret* a corpus of texts sanctifying a correct or legitimized vision of the social world [817, emphasis in original].

The development of a body of rules and procedures with a claim to universality is the product of a division of labor resulting from the competition among different forms of competence, at once hostile and complementary [821].

That technical competence is inevitably social and that competing forms of competence can be at once hostile and complementary are both important elements in the work of Dezalay (see 158 below).[6] Bourdieu describes in particular the competition between the theorists he sees as engaged in a constant struggle to rationalize the law and make it logically consistent, and practitioners, among whom he includes judges, who are committed to practical evaluation of cases. However, the hostility between different groups 'does not preclude the complementary exercise of their functions. In fact, such hostility serves as the basis for a subtle form of the *division of the labor of symbolic domination* in which adversaries, objectively complicitous with each other, fulfil mutual needs' (823, emphasis in original). Bourdieu describes in detail (824–5) how the work of the practitioners adapts to reality what might otherwise be a rigidly rationalist system, while the work of the theorists protects the practitioners from charges of arbitrariness. He also makes it clear that one of the factors in professional struggles is the interests of the participants, including the interests of their clients. These interests may diverge between the different bodies of practitioners and between the different groups in any particular body, in a way which depends on 'their position in the internal hierarchy of the body, which always corresponds rather closely to the position of their clients in the social hierarchy' (821–2). In describing processes of interpretation (827), he concludes that the meaning of a rule 'can be discovered in the specific power relation

---

[6] That knowledge has to be validated by a legal community is also emphasized by Luhmann (1976, 100): while what is characteristic of lawyers is their knowledge of texts, that knowledge has to be recognized by others.

between professionals. Assuming that the abstract equity of the contrary positions they represent is the same, this power relation might be thought of as corresponding to the power relations between the parties in the case.'

Thus, Bourdieu's account, here given in a very simplified form, contains two main points relevant to this paper: the competition over the right to determine what is knowledge in the juridical field offers social support to the whole field, because it makes it clear that ethical, logical, and pragmatic considerations are all taken into account in its decisions, and that the rules developed within the field do not have meaning except in their application by participants with interests of their own. He may be too simplistic, as we shall see, in allowing the power relations between the parties such a direct relevance: the overall interests of the direct participants, for instance, the lawyers, may not coincide with that of their clients from time to time. He also makes an important point in showing how the specific interests of each group are linked with an ideology, logic, for instance, or pragmatism.

In this strand of sociological thought it is hard to disentangle what lawyers do from what they know, because, characteristically, they are seen as constructing the field, and hence their knowledge, as they act. Thus, Cain (1979), in an influential article, points out that much of what lawyers do for their bourgeois clients is to translate their claims and contentions into legal language. But though she does not emphasize the point, she sees this as a dynamic process in which the language is changed to accommodate the claims; for her, lawyers are 'conceptive ideologists': the legal world and its relation to the social world are constructed in lawyers' activities.

How does this construction take place? Powell (1993), in an article which was well-known before it was published, describes how a particular innovation (the 'poison pill', an anti-takeover device for companies and their incumbent management) was invented in a law-firm and then developed, homologated in the courts, and diffused. A number of similar examples are described or cited by McBarnet (1984, 1992) and McBarnet and Whelan (1991, where footnote 1 has other citations).

What McBarnet portrays is a more pervasive process. She is concerned with the role of the legal profession in determining the practical meaning of the law and the interests it is to serve (1984, 233). She describes lawyers as not just 'translators, but transformers and transcenders of law', 'legal entrepreneurs routinely "making law" by establishing legal practice'. She describes how specific devices become standard practice: even if they are endorsed in statute or case law, the origins of the law 'lie rather in the pragmatic practices of legal entrepreneurs serving their clients' interests' (*ibid.*).

Elsewhere she ascribes the ineffectiveness of the law in promoting egalitarianism to 'the *post hoc* creative work upon the law by the legal profession on a day-to-day pragmatic basis to meet the interests of clients who can afford to buy its services in creating or avoiding law' (1988, 119). What is being described is not a stable legal world, set off by instances of creativity or discrete devices, but a world essentially subject to continual construction and reconstruction by participants. Thus, although some parts of McBarnet's work can be read as if there were actual rules, other parts suggest that there are no rules, but a series of negotiations about the limits of acceptable conduct, and the basis on which texts will be used to found judgements of acceptability. What one would have in such a context is not so much knowledge as, in accord with the views of Bourdieu and Luhmann mentioned above, a recognized ability to participate in the negotiations.

Dezalay's work (for instance, 1991, 1992, 1993, 1995) locates knowledge in a far richer context than any of his predecessors. He does not rely to the same extent as Bourdieu on notions of field and *habitus*, but otherwise develops and links many of his insights (and those of Abbott and Powell) by applying them to the examination of a number of recent developments—for instance, changing attitudes to insolvency and insolvency law in France and the United States, the growth of mediation, changes in the character of international arbitration (with Garth), and above all competition in the market for advice in the financial and regulatory sectors, between merchant bankers, lawyers, and accountants, and between American and European and traditional and entrepreneurial practitioners.

A presupposition of Dezalay's work is that we all make law, not just practitioners, but legal journalists, policy analysts, legal scholars, and sociologists too. By analysis, description, exposure, and advocacy, we promote particular views of problems and their appropriate solutions, and of the part which is or should be played by various competing occupations or disciplines. We do so, too, whether deliberately or not, in our own interests. This is easy to see for practitioners, if they press for the application of practical solutions with which they are familiar, which they may perhaps have devised, and in the working out of which they are likely to be employed. But if I can be persuasive in support of my view that thinking about lawyers is important, my own career may be enhanced, and my chances of research grants improved.

In the competition between professionals, he also asserts, expertise and a supporting ideology are powerful tools. Nor can class and hierarchy be overlooked. The applicability and superiority of expertise itself are put forward by hitherto excluded groups against established elites using their existing social and business connections as means both of doing business and justifying their own indispensability. In a recent article (1995, 89), he has an apt newspaper quotation (Chirot, 1988): '[o]nly long-existing relationships confer this privilege [of regular dinners with bosses of large companies]. Newcomers to this business are obligated to use more pragmatic methods. 'We are not "grands seigneurs", so we rely on techniques', pleads Simon Luel, a Credit Lyonnais Director.' The theme of expertise, meritocracy, and hitherto excluded groups as against elites is played out between old Wall Street firms and innovative Jewish firms, as it is in French bankruptcy practice, international arbitration, and the invasion of traditional European law practice by American or Americanized law firms. But once technique and expertise are accepted as tools, whose expertise will prevail? Between competing occupations the battle is fought out on the basis of aptness and experience. American law firms in Europe purvey their experience in take-over and antitrust practice, not just to private clients, but also to regulatory authorities seeking to construct a new regime out of overlapping jurisdictions and procedures that it is in someone's interest to see as outmoded or inadequate. If these firms can help in the process of construction, either by direct commission or by dictating the terms of the debate, they can also put themselves forward as the best people to manipulate the new regime, when it has come into force (see e.g. 1995, 85 ff.). They differ from Halliday's enlightened professions in that they have themselves constructed the knowledge they put at the service of the state, and will thereafter take advantage of it.

On the whole, the knowledge which Dezalay describes lawyers as constructing and using is of juridical techniques, for that is how they can distinguish themselves from their competitors. Nevertheless, it is knowledge developed in the service of economic interests, and its aptness depends on considerable understanding of those interests and their underlying dynamics. For instance, while scholars do good work in enhancing the legitimacy of juridical techniques, the fields in question are too important to be left to those without practical experience (1993, 210). Professionals turn to the writing of papers and treatises; academics respond by assimilating their outlook to that of the practical world.

The range of matters at issue, the skills deployed, and the interests at stake are well illustrated in McBarnet and Whelan (1991), written after and citing some earlier articles by Dezalay. They are describing swings between formalism and anti-formalism in regulatory policy (particularly in taxation and accountancy matters), and show how some of the opposition to anti-formalist or purposive controls combines practical argument with ideology. They also show how some of the ideology supporting formalism is put forward by the legal profession, and may also support it in its competitive struggles with accountants over concepts and clients. Lawyers, they point out, bring extra resources to any struggle, at least if they can judicialize it, because it is then their form of interpretation which will be used to determine it. While a text, along with its possible interpretations, is a recognized resource, so too are the principles of an institution, arguments of practicality, and arguments of ideology. The ideological argument of the rule of law has particular force because of its connections with both political institutions and economic power. They also show how this process can affect broad characteristics of the law; law does not just drift, but is deliberately steered from substance to form, from broad to narrow, from open to closed.

LAWYERS' KNOWLEDGE IN AN INDUSTRIAL FIELD

In what follows, some of the themes which recur in the literature are illustrated from interviews with ninety or so people, mostly advisors in the computer (including software) and electronics industries in England and Wales, conducted between 1990 and 1993. At first, the interviews were generalized, but in 1992 the research became focused on the growth of a specialization in computer law, covering both the knowledge and skills applied in practice, and the way they were organized (both in firms and companies) and marketed. Most of the discussion of knowledge is taken from interviews conducted in 1992.[7]

The general aim of the research from 1992 onwards was to replicate Dezalay's work on the mobilization of expertise in a different context, one in which the novel and complex industrial subject-matter might impose limits on the extent to which lawyers had a free hand in constructing the legal field. I also intended to look more closely at the constituents and development of that expertise. It was plain that during the 1980s a specialization in computer law had developed in Britain, and the aim was to look at not only the creation, development, and diffusion of expert knowledge, but also its social organization within companies and in private practice, including its use in marketing. Like Dezalay, I thought that the internationalization of this industrial sector and the growth of a supranational legal system would have affected the knowledge and practice of law.

Those with relevant knowledge in England and Wales[8] are most easily

---

[7] A few interviews were also conducted along the same lines in 1993. Those interviewed were promised confidentiality for themselves, and non-identification for their firms, companies, and clients. References to interviews numbered 'T1' etc. are to transcripts from tapes.

[8] I did not succeed in identifying relevant Scottish individuals. Major Scottish firms of solicitors must have people capable of advising on the legal aspects of installing computer systems, and more recent editions of *Chambers Directory* list a few firms with computer-

labelled by professional qualification and institutional affiliation. They include solicitors and barristers in private practice and employed by companies, some also with qualifications as patent agents or US lawyers, patent agents in private practice and employed by companies, contracts officers without a legal qualification employed by companies, some US lawyers employed in US law firms or companies, academics, who may also have a professional qualification and act as consultants to firms of solicitors, and, finally, individuals without a legal qualification working in companies,[9] trade associations or in government. A rough count might be 400 to 500 people.[10]

Some of what lawyers know can be found in a library, but a law library may not contain all they know or need to know. Nor can one there find out how widely distributed knowledge is, how much it is used in practice, or the significance it has in use. Indeed, it is hard to know whether publication is an important part of the development of knowledge, though particular types of publication, for instance precedent books, are cited in interviews as useful. But some of those interviewed indicated that they would not be giving away in seminars (and presumably still less in print) information for which they could expect to charge. And, as we shall see, publications may be being used to promote a point of view.

Interviews, on the other hand, allowed an opportunity to ask what skills were actually used in practice, and which were most significant. Practitioners were asked in particular about the importance of intellectual property law. Some solicitors were asked questions addressing the same points indirectly, for instance, what skills assistants had to acquire, or what made other solicitors less good.

In an article in *Legal Business* (1991), in which information-technology lawyers nominated experts in the field, most of the pieces started with a mention of the law.[11] But they were somewhat dismissive of its significance in identifying the real experts, saying that there was no such thing as information-technology law, or that it was a 'rag-bag'. Real expertise

law expertise. Casual inquiry of one large electronics company with manufacturing and sales departments in Scotland suggested that there was no internal legal expertise there.

[9] English engineering companies have traditionally had contracts officers without legal qualifications. The legal affairs committee of one industry association had many non-legal members, some mentioned in complimentary terms by lawyers.

[10] One person interviewed in 1991 estimated that there were then a couple of hundred people claiming expertise in computer law; this does not seem out of line with estimates given by others. Contributors and participants at a recent forum on software patents numbered 147, of whom I had only interviewed 9. While some of the others I know to be lawyers and patent agents, others seem to have been there to put an industry policy on patents (Patent Office, 1994).

[11] Cunningham (1993) offers a picture of US computer lawyers, which, making allowance for the different state of the industry, is quite similar to the general account in this section.

was to be found elsewhere. The interviews reflected a similar approach. Thus, one referred to an inaugural lecture by a well-known academic as showing that there was no such thing as computer law, saying that it dealt with three topics which had nothing to do with each other except that each related to computers. There are quite difficult technical legal questions, such as those raised by the existence of different versions of software over the years when copyright law was changing and the transitional provisions were complex.[12] But such questions are not what even acknowledged experts see as significant either in general practice or in identifying expertise. Instead, what is seen as important is the ability to apply general principles and concepts to the subject-matter of practice.[13] While these may come from some of the few computer-related statutes, or from intellectual property law, they were more likely to be described as coming from contract or tort. For instance, a chapter (Reed, 1993b) on Electronic Data Interchange ('EDI'), that is, the transaction of business by often automated electronic communication, relies on very basic principles of contract law, derived, for instance, from a case about entrants to a yacht-race, and sale-of-goods legislation, along with a very detailed knowledge of the technology and the course of business. The articles in *Legal Business* (1991) referred to one of the pioneers in the field as able to apply basic principles of negligence law to questions of liability for defective software.

Respondents were asked what fields of law were important in practice. Contract and commercial law generally were emphasized in the answers, even by the most expert. When I asked about the importance of intellectual property law, the general response was that it was significant, but not overwhelmingly so. When I asked what particular parts of intellectual property law were important, there were occasional references to the effects of insolvency, but most respondents referred to only one rule, that software belongs to the author, not to the party commissioning and paying for it, unless the author is that party's employee. The practical significance of the rule is that much software is written, wholly or partly, by consultants as independent contractors, who thus acquire legal title in the absence of an assignment in their contract.[14]

---

[12] The example is taken from a 1991 interview with an in-house lawyer for a major software company. Though he does not deal with this particular point, Millard's account (1993) is an informed and useful outline of copyright law in relation to software from the point of view of a leading practitioner.

[13] 'Horizontal legal and vertical industry skills', as it was put by one well-known practitioner.

[14] In clear-cut cases the problem can be dealt with by joining the consultant in legal proceedings, but the absence of legal title may be a problem if the software is to be licensed or the owners are seeking finance.

In spite of this apparently limited relevance, there is a prevalent impression that intellectual property law is associated with computer-related practice. In many firms computer-related matters are dealt with in an intellectual property department. One leading expert, after expressing the view that there was only a limited association in fact, gave a plausible explanation: computer-related matters were seen as technical, and intellectual property lawyers were seen in their firms as the appropriate people to deal with technical matters. He added that as lawyers tended to emphasize what was familiar to them, more intellectual property law than was necessary had thus been introduced into the field.

In practice, respondents advising computer companies, whether internally or externally, also placed great emphasis on European law. Two areas are particularly significant: the provisions on public procurement, for those providing systems too, since public authorities are responsible for substantial proportions of all British computer acquisitions;[15] and those on distribution and licensing, since the setting up of distribution networks on behalf of the UK-based subsidiaries of overseas companies is an important area of work, in which English lawyers have substantial expertise.

If what is relevant is the ability to apply general legal principles to the subject-matter of practice, what in the subject-matter it was important for the lawyer to know varied according to the nature of respondents' practice. For those in general commercial practice, contracts for the purchase of computer systems are a staple, and even some of those who are considered experts point out that such contracts are much of their work. The course of negotiating such contracts, measures of specification and performance, and mechanisms for setting up procedures for the implementation and even alteration of the contract, were all part of what practitioners needed to know. In this context, the general view was that it was not the technology that was legally significant, but it would be hard to practise in the field unless one knew how computers worked. One did not need a technical knowledge, but to understand something which is a blend of industry practice and the practicalities of protection by contract, that is, how the requirements for the computer system should be specified and tested. Even if consultants have drawn up the specification for a tender, say, as one metropolitan solicitor commented (T32), at the end of the day it was the solicitor who had to understand these matters sufficiently to put them into the contractual documents. What had to be understood was not just the purposes for which the system was acquired, but the way in which accuracy and usability could be measured, for

[15] These provisions can be a weapon in the hands of those who have lost out in the tendering process.

instance, in the number of simultaneous transactions which could be carried out, and what the response times would be with multiple simultaneous use.[16]

Advising on drafting on software development is also widespread. Customers often acquire integrated systems whose software may not be standard, and software houses, which can be quite small and not have an in-house lawyer, are found up and down the country. The lawyer has to understand the subject-matter of the intellectual-property rights involved, and what rights in it will be retained or transferred. But they also have to understand the course of a software project, its pitfalls, and the kinds of protection available to the parties, to the customer, for instance, by way of transfer or deposit of completed code, if the developer is unable or unwilling to continue the project to completion or may not maintain it thereafter.

Whatever the transaction, respondents emphasized the importance of understanding the business environment of the particular transaction, and often the general business environment in which the industry operated. A common criticism of other practitioners was that they did not recognize the commercial point of a transaction, what it was important to achieve, and what might be ignored. More than one respondent emphasized this in relation to technology licensing, which for that reason, in their view, could not be standardized. Even in the comparatively standardized area of computer contracting, it was important to understand one's client's needs from the system being acquired, and one lawyer went so far as to say that the supplier's lawyer should also have an understanding of the customer's needs if the contract was to work out well. Two respondents also referred to need to understand a client organization's internal hierarchy and politics if the person giving the instructions seemed misguided.

More generally it was said to be important to know what risks people in the industry would accept, so that it was unnecessary to draft long and possibly contentious clauses to cover them. An interest in the industry and some idea of where it was going, gleaned not only from contact with clients but also from the general computer press, was also helpful, and strongly emphasized by some; though the reasons were not spelled out in the interviews, it might enable a lawyer to understand the purpose of transactions and assess the importance and possibility of securing com-

---

[16] Another specialist went into it in more detail: 'I was distinguishing between the functionality of a product in computer terms and functional specification in computer contract terms, which should include response times, memory capacity and just about everything. So the answer is that it is the case that a little learning is a dangerous thing and it is no good remembering to warrant the technicalities if you can't understand the technicalities and read the technicalities and advise your client on them' (T44). He had indicated that the wording in the functional specification might take away rights.

mitments. The respondents who thought in such broader terms, whether of the industry as a whole (though its limits were not specified) or vertical markets or product life-cycle, seemed on the whole to be the more expert.

What then was the importance of knowledge of the actual technology? Amongst those interviewed there were about twenty in-house lawyers, mostly with substantial technical knowledge, and also forty-nine solicitors in private practice with varying degrees of knowledge.[17] Of these, five were litigators, and two were also qualified as patent agents, and fell into rather a different class; there were also nine who did not hold themselves out particularly as having computer knowledge (though some of them did), and were more involved in technology start-ups (which might include software companies), and technology licensing—they were commercially astute lawyers accustomed to handling transactions with significant technological elements. I sought to classify the other thirty-three under headings relating to their degrees of expertise: those recognized as expert outside their immediate circle, those having a good knowledge of the technology, those having a good knowledge of computer and software contracts, those with an adequate knowledge of such contracts, and others. While membership of the first category was comparatively clear, the others represent a very uncertain judgment on the basis of my response to the comparative texture of the interviews, since I often did not probe for their degree of knowledge. With that caveat, I would say that seven were recognized experts, with the appropriate knowledge of the technology, six more had a good knowledge of the technology, eleven had a good knowledge of computer acquisition and software contracts, six had an adequate knowledge of such contracts, and perhaps three had no special knowledge of them, in spite of some claim to it. Probably somewhat over a third of those mentioned in this paragraph had technological knowledge.

In spite of this degree of technological knowledge, its importance was generally downplayed. A number of lawyers (including most of those referred to above as used to transactions with a technological element) felt that what was needed was not so much knowledge of the technology with which they were dealing (since they could never equal their clients in that, and the clients did not want it anyway), but an ability to go on asking questions until they understood the problem.[18] Even those with a

[17] Membership of particular categories is not always clear-cut. Lawyers from other countries, patent agents, employees of trade associations, and civil servants were also interviewed.

[18] I doubt, however, whether clients would be so tolerant of patent agents with such a limited understanding. A patent agent in private practice indicated that one would not be able to operate in a field of which one had no knowledge, since one might have to discuss technicalities with the client. However, even in a field where the patent agent operated habitually the client's knowledge would always be more advanced and up-to-date.

scientific or computing background pointed out that their knowledge rapidly became out of date.

Nevertheless, specifying the subject-matter of intellectual property rights in software requires some understanding of the technicalities of code, as does, for instance, litigating disputed software-copying cases. In addition, those who see each other as really expert (the groups are mentioned later) have a very good understanding of the technology, and of what aspects of it may be relevant to legal principles and concepts.[19] Without it, one could not usefully discuss, to take only one example, whether it would be possible to chart the interfaces of a program by the electronic impulses to which it gives rise in running, as was at issue in debates over the Software Directive.

Possession of this degree of technical knowledge, and the ability to relate it to legal issues, was seen by an academic as marking out a group of academics with whom he could communicate easily. But this knowledge might be acquired 'on the job'. Though someone with a lifetime in electronics felt that he had an edge in that respect over other experts, many of those interviewed had no technical background, and this applied to some of the principal participants in the debate over the Software Directive.

One striking phrase, often repeated, was the importance of knowing 'the jargon' or the 'buzz-words'. It is worth pausing on, and may serve to highlight not only a division in the profession, but also a gap between the profession and its clients, and between the law and the technology to which it must adjust. On the surface, the point is that clients can be put at their ease by someone to whom every word does not have to be immediately explained, and may so be helped in explaining their problem in a context which may be quite strange to them. But the deprecating terms also imply a disclaimer of an involvement in the clients' world which might seem excessive and even unprofessional, and suggest a consciousness that knowing the language is not the same as knowing the substance. Those who seemed most at home with the technology did not speak in these ambivalent terms, but their widespread use can not only symbolize the uneasy fit between the law and this novel technology, but also show why the fit may be poor. The work of concept formation is

[19] Thus, Reed (1993a, 87) says: '[t]he problems, however, lie not so much in the technology as in the application of existing principles to facts that are entirely novel and which have few conceptual similarities with the kind of facts the judiciary are accustomed to encounter. . . . A lawyer who is entirely ignorant of the processes involved in the creation and running of software can hardly be expected to understand how the principles of negligence, or indeed any other rules of law, should be applied to it.' Some of those interviewed, indeed, commented on the tendency of judges to look for conceptual similarities with facts they were accustomed to encountering, seeking, for instance, to equate contracts for the installation of computer systems with building contracts, an equation not usually accepted by those interviewed.

being carried out by a minority of those engaged in the field; the 'conceptive ideology' (Cain, 1979) of the rest may be at best pragmatic, and at worst random.

Two other forms of knowledge should be mentioned, though they are in no way confined to the lawyers I have been describing. One arises from the international nature of the industry. Knowing and being known to US lawyers who might refer work was very significant for those wishing to act for US companies, and it was also important, since UK lawyers were often the links between US companies and Europe, to have a network of competent lawyers in different European countries to whom work could be referred.

The second is that, as I suggested earlier, some of what lawyers know is how to assess, acquire, manage, and promote the knowledge so far described.[20] Some of those interviewed recognized that they had to assess the skills required to perform certain tasks in the course of managing their departments, both in allocating work and in recruitment.[21] They were reflective about matters such as training, and the kind of literature they needed to keep up with. Above all, they were conscious of the need to promote their firms as having expertise, positioning themselves, where necessary, carefully to match the spectrum of skills available to them to a viable and identifiable presence in the market-place.[22]

CHARACTERISTICS OF LEGAL KNOWLEDGE

From the detailed account of lawyers' knowledge in this area, I turn to discuss some of its general characteristics. I here pick out three: its temporal aspects, the manner of its social construction and its segmentation. A fourth topic, the relationship of the knowledge to the interests of parties and the separate interests of lawyers, is discussed in the concluding section.

First, this knowledge changes: it has a temporal aspect, a history. One can date its beginnings in England, towards the end of the 1960s, its growth in sophistication, and its diffusion amongst more and more practitioners. In addition, within the history one can examine changes in characteristics which themselves have temporal aspects. Thus those interviewed could discuss whether the practice was tending towards stability, so that, at, say, the turn of the century, there would be no new

[20] Stebbings (1994) cites articles by Eraut for these second-order skills.
[21] For instance, a City firm had allocated its telecommunications work as needing four separate kinds of skill, ranging from general skills applicable to privatizations of all sorts, to highly technical skills for which it needed to recruit from the industry itself.
[22] Thus, multimedia work might need not just software skills, but the skills associated with work for the publishing and entertainment industries.

problems, or whether, on the other hand, the subject-matter ensured that new problems would always be arising.[23]

The second major characteristic is that the knowledge is largely, as indicated by Luhmann and Dezalay, socially constructed and internally validated. It is perhaps the more so because judicial decisions in this area tend to follow rather than be the subject of professional knowledge, and there is substantial professional input even into statute. In addition, 'real' expertise seems to be the domain of a comparatively small number of people who recognize each other as having a 'sufficient' grasp of the technology and how to apply general principles of law to it. Some of this mutual recognition is to be found in the membership of the London Computer Law Group, and the overlapping list of those mentioned as experts in the *Legal Business* article (1991). Others are associated with the Intellectual Property Committee of the British Computer Society, and the legal and intellectual property departments of major computer and software companies, this last group overlapping with lawyers associated with the Business Software Association, FAST (the Federation Against Software Theft), and FLAG (its Legal Advisory Group, to which several solicitors interviewed belonged), including US lawyers and lawyers for US companies in Europe. However, outside these groups, there is a wider range of practitioners involved in drafting computer systems contracts and representing smaller software houses, whose knowledge is less the subject of testing and sharpening by social and professional interaction.

As will have been seen from this discussion, a third characteristic of lawyers' knowledge is that it is segmented. It should not be seen as a system of concentric circles in which knowledge decreases the further one goes from the centre, whether the centre is conceived of as California, City firms, or any of the groups of specialists already mentioned. In very broad terms, California contains substantial expertise in the processes of capital formation for the start-up high-tech businesses associated with Silicon Valley's success and in generation of forms of protection, especially for semiconductor and software products, whereas Europe, and England in particular, has substantial expertise in the legal aspects of the distribution of computer-related products. Some City and niche firms have substantial expertise across the board, but in the field of large-scale international technology joint ventures, which has grown rapidly in importance since the mid-1980s, the opinion of a lawyer at a large computer company was that City firms did not have the expertise to handle them, and only a small group, all known to each other, of in-house lawyers at such companies could manage them. The intellectual prop-

---

[23] The answer probably depended on the particular field: computer-system contracts might indeed become a stable practice field, whereas some technologies, such as neural networks, seem capable of giving rise to unlimited problems.

erty protection (through patents, semiconductor mask legislation, and copyright) of computer products was substantially located in company in-house legal and intellectual-property departments, whereas the legal problems of incorporating large computer systems into companies' workings was more the domain of City, niche, and metropolitan solicitors. Finally, though, there are tendencies towards differential spatial location of knowledge; the more detailed knowledge is associated with London, and the area within the 'Western Crescent' (Hall *et al.*, 1987) where computer companies have tended to locate their headquarters functions (*ibid.*, 177).[24]

ACCOUNTING FOR KNOWLEDGE

While in accordance with Dezalay's approach I accept that much of the generation and mobilization of knowledge is entrepreneurial in nature, I would argue that one needs to pay more attention to the material underpinnings of these processes. One can ask what accounts for the state of lawyers' knowledge, and come up with a range of useful, even if not definitive, answers.

Since the industry was new, it gave lawyers little to start from and required bolder analogies than more traditionally-based industries might have done. Two of its products, semiconductor chips and software, were stores of innovation and value not easily translatable into existing forms, while the information computers could now carry, independent of any association with physical objects such as books, also gave rise to new analyses in the fields of data and database protection.

But there were also social characteristics of the industry which were important: its ubiquity, its rapid changes, its association with high technology, and the presence of competing interests within the industry and its customers. Here I touch only on the last. The history of the industry could be written as a changing balance of co-operation and competition. Without some standardization innovation would be hampered, since customers would be unable to make rational choices in a fragmented market-place, but without some degree of monopoly, it is argued, what was the incentive to innovate? At the time of the drafting of what became the European Software Directive of 1991, these tensions became apparent in the struggle between those who saw themselves as innovators in software seeking protection against competitors seeking to 'reverse

---

[24] A couple of exceptional individuals in metropolitan firms had trained in London firms, but it was one of them who thought that front-line expertise in the intellectual-property aspects of information technology would not be possible outside London.

engineer' their products so as to produce competitive software.[25] Users, too, have at least a short-term interest in the results of such competition, as well in some cases in being able to adapt code for their specific purposes. Governmental agencies, used to enacting into law a unified industry view on technical matters, were faced by lawyers and others advocating contrary interests, and a substantial body of literature representing those competing interests appeared and continues to appear. Thus, the pages of the *European Intellectual Property Review* were filled with articles which were aimed, often avowedly but sometimes not, at promoting one side or the other. Once it was made, further articles disseminated knowledge of developments favouring at least one of the sides. What purports to be a standard textbook seems to emanate, wholly or substantially, from the same camp, and each side has produced its own history (Clapes, 1993; Band and Katoh, 1995). But even in this context it does not seem that lawyers were taking positions favouring their own interests in any of the senses Dezalay describes.

The economic state of the industry could also affect lawyers' work, and so the content of their knowledge. It is probably true generally, and not just in this industry, that the middle 1980s were marked by an increased emphasis on intellectual property, both as a means of securing monopolies in a field and also as a means of securing a return on investment in research and development, as against an earlier period in which intellectual property was seen rather as a bargaining tool to secure access to technology developed by others. Intellectual property became a much more mainstream aspect of lawyers' work, and the level of competence, it was observed by a senior City solicitor, rose all round. As best I can tell, lawyers were responding to a client interest rather than actively promoting the area; attempts, for instance, at the active promotion of 'intellectual property audits' seem to have been unsuccessful. The client interest may have arisen from an increasing rationalization of industry in the mid-1980s. Later in the decade the recession was a principal cause of a change in the balance of power between suppliers and users. Whereas the former could previously rely on being able to contract on their standard forms, drawn up in-house or by specialist solicitors, increased competition made it possible and worthwhile for users to bargain over the terms, and several of those interviewed regarded this as having led to a widening of work on computer contracts.

---

[25] Reverse-engineering involves analysing the code of a program to discover its functionality, and then creating a new program with similar functionality but different code. Reverse-engineering is common in industry, but a problem mainly confined to software is that it cannot be carried out without performing acts which *prima facie* infringe the copyright in the program.

It is convenient to discuss together the role of technology and regulation in affecting lawyers' practice and knowledge, because of differences amongst those interviewed. For some it was not the technology that is important but the way it is regulated. They pointed out that although there was a convergence in the technology between computers and telecommunications the work was very different, because computers were a basically unregulated area, whereas telecommunications, which had been heavily regulated were in the process of being partially deregulated. Much of the work in the latter area was more in the nature of lobbying, requiring a knowledge of economics and an ability to think in broad terms on matters of principle, whereas the former involved matters of private right. The difference in the work and the kind of knowledge it involved is undeniable. It does not follow, however, that changes in the technology are unimportant.

A few examples should suffice. A principal event in the industry, with immediate legal consequences, was the 'unbundling' of software. Whereas, more or less up to the end of the 1960s, users bought or leased a machine to perform certain functions, it then became possible to acquire the hardware and software separately. Software became recognized as a clearly separate commodity, and questions of appropriate transactions and protection emerged. The research threw up an example of a consultation with a Q.C. on the possibility of emulation software soon afterwards, in 1972. The emergence of the personal computer, with the Apple II and the IBM PC in the United States, and the English ZX and Spectrum computers, created a mass-market for software, and a wider public willing to take the benefits of easy copying without contributing to its authors. Scepticism about the practicalities of legal protection led to a reliance on technical methods of copy protection, but there was still academic, professional, and commercial discussion of how to protect in legal terms software which was licensed, not sold, without direct contacts between the manufacturer and the user. Much ingenuity was spent on the construction of 'shrinkwrap licences', an import from the United States (as was most of the non-games software), which would be created by the opening of a shrink-wrapped packet which the user might reasonably suppose he had already 'bought'. Finally, the rise towards the end of the 1980s of client-server technology and of 'open systems', in which components might be bought from different vendors, also added to the bargaining power of users, with the consequences which have been referred to.

Changes in the political climate have also affected lawyers' work and the knowledge involved in it. The creation of a legal field by the deregulation of telecommunications has already been referred to, and the expertise has subsequently been available in the export market for East

European governments privatizing their formerly state-owned systems. More recently it seems that pressures from central government on local government and other authorities to contract out part of their operations were a significant element in facilities management work, in which all the data-processing work (often along with the employees) of an organization, whether a company or a local authority, was handed over to an external company. The legal work was described as complex, covering a wide range of issues. Outside the United Kingdom, the creation of the European Community and the extension of the Single Market had very significant effects on legal work. The significance of EC law has already been mentioned. In addition, companies from outside the EC had strong incentives (both the avoidance of tariffs and direct grants) to set up within it, and while their manufacturing plants might be in Eire or Scotland, it was common for their European headquarters to be in Southern England. The arrival of such companies, mainly from the early 1970s on, and their need for advice on local law and how to extend their operations through Europe, were cited by a number of firms as the beginning of their involvement in computer matters.

There will not be a legal field without some recognition. One form of recognition was given by academic interest, particularly the work of Colin Tapper. More generally, it became permissible and acceptable in the 1980s to become and to be seen as entrepreneurial, and to project and market specialities. City firms, in particular, reported that they were responding to client expectations in developing a computer-law speciality. While some firms promoted themselves actively, and there were complaints from others that clients would take legal advice on the purchase of a shed, but not on the purchase of a computer system with a cost in the hundreds of thousands or more, which might ruin their business if it was unsatisfactory, practically no one admitted to being in advance of what clients wanted, or even that that might be possible. On the whole, entrepreneurship, in Dezalay's sense, did not explain the existence of the field, or its main characteristics, though some firms positioned themselves better than others to meet clients' incipient demands.

One final point concerns the origins of some kinds of knowledge. In an area where lawyers have experience of multiple transactions and the clients do not (they buy, for instance, only one large computer system, or seek to profit out of their first major piece of technological innovation) lawyers come to be the repository of a great deal of industry information, licensing rates, for example, or structures for the exploitation of innovation.[26] This has been well described by Suchman (1994) for Silicon Valley, but a number of examples came up in the English interviews. It requires

[26] Universities and inventors were cited by one metropolitan solicitor as people for whom a lawyer might provide such advice.

a willingness by the client and the lawyer not to see the lawyer's role in too technical a light. Accountants may well also have such a role.

LAW AND LAWYERS' KNOWLEDGE

I started this piece by showing that authors had differed on the relationship of lawyers to the law. For some, the legal profession was expert in a separate subject, 'the law'. But for others, the law was part of lawyers' activities, constructed and in fact constituted by them. Academics in the field incline towards the latter view. Thus, Saxby (1990) describes those writing about information-technology law in the encyclopædia he was editing as 'potential law-makers', and another academic, speaking of a leading practitioner, said that 'his clauses have normative force'. It is plain that at the cutting edge much of what goes on is in fact concept-formation; the same academic said that what he and the leading practitioners did was very similar, 'blue sky' speculation about the way in which legal principles might be applied to an appropriate selection from the facts. As has been indicated, much statutory law was the product of industry pressure, mediated through legal experts whose judgement was accepted as authoritative, even if respect was also being paid to the importance of the companies which employed them. Examples were given to me of matters settled between acknowledged company expert and civil servant, though in this the Software Directive was a total exception. A more informal example was a situation in which the telecommunications authorities had decided on the permissibility of a new form of licence, but not the principles on which it should be granted. The applicant's lawyers found themselves invited to formulate acceptable new principles. This is an informal example of what may happen when firms advise on privatizations, in the United Kingdom or abroad. They advise on what are to be the principles of regulation, and may supplement a state which is weakened in Halliday's sense or wishes on principle to delegate its functions.

Thus, in parts of this field at any rate, the law is constituted by lawyers' activities; their knowledge is not of the law, but is the law. An American practitioner gives an example, talking about the possibilities of a claim for the protection of the appearance of a computer program on a screen, by analogy with the principles protecting a unique packaging. 'But talking about it at conferences is the very way to build a momentum so people will begin making trade dress claims', says Katherine C. Spelman, an intellectual property partner at San Francisco's Graham & James.' It takes four or five years of hearing about it at seminars before people start saying "Oh, that's not new", and they go and do it', she says. 'That's the value of those seminars. So much of it is like Peter Pan. You clap your hands and then Tinker Bell is alive.' (Slind-Flor, 1993).

In conclusion, I pull together a few threads in the previous discussion to answer for this context a question posed by Dezalay: if practitioners' knowledge is the law, is it, on the one hand, self-interested or client-oriented, or on the other objective and neutral? I found little or nothing to suggest that it was self-interested, unless the effort to produce law which was from the practitioners' point of view coherent and workable be seen as such. Perhaps closest came remarks by patent agents that they leaned, by training and occupation, in favour of protecting invention. It is true that it is patent agents who lean in favour of software patents (a comment made by a solicitor), but they seem to do so mainly in the interests of their clients. The evidence for action to further client interests seemed much stronger. Some legislative provisions certainly reflect the unopposed arguments of company representatives. But perhaps the European Software Directive, though unique in its circumstances, may stand for the wider process. In its final form it reflected fairly neatly a balance of economic forces and the political power they could mobilize; though lawyers were active, they were not forwarding any independent interest. The law they develop is not impartial, but it is not self-serving.

REFERENCES

ABBOTT, A. (1988), *The System of Professions: An Essay on the Division of Expert Labor* (University of Chicago Press, Chicago and London).

ABEL, R. L. (1979), 'The Rise of Professionalism', *British Journal of Law and Society* 6, 82.

—— (1989), *American Lawyers* (Oxford University Press, New York and Oxford).

—— and LEWIS, P. S. C. (1989), 'Putting Law Back into the Sociology of Lawyers', in R. L. Abel and P. S. C. Lewis (eds.), *Lawyers in Society: Comparative Theories* (University of California Press, Berkeley, Los Angeles, London).

BAND, J., and KATOH, M. (1995), *Interfaces on Trial: Intellectual Property and Interoperability in the Global Software Industry* (Westview Press, Boulder, Colo.).

BOURDIEU, P. (1987), 'The Force of Law: Toward a Sociology of the Juridical Field', *Hastings Law Journal* 38, 814.

CAIN, M. (1979), 'The General Practice Lawyer and the Client: Towards a Radical Conception', *International Journal of the Sociology of Law* 7, 331.

CHIROT, F. (1988), 'Entremetteurs pour capitaux en fusion', *Le Monde Affaires*, 28 May.

CLAPES, A. L. (1993), *Softwars: The Legal Battle for the Control of the Global Software Industry* (Quorum Books, Westport, Conn.).

CUNNINGHAM, J. M. (1993), 'What Is a High Tech Lawyer? An Essay in Self-Definition', *The Computer Lawyer* 10, 23.

DEZALAY, Y. (1991), 'Territorial Battles and Tribal Disputes', 54 *Modern Law Review* 792.

—— (1992), *Marchands de droit: la restructuration de l'ordre juridique interna-tional par les multinationales de droit* (Fayard, Paris).

—— (1993), 'Professional Competition and the Social Construction of Transnational Regulatory Expertise', in J. McCahery, S. Picciotto, and C. Scott (eds.), *Corporate Control and Accountability: Changing Structures and the Dynamics of Regulation* (Clarendon Press, Oxford).

—— (1995), 'Technological Warfare: The Battle to Control the Mergers and Acquisition Market in Europe', in Y. Dezalay and D. Sugarman (eds.), *Professional Competition and Professional Power: Lawyers, Accountants and the Social Construction of Markets* (Routledge, London and New York).

FREIDSON, E. (1970), *Profession of Medicine: A Study in the Sociology of Applied Knowledge* (Dodd, Mead, New York).

—— (1986), *Professional Powers: A Study of the Institutionalization of Formal Knowledge* (University of Chicago Press, Chicago and London).

HALL, P., BREHENY, M., McQUAID, R., and HART, D. (1987), *Western Sunrise: The Genesis and Growth of Britain's Major High Tech Corridor* (Allen and Unwin, London).

HALLIDAY, T. C. (1987), *Beyond Monopoly: Lawyers, State Crises and Professional Empowerment* (University of Chicago Press, Chicago and London).

LARSON, M. (1977), *The Rise of Professionalism: A Sociological Analysis* (University of California Press, Berkeley, Los Angeles, London).

LEGAL BUSINESS (1991), 'Highly Recommended: IT Lawyers Choose their Favourite Expert', March, 57.

LUHMANN, N. (1976), 'The Legal Profession: Comments on the Situation in the Federal Republic of Germany', in N. MacCormick (ed.), *Lawyers in their Social Setting* (Green, Edinburgh).

MACAULAY, S. (1979), 'Lawyers and Consumer Protection Laws', *Law and Society Review* 14, 115.

McBARNET, D. (1984), 'Law and Capital: The Role of Legal Form and Legal Actors', *International Journal of the Sociology of Law* 12, 231–8.

—— (1988), 'Law, Policy, and Legal Avoidance: Can Law Effectively Implement Egalitarian Policies?', in R. Cotterrell and B. Bercusson (eds.), *Law, Democracy and Social Justice* (special issue of *Journal of Law and Society*), 113–21.

—— (1992), 'The Construction of Compliance and the Challenge for Control: The Limits of Noncompliance Research', in J. Slemrod (ed.), *Why People Pay Taxes: Tax Compliance and Enforcement* (University of Michigan Press, Ann Arbor, Mich.).

—— and WHELAN, C. (1991), 'The Elusive Spirit of the Law: Formalism and the Struggle for Legal Control', 54 *Modern Law Review* 848–73.

McCAHERY, J., and PICCIOTTO, S. (1995), 'Creative Lawyering and the Dynamics of Business Regulation', in Y. Dezalay and D. Sugarman (eds.), *Professional Competition and Professional Power: Lawyers, Accountants and the Social Construction of Markets* (Routledge, London and New York).

MILLARD, C. (1993), 'Copyright', in C. Reed (ed.), *Computer Law* (2nd edn., Blackstone Press, London).

PATENT OFFICE. (1994), *Legal Protection for Software Related Innovation: A Report of the Public Forum held at the United Kingdom Patent Office on October 19, 1994.*

POWELL, M. (1993), 'Professional Innovation: Corporate Lawyers and Private Law-Making', *Law and Social Inquiry* 18, 423.

REED, C. (1993a), 'Liability', in C. Reed (ed.), *Computer Law* (2nd edn., Blackstone Press, London).

—— (1993b), 'Electronic Data Interchange,' in C. Reed (ed.), *Computer Law* (2nd edn., Blackstone Press, London).

RUESCHEMEYER, D. (1964), 'Doctors and Lawyers: A Comment on the Theory of the Professions', *Canadian Review of Sociology and Anthropology* 1, 17.

SAXBY, S. (1990), 'Preface', in S. Saxby (ed.), *Encyclopædia of Information Technology Law* (Sweet & Maxwell, London).

SIMPSON, A. W. B. (1973), 'The Common Law and Legal Theory', in A. W. B. Simpson (ed.), *Oxford Essays in Jurisprudence: Second Series* (Clarendon Press, Oxford).

SLIND-FLOR, V. (1993), '"Trade Dress" Seen to Protect Trademarks', *National Law Journal*, May 17.

STEBBINGS, A. M. (1994), 'Implementing a Competence System in the Professions: From Theory to Practice. The New Law Society Skills Standards', *International Journal of the Legal Profession* 1, 97–107.

SUCHMAN, M. (1994), 'On the Role of Law Firms in the Structuration of Silicon Valley', DPRP 11–7 (Institute for Legal Studies, University of Wisconsin Law School, Madison,Wis.).

8

Creative Compliance and the Defeat of Legal Control: The Magic of the Orphan Subsidiary[1]

DOREEN McBARNET AND CHRISTOPHER J. WHELAN

One of the pleasures of working under the Directorship of Don Harris was the unequivocal encouragement he gave to us to research previously unexplored areas in socio-legal studies. The Centre's programme on business, finance, and the law has been one outcome and it has proved a most fruitful area of study. Yet, at the time it began it was a risky strategy for both the Centre and those involved in the programme. For the Centre it meant a long-term commitment was being made to an area whose 'researchability' was untested, and indeed frequently doubted. For us and others, it involved a major investment in the acquisition of new skills and knowledge as well as a willingness to move beyond research 'origins'—in our case criminal justice and labour law. It is no small irony that the research has itself evolved into a study of the regulation of risk (in the context of corporate finance). The research would not have been possible without Don's creation of an environment which fostered freedom of thought, and the pursuit of new lines of inquiry. In this Chapter we shall explore one of the central themes of the research programme—the concept of 'creative compliance'—and the challenge it poses for legal control.

The practice of 'creative compliance' raises significant issues for our understanding of the operation of law and society. One issue of particular concern for both theory and policy is that of securing effective legal control. While many studies in law and society have researched the failure of legal control, focusing especially on the issue of enforcement, there has been little empirical research or analysis of the particular challenge posed for legal control by creative compliance.

---

[1] This Ch. is based on empirical research on business finance and the law funded by the Jacob Burns Fund for Socio-Legal Studies, the Economic and Social Research Council, and the European Commission. The research was based on analysis of legal and accounting data, the financial press, and on interviews with lawyers, accountants, consultants, bankers, and regulatory authorities. Where data collected from confidential interviews have become the subject of public discussion we have presented references for the reader's information.

Creative compliance involves avoiding law's requirements without actually contravening them. It involves creative use of the 'material' of law (McBarnet, 1984) to construct devices which comply with the letter of the law, while nonetheless escaping from legal control. One strand of Centre research demonstrates and analyses the practice of creative compliance in the context of tax, 'tax avoidance' being a familiar concept to layman and lawyer alike (McBarnet, 1988, 1991, 1992; Mansfield, 1994). But the practice of creative compliance is not confined to tax. Nor indeed is it confined to public law and state regulation; private law, as we shall see, is just as susceptible.

Creative compliance can be an expensive strategy, requiring major inputs in legal technicality and innovation. It is therefore characteristically—though perhaps not inevitably—a feature of the world of economic elites and large-scale corporations, in corporate finance, taxation, takeovers, and bankruptcy, or in battles for market share. In this context legal control—both state regulations and the controls of private law—can become just another obstacle to be overcome in the pursuit of economic and competitive advantage (McBarnet and Whelan, 1992).

In this Chapter we show creative compliance at work in the context of corporate finance. This is a complex and technical area, with many different techniques of creative compliance involved, and our research as a whole deals in detail with a wide range of devices and situations (McBarnet and Whelan, forthcoming). This Chapter will illustrate the role of creative compliance by examining the use of just one device in one specific context, the spate of mega-takeovers in the late 1980s in which astonishing sums of money were raised by sometimes relatively small acquiring companies as accomplishments of 'sheer magic'. It demonstrates how creative compliance provided the magic spell for accomplishing these feats for management. But it also analyses the other side of the coin, the risks that creative compliance can obscure, and the challenge creative compliance poses for effective legal control.

MEGA-TAKEOVERS AND LEGAL OBSTACLES

The late 1980s saw a spate of mega-takeovers with vast sums raised through creative corporate financing techniques, including but extending far beyond the now notorious 'junk bonds'. The corporate debt created was unprecedented. KKR's leveraged buyout of RJR Nabisco cost $25.08 billion, resulting in borrowings for the new RJR of $22.08 billion, more than the combined national debts of Bolivia, Uruguay, Costa Rica, Honduras, and Jamaica (*Sunday Times*, 4 December 1988). A major part of the scene was acquisition of US corporations by UK companies. In

1988, for example, there were 389 such acquisitions (*Accountancy*, October 1990, 66). Some of these were takeovers of very large US corporate groups by relatively small UK companies. While there may have been some regulatory advantages available to British companies in such takeovers against their US competitors, there were also many legal and market constraints; indeed on the face of it, the acquisitions in the late 1980s of US Goliaths by UK Davids seemed to be an achievement of the impossible. Vast sums of money had to be raised—often in excess of the acquiring company's own value.

One remarkable example was the takeover of the second-largest American aggregates (sand and gravel) corporation for $1.81 billion (£977 million) by a relatively small British company whose own total share value was just half that amount (£486 million). 'Unbelievable! Sheer magic!' was how one analyst (Angus Phaure, of County NatWest, *Accountancy*, April 1988, 9) described the deal which the British company C. H. Beazer put together with a British and two American banks to take over Koppers, the Pittsburgh-based corporation in 1988. When its chairman Brian Beazer inherited the sixty-year old, Bath-based, company, in 1983 (from his father, its founder), it was only the fourth largest housebuilder in the United Kingdom. How did the Beazer group manage to raise the finance to take over a US company worth twice its own value?

Raising the money to acquire a company worth double your own value poses a major problem at any time. But there were particular problems for the group at the time of this acquisition. It would have been difficult, if not impossible, for Beazer to have issued shares to raise finance to pay for as large a proposed acquisition as Koppers. This was 1988, just after the October 1987 'crash' of world stock markets. In any case, Beazer may also have been reluctant to raise finance in this way having done so throughout the 1980s when it 'absorbed nine large acquisitions' (*Sunday Times*, 30 June 1991), including French Kier (£144 million—1986), Christian Salvesen (£13 million—1986), MP Kent (£34 million—1984), and William Leech (£25 million—1985) (*Financial Times*, 27 June 1991).

This process of issuing new shares ('*paper*') via rights issues meant that between 1983, when Brian Beazer took over the company, and 1988, the number of shares issued by the company rose from 12 million to 300 million (*Financial Times*, 25 April 1991). In these circumstances the issue of dilution arises—individual share value may fall as the number of shares grows—and this can be a cause for concern among shareholders. This process culminated in the takeover in 1986 of another American corporation, Gifford Hill (a cement producer), for £200 million. But the share issue for this takeover was not entirely successful: it was less than three-quarters subscribed (*Financial Times*, 25 April 1991).

In May 1987, an alternative method of raising finance—an American

Depositary Receipt (ADR)—was attempted in the United States. ADRs are dollar-denominated and dividends are paid to ADR holders in dollars. Through the mechanism of the ADR, American institutional investors were able to hold and trade a bundle of Beazer's shares represented by the ADR. But the ADR issue had to be 'scaled down' because it caused 'uproar' among British institutional investors (*Sunday Times*, 6 March 1988).

This outcry, together with an expression of concern over the Gifford Hill share issue, led chairman Brian Beazer to state that he would not use this method of financing again: 'there would be no more paper' (*Sunday Times*, 6 March 1988). To buy Koppers, Beazer therefore had to use debt rather than equity.

In this the Beazer takeover was not alone. Many major takeovers at this time were also 'highly leveraged', based on vast levels of debt. Maxwell Communication Corporation's takeover of the US publishing company Macmillan for $2.6 billion was also a highly leveraged acquisition. So, on the domestic front, was Brent Walker's takeover of bookmakers William Hill. Highly leveraged acquisitions were a feature of the late 1980s. And this is where the analysts' expressions of astonishment come in. For seeking to raise money on this scale via debt has the potential to introduce a number of major legal and market obstacles to management's goals.

Burdening a company with huge quantities of debt can destroy its market value. It can also trigger public and private legal controls such as restrictive covenants, shareholder rights to consultation or veto or, in the specific context of takeovers, regulatory obstacles to sharebuilding in target companies. The key to triggering many of these market and legal obstacles lies in the company's accounts and in the legal requirement to disclose financial information. Many legal controls over management action, such as shareholder powers or restrictive covenants, are founded on company accounts.

The Regulatory Context

Financial reporting lies at the heart of law governing companies in many countries as a means of protection for third parties, particularly shareholders and potential investors, but also employees and creditors. In the United Kingdom, accounting techniques also come under the regulation of the profession. The Accounting Standards Board (ASB), and its predecessor, the Accounting Standards Committee (ASC)) issues Financial Reporting Standards (previously Statements of Standard Accounting Practice). These are rules of professional conduct applicable to all financial statements: 'authoritative statements on accountancy practice'

(Ernst & Young, 1990, 8). The stated purpose of accounts is, as the law puts it, 'to give a true and fair view' of a company's financial performance and value, or, as the profession has put it more generally, 'to assist the user's understanding of an enterprise's affairs by presenting condensed, structured information on the resources, obligations and performance of the reporting enterprise'. (ASC, 1988)

The UK companies taking over US corporations were regulated primarily by UK company law and accounting standards. The Companies Act 1985 required accounting records to be kept by all companies, to show and explain the company's transactions, and to disclose with reasonable accuracy the financial position of the company at any particular time. There are three parts to company accounts:

(i) a balance sheet—a set of numbers which sets out the company's assets (either fixed assets acquired for use in the business, such as property and machinery, or current assets (cash or cash-related assets such as stock and debtors (money owed)) and liabilities (current and long-term claims against the company's assets) together with any residual interest, that is, the capital and reserves that make up the 'balance' between the assets and the liabilities. This information relates to the *value* or worth of the company;

(ii) a profit and loss account—another set of numbers which sets out the company's results of the last year (including turnover (sales), profit from ordinary activities, income from extraordinary activities, charges, or costs). This information relates to the *performance* of the company and indicates the amount available for distribution as a dividend to the owners (shareholders) of the company;

(iii) notes to the accounts—a combination of words and numbers that provide additional information.

The form and content of company accounts are regulated by the very detailed provisions of Schedule 4 to the Act which sets out the rules and formats to be used in presenting accounts.

The objective that the 1985 Act required (and requires) of accounts was that they give 'a true and fair view': by the balance sheet, of the state of affairs of the company as at the end of the financial year; by the profit and loss account, of the performance of the company for the financial year. The requirement to provide a true and fair view was overriding (Companies Act 1985, section 228(3)): even specific statutory rules could be departed from in order to give a true and fair view. The requirement has been described by leading academic accountants as the 'paramount principle' of accounting (Nobes and Parker, 1984, 82).

Most large and many small businesses operate not as a single company but as a group of companies, comprising a parent or holding company and one or more subsidiaries. A group normally operates as a single economic unit with shared top management and control (EC, 1976, 19) so that, although each subsidiary may be a separate company (with its own individual accounts), the interests of companies in a group are closely linked, and the value and performance of any one company may be affected by its relationship with others in the group. In addition to each company producing individual accounts, therefore, there has been a legal requirement under the Companies Acts since 1947 for the directors of the parent company in a group to produce accounts for the whole group. These are group financial statements which take the form of consolidated accounts: a consolidated balance sheet and a consolidated profit and loss account. The group accounts must include all companies which are subsidiaries (or 'subsidiary undertakings' post-1989) of the main or parent company in order to give a true and fair view of the overall picture of the group's financial status and performance for a particular year.

The Companies Act 1985 not only provides detailed rules on disclosure of financial information, it also regulates the policing and enforcement of the law. It does this in several ways. Company accounts have to be approved by the board of directors and a copy delivered to the Registrar of Companies, who will file them in publicly available files. Company accounts are examined by the company auditors who must make a report. In this they must state whether in their opinion the accounts have been properly prepared in accordance with the Act, and whether a true and fair view has been given. The auditors' role, their rights and duties, their relationship with the company are all subject to regulation by the Companies Acts.

Corporate Governance

The legal requirement to disclose financial information is a fundamental element in corporate governance, the basis of management accountability to the company's owners. It is also the basis of many legal and market controls over management. Market assessment and comparability between companies is based on ratios drawn from the figures in the accounts in order, for example, to assess performance (e.g. via earnings per share), estimate the investment potential via the value of shares and expected future earnings (price earnings ratio), measure the degree to which owners (equity financing) or creditors (debt financing) have financed a company (known as gearing in the United Kingdom, or leverage in the United States), and evaluate the financial condition and liquidity of a company (current ratio).

Massive debt on a relatively small equity base means 'high leverage' or 'high gearing'. In Beazer's case, for example, purchase of Koppers by Beazer taking on massive debt would produce a ratio where the debt would dwarf the equity, with potentially adverse consequences in the market. Existing shareholders may become unhappy if they feel too much debt is being taken on, or their stake is being put at risk. Unhappy shareholders may exercise market power by selling their shares or threatening to do so, thereby reducing share price and the value of the company. We have seen how shareholder concern had already been expressed prior to the Koppers takeover when the number of shares issued by Beazer had risen dramatically to fund acquisitions. As a result, earnings per share, which is important to a company share price, had risen more slowly than it would have otherwise (*Financial Times*, 3 June 1988). But there may be more for management to contend with than the unhappiness, and potential market response, of shareholders. There may also be the matter of their legal rights and powers.

A company's accounts are significant not simply as a means of informing shareholders of the performance and financial status of a company. They also form the basis of specific mechanisms of control over management. The public law requirement to file annual accounts is also a foundation for private law controls, on an ongoing basis. The ratios referred to above are often used in a company's memorandum and articles of association as the basis of shareholder power. For management, at any particular time, to exceed a specified ratio of, for example, debt to equity, it may be legally required by the company's constitution to have shareholder approval.

There are other controls over management based on ratios drawn from the accounts. Existing creditors such as lending banks might well have restrictive covenants in place in the contract of loan to protect themselves by preventing excessive additional debt being undertaken. Specified gearing ratios may be built into these covenants. If the borrowing company goes ahead and takes out more debt, the ratio may be exceeded and the company will be in breach of the covenant. The existing bank lender may then invoke contractual clauses which allow it to commence action to recover the sums lent. This might include placing the company into bankruptcy.

In addition, in the specific context of takeovers, there can be, in general law or in, for example, Stock Exchange listing regulations, other regulatory obstacles to predatory stakebuilding in a target company without public disclosure, or there may be regulations requiring shareholder consent.

There are, then, a number of significant legal obstacles to be faced in raising vast sums of debt or engaging in major takeovers. Yet none of these may affect management at all—*not* necessarily because shareholders, lenders, and the market have given their blessing to management plans, but because the potential legal controls over management are simply kept out of play. Highly leveraged takeovers can in practice be accomplished without upsetting market ratios, without triggering shareholder controls, without breaching covenants, and without breaking the law. How? The answer lies in creative compliance.

CREATIVE COMPLIANCE IN ACTION: THE ORPHAN SUBSIDIARY

There is a whole range of creative devices through which the legal requirements to report financial information, including potential liabilities such as large-scale debt in a company's accounts, can, in practice, be circumvented. One simple but potent device, which was used in a number of highly leveraged takeovers, was one known as a 'controlled non-subsidiary', 'non-subsidiary subsidiary', 'controlled dependent company', or 'quasi-subsidiary'. We will refer to it as an 'orphan subsidiary', for reasons which will become clear below. Using an orphan subsidiary provided an escape route from legal constraints, yet it operated in compliance with them. Indeed it was constructed with legal building blocks.

The device of the orphan subsidiary operates in the context of the requirement to produce consolidated accounts for a group of companies. Without this requirement it would be possible for company A to enhance its own reported balance sheet and performance, by keeping major debts, for example, hidden away in a controlled but legally separate subsidiary company B, whose full liabilities would appear in B's but not in A's accounts.

Although the exposure of each company in the group may theoretically be limited by a corporate structure in which each company in the group is a separate legal entity with limited liability and directors are not entitled to sacrifice the interests of their company to the interests of the group, in practice the interconnection of interests may be such that a parent company may be constrained to rescue a failing subsidiary. Tolley notes that this is assumed to be 'good commercial practice' (Tolley, 1988, 662); the Cork Committee acknowledged that it was common practice for directors to consider the interests of other companies in the group (Cork, 1982, paragraph 1951); it may even be argued that it is the duty of directors of company A to rescue subsidiary company B if their interests are intertwined. In practice, therefore, the risk of losing credibility—and creditworthiness—may force a parent to rescue a subsidiary. In short, the risk-exposure of one company may in practice be affected by others in the group to a greater extent than the principle of limited liability might suggest: the whole picture of the whole group is therefore necessary to be able to make commercial assessments. Likewise, where management controls several dependent companies, management performance can only be fully assessed in relation to the whole picture of the group.

It is this whole picture which group consolidated accounts should provide. It cannot be obtained from the individual accounts of each company on its own. Only through the provision of consolidated accounts, said the European Commission, was it 'possible to obtain a true and fair view of the economic and financial position of the group, and through it, a more complete picture of the position of the individual company' (EC, 1976, 19). The legal requirement to produce consolidated accounts should mean that 'bad news' cannot be hidden away in a controlled dependent subsidiary: the performance of the group as a whole, *all* the assets and liabilities, and *all* the revenue and expenses should be disclosed. But what if 'bad news', such as massive debts, can be housed in a company which is controlled, dependent, but *not*, according to the strict letter of the law, a subsidiary? Debts and risky transactions would no longer appear in the group accounts. They would be 'off the balance sheet' of the 'parent' company, even if the 'parent' should prove ultimately responsible for them; they would be *orphan subsidiaries*. How could this be done?

The Orphan Subsidiary

In the 1980s, the Companies Acts (before amendment by the Companies Act 1989, of which more later) spawned a number of ways of structuring companies which were the offspring of their 'parent' companies, were controlled by and totally dependent on them, but in law were not subsidiaries and were thus conveniently excluded from group accounts. According to the letter of the law, they had no parents. They did not have to be consolidated in the group accounts of the companies that controlled them.

Under the Companies Act 1985 (section 736(1)) provisions, there were two questions to determine if a company was a subsidiary:

(a) does the holding company control more than half in nominal value of the subsidiary's equity share capital; or

(b) is the holding company a member of the subsidiary and does it control the composition of the board of directors?

If a company could be constructed so that the answer to both questions was in the negative then a parent–subsidiary relationship had not been created; the company would be an 'orphan subsidiary' and the debts of the orphan would not therefore have to be disclosed in the controlling group's accounts. A number of legal methods could be used to avoid the creation of this relationship by achieving the requisite negative answers. Some structures were simple, others very complex indeed. Each could be customized to meet the particular circumstances and needs. One of the simplest structures was as follows. First, the subsidiary company would issue share capital combining two types of shares, ordinary shares and preference shares. Preference shares confer preference as to income and capital, or both, over the ordinary share capital of the company. The ordinary shares and preference shares would be issued in equal numbers with an identical nominal value, the ordinary shares to the parent company and the preferential shares to the parent company's bank. Thus, half the shares were held by the parent, half by the bank; the parent did not own more than half.

Secondly, the articles of association (the constitution) of the new company would be drafted to ensure that the parent company and its bank had the right to appoint an equal number of directors. In this way, the parent company did *not* have the power unilaterally to appoint or remove the holders of all or a majority of the directorships of the 'subsidiary', so that control over the number of directors—the composition of the board of directors—was not in the hands of the parent company. Despite lack of control over the composition of the board, the parent company could still have effective control of the decisions of the board by giving directors appointed by the holders of ordinary shares (that is, the parent company's directors) special voting rights, say, two votes, to the preferential shareholders' directors' one vote. Moreover, if the parent company was not a 'member' of the 'subsidiary' (those who subscribe their names, for example, by buying shares, to a memorandum of association: Companies Act, section 22) then it could control the composition of the board of directors without having to treat the company as a subsidiary.

The law, of course, also included more general provisions. It required companies 'to give a true and fair view' of its profit and loss account and balance sheet, and auditors were required to sign off accounts on this basis. If companies structured as orphans were 'really' controlled by a group and dependent on it, should the group not be required, regardless of its compliance with other specific provisions of the Act, to consolidate? In the context of the 1980s this was not, however, how law was being interpreted and applied. Indeed in the *Argyll* case (see Ashton, 1986), directors consolidated a company in its 1979 accounts on the ground that the accounts would be more true and fair as a result of so doing. But they were successfully prosecuted on the basis that the company did not meet the strict criteria for consolidation in the Companies

Act of the time. Moreover the Department of Trade had issued an author-itative statement to back this up, stressing the need for strict compliance with the law (Department of Trade, 1982). We deal with this, why this line was taken, and its consequences, in detail elsewhere (McBarnet and Whelan, forthcoming). One result, however, was that in this context there was a clear basis for claiming that an orphan subsidiary *could not* be lawfully included in a group's accounts, and indeed that directors faced prosecution and conviction if they did so.

In the 1980s a number of structures, from the simple so-called 'dia-mond' to highly complex multiple-tiered structures (combining differ-ent distribution and voting rights, and various types of shares (Tolley, 1988, 648–9)) were created to meet the Companies Act requirements but avoid consolidation and thus disclosure. Through the structure of the orphan subsidiary, massive debt could be created without it being con-solidated in a group's accounts. The acquiring company was structured such that it was not part of the group, but was an orphan subsidiary.

The Beazer Takeover

The structure of Beazer's acquisition demonstrates the role of the orphan. With the American banks, Shearson Lehman Brothers and Citibank, and the British NatWest Investment Bank, Beazer set up a financial and legal package 'of mindnumbing complexity' (James Buchan, *Financial Times*, 3 June 1988) but certainly not atypically so in the world of corporate finance. The diagram below sets out the basic structure.

At the heart of this complex structure was an American orphan sub-sidiary, set up by Beazer, NatWest, and Shearson, as BNS Inc. Beazer held 49 per cent of the shares, a subsidiary of SLB 46.1 per cent, and a sub-sidiary of NatWest 4.9 per cent. It was BNS that would raise the money and make the takeover. The total consideration required to finance the purchase of Koppers' shares came to approximately $1.81 billion. This was provided by the partners' equity investment in BNS of $50 million (of which Beazer contributed $24.5 million), $241 million 20 per cent redeemable cumulative preferred stock in a BNS subsidiary (provided by Beazer), $97 million loan to a BNS subsidiary (also provided by Beazer), $879 million syndicated bank loan (from Citibank and a syndicate of banks), and the issue of $540 million subordinated loan to a BNS sub-sidiary subscribed from Shearson Lehman. This financing would be on BNS's balance sheet rather than on Beazer's, and the Beazer Group's accounts would be protected.

Table: Financing the Koppers Takeover

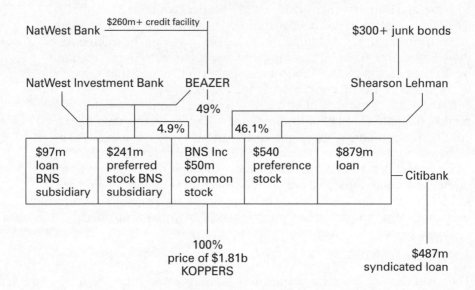

(*Source*: Directors' Report, Beazer Group Accounts, year ending 30 June 1988; table adapted from *Corporate Finance*, April 1988, p. 6)

Legal Obstacles and the Orphan Subsidiary

The orphan subsidiary has been used frequently as a vehicle for raising finance on a large scale. It was the device employed by Beazer, by Maxwell, by Brent Walker, and by many others to make their highly leveraged takeovers in the late 1980s.

Using an orphan subsidiary does not necessarily mean there is no disclosure of information. In many of these high-profile takeovers, including Maxwell's and Beazer's, much was discussed in the press or in announcements made to shareholders or the public more generally, so disclosure in one form did take place. In September 1988, for example, Brian Beazer made presentations to shareholders to reassure them about the company's borrowings. However, such informal disclosure does not always occur.

It is also possible that disclosure may be made, not in the balance sheet or profit and loss account, but in the notes to the accounts. When the tender offer was announced for Koppers, Brian Beazer stated that 'shareholders would be provided with pro-forma balance sheet information over and above that required by statute' (Chairman's Report, Beazer Accounts, 30 June 1988). This was done as promised 'as if the interests of the outside shareholders of BNS Inc had been acquired by the group'. But not all note disclosure is so informative. The Accounting Standards Committee (ASC, 1987) criticized some disclosure in notes as providing only inadequate and 'anodyne' descriptions of the arrangements. What is more, the two types of disclosure may have very different implications, for control and for market assessment. Disclosure in the notes provides information; disclosure in the accounts affects the key ratios which so often form the basis of corporate governance controls.

Through the orphan subsidiary massive finance can be raised without it appearing on the balance sheet, upsetting the ratios, and operating legal triggers. Accounts-based market indicators such as earnings per share and gearing are protected. Potential legal controls which predatory companies might face, such as restrictive covenants and shareholder rights in the memorandum and articles of association, can be success-fully managed. The orphan subsidiary provides the magic spell for accomplishing management goals despite a range of potential legal hurdles.

RISK

The magic of devices such as the orphan subsidiary may, however, have a downside. While disclosure and corporate governance hurdles may be bypassed and group accounts may exclude the orphan's liabilities, expo-sure to risk may nonetheless remain. After all, how does an orphan sub-sidiary raise money when it has no assets of its own? There are several possibilities with the parent playing a key role. Some of these will have to be disclosed by the parent. For example, if the parent provides a 'guar-antee' for the orphan, it will have to be disclosed as a contingent liability. Others, however, will not, or would not in the late 1980s, require disclo-sure. For example, a parent could 'sell' assets to the orphan while retain-ing an option to buy them back at a later date at a fixed price. In law, ownership of the assets may have passed; in substance, however, the transaction is not a transfer of ownership via a sale but a loan secured on the assets.

In the Beazer case, other methods were employed. First, Beazer pur-chased 49 per cent of the common stock of BNS (at a cost of $24.5 mil-lion). Secondly, Beazer provided unsecured loans to the subsidiary ($97 million). Thirdly, and most importantly, investment in the orphan by third parties was encouraged by the use of options. Beazer had a 'call' option to purchase the BNS shares held by the banks. If this option was not exercised within five years, the banks could exercise their 'put' option which would require Beazer to purchase their shares at any time between five and a half and six years.

The options provided two advantages, one for the Beazer group and one for the banks. For the Beazer group, they provided a five-year 'window' in which to sort out the takeover, sell off some assets, reduce debt or restructure it with more manageable interest rates, before taking Koppers onto its own balance sheet in a state which would, if all went to plan, have little or no adverse impact on the group's accounts. The banks knew that, after five years, if they still owned BNS shares, they could dispose of them if they wanted to, at an agreed price, regardless of performance. The price of the BNS stock was agreed in advance whether the call or put options were exercised: the banks would get a price equivalent to a 25 per cent *per annum* compound interest equivalent on their equity stakes (*Corporate Finance*, April 1988, 6). In this sense the $25.5 million subscribed by the banks was just like a loan to Beazer.

During the bid Brian Beazer announced that the bulk of the borrowings raised to fund the purchase was not guaranteed by the company and would never be so unless the board wanted to do so: '[t]here is no attempt to hide the figures' he was quoted as saying (*The Times*, 23 March 1988). He also stated that he would have sought shareholder approval had the financing been on a recourse basis by guaranteeing BNS. But there was in practice no need to do this (although it was considered as a way of getting round a US court injunction (*Financial Times*, 1 June 1988)). Using an orphan subsidiary and options rather than guarantees avoided this.

In practice, however, BNS immediately became a *de facto* subsidiary of Beazer. This was recognized by Brian Beazer himself when he stated that the group had 'had management control of Koppers for some 4 months', adding that 'Koppers will prove to be an excellent acquisition' (Chairman's Statement, Accounts for the year ended 30 June 1988). Whether or not the options were exercised, Beazer in effect had both control of BNS and responsibility for its debts. The options provided the legal mechanism for that control and for ensuring that ultimately BNS would become a *de jure* (wholly-owned) subsidiary of Beazer. When that occurred, not only would Beazer have to assume another $25.5 million of investment, but it would then have to consolidate BNS and bring the BNS debts into the Beazer group accounts. In the meantime, however, that requirement was avoided.

The solution to the question of how a company like BNS, with no assets, could raise so much finance, is simple: Beazer, not BNS, carried the risk. Ultimately, of course, the banks carried the risk. If Beazer had collapsed during the five-year window—or walked away from its commercial responsibilities to BNS—the banks would have borne losses—so-called 'bad debts'. But this would hardly improve the situation of Beazer shareholders, creditors, and employees.

In short, whether the acquisition proved profitable or not, the legal reality was that Beazer could still not escape the ultimate requirement to buy out its partners after 1993. The commercial reality was that, while the loans to BNS were not technically guaranteed, commercial risks did fall on Beazer. The use of the device of the orphan subsidiary together with the put and call options, however, meant that these risks were, quite lawfully, off-balance sheet.

The significance may be underlined by the subsequent collapse of another company in which Beazer had an interest. Beazer announced an extraordinary provision of £29 million pounds in its interim results for March 1990 against its involvement in the Australian company, Girvan, which had been placed in receivership (a form of bankruptcy procedure). The involvement was off-balance sheet: it was not incorporated in Beazer's accounts. Shares dropped 4 per cent at the news. One financial commentator observed that a 4 per cent drop 'might seem excessive. . . . But it is unsettling to hear of the demise of an Australian investment whose existence could not have been inferred from the accounts' (Lex, *Financial Times*, 31 January 1990). Yet, as the law stood, these off-balance sheet vehicles were perfectly legal.

The structure of a deal can therefore involve risks even if, in strict compliance with the letter of the law, they are not written into the accounts. The actual exposure may depend on how well strategies pan out in practice. In the Beazer case developments after the takeover suggest that the $1.8 billion deal in fact proved too big to handle.

A Deal Too Far?

The intention had always been, if the bid was successful, to replace the original borrowings in December 1988 by 'merger finance' of $1.83 billion. This would have included the refinancing of most of the $540 million subordinated loan subscribed by Shearson by the issue of $570 million high-yielding debt securities (junk bonds) by Koppers, thereby reducing the high level of interest repayments required under the bridging scheme, and to pay it off by way of asset sales (disposals of parts of the Koppers group). In other words, the plan was to restructure the debt in order to avoid the high-interest loan notes. Beazer had not expected to complete this task before the summer of 1989 at the earliest (*Corporate Finance*, December 1988, 8).

But this plan still involved refinancing at junk-bond levels of interest—18 per cent plus at the time. This could have undermined the overall earnings of the company. There was an alternative: Beazer could buy out the banks earlier and save on interest charges, but this would undermine the balance sheet.

As it turned out, the latter route was adopted. Restructuring occurred early, following a $2.3 billion refinancing of the debt, in October 1988, underwritten by a syndicate of banks: Citibank, National Westminster Bank, Barclays Bank, and Mellon Bank (*Financial Times*, 15 November 1988). This included $400 million loan finance pending disposals. The funding allowed the call options to be exercised and Koppers to be consolidated on 1 January 1989. As a result, an estimated $25 million a year in interest charges was saved by the Beazer group (Alan Chapple, Beazer Finance Director, *Corporate Finance*, December 1988, 8), but the gearing ratio soared to 150 per cent (a 'healthy' gearing ratio would normally be seen as a low percentage—the lower the better—indicating more equity than debt). Moreover, the attempts to reduce gearing thereafter were not entirely successful.

Disposal of Koppers' assets hit problems. It took longer than expected and Beazer had to support financially some of the purchases. As a result, the heavy interest repayments on the finance to bridge $400 million of expected asset sales continued for longer than anticipated, and some of the sales that did take place were not the absolute disposals that had been sought.

In 1990 and 1991, the Beazer empire began to break up. In April 1991, with interest repayments remaining a problem, Brian Beazer proposed selling off half the group's UK and European operations in order to raise £250 million. By June, with the company debt rising once again from £770 million to £1 billion (as a result of a rising dollar—most of the debt was denominated in dollars), with capitalization at just £236 million and a further sharp fall in profits expected, more radical surgery was attempted, perhaps forced by the banks (*Financial Times*, 17 September 1991). Beazer proposed selling off the entire European operation to pay off £500 million borrowings. This would have led to a US–Europe split in the group, an end to the family control of the company which had lasted for over half a century (described as 'selling a family heirloom' (*Financial Times*, 26 June 1991); 'selling the family silver' (*Independent*, 28 August 1991; *Financial Times*, 25 April 1991)) and the relocation of Beazer's base to the United States.

But by September 1991, with the banks requiring repayment of $600 million (*The Times*, 11 September 1991) and Beazer reporting a 43 per cent drop in pre-tax profits to £60.6 million, Beazer itself was taken over by the Hanson Group, a UK giant industrial conglomerate. Hanson made a successful offer to acquire Beazer, debt and all, for the agreed sum of £351 million. While it was Beazer and its advisers that did all the hard work in the Koppers takeover—and took the risks—it was Hanson that ended up with the 'prize'. Hanson, of course, also acquired the debts but, with its better credit rating, the cost of servicing them was lower than it had been for Beazer.

From the day of the Koppers takeover—the result of innovative financing and creative compliance—Beazer had been on a 'treadmill' (*The Times*, 26 June 1991). Disposals could not reduce the 'horrendous group debt' (*The Times*, 26 June 1991) after 1988. Shareholders saw the share price dip from its peak of around 275 pence in 1987 to 88 pence in 1991. Hanson's bid valued each share at 123.5 pence. Beazer was simply unable to achieve sufficient sums to pay for a level of debt raised to acquire Koppers that turned out to be a 'deal too far'.

It was not the only one. In the case of Maxwell Communication Corporation, the highly leveraged acquisition of Macmillan has been seen as a deal too far. Every year $290 million was needed to repay the interest on the $2.6 billion borrowed (Bower, 1992, 488), more than the business appeared to be producing. The acquisition was blamed as a contributory factor in the collapse of the Maxwell empire and when Macmillan was sold by the administrators in 1993 it fetched only $552 million (*The Times*, 11 November 1993). In many other companies recession has exposed the real risks hitherto obscured in the accounts through devices of creative compliance.

CREATIVE COMPLIANCE AND THE DEFEAT OF LEGAL CONTROL

From the perspective of those on the receiving end of regulation, creative compliance through devices such as the orphan subsidiary can provide a means of removing obstacles and accomplishing goals. It provides legal magic for achieving the apparently impossible. From the perspective of regulators, however, and of those looking to law for protection, it may be seen in more negative terms; creative compliance can mean no less than the defeat of legal control, and of the policies that lie behind it.

The stated objective of financial reporting regulation is that companies provide a true and fair view of their financial situation and performance. This is seen as a means of helping protect creditors, lenders, employees, by providing relevant and reliable information on which market decisions can be made (see, for example, European Commission, 1976, 19; ASB, 1991, 99). Risks may, of course, still be taken, but in theory relevant and reliable information should be provided to assess them. Legal requirements on financial reporting play a key part in corporate accountability and corporate governance, as was underlined in the Cadbury Report (Cadbury, 1992). Yet, if significant potential liabilities can, without any suggestion of contravention of the law, be kept off the balance sheet, accounts are not providing the information necessary for users of accounts to be fully aware—or perhaps aware at all—of the risks involved. Off-balance sheet devices, by keeping vital information out of the accounts, go to the heart of what financial reporting is purportedly about.

In 1987 when we began researching corporate finance from a number of perspectives, the stock markets of the world were still booming, there was little talk of recession, and new financial instruments were being rapidly developed and marketed. There was an explosion of mergers and acquisitions fuelled by an abundance of credit. Since then high interest rates and recession have exposed the heavy debt burden assumed by many corporations. Many of the companies identified in our research as engaging in creative compliance have since faced severe, and in some cases terminal, financial difficulties. Yet the financial risks, and the implications for shareholders, creditors, employees, the economy at large, were not readily apparent from the figures in their accounts. We have referred in this chapter to *known* cases where creative compliance devices, such as the orphan subsidiary, have been used. But one reason for the concern raised by these devices is that their use may not be known, or not known until long after the event, with the bad news eventually emerging only when it is too late to be useful.

Some of the major cases of financial collapse have, of course, involved allegations of fraud, but use of creative compliance devices has also served routinely to obscure the risks to which businesses have in reality been exposed. To the extent that financial reporting regulation is aimed at ensuring that information on such exposure is available through the accounts, that regulation has failed. Legal control has been circumvented, and the policies declared to lie behind it defeated, not just through breach of the law but through creative compliance.

What is more, analysing creative compliance in the context of corporate finance demonstrates that it is not just state regulation which can be overcome in this way. Controls based on private law are just as vulnerable. Contractual covenants, and terms in the memoranda and articles of association through which companies are constituted, can also be sidestepped and basic mechanisms of corporate governance undermined.

Legal control can, of course, fail for many reasons. Companies may get away with non-compliance because enforcement is inadequate. In the context of corporate finance, the finger has certainly been pointed at weak enforcement by auditors (Mitchell, 1995). Professional regulation has been criticized as lacking teeth (Dearing Report, 1988). Laws and standards themselves may be poorly drawn. The rules defining a subsidiary in the 1985 Companies Act (and before) seem like invitations to avoidance, so simple are they—with hindsight—to circumvent. Regulatory strategies may be misconceived or have unintended consequences. Regulation may be compromised, half-hearted, or merely symbolic. All of these factors have played a part in undermining financial reporting regulation. A significant part has also, however, been played by creative compliance.

Creative compliance poses its own special challenge for the achievement of effective legal control. While non-compliance may succeed because of inadequate enforcement, creative compliance effectively pre-empts enforcement, or at least straightforward enforcement. (This is discussed further in McBarnet and Whelan, forthcoming.) The whole point of the strategy of creative compliance is to be able to lay claim to the fact that it does not contravene the law as stated but complies with it, that it is 'whiter than white collar crime' (McBarnet 1992). The problem this poses for enforcement is that, in so far as there is no such contravention of existing law, there is arguably nothing to enforce. Despite the frustration expressed by accounting regulators over off-balance sheet devices such as the orphan subsidiary, we are not aware of any public suggestion that anyone acted unlawfully. On the contrary, there were strong arguments that keeping orphans off the balance sheet was what the law required (Aldwinckle, 1987; see also Law Society, 1990a, 1990b).

Creative devices can be thwarted, at least for the future, by changing the rules. Law is, indeed, frequently amended to close off 'loopholes'. The definition of a subsidiary in the Companies Act 1985 has been amended by the Companies Act 1989. A subsidiary undertaking, the concept now employed, is defined in much more inclusive terms (Companies Act 1985 (as amended) section 258). These definitions would require a structure such as BNS to be incorporated into Beazer's group accounts. As a means of managing accounts, the orphan subsidiary structure of the 1980s is certainly dead. But creative thinking aimed at managing accounts is not. New rules simply invite new structures and techniques to achieve the same result. The structure of BNS was constructed with a careful eye on the 1985 Act. The structure for such a deal today might be adapted to the amendments introduced by the 1989 Act, with an off-balance sheet vehicle achieved by other means, or alternative techniques of managing financial reporting requirements employed.

Even before the rules of the new Companies Act were in the statute book, our interviews (with accountants, bankers, lawyers, regulators) indicated new devices were being dreamed up with the aim of circumventing the new criteria for consolidation of subsidiary undertakings in group accounts. One example of the new generation of creative compliance devices being worked on was the deadlocked joint venture. This aimed at circumventing the toughest—in the sense of being the most inclusive—of the new definitions of a subsidiary undertaking, that requiring consolidation where there was a participating interest in, and actual dominant influence over, another undertaking (Companies Act 1985, section 258(4)(a)).

In the deadlocked joint venture company, companies A and B control half the voting rights and directors' voting rights of company C, which they created together. Company C is also 'deadlocked', that is, the ability of A or B (or any other 'external' agent) actually to exercise a dominant influence over C is restricted since C cannot depart from specified policies. As a result, since neither A nor B controls it, C need not, under the terms of the amended Companies Act 1985, be consolidated in the balance sheet of either A or B. Since there is no 'actual exercise of a dominant influence', there is, in terms of the literal wording of the Act, no requirement to consolidate. Yet the purpose (and commercial effect) of establishing C may have been to remove assets and the loans used to acquire them from the balance sheet of the company or group working through them. Joint venture companies can work to hide liabilities. For example, after the collapse of the property development group, Rush & Tompkins, an estimated £700 million of debt in joint ventures emerged, which had not been on the balance sheet (*The Times*, 30 April 1990). If BNS had been deadlocked, then it, too, could be off-balance sheet in the 1990s.

Creative compliance is directed at, and based on, current law, *whatever* that law may be. If legal control seems to be constantly lagging behind current practice, it is quite simply because current practice is geared to staying ahead of legal control and using the law in creative ways to achieve this. New laws may effectively control old devices, but new laws will also stimulate attempts to find new devices based upon them.

Creative compliance thus poses its own challenge for control. By complying with the letter of the law rather than breaching it, it poses a challenge for enforcement, while its inherent dynamism poses a challenge for those seeking to formulate laws comprehensive enough to capture all possible devices. Yet unless creative compliance can be effectively controlled, legal policies will be constantly vulnerable to being routinely nullified by legal creativity.

The challenge of creative compliance is periodically addressed. Enforcement is not necessarily mechanistic, confined to applying the letter of the law. As we have noted elsewhere (McBarnet and Whelan, 1991), the courts have thwarted some devices, and caught in the enforcement net those using them, by rejecting literal interpretations of the requirements of law in favour of a purposive approach (e.g. *Litster* v.

Forth Dry Dock Engineering Co Ltd [1990] AC 546), or by moving the goal-posts after the event by introducing a 'new approach' (*Furniss* v. *Dawson* [1984] AC 474; *Ramsay (WT) Ltd* v. *IRC* [1982] AC 300). In practice, however, these turning-point decisions tend, like legislation, to generate new criteria on which to base new devices, and constant new approaches may meet resistance.

One reason for our continuing interest in financial reporting regulation is the fact that there has been an explicit acknowledgement there of the particular problems posed for control by creative compliance, and recent developments have demonstrated an explicit attempt to find a means of formulating law and regulations in ways which can not only combat it, but which are immune to it. Our current work is concerned to analyse these developments, the strategies being adopted to enhance control and their prospects for success.

What an analysis of the practice of creative compliance underlines is that law is a double-edged sword. It is not only a mechanism for control, but a mechanism for escaping it. It comprises prohibitions and requirements; but it also constitutes the material for constructing devices to escape them. The orphan subsidiary illustrates how the raw material of law can be worked on to produce a potent device of creative compliance as a mechanism for overcoming legal barriers and defeating legal control. The challenge for regulation is to come up with an approach which can control creative compliance; the challenge for law and society researchers is to explore more fundamentally whether this is possible.

REFERENCES

ACCOUNTING STANDARDS BOARD (ASB) (1991), *The Objective of Financial Statements and the Qualitative Characteristics of Financial Information (ED—Statement of Principles)* (ASB, London)

ACCOUNTING STANDARDS COMMITTEE (ASC) (1987), *Exposure Draft 1487: Accounting for Off-balance Sheet Finance* (Institute of Chartered Accountants, London).

—— (1988), *Exposure Draft 42, Accounting for Special Purpose Transactions* (Institute of Chartered Accountants, London).

ALDWINCKLE, R. (1987), 'Off-balance Sheet Finance—The Legal View', *Accountancy*, June.

ASHTON, R. K. (1986), 'The Argyll Foods Case. A legal analysis', *Accounting and Business Research* 3–12.

BOWER, T. (1992), *Maxwell: The Outsider* (BCA, London).

CADBURY COMMITTEE (1992), *Report of the Committee on the Financial Aspects of Corporate Governance* (Gee & Co Ltd, London).

DEARING COMMITTEE (1988), *The Making of Accounting Standards* (Institute of Chartered Accountants, London).

DEPARTMENT OF TRADE (1982), *The True and Fair View and Group Accounts* (Department of Trade, London, 15 January 1982; reprinted in *Accountancy*, February 1982 and in Tolley's (1988), *Company Law* (Tolley, Croydon), 1377–80).

ERNST & YOUNG (1990), *UK GAAP* (Longman, London).

EUROPEAN COMMISSION (EC) (1976), *Group Accounts: Proposal for a 7th Directive*, Bulletin of the European Communities, Supplement 9/76.

LAW SOCIETY COMPANY LAW COMMITTEE (1990a), *Comments on ED49—Reflecting the Substance of Transactions in Assets and Liabilities* (Law Society, London, September 1990, No 232).

—— (1990b), *Comments on ED50—Consolidated Accounts* (Law Society, London, October 1990, No 236).

McBARNET, D. (1984), 'Law and Capital: The Role of Legal Form and Legal Actors', *International Journal of the Sociology of Law* 12, 231–8.

—— (1988), 'Law, Policy and Legal Avoidance', *Journal of Law and Society* 15, 113–21.

—— (1991), 'Whiter than White Collar Crime: Tax, Fraud Insurance and the Management of Stigma', *British Journal of Sociology* 42, 323–44.

—— (1992), 'It's Not What You Do but the Way That You Do It: Tax Evasion, Tax Avoidance and the Boundaries of Deviance', in D. Downes (ed.), *Unravelling Criminal Justice* (Macmillan, London), 247–68.

—— and WHELAN, C. (1991), 'The Elusive Spirit of the Law: Formalism and the Struggle for Legal Control', 54 *The Modern Law Review* 848–73.

—— and —— (1992), 'International Corporate Finance and the Challenge of Creative Compliance', in J. Fingleton (ed.), *The Internationalisation of Capital Markets and the Regulatory Response* (Graham & Trotman, London), 129–41; reprinted in S. Wheeler (ed.), *Law and the Business Enterprise* (Clarendon Press, Oxford, 1995) 403–416.

—— and —— (forthcoming), *Law, Creativity and Control* (provisional title).

MANSFIELD, G. (1994), 'Five Ways out of Tax', *Journal of Financial Regulation and Compliance* 2, 133–49.

MITCHELL, A. (1995), 'Oh Dear, Another Huge Dollop of Auditing Whitewash', *The Times*, 4 January 1995.

NOBES, C. W. and PARKER, R. H. (1984), 'The Fourth Directive and the United Kingdom' in S. J. Gray and A. G. Coenenberg (eds.), *EEC Accounting Harmonisation: Implementation and Impact of the Fourth Directive* (North-Holland, Elsevier, Amsterdam).

TOLLEY (1988), *Tolley's Company Law*, (Tolley Publishing Company, Croydon).

9

Doctrine and Practice in Commercial Law

ROSS CRANSTON

The legal doctrines of commercial law are contained primarily in the legislation and decided cases, coupled with the literature of the academic and professional commentators. Those seeking to understand the role of commercial lawyers will not get far without an appreciation (at least in broad outline) of these legal doctrines, for they contain the categories which lawyers invent and which are constitutive of practices and institutions (Cain, 1994, 33). Focusing on the doctrines alone, however, tells only part of the story of how commercial lawyers practise law and the ends they pursue. A case-centred approach—still so common in legal education—misses out, for instance, on those many types of commercial transaction which are rarely litigated. Even if matters are litigated it misses out on the impact of legal decisions, which is often quickly mitigated by lawyers redrafting documents, by deals being restructured on their advice, and by the invention of new legal institutions. Moreover, an over-abundant concern with doctrine neglects the reality that practising lawyers are not devoted to its purity or its rational development. Instead they see it as a malleable resource which can be used instrumentally to achieve their clients' ends. Innovation and boldness with regard to doctrine are the hallmarks of commercial lawyers, but these qualities are wrapped up in appeals to core societal values such as markets and economic growth.

There is too little systematic knowledge of the role of commercial lawyers, in particular how they use legal doctrine. A limited amount of information can be gleaned from the course notes on drafting and negotiation published for trainee lawyers and on the manuals available to assist practising lawyers in their craft, principally in drafting legal documentation (e.g. Bradgate, 1991). Some information is available in historical studies (amongst which are the histories of the eminent firms) (Sugarman, 1990). There are references, for instance, to the transplant of the investment trust from the United States to Britain and to the invention of new forms of security (Sugarman, 1994; Gordon, 1983). There is a splendid study of how retention-of-title clauses are dealt with in insolvencies, although centre-stage there are the non-lawyer 'insolvency practitioners' (Wheeler, 1991a, 1991b, 1994). Flood's ethnographic study of commercial lawyers contains fascinating detail, for instance on how they negotiate in drafting contracts on behalf of their respective clients. Boiling down these tasks to advising, negotiating, and drafting, however, does not do justice to the legal doctrines lurking in the shadows of these activities (Flood, 1991).

By examining three disparate areas, taken from various periods over the last 150 years—the trust receipt used in financing international trade, international loan finance, and swaps (one type of derivative)—the present essay adds something to our stock of knowledge of lawyers' involvement in commercial practice. The methodology—relying on archival material—is such that the picture is incomplete. Nevertheless it is possible to draw some conclusions about how lawyers invent legal devices, draft documents, and manœuvre around doctrine to oil the wheels of commerce. I hope it is a fitting subject to honour Donald Harris, for whom it is being published (and who, incidentally, expertly guided my own doctoral studies in the area of business' compliance with the law (Cranston, 1979)). During his career Harris has straddled its two concerns of doctrine and doctrine's practical implementation—doctrine, through his contributions to those bibles for English commercial lawyers, *Chitty on Contracts*, and *Benjamin's Sale of Goods*, and doctrine's implementation through his forays into areas such as complex contracting (e.g. Beale, Harris, and Sharpe, 1989).

TRUSTS RECEIPTS

Except for the most credit-worthy of customers, banks are generally happier lending money if they can take some sort of security. This applies to importers as much as to anyone else. With importers the obvious security for the banks financing them is to take security over the goods themselves. This can be done relatively easily by a bank taking the bill of lading representing the goods, which may still be on the high seas. Indeed at common law the bill of lading is a document of title, so a pledge of it is equivalent to a pledge of the goods themselves. But the importer will need access to the bill of lading to deal with the goods when they arrive at the port or in relation to third parties. The trust receipt is a document, signed by the importer, which facilitates this without destroying the bank's security interest. The importer undertakes that in consideration of the bank releasing the bill of lading to it, it will hold it on trust for the bank, together with the goods and the proceeds of their sale.

The trust receipt was first used by Samuel Ward, Baring Brothers' agent in Boston, in the early 1830s. Unfortunately we do not know who devised it for him, but his confidence in the security provided by the device strongly suggests he had legal advice.[1] For some time Barings were the only firm to use it, but later another merchant bank, Fletcher, Alexander & Company, adopted it. Initially the trust receipt was in the form of a receipt at the bottom of each uncovered credit. The term trust receipt was not applied at this stage (Hidy, 1949, 142).

Story J gave his imprimatur to the device in 1843, when Fletcher, Alexander & Co. brought an action against the assignee of an insolvent merchant who had signed a 'trust receipt'.[2] Fletcher, Alexander & Co. had possibly decided to test the device—and indeed to do so before Story. Story was one of the great judges of nineteenth-century America and wrote many works in the area of commercial law. Story began his judgment by saying that he did not see any real difficulty in the case. He continued that he had no doubt that equity would enforce the agreement as far as it related to the shipments or proceeds still in the hands of the party himself, his personal representative, an assignee in bankruptcy, or third parties taking as volunteers or with notice. That was because every agreement for a lien or charge *in rem* constitutes a trust. To a contention that the agreement, if enforced, would operate as a fraud upon the creditors and hence was void against the policy of the law, Story J said—and notice his concern with the needs of commerce:

It was as fair and honest a commercial transaction, in its origin and progress, and consummation, as was probably ever entered into. How, then, it is against the policy of the law, I confess myself unable to perceive, unless we are prepared to say, that taking collateral security for advances, upon existing or future property, on the part of a creditor, without taking possession of the property at the same time, or when it comes in esse, is per se fraudulent. Possession is ordinarily indispensable at the common law to support a lien; but even at the common law, it is not absolutely indispensable in all cases.

The device of the trust receipt had been given the green light. Other bankers adopted it and had standard forms of trust receipt prepared. By the 1870s, the term 'trust receipt' was applied as a matter of course to Ward's device. Legally the term 'trust' was a misnomer, although no doubt some lawyer thought it might offer some protection in insolvency (since property held on trust is excluded from the insolvent's estate) and in relation to the proceeds of sale. And it might also have been used to

[1] Ward's letters on this are in the Canadian Public Archives, Baring Bros. collection.

[2] *Fletcher et al.* v. *Morey*, 9 Fed Cas. 266 (1843). The document provided that the merchant, in receiving the letter of credit, agreed to put Fletcher, Alexander & Co. in funds, 'and also to give security here for the same at any time previous thereto, if required by them or their agent, and all property, which shall be purchased by means of the above credit and the proceeds thereof, and the policies of insurance thereon, together with the bills of lading, are hereby pledged and hypothecated to them as collateral security for the payment as above promised, and held subject to their order on demand, with authority to take possession and dispose of the same at discretion for their security or re-imbursement.'

bring home to lay merchants their obligations to their bank in relation to the goods. But legally no trust was involved, and at most one could say that the buyer had certain fiduciary obligations to its bankers as a result of signing the trust receipt.

In the typical case a merchant would buy goods, having the bill of lading made out to the order of the banker (but the buyers to be notified). Insurance would be effected in the name of the bank. In consideration of the banker giving the buyer credit (e.g. by issuing a letter of credit in the seller's favour) the buyer would sign an agreement with the bank to the effect that the bank remained the owner of the goods, the bill of lading, the policy of insurance, and the proceeds of these until repayment of the credit. The agreement would probably refer to the buyer giving a trust receipt and security, if required, once the goods had arrived and being released to it for resale or use. Once notified of the arrival of the goods, the buyer would obtain the bill of lading and other documents upon signing a trust receipt.[3]

The first decision in Britain to consider the device of the trust receipt was an appeal from Scotland to the House of Lords in 1894, *North Western Bank Ltd.* v. *John Poynter, Son & Macdonalds* [1895] AC 56. Merchants obtained credit of £5,000 from the bank on security by way of pledge of a cargo of phosphate then afloat in the *Cyprus*. Bills of lading, indorsed in blank, were handed to the bank. Subsequently the bank handed the merchants the bills of lading on the condition that they held it as trustee for the bank. The same day the merchants delivered a sale note to the bank, to the effect that they had sold the phosphate on behalf of the bank to buyers in Glasgow, and they also forwarded the bill of lading to the defendants for delivery to the buyers on arrival of the *Cyprus*. The buyers received the bill of lading and took delivery of the cargo, and paid the merchants part of the price. The defendants now claimed the remainder of the purchase price from the buyers, on the basis that they were creditors of the merchants. The House of Lords had no difficulty in concluding that the bank was entitled to the proceeds of sale. Under English law, it said, there could be no doubt that a pledgee like the bank might hand back to the pledgor as his agent goods he had pledged for the purposes of sale, without diminishing the power of the security. The appeal court in Scotland had held that the rule there was different. Even if the matter had been governed by Scots law, the House of Lords disagreed. Lord Herschell LC canvassed the Scottish legal authorities in some detail, but was clearly also influenced by commercial practice (at 69). '[i]t does not seem to me to be a reasonable rule. If the rule exists, it is one which runs counter to every-day commercial practice and, I am

---

[3] Warehousing of the goods in the bank's name may precede their resale.

satisfied, to every-day commercial understanding of business transactions'. So long, then, as there was a valid pledge of documents or goods to the bank, the trust receipt would be effective.

The commercial efficacy of the trust receipt led the courts in England to deflect attacks on it. When in a case involving sale of cotton goods to India it was argued that trust receipts created a security which was void because they were not registered under the bills-of-sale legislation, the court held that security (pledge) rights of the bank were complete on the deposit of the bills of lading and other documents of title, before the trust receipts came into existence. Their object was to enable the bank to realise the goods over which it had a charge 'in the way in which goods in similar cases have for years and years been realized in the City [of London] and elsewhere'.[4] The exception where a bank would be defeated was if the merchant was fraudulent and sold or otherwise disposed of the goods obtained under a trust receipt to innocent third parties. In a leading decision to this effect in the Court of Appeal, one of the judges refuted the suggestion that this exception would have a deleterious effect upon the continued use of the trust receipts:

The truth is that almost every aspect of commercial dealing is not proof against the possible result of the frauds, that a lawyer, thinking of the possibilities of such things, might suppose to be so easy, but which in business in fact occur so rarely. ... I have no doubt that this very convenient business method will continue, and can do so because the whole basis of business rests upon honesty and good faith, and it is very rarely that dishonesty or bad faith undermines it.[5]

That case, too, involved transactions with India. Indeed, the trust receipt seems to have been taken up with enthusiasm on the sub-continent. It was used by some sellers to make their buyers trustees of the goods and their proceeds until payment, but the Indian courts eventually disapproved of this embellishment to what in fact was simple retention of title.[6] In two appeals from the Madras High Court involving the same insolvent merchant, the Privy Council gave advice which was conducive to the use of trust receipts. There the merchant had bought groundnuts from upcountry sellers, but to obtain finance gave banks the railway receipts for each waggon-load sent, duly endorsed in blank, with a letter of hypothecation and a promissory note. When the wagons arrived at the port, in order to enable the merchants to unload them into a warehouse bearing the name of the bank, the practice was to hand back the railway receipts. Although no trust receipts were given, the Privy Council

[4] *In re David Allester Ltd* [1922] 2 Ch. 211 at 218.
[5] *Lloyds Bank Ltd.* v. *Bank of America National Trust and Savings Association* [1938] 2 KB 147, 166.
[6] *In re Nripendra Kumar Bose*, AIR 1930, Calcutta 171; *In re Sumermull Surana*, AIR 1932, Calcutta 680.

nonetheless held that handing the railway receipts back for the limited purpose of unloading did not release the pledge.[7] Nor when the merchant fraudulently used the railway receipts to obtain finance from another bank by 'pledging' them did that bank get good title.[8]

Yet here we strike an interesting phenomenon: obiter dictum of a single judge in the Calcutta High Court was taken to be an impediment to the use of trust receipts in India. *Chartered Bank of India, Australia and China* v. *Imperial Bank of India* (AIR 1933, Calcutta 366) involved use of trust receipts in the normal way by an importing merchant in favour of the plaintiff bank. The merchant was fraudulent and purported to pledge the goods to the defendant bank. Lord Williams J could have resolved the matter by simple inquiry into whether the defendant bank, acting *bona fide* and without notice, took free of the claim which the plaintiff bank might have under the trust receipt. Instead, he launched attacks both on trust receipts as a device to defeat the claims of creditors under the relevant insolvency legislation and on commercial morality generally. Although his judgment is inconsistent with English decisions and the advice of the Privy Council—indeed the Privy Council subsequently refuted the reasoning he adopted about the impact of the insolvency legislation[9]—his views became enshrined in Indian legal consciousness. Trust receipts were a chancy device, to be used in only limited circumstances, and then with caution. A failure of legal analysis, tinged with an anti-merchant, anti-Privy Council turn of mind? In any event, after Independence various government committees recommended legislation to place trust receipts on a firmer basis, so that they could be used both in domestic as well as international dealings. For example the Indian Government Banking Laws Committee recommended that the law in this area be codified to 'enable banks to play more effectively their role as catalysts of our country's economic development' (Indian Government Banking Laws Committee, 1977, 42). The committee recounted decisions of Indian courts as a result of which it concluded that the utility of the trust receipt had been undermined. The commercial community wanted codification, and indeed the Reserve Bank of India had prepared a draft bill. Nothing, however, was done.

Meanwhile in the United States the device went from strength to strength. *Farmers and Mechanics' National Bank of Buffalo* v. *Logan*, 74 NY 568 (1878) is a leading case, involving the domestic sale of wheat. The bank succeeded against a third-party purchaser on the New York

---

[7] *Official Assignee of Madras* v. *Mercantile Bank of India* [1935] AC 53. The Privy Council also held that the railway receipts were documents of title and that the merchant could pledge them (and hence the goods) under the Indian Contract Act.
[8] *Mercantile Bank of India Ltd* v. *Central Bank of India Ltd* [1938] AC 287.
[9] *Official Assignee of Madras* v. *Mercantile Bank of India Ltd* [1935] AC 53 at 67.

Produce Exchange, the court remarking that the third party should have made inquiries of the buyer—it had 'no cause to complain of a purpose [of keeping title from the buyer until he paid the bank] so reasonable and productive of so good results' (581). It had been argued that there was a custom or usage among grain dealers in New York, or on the Produce Exchange, which would have given to third-party purchasers a better title than their sellers. While conceding that this would tend to the security of transactions on the Produce Exchange—which 'makes very easy and rapid the transaction of an immense trade in the agricultural produces of the country'—the court held that it was not the law. Subsequent courts validated the trust receipt in most US jurisdictions, and also held that there was no necessity for it to be recorded under chattel mortgage legislation (Frederick, 1922a, 406–8). There was some reluctance to examine its doctrinal basis too minutely lest it not bear the weight of scrutiny. A leading case in the Second Circuit Court of Appeals noted that courts, without always defining exactly in the same way the relation between the parties, 'still are astute to protect the rights of the banker in such cases.'.[10] The Third Circuit Court of Appeals observed:

The exigencies of trade and commerce have caused many exceptions to be made to the rigid rule founded on the policy underlying the Statute of Frauds, by which the device of title from possession is declared either evidence of fraud or to be fraudulent *per se*. . . . The courts have not attempted to define exactly what the relation between the credit lending banker and the merchant is, as to the goods.[11]

Bona fide transferees in breach of a trust receipt would often defeat the bank, as in England, as a result of legislation such as the Factors Acts (Frederick, 1922b).

Yet the cases contained within them the seeds of doctrinal rigidity. No pledge was involved, said the Supreme Court in *Farmers and Mechanics' National Bank*, thus eschewing the doctrinal path to be hewn by the English courts when they came to consider the trust receipt. And subsequent courts in the United States imposed the requirement that title to goods had to pass from the sellers to the bank (or other financier) without ever having been in the 'buyer', the person giving the trust receipt. If title was in the 'buyer' at any time, the trust receipt was ineffective as an unregistered chattel mortgage.[12] It followed that a trust receipt could never be used in a bilateral arrangement—where a buyer had property in goods, pledged them to the bank, and then obtained their release through giving the trust receipt. By contrast the analysis of English courts

[10] *In re Cattus*, 183 F. 733 (1910).
[11] *Century Throwing Co.* v. *Muller*, 197 F. 252 (1912).
[12] e.g. *In re Carl Dernberg & Sons Inc*, 66 NYLJ 1200 (1921).

in terms of pledge led them to conclude that a trust receipt in such circumstances may be valid.

Effective trust receipts were thus possible, and widely used, in the
United States in the case of the import of goods. But since title had to be
kept out of the buyer, there were significant obstacles to using trust
receipts domestically. This was of particular relevance to financiers of
automobile dealers, who wanted to take security over the vehicle
financed by way of a trust receipt. Dealers entrusting a trust receipt
would be authorized to display the automobiles for sale and usually also
to sell them. The uncertainties meant that banks accepted trust receipts
from only the most responsible and reliable dealers, or when the dealers
were owned or absolutely controlled by a manufacturing company.
Clearly in such cases the security was largely redundant; reliance was
being placed on moral security (Cornwell, 1923). The financiers agitated
for legislation, a task undertaken by the Conference of Commissioners
on Uniform State Laws. The Uniform Trust Receipts Act, drafted by Karl
Llewellyn, removed the requirement that title never be in the buyer
(Llewellyn, 1934). It was promulgated in 1933 and by 1940 had been
enacted by ten states. Despite its obscurity, the Act worked without
major problems, because the trust receipt was invoked by a relatively
small number of metropolitan banks financing imports and the handful
of national sales finance companies which had pioneered support for
automobile dealers (Gilmore, 1968). Writing in 1947, McGowan observed
that not only did the trust receipt stand between practically every dollar's
worth of banker's acceptance involving purchases of imported and
domestic goods, it also financed practically 'the entire wholesale automobile business'.[13]

INTERNATIONAL BANK FINANCE

A large component of international bank-lending in the nineteenth century was to sovereign borrowers. Governments from the first part of the
century called for subscriptions for their loans and the ties formed by the
banker resulted in alliances and joint account activities (Carosso, 1970).
Thus the banking syndicate was born; its use enabled large amounts of
capital to be raised and risks to be spread. A syndicate was formed by
what these days would be called the lead or arranging bank sending out
basic details of the intended borrowing and the invitees sending back a

---

[13] G. McGowan, 1945. The Uniform Commercial Code, which replaced legislation like
the Uniform Trusts Receipts Act in the early 1960s, protects the security given by a trust
receipt for a period of 21 days without filing if the goods are released for the purpose of ultimate sale or processing: UCC §9–304(5).

brief letter of acceptance to become members. The actual agreement was in legal form, if rather brief. Take as an example an agreement between J. S. Morgan & Co. and some eight others in relation to a Chilian 6 per cent agreement loan for some £2 million in 1867.[14] Under the agreement the parties agreed to purchase on joint account the proportions of £1 million set out opposite their signatures. Their obligations to purchase were stated to be several (clause 1). They undertook also to offer the loan for public subscription (clause 2). Management of the issue to the public was to remain with J. S. Morgan & Co. (clause 4); the allotment of the bonds to the public was to be by J. S. Morgan & Co. and two others. This wide delegation of discretion for managers was typical. An addendum makes clear that the firm undertaking relating to £1 million was in the character of an underwriting commitment only:

Should the public subscription not admit of the allotment of the whole of the One Million Pounds bonds taken firm, then the remainder of such Bonds together with any Bonds purchased in the market on the joint account, shall remain in the hands of Messrs J. S. Morgan & Co. for sale on account of all parties concerned until the 1st day of March next, at which date the number of Bonds undisposed of shall be handed over to the several parties in the proportions appertaining to each.

The agreement sets out in detail the commission payable (clause 3). Overall, though, the agreement is clear and succinct.

By 1914, the typical corporate issue had two syndicates, one with a lead bank and co-managers to originate, purchase, and perform the banking function, the other to sell the issue. The first syndicate would either underwrite the issue or, in the case of established corporations, purchase the issue and be responsible for its sale (Carosso, 1970, 61–2). Agreements were becoming more detailed, partly through experience and partly because corporate issuers as well as governments were now involved. The manager was now given discretion to extend the syndication period if necessary; the agreement set out the time and method of payment to the borrower, and whether members were to advance funds; managers were often given power to stabilize the market price of the issue during its distribution; and other powers were entrusted to managers such as to assign exclusive sales territories to certain firms, to permit participants to withdraw from the syndicate, if necessary to borrow from commercial banks, or to sell at a loss.

In addition to the syndicate agreement—usually a rather informal document—there was the agreement between the borrower and the banks. This too could be straightforward. The contract of April 1878

---

[14] Letter Morton Rose & Co. to J. S. Morgan & Co., 30 April 1884, Morgan Grenfell & Co. Archives, Guildhall Library, London, ms HC4 1.5(a).

between the US Treasury and Rothschild & Sons, J. S. Morgan & Co., Seligman Bros, Morton Rose & Co., and the First National Bank of the City of New York for the raising of $10 million, may be taken as illustrative.[15] Under it, the banks agreed to take $10 million US Treasury bonds in specified proportions, and to subscribe for the remainder of the $50 million issue at a rate of not less than $5 million a month. The US Treasury covenanted that it would not sell (except in two specified cases) any other bonds during the period of the agreement. Commission and arrangements for expenses were set out, as well as a term that no bonds would be delivered to banks until payment in full to the Treasury. With time, of course, the borrower—banks agreement was to balloon.

Legally the most detailed of the documents associated with these international lending transactions was probably the bond itself.[16] For example, the 6% bearer bonds issued by the French government in 1870, in relation to a £10 million loan, promised due and punctual payment of interest and a sinking fund for redemption.[17] The key clauses are worth quoting in full:

FIRST.
That the French Government will, during the currency of the said Loan, duly and punctually remit to London by equal semi-annual payments to Messrs. J. S. Morgan & Co., so as to be in their hands at least fifteen days previous to the periods respectively fixed for the payment of Interest on the Bonds, the sum of £600,000, or 15,000,000 of francs, without any deduction whatever, and exempt from all taxes, duties, or imposts, now or hereafter made, levied, or charged by or on behalf of the Nation of France, or the Government thereof.

SECOND.
That, in addition to the said semi-annual payments before mentioned, the French Government will from and including the year 1873, and thenceforward to the period at which the whole of the Bonds shall have been redeemed and paid off, duly and punctually remit by annual Instalments to London to Messrs. J. S. Morgan & Co., so as to be in their hands at least fifteen days previous to the First day of April in each year, the sum of £95,000 or 2,375,000 francs, without any deduction whatever, and exempt from all taxes, duties, or imposts now or hereafter made, levied or charged by or on behalf of the National Bank of France, or the Government thereof.

There then followed a clause about payment of interest, which was to be at the option of the bearer in London or in Paris, and several clauses

[15] Morgan Grenfell & Co. Archives, Guildhall Library, London, No. 21, 760, HC 3.1.1(1) Box 3. For background to this loan see Carosso, 1987, ch. 6.

[16] The prospectus was usually a fairly brief, descriptive, affair with a specimen bond attached, an application form and possibly a receipt for deposit.

[17] Morgan Grenfell & Co. Archives, n. 15 above, No. 21, 760, HC 9.1.(1) 4.

about redemption and redemption procedures (by lot). Interest and redemption were to occur in time of peace as well as war, and whether the holder was the subject of a friendly or hostile state—although one cannot imagine too many German buyers at the time. Finally, the government reserved the right to repay the bonds at any time.

What was the role of law and lawyers in all this? Legal issues rarely arose between the syndicate members or between the borrowers and the syndicate; the sanctions for breach of the letter or spirit of these agreements were informal, not legal, in nature. A New York attorney wrote in 1910: 'should one of the participants fail to keep his promise, the result would probably be not a suit for breach of contract, but banishment from the syndicate list' (Gerstenberg, 1910, 328). Lawyers were, however, involved in providing advice. In the archives of J. S. Morgan & Co. we find examples of advice from solicitors to the bank on the form and content of borrowing documents and whether or not stamp duty was payable on them (Drake 1884). Counsel's advice might also be sought on particular points; for example, the Argentine Great Western Railway Company Ltd was to raise money through Morgans, but a question arose whether its existing articles enabled the company to pay underwriting commission when the issue was to be to existing shareholders, not the public. Counsel confirmed the opinion of the company's solicitors, that commission could not be given, but played the invaluable role of legal problem solver by suggesting that the difficulty could be avoided by offering the issue to the public generally, but giving the present shareholders a preference (Kirby, 1901).

Let us now move on more than half a century to the modern period of international bank-lending. Since the 1960s when it began, Euromarket lending has grown to encompass billions of dollars, marks, yen, and other currencies, not forgetting synthetic currencies like the ECU.[18] The legal features of Euromarket lending replicate those of international lending, certainly as it dates from the nineteenth century (Todd, 1989, 11). Syndicated lending was a feature of the 1970s. With the Third World Debt crisis of the early 1980s, however, sovereign borrowers faced difficulties repaying their loans. The Euromarkets saw the proportionate increase in the popularity of bonds, notes, and other debt instruments issued by corporate borrowers. Instead of having loans on their balance sheets banks now acted as underwriters to issues and earned fees rather than interest (so called disintermediation). In the last decade, the Euromarkets have been characterized by further innovations, notably

[18] No one knows exactly how much is involved: the periodic reports of the Bank for International Settlements provide but an inkling of the realities. One figure is illustrative: from 1980 to 1989, total outstanding debt on the market is estimated to have grown from US$10 billion to US$791 billion: *Euromoney*, June 1989, 22.

securitization, swaps, and other derivatives (swaps are dealt with at 000 below).

The definitional key to Euromarket finance is that it involves a currency which is not the currency of the place of issue. 'That is all Eurodollars are—a credit in dollars outside the United States, whether in Europe or elsewhere'.[19] A particular source of Eurodollars in the 1950s and 1960s was the Soviet Union, its East European allies, and China. Dollars from trade, reserves, and the sale of gold were deposited with the Moscow Narodny Bank in London and the Banque Commerciale pour l'Europe du Nord in Paris (both owned by the Soviet Union), which then redeposited them with other banks. Moreover, as a result of favourable trading, companies around the world accumulated dollars. By the early 1960s apparently some $US3 billion were circulating outside the United States, of which $1 billion was not in official institutions. Once it had begun, the growth of Eurodollar finance was promoted by banks such as S. G. Warburg, which approached companies they thought were potential borrowers. Eurodollar finance was given a boost by measures taken by the United States with the aim of protecting its balance of payments. On 18 July 1963, President Kennedy proposed an income equalization tax to penalize the sale of some foreign securities to American investors, and in 1965 President Johnson imposed voluntary restraints on lending to foreign borrowers. The Eurodollar market was also facilitated by US banking legislation, under which banks did not have to pay insurance premiums, or make reserve payments, against deposits with their branches outside the United States. As far as Eurobonds were concerned, there was a ready market because as bearer instruments investors with doubtful capital could buy them anonymously, as well as investors wishing to avoid taxation on the interest received. Euromarket dealings became much easier with the establishment of the international securities clearing systems, Euroclear (1968, run by Morgan Guaranty) and Cedel. Over time Euromarket finance became increasingly varied. The first Eurobonds convertible into shares were issued in 1966; zero coupons began the same year; and in 1970 floating interest rates were introduced.

It is generally said that the first modern Eurodollar issue was led by S. G. Warburg & Co for Autostrade, the Italian state motorway company, in 1963.[20] Warburgs had made extensive preparation for a Eurodollar issue, especially in the light of criticism by the US Treasury of foreign companies borrowing in the United States. The expectation was that the first Eurodollar issue would be by the European Coal and Steel

---

[19] *Libyan Arab Foreign Bank* v. *Bankers Trust* [1989] QB 728, 735. See also *Hazell* v. *Hammersmith and Fulham LBC* [1992] 2 AC 1, 24.

[20] There are other claimants for that honour: Kerr, 1984.

Community, which had been an innovator in the markets, but that would have involved taking a client from Warburgs' New York associate (Attali, 1986, 324). Warburgs therefore turned to IRI, the industrial and financial holding company owned by the Italian state. Agreement was reached for a $15 million issue of bearer bonds on 14 January 1963, to the most prosperous of the IRI subsidiaries. It was not for another six months that the arrangements were finally consummated.

Our concern here is with the legal aspects of the arrangements, in particular how the regulatory and fiscal difficulties were overcome in England.[21] The first legal hurdle was in relation to the prospectus provisions of the Companies Act 1948 and the ramifications of the Borrowing (Control and Guarantees) Act 1946. The application of both turned mainly on whether the bonds to be issued by Autostrade were to be offered for sale 'to the public', as that phrase is interpreted legally. This is because the Companies Act 1948, Part X, would have deemed the offer document a prospectus if the bonds were to be issued to the public, with the consequence that it would have been unlawful to issue it or any application form without the offer document being registered. That would have been undesirably inflexible, it was thought, as well as contrary to the notion of a European-wide offering, tied to no one country. The Borrowing (Control and Guarantees) Act 1946, designed to give the government some control over the raising and allocation of capital, demanded the consent of the Treasury (through the Capital Issues Committee) if anyone were to circulate an offer for sale which constituted a public offer (Control of Borrowing Order 1958, paragraph 6). Initially, the Treasury took the view that the issue was to be a public offer and that therefore its consent was necessary. This was because Warburgs told the Capital Issues Committee that its syndicate would subscribe for the whole of the issue, and then subject to listing on the London stock exchange,[22] '[Warburgs] would place . . . approximately $3,750,000 of the Bonds in the United Kingdom and on the Continent, the balance of approximately $11,250,000 being placed by other members of the consortium, either by themselves or by us on their behalf, on the Continent' (Warburg, 1963a). On being asked to clarify, Warburgs replied that the transaction would not conform to any precedent and in a sense would represent a compromise between a conventional London 'placing' and a conventional American 'offering'. It then set out the steps as follows (Warburg, 1963b):

---

[21] The relevant documentation was kindly provided by Mr A. J. Herbert of Warburg's London solicitors, Allen & Overy. I do not deal here in detail with the drafting of the documentation. The documentation was governed by English law; the bonds by Italian law.

[22] The bonds were also to be listed on the Luxembourg stock exchange and later, if required, on other European stock exchanges.

1. The consortium of four banks, of which we will be the leader, will underwrite the issue, each bank severally (but not jointly) taking a commitment for U.S.$3,750,000. We propose to lay off part of our commitment with sub-underwriters in the United Kingdom and elsewhere.
2. Immediately thereafter the four banks will send out written invitations to other banks, brokers, finance houses and institutional and other clients inviting them to state their requirements for bonds on the basis of the draft Advertisement (see below). We will offer bonds in this manner principally in Italy, Switzerland, France and the United Kingdom. It is not expected that more than a relatively small amount of bonds will be applied for in the United Kingdom.
3. Shortly thereafter a full Advertisement will appear in London newspapers in accordance with the quotation requirements of The Stock Exchange, London. The Advertisement will not itself solicit subscriptions and members of the public wishing to subscribe for bonds will have to address themselves to their bankers or brokers. Similar arrangements will be made for the purpose of obtaining quotation for the bonds on the Luxembourg Stock Exchange.
4. The four banks will accept applications until the fourth or fifth day after publication of the Advertisement and will thereafter proceed to allotment . . .
5. We, as the leader of the consortium, will then confirm allotments to applicants requesting their written confirmation and requiring them to make payment at a Luxembourg bank against delivery of the bonds.

To this the Capital Issues Committee replied that they had been advised (no doubt by their lawyers) that notwithstanding that the advertisement referred to would not itself solicit subscriptions, the procedure contemplated amounted to the circulation in Britain of a public offer for the subscription or sale of bonds.

Warburgs were now in a corner. The Capital Issues Committee had indicated its view, although not yet made a final ruling. What could be done? Warburgs' solicitors used the oldest trick in the London legal book; they had a leading QC prepare an opinion expressing a contrary view, thus trumping that of the Capital Issues Committee. Michael Wheeler QC opined that, since the only persons in Britain to whom Warburgs would offer to sell any of the bonds would be two firms of brokers who, with Warburgs, would make available to jobbers any bonds required to obtain stock exchange quotation, there would not be an offer to the public. The offer to sell bonds to other members of the selling group, resident abroad, would be an offer to the public, but mere despatch of any document would not constitute its *issue* in Britain—another prerequisite to application of the Act. Just so that the various documents could not be said to constitute a prospectus, Wheeler suggested various amendments to them (Wheeler, 1963). In addition to the changes suggested in Wheeler's opinion, Warburgs also decided to effect its offer of bonds to the two firms of brokers orally, and that the brokers in turn would make only oral offers to jobbers and the few selected clients contemplated (Warburg, 1963c). In the light of all this the Capital Issues Committee concluded that contrary to their previous view Treasury consent would not be necessary (Capital Issues Committee, 1963).

Exchange control was more readily obtained, the Bank of England treating the Eurobonds as foreign currency securities for the purposes of the Exchange Control Act 1947 (Bank of England, 1963). The Inland Revenue agreed that Warburgs as paying agents under the documentation need not deduct United Kingdom income tax on the interest paid to other parties (Inspector of Foreign Dividends, 1963). The Board of Trade was also contacted. It was fairly clear that their permission was unnecessary under the Prevention of Fraud (Investments) Act 1958, since Warburgs were exempted dealers under it, but since the present issue was probably the first of many, it was though prudent to get that in writing. The Board of Trade obliged (Board of Trade, 1963). The final hurdle was stamp duty. The acknowledged expert at the bar, J. G. Monroe, 'Stamps' Monroe as he was called, was consulted. He advised that on the basis that the bonds would be issued in Luxembourg no UK stamp duty would be payable merely because they were to be quoted on the London stock exchange (although if bonds were brought into the country they would of course be stampable.) Monroe also advised that the subscription agreement would be stampable with only a nominal amount if one of its clauses was amended.[23] This was done.

SWAPS

Swaps developed in the early 1980s—one of a number of financial innovations of that decade. The simplest case of an interest-rate swap involves a borrower which can easily raise fixed-interest finance swapping its interest obligations with another borrower which can only borrow at variable rates. Both parties are better off because the swap enables them to obtain a preferred structure of interest rates, which is not available directly because of differential access to markets. More complex cases involve an interest-rate swap where the moneys are in different currencies, or an interest-rate swap coupled with a currency swap. Through swaps borrowers raise funds in markets where they can obtain the best rates but are able to make interest and principal payments in the preferred form and preferred currency.

---

[23] Monroe advised that the clause whereby Autostrade undertook to pay Warburgs principal and interest (to be onpaid) might constitute the agreement as a 'security'. The clause was amended to make Warburgs' functions as paying agents depend on receipt of the appropriate payments, in due time, from Autostrade.

Legally, the term swap is a misnomer. The parties are not swapping anything in an interest-rate swap, but rather agreeing to pay each other a sum equivalent to an amount calculated on the nominal principal chosen for the transaction (see Henderson and Price, 1988). Similarly, with a currency swap, the parties are agreeing to pay a sum equivalent to the amount originally paid and in the currency agreed. Normally the parties do not pay the sums so calculated but make a settlement on a net basis, so that the party owing the greater amount pays the difference between the two amounts due (if the interest rates or value of the currencies have moved).

As with other financial innovations of the 1980s, the invention and introduction of swaps was market-driven. The volatility of financial markets provided an incentive for techniques to be developed which would minimize costs and reduce uncertainty. Speculation was also a motor driving the search for new financial products like the swap. Deregulation created opportunities for arbitrage between capital markets. Once invented, an attractive tool such as the swap takes on a life of its own as it is refined, adapted, and extended.[24] Soon most international bond issues were coupled with a swap as a means of obtaining more advantageous finance for the borrower. The explosion of derivatives markets in the 1990s is beyond the scope of this essay. As with swaps, terminology and complexity are barriers to a general understanding of what is entailed in the many forms of a particular financial technique.

Throughout the 1980s lawyers claimed a key role in financial innovation. The 'Deal of the Month' column in the *International Financial Law Review* proclaimed the latest success of a law firm constructing a transaction for a particular commercial end. It would seem, however, that lawyers rarely played a critical role in the process of invention. Rather it was the so-called rocket scientists in financial institutions who were responsible for product development. The application of a new technique then required a range of matters to be determined, such as tax issues, where transactions ought to be booked and settled, which accounts to use, how to hedge, and what capital to allocate (Hu, 1989, 339). Here lawyers played a part in the picture, but along with bankers, accountants, and others.

The first currency swap is said to have occurred in 1976 between clients of Continental Illinois and Goldman Sachs, but the parties to that transaction did not publicize it so as to protect their property in the idea.[25] Once the World Bank became involved in 1981 in a currency swap with IBM, the nature of the swap became public knowledge.

---

[24] Swap options and caps, floors, and collars for swaps were examples.
[25] But there may have been earlier examples: Chernow, 1990, 549.

Subsequently a connection has been made between currency swaps and the parallel loans used in the 1960s and 1970s to avoid foreign-exchange controls, but this owes more to pedagogical neatness than historical reality. As to interest rate swaps there is no agreement on when they emerged, the late 1970s or early 1980s. An interest-rate swap involving Deutsche Bank, Luxembourg, in 1982 is mentioned as a watershed in swaps becoming rapidly popular. The leading financial journal of the Euromarkets, *Euromoney*, has said that the whole issue of who invented swaps is shrouded in obscurity (*Euromoney*, 1989, 246). Whatever the truth, it has never been claimed that lawyers were present at their birth. Lawyers have been important, however, to the growth of the idea.

The contribution of lawyers to the diffusion of the swap has comprised three areas of activity—spelling out the documentation, addressing regulatory issues, and defending the swap against challenges to its validity. Documentation of the early swaps seems to have been rudimentary, but soon master agreements were drafted to cover all swaps between particular parties. These master agreements recited the nature of the transaction and contained important representations and covenants by the parties. There followed the standard terms developed by the British Bankers' Association and what is now the International Swaps and Derivatives Association (ISDA). Most importantly these contained standard definitions of terms used in swap agreements (e.g. Cunningham, 1986, 26). Thus lawyers have ensured the accurate legal description of what was occurring through important problems such as exemptions and damages clauses, and generally ensured an accuracy of language and consistency of terminology. Since that time lawyers have been involved in drafting a whole range of standard form documentation for swaps and other derivatives.

The regulation of swaps, as of other matters, has been both unintended and deliberate. Unintended regulation occurs because the language of legislation, couched as it is in general terms, may arguably apply to a phenomenon even though its proponents did not have it in mind. For example some legal thought was given in the early days of swaps to whether they constituted a breach of the gaming legislation. Having a long pedigree, the gaming laws are directed at gambling and speculation in the nature of gambling, rather than at genuine financial transactions. Their wide language, however, means that they raise their heads in the financial sector when new techniques emerge. Legal advice is necessary. In the United Kingdom, section 63 of the Financial Services Act 1986 contains a specific provision disapplying the gaming laws to matters falling under it. Legal attention had also to be given to the potential application of the securities laws to swaps. While the US legislation was designed to have a wide scope, swaps did not exist at the time it was enacted, and its application to swaps would have been fortuitous rather than intentional.[26]

The deliberate regulation of swaps has come in various guises. In Britain, the Bank of England set general standards for the swaps market (Bank of England, 1988, 38–9). More importantly, swaps were regulated through the capital adequacy requirements for banks, first set out in the Basle concordat and then contained in the Second Banking Directive of the European Community. These measures were a recognition that banks were assuming higher risks in the 1980s when engaged in transactions such as swaps, and that one method of protection was to require them to have more capital (Dale, 1984; Norton, 1989; Gardener, 1991).[27] With swaps, the risks seem to have been far higher than those engaged in the swap industry seem prepared to acknowledge, or that pricing levels justified. A closer attention in the industry to the legal nature of the swap—an unsecured promise to pay money—may have highlighted the true nature of the risks.

Lawyers came into the spotlight with swaps when transactions involving local authorities in Britain were attacked on the ground that they were *ultra vires* their powers. The attack was by the district auditor (a central government appointee, monitoring local government) on the legality of swap transactions by a particular local authority. Given the serious repercussions for banks, however, they were joined as parties to the litigation. The swap transactions impugned were undertaken in the hope that the particular local authority (Hammersmith and Fulham) could minimize its interest bill by successfully predicting that interest rates would fall. The local authority had entered some 592 swaps by the time of the ligation, the notional principal amounting to some £6,052 million (its borrowing at the time was £390 million) and potential losses were considerable. By contrast with Hammersmith and Fulham, only ten other local authorities had entered into more than ten swaps, and only eighteen more than five.

Argument revolved around whether the swaps by the particular local authority were specifically permitted under the borrowing powers conferred by statute on local government or, under a more general enabling provision, because they were calculated to facilitate or were conducive to or incidental to the discharge of its functions. The banks contended that swap transactions were generally lawful if undertaken for 'replacement' or 'reprofiling' purposes, in other words to reduce the interest burden on specific borrowings ('replacement') or to increase the proportion of variable interest rate obligations to fixed interest obligations ('reprofiling').

---

[26] Early discussions include Klein, 1986, 35. Contrast UK law: Morton and Creamer, 1989, 30.

[27] *Quaere* whether capital adequacy is an effective means of protecting against risks.

The House of Lords would have none of it. While quoting an analysis of swaps in the *Bank of England Quarterly Bulletin*, that in most cases they are used to eliminate speculation and uncertainty, the House of Lords concluded of replacement swaps (the least objectionable form of swap): '[the replacement swap] does not in fact replace the interest under the original borrowing and the swaps transaction is a speculation no different in quality though different in magnitude from a swap contract which is not entered into by reference to any existing borrowing.'[28] That building societies were authorized by statute to enter swaps simply demonstrated that it was for Parliament, not the courts, to decide whether it was necessary or wise for local authorities to have the power.

The case exposed a clash of cultures, the culture of the market where swaps are an everyday occurrence on the one hand, and the judicial culture where swaps are regarded as dangerously speculative, at least for public bodies.[29] The House of Lords gave short shrift to the great difficulties caused to banks and the swap market by their conclusions. None of the judges in the House of Lords would have ever dealt with a swap while in practice at the bar, and since this was the first swaps case to be litigated none would have had experience of swaps while on the bench. They would nonetheless have been aware of how importantly their decision was regarded by the financial community because from the outset there was wide press coverage of the litigation.

The *Swaps case* caused considerable consternation in the City of London, for it cast doubt on the certainty of straightforward, if relatively novel and high-risk, financial transactions. There was also the fear that the decision might presage a less accommodating stance by the English judiciary to commercial dealings.[30] The Bank of England established a Legal Risk Review three months after the decision:

The markets as a whole are undoubtedly concerned that there are some unacceptable uncertainties and legal anomalies which interfere with transactions

---

[28] *Hazell* v. *Hammersmith and Fulham LBC* [1991] 2 AC 1 at 27, *per* Lord Templeman. Lord Ackner said: '[swap transactions] in fact are indistinguishable from any other transaction which involves the hope of gain. . . . Although the phrase "debt management" may be a convenient one, swap transactions in fact leave the debt wholly unmanaged' (at 45). Another interpretation is that it was public law trumping commercial law. The fall-out of *Hazell* is still being litigated at the time of writing.

[29] The Divisional Court had found all transactions to be unlawful ([1990] 2 QB 697); however, the Court of Appeal had been more sympathetic and had found those lawful which had been entered into after the issue of illegality was raised to reduce or eliminate the risks of the earlier ones (*ibid.*)

[30] Two other decisions also caused concern, although they had less far reaching implications than the Swaps case: *Arab Monetary Fund* v. *Hashim* (No 3) [1991] 2 WLR 729 involved the capacity of corporate bodies created by the laws of foreign states to sue; ultimately, the House of Lords held that the Fund had that capacity. *The International Tin Case* was resolved less satisfactory: see *Shearson Lehman Brothers Inc.* v. *Maclaine Watson & Co. Ltd* [1988] 1 WLR 16, [1990] 1 Lloyd's Rep. 441.

freely entered into. Similar problems exist in other jurisdictions but it is important that the UK, as host to so many international financial markets, does all it can
to minimise its own. If markets in this country are to continue to flourish and
innovate as successfully as they have in the past it is essential that participants
should be as certain as they can be that what they are doing will be upheld by the
law. [Legal Risk Review Committee, 1992, paragraphs 2–3]

The Committee recommended legislative change of the rule relating to
the *vires* of statutory institutions. It also proposed the establishment of a
Financial Law Panel, which would be a forum where the City of London
could bring in the final instance issues of legal uncertainty, and a
Financial Law Liaison Group, where these concerns could be voiced to
government. The committee's premise was that it was often possible to
resolve issues of uncertainty by contract or market practice, but that in
some cases a change in the law was the only satisfactory solution. The
Financial Law Panel has been operating successfully for several years.

SOME CONCLUSIONS

These three, rather different, areas of commercial law enable us to
identify, over a 150-year period, some of the ways in which lawyers have
facilitated commercial activity. The dominant theme to emerge from
the study of trust receipts is one of creative lawyering. Lawyers manipulate and mould legal concepts in order to protect their clients' business
activity. It is what some jurists describe as private law-making. The
scope and flexibility which lawyers have varies of course, with the
subject-matter. Someone—probably Baring Brothers' American
lawyer—conceived the idea that a merchant, by signing a form of words
on the application for a letter of credit, could give Barings a security over
the goods being imported until it was repaid. It is this capacity to form
and reformulate concepts which is at the base of commercial law. Yet
the device needed legal approval to be effective; after all it resulted in
banks being preferred over the other creditors of an insolvent merchant
(and in some cases over third parties taking from the merchant). That
came when courts in both the United States and Britain, attuned to the
needs of commerce, gave their imprimatur to the trust-receipt device as
a form of security.

The capacity of the common law to respond positively to commercial
need is a recurrent theme in its development in the modern era (and,
incidentally, a reason that the commercial community looked askance at
the *Swaps* case, because here commercial need was very much relegated
to the back seat). But note—and this must be the theme of another
study—the courts are often just giving their imprimatur. The practising

lawyers are the main creative element, reacting to the needs of their clients; the courts then respond to the devices which the lawyers develop, approving (with or without qualifications) or disapproving. Importantly, common law courts have in the main approved—instead of being too concerned with elaborate edifices or logical consistency, common law courts have crafted doctrinal lines consistent with commercial needs in a largely pragmatic manner (e.g. Chorley, 1940).

Lawyers manipulate language, as well as concepts. Legal language has a value, even if not used accurately. Lay people can be influenced in their behaviour because they believe (wrongly) that certain consequences follow. Courts, too, may be swayed by the bold, though imprecise, use of legal language. Writing about trust receipts Karl Llewellyn suggests that use of the word 'trust'—legally a misnomer, as we have seen—helped courts uphold the rights of banks under them:

New words and labellings which are things of guile are far from being reliable before a case-law court, and a counsellor would be a fool who trusted wholly to them; but a moderately pure transaction's strength is as the strength of a much purer one if its words and its labellings bear the mark of legal artistry rather than of stupidity or artifice. [Llewellyn, 1939, 730]

Legal concepts are not necessarily straightforward. Over time they may become encrusted with detail and qualifications. A feature of the common law is the accretion of case law based on single instances; this means that the main principle can be lost sight of. Complexity and obscurity in the law demand routinization if the consequences of a slip are significant. Procedures have to be devised so that the legal niceties can be observed. Thus lawyers must advise not only on the contents of standard forms for business but on how they are to be used. Their clients must appreciate the need meticulously to observe the procedures, even if they have no idea about the underlying legal rationale. Thus in England it was fundamental to the efficacy of the trust receipt that there be a valid pledge to the bank, which involves a transfer of possession (actual or constructive). To leave the goods or documents of title in the possession of the buyer throughout, and merely getting it to sign a trust receipt, would be fatal. Similarly in the United States we saw that before the Uniform Trust Receipts Act it was vital that title never rest in the buyer if the trust receipt was to be effective. If transactions are guided by a party conscious of the need to observe procedures—even if the other party is in a state of blissful ignorance—things can run smoothly, however difficult or arcane the law. Trouble occurs when the procedures are not properly policed—when clerks use the wrong standard form (to continue with that example), misuse the correct form, or otherwise trample on delicately constructed routines.

In 1829 the editor of the London-based *Law Magazine* noted the advent of a new series of law reports 'well meriting the attention of those whose engagements render an acquaintance with mercantile law necessary or expedient'—the Reports of Cases relating to Commerce, Manufactures, etc. determined in the Courts of Common Law. He added: '[s]o complete is now the division of labour amongst lawyers, that many barristers have made mercantile law their peculiar, if not exclusive, study; whilst solicitors in trading towns are obliged to have it at their fingers' ends' (Law Magazine, 1829). Certainly from the mid-nineteenth century it was the growth of the railways and the joint-stock company, rather than trade alone, which created a more sustained demand for commercial lawyers and led to the establishment of many of the leading City of London law firms (e.g. Michie, 1992, 182–3); Slinn, 1987, 60–6; slinn, 1984, 84–5, 111–12). International lending raised, as we saw, points of company law. The advent of the modern regulatory state in the twentieth century compounded the need for legal advice. The example of the first Eurobond issue in 1963 draws attention to the range of regulatory hurdles which had to be surmounted—company law, exchange control, and securities regulation. We saw also how the strategy for the issue was amended in the light of the legal advice which Warburgs received from Allen & Overy and Michael Wheeler QC. The fiscal implications of the issue had also to be explored; the general impact of fiscal legislation as a motor for particular deals, or the way they are structured, is a story in itself.

The response of business to legal regulation has been described as 'creative compliance' by two writers working with Don Harris at the Centre for Socio-Legal Studies. With the help of lawyers, those regulated by the law turn it to serve their own interests and to avoid unwanted control. Creative compliance thrives, it is said, on legal formalism—the narrow legalistic approach to rules—because transactions, relationships and legal forms can be constructed to avoid them (McBarnet, 1988; McBarnet and Whelan, 1991). Whether 'creative compliance' is a function of formalism is open to question; lawyers devise avoidance strategies for their clients, come what may. More importantly, it would be wrong to think that creativity is a function of regulation; the story of the trust receipt shows that areas quite divorced from regulation can be the occasion for creative lawyering. The raw material of the law is shaped to meet clients' needs over the whole range of commercial activity. Concepts and language are used to enable clients to plan their activities within a legally acceptable framework.

The swaps story introduces two cross-currents into our analysis. For here we have lawyers not being especially central to a particularly important financial innovation and then (in the judicial guise of the

House of Lords) being obstructive in the legal rationalization of that innovation. The first point is no doubt a feature of one's perspective: focusing on the legal dimensions alone can lead to the conclusion that the lawyer is central, whereas examining a business deal or commercial activity in the round casts the lawyer as just one among a number of the players necessary to its execution. Certainly areas such as financial markets, cross-border investment, and corporate restructuring are so complex that a range of financial, accounting, taxation, personnel, and legal advice are necessary. Whether one type of advice is crucial obviously depends on the circumstances, but it is a matter for inquiry whether on the whole the legal practitioner is less crucial than in the past or in other areas of societal activity.

In *Prager* v. *Blatspiel* [1924] 1 KB 566 at 570 McCardie J said:

The object of the common law is to solve difficulties and adjust relations in social and commercial life. It must meet, as far as it can, sets of facts abnormal as well as unusual. It must grow with the development of the nation. It must deal with changing or novel circumstances—unless it can do that it fails in its function and declines in its dignity and value. An expanding society demands an expanding common law.

The dominant view in the City of London would be that the House of Lords in the *Swaps* decision did not 'deal with changing or novel circumstances'. So great was the concern that, as we have seen, the Bank of England constituted a committee which recommended both changes in the law and the establishment of a mechanism to ensure a congruence between the markets and the law. Perhaps the *Swaps* case is an exception. The courts daily resolve many commercial disputes. Their attitude—at least in the Commercial Court in London, and it can probably also be said of, say, the federal District Court for the Southern District of New York—is generally facilitative of commerce. As one of the most eminent of present-day English judges, Lord Goff, has said: '[w]e are there to help businessmen, not to hinder them: we are there to give effect to their transactions, not to frustrate them: we are there to oil the wheels of commerce, not to put a spanner in the works, or even grit in the oil' (Goff, 1984).

There are, of course, other aspects of the relationship between lawyers and commercial practice which are not touched on in the present essay. One is the segmentation in recent decades of the legal profession into the large law firms which serve commercial clients, on the one hand, and those representing individuals or small businesses on the other. The large law firms are divided internally into specialist units, spend large amounts on internal training, have enormous research capability, and can engage in strategic thinking and preventive planning, and lobbying work on their behalf. The large firm and the mega-lawyering which it entails are a response to the changed business environment, which is more competitive and more uncertain (Galanter and Palay, 1990). There is ample scope for a study of the consequent degree of legal innovation in modern day commercial activity. But that must wait for another day.[31]

REFERENCES

ATTALI, J. (1986), *A Man of Influence. Sir Siegmund Warburg, 1902–82* (Weidenfeld and Nicholson, London).

BANK OF ENGLAND (1963), Letter to S. G. Warburg & Co. Ltd, 13 May.

—— (1988), *The Regulation of the Wholesale Markets in Sterling, Foreign Exchange and Bullion* (Bank of England, London).

BEALE, H., HARRIS, D., and SHARPE, T. (1989), 'The Distribution of Cars: A Complex Contractual Technique' in D. Harris and D. Tallon, *Contract Law Today* (Clarendon Press, Oxford).

BOARD OF TRADE (INSURANCE AND COMPANIES DEPARTMENT) (1963), Letter to Allen & Overy, 21 June.

BRADGATE, R. (1991), *Drafting Standard Terms of Trading* (Longmans, London).

CAIN, M. (1994), 'The Symbol Traders' in M. Cain and C. Harrington (eds.), *Lawyers in a Postmodern World* (Open University Press, Buckingham).

CAPITAL ISSUES COMMITTEE (1963), Letter to I. J. Fraser, May.

CAROSSO, V. (1970), *Investment Banking in America* (Harvard University Press, Cambridge, Mass.).

—— (1987), *The Morgans* (Harvard University Press, Cambridge, Mass.).

CHERNOW, R. (1990), *The House of Morgan* (Simon and Schuster, London).

CHORLEY, R. (1940), 'Liberal Trends in Present-Day Commercial Law', 1 *Modern Law Review* 272.

CORNWELL, W. (1923), 'The Bank and the Automobile Market' *The Burroughs Clearing House*, vol. 7, no 7 (April).

CRANSTON, R. (1979), *Regualting Business* (Macmillan, London).

CUNNINGHAM, D. (1986), 'Swaps: Codes, Problems and Regulation', 5 *International Financial Law Review* (August), 26.

DALE, R. (1984), *The Regulation of International Banking* (Woodhead-Faulkner, Cambridge).

DRAKE, SIR WILLIAM (1884a), *Letters from Sir William Drake, Solicitor,* 5 June 1882, 10 July 1884, 29 September 1884.

EUROMONEY (1989), 'First Swap', *A Special 20th Anniversary Supplement,* June, 246.

FLOOD, J. (1991), 'Doing Business: The Management of Uncertainty in Lawyers' Work', 25 *Law and Society Review* 41.

FREDERICK, K. (1922a), 'The Trust Receipt as Security', 22 *Columbia Law Review* 395.

—— (1922b), 'The Trust Receipt as Security II', 22 *Columbia Law Review* 546.

---

[31] I am grateful to Professor David Sugarman and Dr Joshua Getzler for their help in relation to my excursions into legal history.

GARDENER, E. (1991), 'International Bank Regulation and Capital Adequacy' in J. Norton (ed.), *Bank Regulation and Supervision in the 1990s* (Lloyd's of London Press, London).

GERSTENBERG, C. (1910), 'The Underwriting of Securities by Syndicates' in *Trust Companies* vol. 10, June, 328.

GILMORE, G. (1968), 'Security Law, Formalism and Article 9', 47 *Nebraska Law Review* 666.

GOFF, SIR ROBERT (1984), 'Commercial Contracts and the Commerical Court' [1984] *Lloyd's Maritime and Commercial Law Quarterly* 382.

GORDON, R. (1983), 'Legal Thought and Legal Practice in the Age of American Enterprise 1870–1920' in G. Geison (ed.), *Professionals and the Professional Ideologies in America* (University of North Carolina Press, Chapel Hill, N.C.).

HENDERSON, S., and PRICE, J. (1988), *Currency and Interest Rate Swaps* (2nd edn., Butterworths, London).

HIDY, R. (1949), *The House of Baring in American Trade and Finance* (Harvard University Press, Cambridge, Mass.).

HU, H. (1989), 'Swaps, the Modern Process of Financial Innovation and the Vulnerability of a Regulatory Paradigm', 138 *University of Pennsylvania Law Review* 333.

INDIAN GOVERNMENT BANKING LAWS COMMITTEE (1977), *Report on Personal Security Law* (New Delhi).

INSPECTOR OF FOREIGN DIVIDENDS (1963), Letter to Brown, Fleming & Murray, 26 June.

KERR, I. (1984), *A History of the Eurobond Market* (Euromoney Publications Ltd, London).

KIRBY, A. R. (1901), 'Opinion', HC 4.1.7.

KLEIN, L. B. (1986), 'Interest Rate and Currency Swaps: Are They Securities', *International Financial Law Review* (October), 35.

LAW MAGAZINE (1829), 1 *Law Magazine* 265.

LEGAL RISK REVIEW COMMITTEE (1992), *Reducing Uncertainty. The Way Forward* (February).

LLEWELLYN, K. (1939), 'Across Sales on Horseback', 52 *Harvard Law Review* 730.

LLEWLLYN, K. (1934), 'The Uniform Trust Receipts Act', 82 *University of Pennsylvania Law Review 270.*

MCBARNET, D., and WHELAN, C. (1991), 'The Elusive Spirit of the Law: Formalism and the Struggle for Legal Control', 54 *Modern Law Review* 848.

MCGOWAN, G. (1945), *Trust Receipts and the Variations in their Legal Status* (New York).

MICHIE, R. (1991), *The City of London* (Academic and Professional, London).

MORTON, G., and CREAMER, H. (1989), 'FSA: The Scheme for Derivative Instruments', *International Financial Law Review* (October), 30.

NORTON, J. (1989), 'Capital Adequacy Standards: A Legitimate Regulatory Concern for Prudential Supervision of Banking Activities?', 49 *Ohio State Law Journal* 1299.

SLINN, J. (1984), *A History of Freshfields* (Freshfields, London).

—— (1987), *Linklaters and Paines* (Longmans, London).

SUGARMAN, D. (1990), 'Lawyers and Business in England 1750–1950' in C. Wilton, *Beyond the Law* (The Osgoode Society, Toronto).

SUGARMAN, D. (1994), 'Blurred Boundaries: The Overlapping Worlds of Law, Business and Politics' in M. Cain and C. Harrington (eds.) *Lawyers in a Postmodern World* (Open University Press, Buckingham).

TODD, W. (1989), 'A Brief History of International Lending, From a Regional Banker's Perspective', 11 *George Mason University Law Review* 1.

WARBURG, S. G. & CO. (1963), Letters to Capital Issues Committee, 18 April, 26 April, 15 May.

WHEELER, M., QC (1963), 'Opinion', May.

WHEELER, S. (1991a), 'Lawyer Involvement in Commercial Disputes', 18 *Journal of Law and Society* 241.

—— (1991b), *Reservation of Title Clauses* (Clarendon Press, Oxford).

—— (1994), 'Capital Fractionalized: The Role of Insolvency Practitioners in Asset Distribution' in M. Cain and C. Harrington (eds.), *Lawyers in a Postmodern World* (Open University Press, Buckingham).

10

Property and Financial Adjustment after Divorce in the 1990s—Unfinished Business

JOHN EEKELAAR AND MAVIS MACLEAN

In 1995, an experienced judge in the English Family Division described his role in a case concerning post-divorce financial provision in these terms: '[t]he function of the Family Division judge is not so much to state principles as to reflect the relevant circumstances of the particular case in the discretionary conclusion', (*Atkinson* v. *Atkinson*, 1995).[1] The judge did not say that he should not *follow* principles, and in fact he went on to observe that the 'authorities do show a broad approach'. Nevertheless, if a judge is not to 'state' principles, even by way of recollection and self-guidance, the parties are left with no indication of the basis of the judge's decision, beyond perhaps an assertion of his instincts for justice. It is not our purpose to revisit the debate over the nature of judicial discretion, about which much has been written (see, e.g., Hawkins, 1992). It is, however, clear that the wide scope allowed in the common law world for judicial bodies to decide how finances should be ordered when married people divorce had been seriously circumscribed during the early 1990s, and the judge's statement carries less conviction than it would have done ten years earlier. The reasons for this change lie in events of the 1980s, including the contribution made by socio-legal research. We wish in this Chapter first to consider those events and then to examine the state of the debate on these issues as it stands in the mid-1990s.

Before we do this, however, we wish to place on record our appreciation of the encouragement which Donald Harris has given to family law research. From the mid-1970s, when research was undertaken at the Centre on the outcome of custody dispositions on divorce (Eekelaar and Clive, 1977) and the way the registrars (now District Judges) exercised their discretion in financial matters (Barrington Baker *et al.*, 1977), Harris saw family law research as being capable of making an important contribution to socio-legal studies. Our own subsequent research and any part it may have played in contributing to the policy agenda is therefore a

---

[1] *Atkinson* v. *Atkinson* [1995] 2 FLR 356 (Thorpe J). In *Thomas* v. *Thomas* [1995] 2 FLR 668 Waite LJ described the discretionary powers to redistribute the assets of the spouses as being 'almost limitless'.

direct consequence of his support and capacity to energise his research staff, for which we remain very grateful.

RESEARCH AND POLICY IN THE 1980s: SETTING THE AGENDA FOR THE 1990s

In England and Wales, the Matrimonial and Family Proceedings Act 1984 was seen as introducing the 'clean-break' concept into post-divorce financial provision. In it, the policy-goal which accompanied the introduction of the reformed divorce law of 1971, *viz.*, that the financial settlement should aim as far as possible to leave the parties in the position they would have been in had the marriage not broken down, referred to variously as the 'persisting obligation' or 'minimal loss' principle,[2] was repudiated and the courts were directed in each case where periodical payments were sought to consider whether it would be appropriate to make an order which would allow the parties, without hardship, to sever their financial relationship. The courts were given specific powers to prevent financial issues being re-opened at a later time. This shift in express legal policy was immediately precipitated by a public perception that many divorced women were 'living off' their former husbands when they could be supporting themselves. The persistence of a financial obligation on one former spouse (usually the man) to support the other after the dissolution of the marriage was seen to be inconsistent with the newly-acquired 'right' to divorce irrespective of fault, and indeed the clean-break principle has become attractive in many jurisdictions. Its acceptance has, however, posed serious questions about the legal significance of marriage, for if the fact that parties have been married does not *in itself* generate obligations which survive its factual collapse, it becomes hard to see what its legal purpose is.

Although the 1984 Act was clearly intended to herald a significant shift in policy, it endeavoured to do this while maintaining a discretionary framework of adjudication. Judges were to be encouraged to 'think about' the desirability of the clean break; there was no legal presumption in its favour (*Barrett* v. *Barrett* (1988)). Judges had to work out for themselves (as they indeed did in practice before the 1984 Act) how far it was 'appropriate' to impose a clean break. Furthermore, it was unclear how far the clean-break principle was to be applied to the child-support obligation. While it has long been established that a parent can never bargain away such liability completely (*Crozier* v. *Crozier* (1994)), courts were sometimes content to countenance arrangements in which a par-

---

[2] Matrimonial Causes Act 1973, s. 25. For an account of the background to the enactment of this policy in 1970, see Eekelaar and Maclean, 1986, ch. 1.

ent forwent receiving child-support payments (*Suter* v. *Suter & Jones* (1987)), perhaps in return for a capital or property settlement (*Delaney* v. *Delaney* (1990); *Smith* v. *McInerney* (1994)). Also, the method of calculating the amount of child-support orders, and, where made, of spousal-support orders, seemed to follow no clear pattern.

The instability of this situation was aggravated by two developments. The first was the advent of empirical evidence of the economic consequences of divorce. The results of our research, undertaken at the Oxford Centre for Socio-Legal Studies, fully published in 1986 (Eekelaar and Maclean, 1986), raised doubts about the assumptions which lay behind the change in policy. Our empirical evidence had convinced us that it was very rare for a divorced woman to find her financial support primarily from her former partner. Where payments were being made at all, they mainly benefited only the state, since they were diverted to the social-security authorities as a consequence of their payment of supplementary benefit (now known as income support) to the woman (57 per cent of mother and child-only households were receiving that benefit; maintenance payments amounted to more than half of household income in only 4 per cent of such households: Eekelaar and Maclean, 1986, 93–4). The payments were effectively enjoyed by the woman only in those cases where she was employed full-time, in which case they characteristically provided a small but useful supplement to modest earnings. Perhaps even more importantly, the evidence revealed that payments of any significance were almost entirely confined to cases where the woman either was looking after a child, or had done so. In other words, the fact of *parenthood* rather than *marriage in itself* appeared to dictate the imposition of a post-divorce legal obligation of support.

This was not the only evidence of this nature. In the United States in 1985 Lenore Weitzman's research emphasized that the economic effects of divorce were very different as between men and women (Weitzman, 1985), and similar findings were published about the same time in Australia (McDonald, 1986) and with respect to Germany (Willenbacher and Voegeli, 1988). These results led us to suggest that the costs of child-care, both direct and indirect, should be examined more closely, and that the obligation to meet these costs, or a proportion of them, which could be fixed on an absent parent should be more precisely articulated. We argued that the children of a parent who left the home had a first claim against that parent, and that they were entitled to share an equivalent living standard to that of the absent parent, subject to an upper limit representing the standard income level in that society (the 'normative standard' : Eekelaar and Maclean, 1986, 117–23) The caregiving parent would automatically benefit from that claim. Once child support was discharged (when the children left home), we argued that a residual claim should be available on behalf of the caregiving adult, based on the fact that the burdens of the exercise of parenthood had fallen unequally between the parents and that the breakdown of the joint exercise of this parenthood had exposed one of them to the consequences of this inequality (Eekelaar and Maclean, 1986, 142–9). We found it difficult to construct a principled basis for assessment of the claim, but concluded that one might be established by reference to the standard of living a person of the age of the claimant and occupational category of the debtor could have expected if their partnership as parents had continued.

This position amounted to a re-assertion of the policy-goal which had been repealed by the 1984 Act, but with two significant differences. The repealed goal attempted to keep in force an obligation *based on marriage alone* after the marriage was over. It could thus apply (in theory, though, as our research showed, hardly ever in practice) when a short, childless marriage was dissolved. Our principle would apply only in the event of the exercise (and subsequent rupture) of joint parenthood. Secondly, our upper limit based on a 'normative standard' required the absent parent to do no more (if he had the resources) than to keep his children and the other parent at a standard of living somewhere around the average for the community. They would not acquire a right to shadow his standard of living *however high it rose*.

It is unlikely, however, that these concerns for the welfare of children and their caregivers would have been sufficient in themselves to re-cast the policy agenda for the 1990s were it not for the second development. This was triggered in the United Kingdom by the somewhat belated official recognition of the drain on the social-security budget apparently caused by single parenthood. In 1990 the Government published a White Paper which pointed out that not only had the total number of single-parent families almost doubled in the period 1971–86, but about two-thirds of them were receiving income support.[3] This information, coupled with a political ideology hostile to large-scale public spending and rooted in a belief in placing financial (and moral) responsibility on individuals, impelled the government to seek a solution through rigorous enforcement measures against 'absent fathers'. The Australians had already taken this route in 1989 (Child Support Assessment Act 1989; see Parker, 1991) on which the Americans had set out as early as 1974 (see the review by Krause, 1989). The UK initiative led to the enactment of the Child Support Act 1991, a measure dogged with miscalculation and controversy.

---

[3] *Children Come First: The Government's Proposals on the Maintenance of Children,* (HMSO, London, Cm. 123), i and ii (1990).

The policy of rigorous enforcement of the child-support obligation had at least two significant implications on the approach to the practice regarding post-divorce financial arrangements. First, it *overtly* reduced the scope for the application of the 'clean break'. At least as long as one parent was looking after dependent children, it was now officially conceded that a financial relationship between the separated parents was likely to continue. Secondly, it forced legislators to address the issue of how the amount of the payment should be calculated. This could no longer be left entirely to judicial discretion. The American strategy was to require the development of guidelines which courts would be bound to apply when exercising their discretion. Australia, New Zealand, and the United Kingdom adopted a more radical solution. The award was to be set by the application of a formula, implemented primarily through an administrative agency. The way these issues have been tackled has been described elsewhere (see Maclean, 1994; Eekelaar, 1997).

BEYOND CHILD SUPPORT: THE QUEST FOR FURTHER PRINCIPLES

This is not the place to analyse the principles upon which child-support guidelines or formulae are grounded. We wish merely to observe that, by making a serious attempt to instigate the transfer of substantial income from one parent to the other (or to the state claiming in subrogation of that other's rights), it was necessary to make certain principled choices. For example, was the obligation to be fixed according to some minimal cost necessary for providing for a child, or was it to be related to the actual income and wealth of the parent (or parents)? Was the cost of supporting the child's carer to be included? How was the obligation to be allocated between the parents? How were the interests of any 'new' persons to support from the absent parent to be balanced against those of the entitled children? The inevitable further question this exercise prompted was: if setting child-support demands principled choices, does this not also apply to support and to property claims between divorcing spouses? The answer can only be: yes.

We shall examine some approaches which are currently under consideration, first with regard to property allocation, and then with regard to financial provision.

Property Allocation

The issue of property allocation has been confronted by two major problems. One revolves around the issue of 'contributions' (the *contribution issue*). The other arises from the realisation that equality is not always synonymous with equity (the *equity issue*).

The Contribution Issue

In discretionary-based systems, such as those in England and Wales and in Australia, courts are usually directed to consider a wide range of factors in making property allocations after divorce. One factor is likely to be the 'contributions' made by each party to the marriage.[4] These contributions need not be financial; they may normally include enhancing the welfare of the family generally. Our research revealed little about the way this discretion was exercised, largely because so few of our sample (of 274 people) had capital assets of any significance, other than the home.[5] For its research, the Australian Institute of Family Studies used a sample of 825 respondents, weighted towards upper-income groups (McDonald, 1986). The Institute found that in the case of *basic* assets (home, furniture, bank accounts) the wife received about a half-share in under one-third of cases, but in half of them she received *more* than a half share: from 60 per cent to 100 per cent, usually getting more where these assets constituted a higher proportion of the total wealth of the couple. But with respect to 'non-basic' assets (farms, businesses, superannuation, life insurance) the women received less than half, though the data on these splits were unsatisfactory, as men and women sharply diverged in their reports of them.

Although these findings are not confined to court-ordered outcomes, negotiated settlements probably do not differ significantly from the substantial nature of judicially resolved cases. They suggest that evaluations of contributions either play little part in actual property division under discretionary systems or that what are considered to be contributions are influenced by the nature of the capital against which a claim is being made, or even by the extent of capital available. So a woman might find it easier to convince a court that she had contributed to the domestic assets than to business assets simply because she appears to have more control over the former than the latter. Such a perception of what a contribution is will normally make it very difficult for a woman who devotes

---

[4] See Matrimonial Causes Act 1973, s. 25(2)(f) (England and Wales): 'the contributions which each of the parties has made or is likely in the foreseeable future to make to the welfare of the family, including any contribution by looking after the home or caring for the family'. Family Law Act 1975, s. 79(2) (Australia): 'the financial contribution and the contribution other than a financial contribution made directly or indirectly by or on behalf of a party to the marriage or a child of the marriage to the acquisition, conservation or improvement of any property of the parties . . .; the contribution made by a party to the marriage to the welfare of the family constituted by the parties to the marriage and any children of the marriage, including any contribution made in the capacity of homemaker or parent'.

[5] Fewer than one in 5 had more than £500 in savings (Eekelaar and Maclean, 1986, 86).

more time to running the home than participating in business to stake a claim to non-domestic assets, which may be considerably higher in value than domestic ones.

This may, of course, be thought to be the proper outcome: on one perception, the homemaker *has* 'contributed' less to the non-domestic wealth. But this has resulted from a division of labour either socially (or personally) imposed or believed to be mutually beneficial. A solution may be sought in expressly requiring domestic activities to count as contributions towards non-domestic acquisitions, but this poses serious problems of measuring one type of activity against a very different one, and the language of contribution begins to look artificial in that context. Conversely, on what measure of the value of respective contributions does one justify giving a homemaker a larger share in domestic assets where these constitute the greater (or entire) part of the couple's wealth? The reason for this finding may lie less in measuring contributions than in dealing with the equity issue (discussed on 235–6 below).

These considerations explain why a Tentative Draft put before the American Law Institute in March 1995 (American Law Institute, 1995) by the principal reporter, Ira Mark Ellman, makes a radical departure from the 'contribution' approach. This draws on a thorough review of judicial practice throughout the United States and analysis of the extant literature. A second Tentative Draft was agreed in March 1996 (American Law Institute, 1996),[6] after this Chapter was completed, but it retains the essential features of the first Draft, which will be drawn on here. The form of the Draft is to enunciate principles which can apply uniformly but be supplemented by a certain amount of detailed regulation by states.

The Draft distinguishes between property division and 'alimony', treating them separately, but recognizes that in practice they may be traded against each other. On the issue of property, subject to any agreement between the parties, the fundamental principle is that 'marital property' must be divided equally (in the sense that its *value* should be so shared), without investigation into the respective contributions (financial or otherwise) to the marriage made by the partners. The law should irrebuttably presume there was an equal contribution to the 'entire relationship'. The only exceptions would be where (i) one partner should receive an enhanced share by way of compensation for losses (dealt with separately) and (ii) where one spouse has made an improper disposition of some of the property.

This approach sees marital property as acquiring its 'marital' character by reason of the efforts made by either party in relation to the

---

[6] We are grateful to Professor Ira Ellman for information on the American developments.

property during the marriage. So property acquired from labour *performed prior to* the marriage is separate, not marital, property. Conversely, increases in value of separate property brought about by the efforts of either spouse during marriage are marital property and property received *in exchange* for separate property, even during marriage, remains separate. But the radical thrust is that the spouses are deemed to expend energy not just for themselves but for both of them. Or, to put it another way, each partner is deemed to be assisted by the other in the efforts (contributions) he or she makes in relation to the property. As the Draft declares:

The spousal contribution of domestic labor may not confer an equal financial benefit, but may have made it possible for the couple to raise children as well as accumulate property. One spouse may have contributed more than the other in emotional stability, optimism, social skills, and thereby enriched the marital life. Property may be the only thing left at dissolution for the court to divide, but it is not usually the only thing produced during the marriage. An equal allocation of the property at divorce might thus be grounded on a presumption that both spouses contributed significantly to the entire relationship whether or not they contributed to accumulation of property during it [American Law Institute, 1995, 136].

The drafters, however, felt uncomfortable with a result which would confine shareable property to property acquired in that way. Suppose a gift or inheritance made up a substantial element of the family's assets, and effectively determined their standard of living. The drafters discerned an intuition that:

after many years of marriage spouses do not typically treat their assets as entirely separate even if they would technically be classified as separate property. Both spouses are likely to believe, for example, that such assets will be available to provide for their retirement, for a medical crisis, or for other personal emergencies. The longer the marriage the more likely it is that the spouses will have made decisions about their employment or use of their material assets that are premised in part on such expectations about their separate property [American Law Institute, 1995, 159–60].

The Draft therefore allows separate property to be re-characterized as marital property according to rules which take into account both the length of the marriage and the duration since the acquisition of the property.[7]

As in the American proposal, New Zealand's scheme, introduced in 1976, sweeps a similarly wide range of property into the matrimonial

---

[7] The rules for achieving this proposed in Tentative Draft No 1 were altered in Council Draft No 3, but the principle remains the same.

net.[8] Thus all property acquired by either spouse during the marriage is matrimonial, as are the matrimonial home and family chattels whenever they were acquired and also other property acquired before the marriage if intended for common use and benefit. Unlike the American proposal, property acquired during the marriage from separate property becomes matrimonial, as do life-assurance policies, but increases in value of and income from separate property are matrimonial only if those increases or the income are attributable to the actions of the *other* (not *either*) spouse. Pension benefits are matrimonial property if entitlement is derived wholly or in part from contributions made during the marriage. Other property is separate, including property acquired by succession or survivorship unless 'with the express or implied consent of the spouse who received it, the property or the proceeds of any disposition of it have been so intermingled with other matrimonial property that it is unreasonable or impracticable to regard that property or those proceeds as being separate property'. Separate property remains with its original owner.

The system diverges from the American proposals mainly in the opportunities given for evaluations of contributions to displace equality of division. Within matrimonial property there is a further distinction. In the case of *domestic* property (the home and chattels) there is a strong presumption in favour of equal sharing, unless the marriage was of short duration (generally defined as less than three years), when, in the case of property acquired by gift or succession, equality is displaced by determination according to contributions, or if equal sharing would be 'repugnant to justice', when again distribution will follow contributions. For other matrimonial property (*balance* property) there is a weaker presumption of equal sharing because equality will apply unless one partner's 'contribution to the marriage partnership has clearly been greater than that of the other spouse'. In 1983 courts were directed that, in making any order, they should have particular regard to the need to provide a home for any dependent child.

These opportunities for resort to contribution evaluation have been criticized for encouraging litigation and leading to undervaluation of women's contributions (see Bridge, 1992). For example, research demonstrated, as it had done in Australia, that the larger the totality of balance property, the smaller was the proportion which tended to be awarded to the wife. Wives tended to be given only a quarter of the value of farms (Bridge, 1992, 245). Herein, therefore, lies a central point of principle to be resolved whenever post-divorce property-allocation is made. Is equality of division to be deemed appropriate as being an implicit

[8] Matrimonial Property Act 1976, s. 8. See Bridge, 1992; Atkin, Austin, and Grainer, 1995. We are grateful to Bill Atkin for information on New Zealand developments.

reflection of lives lived together, or is it to be the result of an assumption that spouses have *in fact* provided an equal input through 'contributions' (though perhaps in different ways) into the effort of accumulating wealth, although this assumption is open to rebuttal.

Reforms proposed in Australia adopt the latter approach with great clarity. Following a Report of a Parliamentary Select Committee in 1992,[9] the Family Law Reform Bill (No 2) 1995 sought to enact that courts should dispose of property disputes on divorce 'in a way which the court determines is just and equitable'. Although the Bill later fell on the dissolution of the Australian Parliament in 1996, its provisions justify examination as a distinctive approach to the issues under consideration. Under them, a court would be required to assume that justice and equity required 'the disputed property to be divided between the parties in proportion to their respective contributions to the marriage as a whole', unless 'it considers that doing so would not produce a just and equitable result'. Expanding on this, the Bill said that the court was to assume 'as a starting point' that the parties to the marriage had made equal contributions to the marriage as a whole but that this assumption would be displaced if it was satisfied that the contributions were not in fact equal. In making its decision the court was to consider the duration of the marriage and the parties' cohabitation, financial and non-financial contributions made to the acquisition, conservation and improvement of property, their financial resources, and the welfare of the family 'including any contribution made in the capacity of homemaker or parent'. A whole range of other factors was set out as relevant for deciding what is just and equitable.

Although the Australian proposals specified an assumption of equal contribution as a starting point, they invited its rebuttal by measurement of the actuality of contribution. This is specifically rejected in the American Draft:

The difficulty of attaching monetary value to these non-financial contributions precludes precise assessment of whether spousal contributions are equal. . . . Furthermore, the difficulty of measurement may make it sensible for the law to presume irrebuttably that the spouses contributed equally to their entire relationship, even though the presumption will sometimes be incorrect. To determine whether the presumption is correct in any particular case would require a retrospective examination of the parties' marital life that would be impractical if not impossible [American Law Institute, 1995, 137].

---

[9] *The Family Law Act 1975: Certain Aspects of its Operation and Interpretation,* (Australian Government Printing Service, Canberra, (November 1992)). We are grateful to Belinda Fehlberg for information about Australian developments.

The Equity Issue

The equity issue arises directly from the findings of research, particularly by ourselves (Eekelaar and Maclean, 1986), Lenore Weitzman (Weitzman, 1985), and the Australian Institute of Family Studies (McDonald, 1986) that, after divorce, women characteristically suffer significantly greater financial hardship than men. The Australian researchers spelt out the reasons with great clarity: marriage and divorce have virtually no effect on workforce participation by men. For women, post-divorce workforce participation is related to whether they are in work at the time of separation; discontinuities in women's employment are overwhelmingly due to child-care responsibilities (McDonald, 1986, 260–1). The implication of this is that, the parties themselves being unequal, equal division of assets is not necessarily an equitable division: rule equality does not bring about result equality (Fineman, 1983; Eekelaar, 1988).

This is almost certainly one reason why women appear to receive a larger share of domestic assets, especially where they constitute the major portion of the entire assets. Another reason why this is so is that courts try to maintain a stable residence for the children. We had found that, in half of our sample involving owner-occupiers, the house was sold (irrespective of the presence of children). Where it was not sold, in those cases where there were no children the husband was more likely to stay in it (giving the wife a compensating payment) whereas if there were children the wife more likely to remain. The Australian research found that the house was sold in one-third of cases, but that (as we too had found) the children left anyway in half the cases. But the Institute also found that the house was more likely to be sold where the equity value was low or where it represented a high *proportion* of the couple's total wealth. So if there existed significant other assets out of which adjustments could be made, the home would be kept, unless it was more of a liability than an asset. These outcomes show that where the home is concerned, a range of factors come into play which affect the equity of straightforward sale and equal division of the proceeds.

Lying behind the problem of what to do about the home and its contents is the fundamental issue of disparity in earning capacity. This was expressed by the New Zealand Minister of Justice in a symposium on 'Family Property, Law and Policy' in November 1994:

I have never been able to quite understand the fairness in a case where the assets are divided more or less equally, but the wife who has custody and primary responsibility for the children, is left with a greatly reduced earnings capacity both then and in the future compared with the earnings potential of the husband. . . . In other words, when it comes to a division of property, should the earnings capacity of each partner be taken into account, and, if so, how? [Atkin, Austin, and Grainer, 1995].

It is unlikely that property allocation can deal with this. Although New York has treated earning capacity within the context of a professional degree as a form of property (*O'Brien* v. *O'Brien* (1985)), this has not been followed elsewhere in the United States. There are serious problems of assessing its value (how can we know how far future earnings will be attributable to the qualification and how much to subsequent efforts? and how do we evaluate a person's claims to have contributed to another's attainment of a degree or earning capacity?). In any event, to treat payments ordered as a share in someone's earning capacity as capital payments defies the reality that these are income transfers.

The 'equity issue' therefore usually implies that equal property division does not settle the equities between the parties. It will normally be necessary to supplement this by some kind of income transfer, and we will discuss how this has been approached in a moment. But it can also be approached by allowing departure from equal property-sharing where this could satisfy the demands raised by the equity issue. In New Zealand this is done through the qualifications to equality permitted by reference to contributions. But, as has been pointed out, this focuses on *past* contributions (with the difficulties of evaluation mentioned earlier) rather than the future income and earning capacities of the spouses (Bridge, 1992, 248). In Australia the 1995 Family Law Bill (No 2) allowed departure from distribution in accordance with (presumed equal) contributions if such a distribution would not produce a just and equitable result by reason of a wide range of factors which included the parties' present financial resources and earning capacities (Family Law Reform (No 2) Bill 1995, sections 86B and 86D). The American Draft explicitly allows an enhanced share in property to be awarded as part of a 'compensatory' award, to be discussed later.

We now consider the principles that have been used to go beyond property awards and to justify awards on other grounds. These might sometimes be income transfers, although they could also be capitalized payments, thus producing unequal property shares.

Non-property-based Awards

The Australian Institute of Family Studies sought to address the equity issue by providing a method whereby 'the marriage partnership' (i.e. not just the other party) should compensate anyone who would in fact be disadvantaged by an equal property division.[10] In line with their find-

[10] This proposal appeared in McDonald (1986), but was developed by Funder (1992), and re-stated in Funder, Harrison, and Weston (1993).

ings, this method is unashamedly tied to the fact of child-rearing. Essentially it involves expressing in tables published in regulations the differences between the earnings of women who do not have children and the earnings of women who have had children. This would be reduced by actuarially calculated chances of remarriage, working later, or receiving state benefits. A proportion of this would be 'attributed to the marriage'. The resultant sum would be regarded as a debt against the net partnership assets. If it came to a figure greater than the net assets, it could be paid off by instalments. This approach has not, however, commended itself to the legislature, which has retained in section 3 of the Family Law Bill (No 2) a discretionary approach to spousal maintenance.

The American Draft also proceeds on the basis that any transfers which are made other than in furtherance of the property division (made on the principles discussed earlier) should be grounded in the notion of compensation. This is seen as being a major 'conceptual innovation', holding many advantages over the present dominant characterization of alimony as being for the relief of need. Need is seen as being impossible to define objectively, and the claims based on it to be pleas for help rather than claims based on entitlement (American Law Institute, 1995, 184–5). Hence it is proposed to replace the word 'alimony' by the expression 'compensatory spousal payments'. But the method of conceptualizing the loss is very different from the one proposed by the Australian Institute. First, it is not tied to the exercise of child-rearing. Secondly, it expressly rejects the use of 'group data' which show that child-carers as a group do less well in the labour market than non-child-carers 'because of the speculation inherent in comparing the actual facts with the hypothetical facts that would have developed had the parties behaved differently years earlier' (American Law Institute, 1995, 251).[11] The proposals seek instead to ascertain the actual losses suffered by individual claimants and to find principles justifying which of the losses should be subject to compensation.

The compensable losses are described as being: (i) in long marriages (a) the loss in living standard by the spouse with less wealth or lower living standard and (b) an earning-capacity loss arising during the marriage but continuing after it, arising from having a disproportionate share of the care of children, or of care provided to a sick, elderly, or disabled party in fulfilment of a moral obligation of the other spouse of or both of them and (ii) in some other cases, certain other losses, such as those caused through unrewarded investment in building up the other spouse's earning capacity.

---

[11] American Law Institute, 1995, 251. We rejected the Australian approach for the same reasons: Eekelaar and Maclean, 1986, 145–6.

The first type of compensation corresponds to recognition of interests arising by what traditional legal analysis refers to as 'expectation' or 'reliance' interests, and thus are properly confined to longer marriages, while the second type could apply in shorter marriages because they correspond to a restitutionary claim. But how would the first type of compensation (i)(a) be calculated? This would need to involve certain axioms. For example, it might be proclaimed that after fifty years of marriage there should be no disparity in income between the parties after divorce, it being reasonable to suppose that after that period of time the reliance and expectation interests demand income equality. This can be expressed as $D \times 0.5$ (where D is the difference in income). One might therefore see this expectation as building up, over the years, at a rate of $D \times 0.01$ per year, although the claim would be triggered only after the marriage had lasted a specified duration: say ten years (when the compensation would be $D \times 0.1$). The duration of the award could also be related, by means of a formula, to the length of the marriage. This, then, is the technique adopted in the proposal, and it is also used for calculating an award under (i)(b) (the effects of child-rearing). In this context you look again at the difference in earning capacity (D) and apply to it a 'child-care durational factor' which has the effect of reducing D in accordance with the length of child-care provided: so, if seven years of care have been provided, the award could be $D \times (7 \times 0.015)$. A claimant might of course be entitled to awards under both (i)(a) and (i)(b), but the combined award would not exceed the maximum allowed under (i)(a). The duration of a (i)(b) award would relate to the period of child care. Finally, it must be recalled that one of the permitted grounds for departing from equal property sharing is where an enhanced share is awarded to one party in order to give effect to a claim for compensatory maintenance.

It is important to remember that these formulae would operate only as presumptions, and could be departed from by explicitly justified grounds showing their application would lead to substantial injustice. However, the proposal also goes to much length arguing that conduct should be ignored when settling the award. The argument is that to allow in considerations of conduct would undermine the compensatory basis of the award (although conduct which imposed 'financial costs' could be relevant). Specific harms arising from marital misconduct, it is said, should be dealt with through tort law.

Scotland: A British Compromise

While England and Wales was applying the discretionary jurisdiction, guided only by the 'persisting obligation' (or 'minimal loss') principle, (see above note 2) the Scottish Law Commission was reviewing the basis for dealing with post-divorce property and finances in Scotland. In Scotland, prior to 1964, no financial provision of any kind could be awarded to a guilty spouse, but the innocent spouse had a claim against the assets as if the guilty one had died. The Succession (Scotland) Act 1964 allowed a 'periodical allowance' to be made in favour of an innocent party, but when the Divorce (Scotland) Act 1976 introduced no-fault divorce, the matter demanded urgent review. This was provided in the Scottish Law Commission's report of 1981 (see Scottish Law Commission, 1981). This made recommendations for legislation which would deal comprehensively and consistently with both property and income matters.

The Scottish report believed that post-divorce financial and property settlements should be based on principles demanding that matrimonial property should be fairly shared, that contributions to and disadvantages suffered from the marriage should be fairly recognized, that the economic burden of child-care should be fairly shared, that there should be fair provision for adjustment to independence, and that grave financial hardship should be relieved (Scottish Law Commission, 1981, paragraph 3.64). However, although these matters are described as principles, and are stated to be such in the legislation which subsequently gave effect to the recommendations (Family Law (Scotland) Act 1985, section 9), there is little to distinguish them from 'factors to be taken into account' under the discretionary systems. But the separate provision about property does introduce a more structured element into the process. This enacts that, in applying the principle about sharing property fairly, 'the net value of the matrimonial property shall be taken to be shared fairly between the parties to the marriage when it is shared equally or in such other proportions as are justified by special circumstances' (Family Law (Scotland) Act 1985, section 10(1)).

The definition of matrimonial property is similar to that used in New Zealand, so it includes all property acquired during marriage and property acquired before the marriage but used as a family home or its contents, but excludes acquisitions by way of gift or succession from third parties. However, in contrast with New Zealand, which allows sharing to be displaced sometimes by reference to contributions, and even more unlike Australia, which defines equitable sharing as being *prima facie* reflective of equal contributions (see above), the Scottish concept of fair sharing makes no reference to contributions. This reflects the view that 'an attempt to work out which spouse had contributed more to the welfare of the family during the marriage would often involve an unproductive examination and investigation of conduct over many years' (Scottish Law Commission, 1981, paragraph 3.9). This largely overcomes the 'contribution' problem. It is true that 'fair account' is to be taken of economic advantages conferred by one spouse on the other, but the restriction of this to economic advantages avoids potentially open-ended evaluations of non-financial 'contributions'. Nor are contributions expressly mentioned as being among the stated 'special circumstances' which permit non-equal distribution to be made.

There is, however, no express recognition of the 'equity' problem. The fact that the property may be shared between parties of very different earning capacities is not stated to be a reason for departing from equality.[12] This may be a reflection of the fact that the Scottish Law Commission Report was compiled at a period when the 'minimal-loss' principle was under attack, self-sufficiency was being promoted, and the empirical evidence demonstrating the extent of the 'equity' problem had not yet been published. 'Equity' issues can, of course, be addressed under the legislation in the context of the account taken of economic *disadvantages* suffered by either party in the interests of the other party or of the family, but these must be quantified at the time of the divorce and redressed by a capital award (albeit one which is payable in instalments) which is not subject to later variation (Family Law (Scotland) Act 1985, section 13(2)). Although, as we saw, the Australian Institute of Family Studies attempted to provide a method for quantifying such losses insofar as they may be suffered in the future, this is an inherently speculative exercise and difficult to achieve through the judicial process.

As far as non-property-based awards are concerned (i.e. income orders) the Scottish scheme restricts these to a period of three years from the divorce if the objective is to make adjustment to independence (self-sufficiency). Income orders may be longer than that if the award can be justified on the basis of fairly sharing the economic burden of child-care, or of relieving grave financial hardship, but the former merges with child support and the latter only applies in extreme circumstances. The disparity in earning power, the consequences of which may extend over a long period, is not fully addressed in these provisions.

CONCLUSIONS

Empirical research tends to undermine old certainties. It draws hitherto excluded information into the judgemental process. The costs of child-

---

[12] Departure is permitted in 'special circumstances'. Without prejudice to the generality of those words, these are said to include any agreement between the parties, the source of funds used to acquire the property where they did not come from the parties' income or efforts, destruction, alienation etc. of the property, the nature of the property and its use, and any liability for expenses regarding the property in connection with divorce: Family Law (Scotland) Act 1985, s. 10(6).

care itself, the lost opportunity costs which fall on the child's carers, the evaluation of contributions to family life: these are all matters which must now be factored in to an assessment of the fairness of post-divorce outcomes. The paradox is that the more numerous these factors become the harder it is to exercise a judgement on a discretionary basis. Some judges are not deterred by this. L'Heureux-Dubé J, in the Supreme Court of Canada, has not hesitated to examine in depth the social-science literature and evidence relating to post-divorce finances and to assert their relevance to the determination of post-divorce support issues within a discretionary remit.[13] As we remarked earlier, the Australian review of the Family Law Act maintains a highly discretionary approach to spousal maintenance, detailing an extensive list of contributions to be taken into account (Family Law Reform Bill (No 2) 1995, Division 3).

As we stated at the outset of this Chapter, however, it has not been our purpose here to evaluate the merits of discretionary, as against rule-based, decision-making. We would observe, however, that, notwithstanding L'Heureux-Dube J's heroic advocacy, one of the indirect effects of bringing into view so much social data has, ironically, been to push policy-makers towards attempting to find solutions grounded on generalized standards. The most spectacular example of this is the proposal of the Australian Institute of Family Studies to use national tables of earnings by childless and child-rearing women as a reference point for arriving at a compensatory award. Our own suggestion that a parent should have a *prima facie* obligation to underwrite (his) children's and the other parent's living standard up to some kind of community average displayed a similar approach. The American drafts lack this communal dimension. In their terms, the approach of the Australian Institute could significantly over-compensate, and our approach might under-compensate. The American preference therefore is to relate the award more closely to the respective post-divorce incomes of the parties, but discretion is limited by the axiomatic setting of the degrees by which the difference between the incomes is to be closed and their relationship to the duration of the marriage.

We have observed that opinion in New Zealand, Scotland, Australia, and the United States has accepted the widespread intuition that fairness demands *prima facie* an equal sharing of matrimonial property

---

[13] *Moge* v. *Moge* (1993) 99 DLR (4th) 456; see at 491 and 495. *Willick* v. *Willick* (1994) 6 RFL (4th) 161. In Canada, division of property on divorce falls under provincial jurisdiction. The predominant approach is very similar to that described in Scotland: *viz.*, that contributions are irrelevant in establishing the presumption of equal sharing, and that little allowance is made for 'equity' issues to influence departure from equality. The result is that in Canada, while post-divorce *income* issues are determined on a wide discretionary basis, *property* distribution tends to follow established rules.

when the marriage ends. However, there is a sharply divergent view about whether this has the nature of a reward for efforts expended towards the well-being of the relationship and should therefore be subject to displacement by demonstration that the spouses did not devote equal efforts towards it (a view held most strongly, it seems, in Australia, but less so in New Zealand) or whether this reflects something inherent in the marital relationship itself, to be departed from only in quite narrowly defined circumstances (which is the American, Canadian, and Scottish view). But the American draft contains the clearest recognition of the 'equity' issue, and the Australian 1995 Bill allowed it to play a part among various factors justifying non-equal division. New Zealand and Scotland, perhaps because their laws preceded the publication of research evidence revealing the problem, refer to it not at all, although it can be taken indirectly into consideration in New Zealand through a retrospective evaluation of contributions and in Scotland disadvantages suffered may be compensated for through an additional capital award if quantifiable and quantified at the time of divorce.

It is unlikely that any of these problems will reach definitive resolution. However a collaboration of lawyers, policy-makers, and researchers has moved the debate into wider waters, and this paper has shown the varying ways technology is used to reach the desired solutions. England and Wales, sadly, seems as yet to have nothing substantial to contribute to the debate.

CASES

Atkinson *v.* Atkinson [1995] 2 FLR 356.
Barrett *v.* Barrett [1988] 2 FLR 517.
Crozier *v.* Crozier [1994] Fam. 114.
Delaney *v.* Delaney [1990] 2 FLR 457.
Moge *v.* Moge (1993) 99 DLR (4th) 456.
O'Brien *v.* O'Brien, 66 NY 2d 576, 489 NE 2d 712 (1985).
Smith *v.* McInerney [1994] 2 FLR 1077.
Suter *v.* Suter & Jones [1987] Fam. 111.
Thomas *v.* Thomas [1995] 2 FLR 668.
Willick *v.* Willick (1994) 6 RFL (4th) 161.

REFERENCES

AMERICAN LAW INSTITUTE (1995), *Principles of the Law of Family Dissolution: Analyses and Recommendations: Tentative Draft No. 1* (American Law Institute, Philadelphia, Penn.).

—— (1996), *Principles of the Law of Family Dissolution: Analysis and Recommendations: Tentative Draft No. 2* (American Law Institute, Philadelphia, Penn.).

ATKIN, BILL, AUSTIN, GRAEME, and GRAINER, VIRGINIA (eds.) (1995), *Family Property: Law and Policy*, (New Zealand Institute of Advanced Legal Studies, Wellington).

BAKER, W. BARRINGTON, EEKELAAR, J., GIBSON, C., and RAIKES, S. (1977), *The Matrimonial Jurisdiction of Registrars* (SSRC Centre for Socio-Legal Studies, Wolfson College, Oxford).

BRIDGE, CAROLINE (1992), 'Reallocation of Property after Marriage Breakdown: The Matrimonial Property Act 1976' in Mark Henaghan and Bill Atkin (eds.), *Family Law and Policy in New Zealand* (Oxford University Press, Oxford).

EEKELAAR, JOHN (1988), 'Equality and the Purpose of Maintenance', *Journal of Law and Society*, 15, 188–200.

—— (1997), 'Child Support: Judicial or Computerized Justice?' in T. Oldham (ed.), *Child Support: the Next Frontier* (University of Michigan Press, Ann Arbor, Mich.).

—— and CLIVE, ERIC (1977), *Custody after Divorce* (SSRC Centre for Socio-Legal Studies, Wolfson College, Oxford).

—— and MACLEAN, MAVIS (1986), *Maintenance after Divorce* (Oxford University Press, Oxford).

FINEMAN, MARTHA L. (1983), 'Implementing Equality: Ideology, Contradiction and Social Change' [1983] *Wisconsin Law Review* 789–886.

FUNDER, KATHLEEN (1992), 'Australia: A Proposal for Reform' in L. Weitzman and M. Maclean (eds.), *Economic Consequences of Divorce: the International Perspective* (Oxford University Press, Oxford)

—— HARRISON, MARGARET, and WESTON, RUTH (1993), *Settling Down* (Australian Institute of Family Studies, Melbourne)

HAWKINS, K. (ed.) (1992), *The Uses of Discretion* (Oxford University Press, Oxford)

KRAUSE, HARRY D. (1989), 'Child Support Re-assessed: Limits of Private Responsibility and the Public Interest', 2 *University of Illinois Law Review* 367–98.

MACLEAN, MAVIS (1994), 'Child Support in the United Kingdom: Making the Move from Court to Agency', 31 *Houston Law Review* 515–38.

McDONALD, PETER (ed.) (1986), *Settling Up* (Prentice-Hall, Sydney).

PARKER, STEPHEN (1991), 'Child Support in Australia: Children's Rights or Public Interest?' *International Journal of Law and the Family*, 5, 24–57.

SCOTTISH LAW COMMISSION (1981), *Family Law: Report on Aliment and Financial Provision*, Scot. Law Com. No 67 (HMSO, Edinburgh).

WEITZMAN, LENORE (1985) *The Divorce Revolution: The Unexpected Social and Economic Consequences for Women and Children in America* (Free Press, New York).

WILLENBACHER, B., and VOEGELI, W. (1988), 'Multiple Disadvantages of Single-Parent Families in the Federal Republic of Germany', in M.-T. Meulders-Klein and J. Eekelaar (eds.), *Family, State and Individual Economic Security* (Story Scientia, Brussels).

11

Judges, Politics, Politicians and the Confusing Role of the Judiciary[1]

ROBERT STEVENS

All of us owe a great debt of gratitude to Don Harris. A superb scholar, he offered leadership to the Centre for Socio-Legal Studies through a long and difficult period. The fact that the field is so firmly established both in Oxford and in the United Kingdom is significantly his work. He has given so many of us support and encouragement and helped to bring us into the mainstream of legal scholarship. For me, his encouragement, so often related to the role of the judiciary, where the socio-legal field may well be on the brink of important breakthroughs. This study of the current state of relations between the judiciary and the executive is intended as an encouragement to these endeavours.[2]

The apparent tensions of the last few years between judges and politicians have a historical inevitability. A memorandum from the Permanent Secretary to the Lord Chancellor read:

The deep and . . . underlying truth seems to be that Judges, however, subconsciously, desire to retain or obtain for the judiciary problems more fit for executive decisions. . . . In recent years . . . it has been difficult for the State to obtain justice from the Judges of the High Court. It is not too much to say that in recent years, the weight of prejudice against the State in the minds of many members of

[1] I should like to thank Walter Aylen, Ruth Deech, John Eekelaar, Keith Hawkins, Anthony Holland, Anthony Lester, Christopher McCrudden, Daniel Prentice, Andrew Sanders, Colin Sheppard, William Twining, and Stephen Whitefield for commenting on this paper. A number of judges and civil servants have also been kind enough to comment. I have assumed that they would prefer to be anonymous. With respect to all the errors and opinions, they are, of course, mine. I should also like to thank my long-suffering secretary at Covington and Burling, Carole O'Callaghan (together with Vicki Smith), for typing and then revising innumerable drafts, mostly with good humour.

[2] This article is based on the 1996 Hardwicke Building Lecture. The ideas for this lecture were developed at three seminars: the first at the University of Bristol in December 1994, the second at the University of Hong Kong in September 1995, and the third at Pembroke College, Oxford, in May 1996. The lecture also draws on earlier work: Brian Abel-Smith and Robert Stevens (1967); Brian Abel-Smith and Robert Stevens (1968); Robert Stevens (1983, 1993).

the Court of Appeal and Judges of the High Court has been such as seriously to affect the Administration of Justice.

That was not Sir Thomas Legg warning Lord Mackay. It was a confidential memorandum from Sir Claud Schuster, dated 25 March 1929 (LCO 2/1133), written to the first Lord Hailsham—Lord Chancellor in the later years of Baldwin's first administration.[3]

In order to understand the continuing friction, it will be necessary first to analyse some of the 'terms of indeterminate reference' which so becloud any serious analysis of the British Constitution; then to look, albeit impressionistically, at the last fifty or sixty years in terms of change—in the nature of the judiciary, in the nature of the judicial process, and in the political scene itself. Finally, some assessment will be made of the implications for the judiciary and the constitution at large resulting from developments over the last few years. It is particularly appropriate to raise these issues as Lord Bingham replaces Lord Taylor as Chief Justice, and Lord Woolf moves into the powerful position of Master of the Rolls.[4] Indeed, by the summer of 1996, even the House of Lords set aside time to debate the relationship of the judges and the executive.[5]

I TERMS OF INDETERMINATE REFERENCE

To begin, however, the context does not help. The words 'constitutional' and 'unconstitutional', as used in political debate in England are terms of political argumentation, they are not normally legal terms. The word 'constitutional' in England is used in a political rather than a legal sense.[6] It is a political argument to be thrown about when a King abdicates, a Minister refuses to resign, or perhaps even when a Government refuses to accept a Report. It does not normally rise even to what Dicey would have called a Convention of the Constitution. It is not a legal concept at all. Since the US Constitution is increasingly turned to by English

---

[3] In the mid-1980s, Sir Michael Kerry, the Treasury Solicitor, noted that the 'Crown has lost too many cases in the courts recently' and urged officials to 'think through the legal basis of and to consider properly the powers and authority for activities'. (Kerry, 1983, 170–1).

[4] 'Judging Judges: Bingham and Woolf Should Be Welcomed, But Act Warily' (leader), *The Times*, 25 May 1996: 'It is to the credit of a Conservative Government that two men of such liberal temper should be appointed to the two most senior judicial posts. Yet if judges themselves chose to become more political, then they may undermine the foundation of their own independence'. See also, Simon Jenkins, 'The Minister and Judge', *ibid*. The *Observer* reported that Lord Mackay had to fight off a right-wing attack (including Mr Howard) in order to get the 'liberal' judges appointed: *Observer*, 26 May 1996.

[5] 'The Judiciary: Public Controversy', H.L. Debs.(5th Ser.), vol. 572, col. 1254. (5 June 1996), hereinafter 'The Judiciary: Public Controversy'.

[6] See especially on this Sedley (1994).

lawyers, it is important to note when an American lawyer says something is unconstitutional or violates the separation of powers, it does not normally signify a political slogan, nor even a desirable and conventional process to be followed, but rather it symbolizes a clear legal point. In particular, with respect to the separation of powers, while there are disagreements about institutional appropriateness and inevitably there is overlap between the three branches of government, the core concept is clear.

In what we may happily agree to call either the American War of Independence or the Revolutionary War, the Colonists were much divided about the issue of separation of powers. Whether the colonists read Montesquieu or whether they were just tired of seeing the judges, appointed by the Crown, interfering with the democratically elected legislature, Massachusetts left no doubt that it wanted to break with an English system. Its Constitution of 1780, drafted while the War was going on, put it bluntly:

In the government of this Commonwealth, the legislative department shall never exercise the executive and judicial powers, or either of them; the executive shall never exercise the legislative and judicial powers, or either of them; the judicial shall never exercise the legislative and executive powers, or either of them; to the end that it may be a government of laws, and not of men.

It is, however, impossible to generalize about the views of the Founding Fathers. When New York drafted its Constitution, it provided for a Supreme Court based on the Judicial Committee of the Privy Council—comprised of eight senators and seven judges. Even here, however, there is a moral. In the great New York Constitutional Convention of 1846 all this was swept away. In the place of such an elitist non-separatist solution, the Convention required the election of judges at all levels and a clear separation of powers.[7]

What is perhaps more significant is that there is today, in the United States, both a sophisticated literature about the separation of powers and serious thought by lawyers about the impact of judicial intervention going back at least to the writings of Thayer at Harvard in the 1890s. In this country there is little serious analysis of the separation of powers.

[7] Separation of powers, particularly after the addition of a Bill of Rights, passed a great deal of power to the courts, including the right to declare legislation unconstitutional, something not envisaged by Jefferson or Hamilton. It is true that the separation of powers as such has not always been significant in decisions since the Commerce Clause has taken pride of place. The separation of powers, however, played its part in the effort to strike down the New Deal. See also the Steel Seizure case, *Youngstown Sheet & Tube Co.* v. *Sawyer* (1952). The provision from the 1780 Massachusetts Constitution, cited earlier, was recently used by that powerful Chicago-trained intellect of Scalia J to attempt to show that the Special Prosecutor's status was inconsistent with the separation of powers: *Morrison* v. *Olsen* (1988).

Maurice Vile's book may be the major exception, although I would certainly add the important work of Geoffrey Marshall, and now Eric Barendt (1995). The historical basis in England, however, is very different. The judges were involved in the legislative process throughout the eighteenth century. They played some role in administering local government until well into the nineteenth century. Despite the rhetoric, the Act of Settlement made them lions under the mace. Mansfield and Ellenborough served in the Cabinet. No-one had a clear idea why there needed to be a second appeal. The House of Lords was reinstated as a judicial body in 1876, having been abolished in 1873, primarily for propping up the power of hereditary peers (Stevens, 1983, 57–67). After all, with Dicey about to propound the absolute sovereignty of Parliament, intellectually a second appeal was indefensible, as both the Liberal and Conservative Lord Chancellors, Selborne and Cairns, admitted.

The failure to have even a clear core concept of what separation of powers means in Britain has led to a series of public outbursts which, however hard we try to analyse them, often elude rational analysis. They, of course, impinge on procedural due process and delegated legislation, what we now normally call judicial review and the *Wednesbury* principle. Yet, to go back now, and to attempt fully to understand Hewart's attack in *The New Despotism* or the strange response, evolved by the alchemy of the Civil Service, the Scott–Donoghmore Committee on Ministers' Powers, requires an element of credulity (Stevens, 1993, 31–3). Nor in the light of recent thinking can one be entirely happy about the Committee on Administrative Tribunals.

That Britain does not have separation of powers is clear beyond peradventure. The example we all use is the Lord Chancellor, where even Gilbert and Sullivan had noticed there was some confusion. Indeed, perhaps the Labour Party, and certainly the Liberal Democrats, have called for the restructuring of the Lord Chancellor's Office into a Ministry of Justice, with politicians heading the Ministry, although, as Lord Irvine approaches the Woolsack, some have suggested Labour's enthusiasm for the change may be waning. Yet the present situation is bound to cause confusion—whether it be the concerns of Lord Lester that the Lord Chancellor was putting administrative and political responsibilities ahead of the protection of judicial independence in his handling of changes at the Employment Appeals Tribunal[8] or Judge Wilson's con-

---

[8] Lord Lester on the operation of the Employment Appeal Tribunal. See H.L. Debs. (5th Ser.), vol. 554, col. 756 ff. (27 April 1994). The concern surrounded Lord Mackay's requirement that the Presiding Judge of the Employment Appeal Tribunal be accountable for his administrative behaviour. There was concern when the Presiding Judge left the bench rather than accept administrative change. Fortunately, the new Presiding Judge, Mummery J, rapidly cleaned up the backlog, and Lord Taylor was able to claim another triumph for judicial administration. Lord Taylor, speech, 'Lord Mayor's Dinner to H.M. Judges', 5 July 1995.

cern that the Lord Chancellor was putting his Cabinet responsibilities ahead of his duty to act as shop steward for the Judiciary (Wilson, 1994, 1453).

This whole issue becomes clearer as one thinks of the use of the judges. In the United States judges are expected to live within their co-equal branch of the Constitution. As far as possible they are discouraged from arguing political points outside court or taking on administrative or legislative chores.[9] It was generally agreed that Jackson J had made a mistake by agreeing to be a prosecutor at Nuremberg and that Warren CJ should not have chaired the Commission investigating the Kennedy assassination. Yet between 1945 and 1979 the English judges, while flaunting their independence as judges, actually chaired over a third of Royal Commissions and Departmental Committees,[10] which in those days played such a significant role in British public life. It was not merely inquiries about spying or errant ministers, or Indian boundaries, or colonial insurrections, it covered the range of pay awards—from dockers to doctors, and all aspects of public life, from the unions and company law to compensation and income tax and from spies to the restructuring of administration. It allowed A. P. Herbert to describe the scene as 'Government by Radcliffery'—although one should note that that itself was a change. In the nineteenth century, and even down to the First World War, the two Houses of Parliament normally did their own investigating even in such delicate matters as the Marconi scandal. Because such concepts as independence and impartiality are not seriously unpacked either academically or politically in England, there has not been a persuasive analysis of which inquiries judges are eminently suitable for and those which it is politically unwise for them to undertake.

While in the period of Butskillism, Reports were sometimes consigned to oblivion, in general, judicially-chaired Committees or Commissions were either implemented, partially implemented or at least came to have an important psychological impact on the evolution of a field. At the very

---

[9] The assumption has always been that the *quid pro quo* was that politicians did not attack judges—especially at the federal level. For an example of the flouting of that principle and those assumptions, see the case of Judge Harold Baer, a federal judge, who, in the Spring of 1996, rejected police evidence in a drug case including duffle bags filled with cocaine. Republican Presidential Candidate Bob Dole suggested Judge Baer should be impeached, while President Clinton attacked the ruling, adding that independence of the judiciary did not mean that a judge 'should be entitled not only to lifetime tenure but a gag rule on everyone else'. The judge reversed his earlier ruling. 'Clinton Chides Foes Over Judge' *International Herald Tribune*, 4 April 1996, and 'Amid Political Flak, Judge in Drug Case Reverses View', *International Herald Tribune*, 3 April 1996. For a review, see Riske (1996). By this time, Speaker Gingrich and 150 other Members of Congress had urged the judge to resign in view of this 'shocking and egregious example of judicial activism'.

[10] Between 1945 and 1965 the figure rises to over a half if lawyers are included (Cartwright, 1975, 69).

least they were treated with respect.[11] The only two recent Committees, which were both enquiries into sensitive political issues, chaired by members of the judiciary, were the Nolan Committee and the Scott Inquiry. To a greater or lesser extent, both were trashed by the elected representatives of the people—at least one of them successfully.[12] The game has changed.[13] The need for greater clarity about the separation of powers will become more important, the more the judges throw off their traditional caution about speaking out[14] and their formal political caution about moving into new judicial areas. One of the political trade-offs of that enhanced power may be that the judiciary should be far less willing to accept extra-judicial chores.

A mandated political front line appears elsewhere. The Law Lords can scarcely be held responsible for having been made members of the Upper House. As the result of the activities of a group of disreputable Tory backbench MPs, the jurisdiction of the Lords was reinstated in 1876, and part of the plan was to keep the Law Lords politicalized. Certainly that plan was fulfilled in the first half of this century, both in judicial decisions (procedural due-process was seriously weakened by the Liberal law lords in *Arlidge* and *Rice*: Stevens, 1983, 251–9) as well as in political activities. It is the latter, however, that is significant in the separation of powers. Lord Carson did not hesitate to attack the 1922 Treaty while a Lord of Appeal and Lord Sumner gave enthusiastic support to General Dyer for his work at Amritsar (Stevens, 1983, 262–6).

Since then most commentators have asserted that law lords have only spoken on non-political or legal matters. That may well be a superficial analysis. Lord Goddard was a strong advocate of both hanging and flogging. His successor, Lord Parker, in his early speeches, emphasized the need for corporal punishment. Lord Goddard doubted the value of criminal legal aid (Abel-Smith and Stevens, 1967, 331–2). Attempts to reform the divorce law were hampered for a generation by the robust legislative opposition of Lord Merriman (Stevens, 1993, 92–3). And so it goes on. Legal aid, divorce, compensation, crime are all regarded as 'on-limits'. Frequently one may agree with what the Law Lords say, but does it help

[11] The major exception may well be the Devlin Report on Nyasaland (Stevens, 1993, 170).

[12] Lord Williams of Mostyn recently noted: '[i]t was a very wrong consequence of Sir Richard Scott's report that there was an officially orchestrated, mischievous, wilful campaign to undermine the judge who had done no more than his public duty': 'The Judiciary: Public Controversy', H.L. Debs. (5th Ser.), vol. 572, cols. 1307–8.

[13] Lord Woolf has pointed out that if judges are required to show restraint, so should politicians when judges are exercising their constitutional responsibilities to chair commissions: *ibid.*, col. 1272.

[14] See 'Judges Told to Dispel "aloof" image', *Independent*, 16 April 1996. Lord Taylor apparently urged judges to 'prove they did not live on another planet'. He warned that 'criticism of the court system was reaching new heights after decades of apparently aloof behaviour by the judges'.

legitimate or legitimize the judicial process? That is one of the issues which underlies the current battle between the Government and the Judiciary.

It may not, in the long run, have helped the political power of the judiciary within the judicial function to have allowed Lord Ackner to whip so many of the Law Lords into such extravagant claims for judicial independence in the debates on the Mackay Green Papers on the Profession. 'Tanks on lawns' and the imminence of Nazism were not only unfair to the Lord Chancellor, they have not helped clarify the judicial role.[15] The presence of law lords (and especially ex-law lords) exposes them to a higher than desirable degree of political exposure in a society which is fumbling its way towards a concept of separation of powers.[16] When the *Fire Brigades* case (1995) came on before the Lords, a decision which eventually struck down Michael Howard's attempt to make cuts in the criminal injuries compensation scheme, it was difficult to find five law lords to sit judicially, since so many law lords had already spoken out, legislatively, against the Howard proposals (Marr, 1995, 283).

So too outside legislation. Whatever one's view about Michael Howard's obsession with stiffer penalties—mandatory and minimum sentences and his 'two strikes and you're out', it is not clear that the vigorous restatement of the policy argument against such unattractive populism by Lord Chief Justice Taylor, before his untimely resignation on health grounds,[17] helped in clarifying the separation of powers.[18] Naked politicization of the judiciary may well be inimical to a political climate which may allow organic growth of an extended role for the judges within the constitution.[19]

---

[15] Stevens (1993), Epilogue. For a criticism of such extreme speeches, see Lord Irvine, 'The Judiciary: Public Controversy', H.L. Debs. (5th Ser.), vol. 572, cols. 1257–1258. For an attempted apologia for such speeches, see Lord Ackner, *ibid.*, cols. 1285-6.

[16] Some would certainly argue that it was unfortunate that Lord Hoffman found himself introducing an amendment to the Defamation Bill 1996, strongly supported by the right wing of the Tory Party, restricting the Bill of Rights, 1689, in favour of sitting MPs.

[17] 'Ill Health Forces Chief Justice to Retire Early', *The Times*, 3 May 1996.

[18] I sometimes think that the only successful application of the true separation of powers comes from Lord Greene's pronouncement that he could not accept an official car while Master of the Rolls, since that would amount to 'a gift from the Executive to the Judiciary, without the authority of the Legislature'. Such a pronouncement later scuppered Sir George Coldstream's plan to have High Court judges picked up at the London rail termini by Godfrey Davis Car Hire and conveyed with appropriate decorum to the Royal Courts in the Strand (Stevens, 1993, 130–1). Thus, today, if one is invited out to dinner by a Minister, even a junior one, or by a Permanent Secretary, one travels in an official car. If one is invited out to dinner by a judge of the Supreme Court, one is subjected either to the vagaries of judicial driving or the charms of the Temple station.

[19] Like 'constitutional' and 'the separation of powers', the concept of judicial independence is fuzzy, and its lack of clarity has not been helped by Dicey's domination of legal thinking in the public-law arena over the last 100 years. To look at the treatment of judicial independence in any constitutional textbook is to confront a combination of platitudes

The independence of the judiciary is also too often assumed rather than analysed. Even with respect to the alleged requirement of security of tenure, guaranteed by the Act of Settlement, we should not forget that, in this century, two successive Lords Chief Justice read of their resignations in *The Times*: Lord Trevethin in 1922 and Lord Hewart in 1940. One may assume that Lord Taylor did not do, nor has Lord Bingham done, as Lord Trevethin unwisely did, and provided the Government with an undated letter of resignation! (Stevens, 1993, 50 ff.)

In short, it is time to clarify what we mean by separation and independence. In the English Constitution, there cannot be watertight compartments. Yet if one reads the debates on transferring the control of judicial salaries from the legislature to the executive, something finally conceded in the 1960s, the absence of any sense of the constitutional implication is somewhat frightening (Stevens, 1993, 134–5); and John Major may not be the last Prime Minister to delay implementing judicial increases! (Stevens, 1993, 138) Herbert Hart taught us the distinction between meanings in the core and the periphery. There ought to be enough evidence to convince even the sceptic that there is a case at least for clarifying the core of the concepts of constitutional, the separation of powers and judicial independence.

II THE CHANGING ENVIRONMENT

It is now time, then, to look at the changing environment for judges and politicians over the last forty years. In the 1950s, there was little fear that there would be a clash between judges and politicians over power. Any

and dubious history, in its attempt to show that the concept has some meaning in English law.

The textbook exposition emphases that judges must not be biased or take bribes—sometimes accompanied by jingoistic comments that it has never happened, remind one a little of Harold Laski's observation that 'the English judges cannot be bribed—with money'. The Granthams and the Barringtons have had their days. We should also remember that until 1825 English judges were largely paid by fees and the opportunities for peculation were considerable. Although not thought of as dishonest at the time, except by Bentham, who talked of the 'sinister interest of Judge and Co.', to think of some of the judges of that period as impartial in a modern sense is not realistic.

These same expositions also normally have something about the independence of the judges from the state, clearly an important matter. Yet again, it should be seen in historical context. The 'job' was political in the broadest sense throughout the 18th century. It was part of a system of spoils. Judges, like ministers, had to be re-appointed when the sovereign died—and at least one lost his job. This was a system which lasted until Victoria's reign. So too with the 'requirement' that appears in such constitutional law works about an 'adequate' salary. For the first half of the last century, after salaries were introduced, there were negotiations about the amount. In the 1830s Denman became Chief Justice because he agreed to take the job for £8,000 rather than the statutory £10,000. Lord Campbell made a similar deal in 1850 (Stevens, 1993, 50n).

hints of this would have been so *sotto voce* that even in a reference in a *Times* leader would have been thought surprising. Today, with the Murdoch press, there are clear battle lines. The Home Secretary is the good guy; the judges the bad guys. As The *Sunday Times* recently announced: 'Howard must win' (Comment, 10 March 1996). Why has that change occurred?

(a) The Judicial Process Evolves

In the early 1950s the tone of the judiciary was set by Lord Jowitt, who had been Attlee's Lord Chancellor, and Lord Simonds, a former Chancery judge who served as Churchill's Lord Chancellor in the years immediately after 1951. Jowitt explained the 'creative' role of the judges in the House of Lords to an Australian audience in these terms:

the problem is not to consider what social and political conditions do today require; that is to confuse the task of the lawyer with the task of the legislator. . . . It is quite possible that the law has produced a result which does not accord with the requirements of today. If so, put it right by legislation, but do not expect every lawyer, in addition to all his other problems, to act as Lord Mansfield did, and decide what the law ought to be. He is far better employed if he puts himself to the much simpler task of deciding what the law is . . . please do not get yourself into the frame of mind of entrusting to the Judges the working out of a whole new set of principles which does accord with the requirements of modern conditions. Leave that to the legislators, and leave us to confine ourselves to trying to find out what the law is. [Stevens, 1983, 338–9]

Lord Simonds, Churchill's first Lord Chancellor, added a parallel role for statutory interpretation:

It is sufficient to say that the general proposition that it is the duty of the court to find out the intention of Parliament—and not only of Parliament but of Ministers also—cannot by any means be supported. The duty of the court is to interpret the words that the legislature has used; those words may be ambiguous, but, even if they are, the power and duty of the court to travel outside them on a voyage of discovery are strictly limited. . . . What the legislature has not written, the court must not write. . . . If a gap is disclosed, the remedy lies in an amending act.

Judicial styles evolve and the evolution is not smooth. Yet one can see milestones on the way. Something led the courts from the attempt in *Jacobs* v. *L.C.C.* (1950) and *Candler* v. *Crane Christmas* (1951) to imprison tort law in a nineteenth-century straightjacket to the almost Californian enthusiasm for liability for physical and financial harm in the 1990s (e.g. *White* v. *Jones* (1995), expanding *Hedley Byrne* v. *Heller*)—even if one accepts the staging posts of *Hedley Byrne* (1964) and *Dorset Yacht* (1970). That change of style may also help explain how the law lords moved from a willingness to abandon even a residual sense of procedural due process in *Franklin* (1948) and to allow Parliament implicitly to take away the right to intervene when local authorities made orders in bad faith in *Smith* v. *East Elloe RDC* (1956),[20] through the rediscovery of control in *Anisminic* (1969) to the Naughty Nineties—*Pepper* v. *Hart* (1993), judicial review, and all that.

One looks for points to alight on the jurisprudential evolution of the English judges. Perhaps Lord Radcliffe offers one: '[t]here was never a more sterile controversy than that upon the question whether a judge makes laws. Of course he does. How can he help it? . . . Judicial law is always a reinterpretation of principles in the light of new combinations of facts.' (Jones, 1966, 733).

He also added the political justification—singularly appropriate for one so involved in 'political' work off the bench—for the then current situation:

Personally, I think that judges will serve the public interest better if they keep quiet about their legislative function. . . . The judge who shows his hand, who advertises what he is about, may indeed show that his is a strong spirit, unfettered by the past; but I doubt very much whether he is not doing some harm to general confidence in the law as a constant, safe in the hands of the judges, than he is doing good to the law's credit as a set of rules nicely attuned as the sentiment of the day.

The next alighting point might well be on Lord Reid. He pushed the style beyond what Karl Llewellyn had said of the English judicial style—'like a Victorian virgin tubbing in her nightgown'. Reid put it directly—to pretend judges did not make laws was a 'fairytale', and 'we do not believe in fairytales any more'. He also raised the beginning of the constitutional issue: 'In so far as we can get the thing back on the rails let us do so' (Reid, 1968, 194–5).

From Reid to Lords Browne-Wilkinson and Woolf is close to a direct line. Some judges have found attractive the Dworkinian argument that what the judges are really doing is finding underlying principles, already

---

[20] As Lord Simonds put it (1956, 750–1): 'I think anyone bred in the tradition of the law is likely to regard with little sympathy legislative provisions for ousting the jurisdiction of the Court, whether in order that the subject may be deprived altogether of remedy or in order that his grievance may be remitted to some other tribunal. But it is our plain duty to give the words of the Act their proper meaning and, for my part, I find it quite impossible to qualify the words of the paragraph in the manner suggested. It may be that the legislature had not in mind the possibility of an order being made by a local authority in bad faith or even the possibility of an order made in good faith being mistakenly, capriciously or wantonly challenged. This is a matter of speculation.' In *Earl Fitzwilliam's Wentworth Estates Co.* v. *Minister of Housing and Local Government* (1952), the House of Lords held that the Central Land Board might use its powers to force owners to sell undeveloped land, although the Board's powers had previously been thought to be limited to the collection of development charges.

lurking in the common law (Mackay, 1987, 285). Whatever the justification, however, there has been a gradual transition to the appeal judges being both more willing to be creative and more willing to admit what they are up to. How did the political process allow that?

(b) The Changing Political Environment

In the sense that Lord Chancellors Jowitt and Simonds had sought to protect the judiciary from anything that might be thought to be political—or even involve a policy choice—there was an understandable change from what was arguably an intellectually indefensible position. One can begin to detect a change during the Chancellorship of Lord Kilmuir. In 1954, he announced that 'the law should be brought in to help in the solution of the great problems of a modern state'. The first step towards changing the role of the judges came with the Restrictive Practices Court in 1956. The idea of a High Court judge being used as President of the new court deeply upset the Lord Chancellor's Office, which produced a memorandum tracing judicial independence back from the War of the Roses to the twentieth century. Simonds had opposed a similar move earlier in the Churchill administration. From the Lord Chancellor's office, Sir George Coldstream thought the proposals 'thoroughly unsound . . . I have assumed it would be wrong to require the courts to pronounce on issues of economic policy'. He was eventually convinced that the only justification for using the judges was 'the wretched state of business in the Chancery Division'. The Chancery judges, however, had 'grave objections' because of the 'political element' which 'must play a part in the deliberation of the court as proposed'. All the Queen's Bench judges except Mr Justice Devlin opposed the new court. He was selected as President (Stevens, 1993, 101–8).

The Labour Party opposed the Bill because the 'Bill hands over to this court governmental and parliamentary power . . . [judgments] will be a political and economic decision'.[21] *The Economist* warned that the 'idea that a decision should change if the climate of opinion changes, even though other things remain the same, is not an idea that will be easily digestible by trained legal minds'. *The Times* thundered: '[c]lose thought must be given to the probable effect on the judiciary itself. Will judges . . . weighing these highly controversial questions of expediency . . . carry

---

[21] 'This is not really a matter suitable for judicial decisions according to the rules and the ordinary way in which we conduct matters in the courts of law in this country. It is a matter of a decision to be made from the greatest accumulation of knowledge and experience which is available, and the greatest knowledge and experience available in this country is only available, in the last resort, to the Minister. It is essentially a government decision': Sir Lynn Ungoed-Thomas, H.C. Debs. (5th Ser.), vol. 549, col. 2033 (6 March 1956). On this, see Stevens and Yamey (1965).

back to the Queen's Bench and Chancery quite the same unassailable reputation for detachment from political considerations that they have hitherto enjoyed?' (Stevens, 1993, 101–12). *Facilis descensus Averno*.

Within a decade one could see a slowly changing attitude to judicial decision-making. *Hedley Byrne* v. *Heller* (1964) and *Ridge* v. *Baldwin* (1964) in the early 1960s suggested that the judges were waking up from several decades of a formalistic approach to the common law. Ironically, and probably unintentionally, the return of Labour in 1964 actually accelerated this trend toward the instrumental. Lord Gardiner, while intellectually belonging to the narrow formalistic tradition of the liberal left, by allowing dissents in the Privy Council and, more importantly, allowing the House of Lords to overrule its own earlier decisions, which he thought would be used to remedy primarily legal inconsistencies, changed the psychology and perhaps the very nature of the appeal process in England (Stevens, 1983, 417–20; 472–3; 543–4; 551–2; 572–5; 617–20). It was not to be long before the judiciary was taking power from both executive and legislature.

The next convenient milestone on the road to the politicization of the Judiciary was the Industrial Relations Court, created by Edward Heath in 1971, before he made the U-turn from dry to wet—or, if you prefer, from idealogue to consensus politician. Before the Court was dismantled by the returning Labour administration in 1974, its President, Sir John Donaldson, later to be Master of the Rolls, joined the Roll of Honour with Barrington and Grantham, of having had a brush with impeachment—when 187 Labour MPs moved an address to remove him from the Presidency for 'political prejudice and partiality' (Stevens, 1993, 172). That move was to persuade Lord Diplock, in discussing the 1974 Trade Disputes and Labour Relations Act, that

at a time when many more cases involve the application of legislation which gives effect to policies that are the subject of bitter public and parliamentary con-troversy, it cannot be too strongly emphasized that the British Constitution, though largely unwritten, is firmly based upon the separation of powers: Parliament makes the laws, the judiciary interprets them [Stevens, 1993, 172].

It is in this rather narrow context that one must look at the evolution of administrative law—especially the growth of judicial review. *Anisminic* had been decided in 1968. The evolution of administrative law over the next thirty years cannot but have been heavily influenced by the political tone of the years that followed. Heath's undistinguished administration from 1970 to 1974 was marked chiefly by Britain's acceptance into the EEC. Whatever was appreciated at the time, it came to mean continental influences and, in particular, a Treaty of Rome whose federalist thrust was hidden primarily amid the powers and potential powers of the

European Court. In recent years, the implications for English law have finally become clear.

It was with the unwinding of the Wilson–Callaghan administration between 1974 and 1979 that the judges felt pushed to strike out on their own. With the appearance of Mrs Thatcher in 1979, the game changed still further. It gradually became clear that Britain now had a radical Government of the right, with a Labour Party, soon to be led by Michael Foot, appearing to lurch to the left. There was a vacuum of power in the centre and, consciously or not, the judiciary began to move into it or, if you prefer, was forced into it. If this was not clear at once, it may be attributed to the fact that, until 1987, there was a Lord Chancellor, Lord Hailsham, protective of the traditional roles of judges and the profession and insisting on the continuation of the Kilmuir Rules on judicial silence out of court. Since 1987 there has been a Chancellor more willing to let market and political forces take their toll. The Kilmuir rules went. Politically, there has been friction between the judges and Lord Mackay (Stevens, 1994, 1620), but at the same time, the judges began taking liberties, both inside and outside the courtroom, actively discussing what they believed they were doing. The Conservative Government, whatever it may have said about concern with local democracy and devolution, pursued a remarkably powerful agenda—explicit or not—of centralization—a process now articulately recorded and analysed by Simon Jenkins (1995). Faced with this situation, how could the judiciary not expand judicial review, pine for a Bill of Rights, encourage the notion that, in implementing EU law, it was serving as a constitutional court, and even dream of fundamental laws? Perhaps the most interesting challenge has been the political conflict with New Labour, as that party seeks to regain the centre ground of politics, currently most obviously occupied by the judiciary.

(c) And who were these Judges?

It is then time to ask who were these judges. One could wish there were a more sophisticated literature in the socio-legal field relating to the judiciary. We know so little about who the judges were and who the judges are. What quantifiable information we have is basically so unrevealing, although we do know that judges today are from a slightly more diverse background than their predecessors and are much more likely to have read law at University. In general, however, one is driven to 'barroom sociology'—or perhaps, in deference to our distinguished and sophisticated profession, one should say 'wine bar sociology'. That enterprise may well involve some tendentious claims, but in the absence of facts who can prove me wrong?

Inevitably one has to begin with ambience. In the 1950s, the profession was indeed dramatically different. Court of Appeal and High Court were barely one-third their current size (in 1948 there were twenty Queen's Bench judges); the County Court bench one-fifth the size of the Circuit Court bench; solicitors about one-quarter of their present numbers; barristers less than one-fifth their present strength. The bench, however, could not have been held in greater awe.[22] As Churchill put it, in Cabinet, the judges were 'a national asset the Conservative Party should feel honoured to uphold' (Stevens, 1993, 128). Yet for all this deference, in the words of Anthony Sampson, who was beginning his *Anatomy of Britain* industry, the judges were 'increasingly out of touch with the movements of contemporary Britain' (Abel-Smith and Stevens, 1967, 290).

The bench surely contained its share of scholarly, fair, and decent men. It also had perhaps more than its share of cantankerous, prejudiced, intimidating, and boorish judges, constrained by no retirement age. In an age when the courts were under-utilized, the bar financially impoverished, when what we would now call High Street practice was the norm for solicitors—judges were, with rare exceptions, accustomed to deference and sycophancy. Conservatism, both political and in personal, with both a capital and a small 'c', was the order of the day among the judges. Henry Fairlie, in *The Establishment* (1963), said that it is impossible to understand the intellectual tone of the period unless one realized that the intellectual revolution sparked by Freud had had no impact on the England of that day. It was a period when the socialist Lord Chancellor Jowitt could boast to the slightly mystified Canadian audience that all the High Court judges he had appointed had been members of the Conservative Party.[23]

Britain today has a remarkably distinguished judiciary, marked by a bench which is gracious, scholarly, imaginative, and fair compared with the 1950s. They are even 'in touch'—the days of 'Who is this Mr Gordon Richards?' and 'What are The Beatles?' have passed,[24] as have the days

[22] The Lord Mayor's Banquet set the tone. During the 1950s the judges were told 'if British judges were ever biased at all, it was always in favour of the accused', 'our judiciary today stood unchallenged by friend and foe and remained the bulwark of our nation and a guarantee of peace', they 'maintained, with glorious continuity, the high standards which they, and they alone in the world, had created', and by 1956 'Her Majesty's judges had a greater understanding of human nature than any other body of men in the world' (Abel-Smith and Stevens, 1967: 290; see also Abel-Smith and Stevens, 1968, 181–5).

[23] Elsewhere he claimed he 'would far rather have a true blue Tory of the extreme Right who was an honest and respectable man than somebody of his own line of thought who was not' (Jowitt, 1948, 318).

[24] If one needs an exception to prove a rule, there is always Mr Justice Harman of the Chancery Division. He recently affected to be ignorant of Oasis. He had earlier, when leaving his home to hear an emergency petition for equitable relief, aimed a kick at journalists and their photographers. Unfortunately, he connected with his own taxi driver, earning the

when High Court judges took pleasure in looking at widows to assess damages by attempting to judge their chance of remarriage from their appearance, or when Divorce Commissioners filled the *Evening Standard, Evening Star,* and the *Evening News* with totally inappropriate comments on their views of the morality of divorce and the behaviour of petitioners, respondents, and co-respondents.

Why the change? Partly it was a change in the approach to authority, partly to what might be called the Joan Littlewood factor. The Second World War had an infinitely better General Staff than the First, largely, so we are told, because the young subalterns in Flanders were so appalled by the awfulness of Haig's and Kitchener's operations they vowed never to repeat them. In the spirit of *Oh What a Lovely War*, it may be that the leaders of our current judiciary made a similar pledge when they saw the worst side of the judges in the 1950s.

Of course there were other influences. The sudden prosperity of the Bar, beginning in the late 1960s and never fully explained,[25] undoubtedly changed attitudes. The massive financial success of the whole legal profession in the 1980s, coupled with the knowledge that London was by then a largely unchallenged international legal centre, was important. No longer was the Bar dominated by the rather childish high-jinks of circuit life. The legal profession was once more attracting more than its fair share of academic talent. Discrimination against Jews, which had driven the likes of Herbert Hart away from the Chancery Bar and caused even Lord Goddard to rail, largely went after Lord Schuster ceased to be Permanent Secretary to the Lord Chancellor. The change opened the bench to an important intellectual tradition that did not shy from the theoretical, and even thought it might be possible to learn from the United States and Continental Europe. With the demise of Lord Jowitt, there was no longer prejudice against Catholics on the bench. After Lord Simonds there was less prejudice against divorcees on the bench. Lord Mackay actively sought out women for the judiciary. Within the narrow parameters of the Bar, the bench was increasingly open to talent and, as specialities in commercial and corporate law took off, the availability of talented barristers who also knew about business, in addition to more general common lawyers, once again changed the style. Today, commercial lawyers (or perhaps one should say Essex Court), with their more scholarly style, dominate the English law lords. In particular at the

profound caption from *Sun*: 'It's me nuts, m' Lord': *Independent on Sunday*, 31 March 1996. He was voted the worst judge on the bench by solicitors in 1993. *Legal Business, passim.* And again in 1996. 'Gentlemen of the Jury find Harman "the Terrible" Guilty', *Sunday Times*, 12 May 1996.

[25] The advent of well-remunerated criminal legal aid in the 1960s and the Courts Act 1971 undoubtedly helped.

appellate level, where England had rarely distinguished itself, by the 1970s a new style was afoot. It only required the advent of the first Scottish Lord Chancellor, Lord Mackay, willing to appoint to both the Court of Appeal and House of Lords not merely those who had reached a certain point on the *cursus honorum*, but those who might have real talent as appeal judges, to allow this style to reach fruition.

What then distinguishes the judges of the 1990s? Even if one had hard empirical evidence, it would no doubt be difficult to generalize about some 100 High Court judges and forty appeal judges. If one were to take only the latter group, however, one would see a group in their late fifties to early seventies. They were likely to have been teenagers in the Second World War, and to have had their sense of England's role shaped more by Suez and ongoing economic decline that the notions of Empire which shaped the attitudes of judges forty years ago. Their views of trade unions (except possibly ones in the legal profession) may well have been shaped by the Wilson years and *In Place of Strife*. Their view of the Welfare State, however, is likely to have been shaped by Gaitskell and Butler rather than Milton Friedman and Michael Portillo. They lean towards being Europhiles and are more sympathetic to the penal policies of a Roy Jenkins or a Leon Brittan than a Michael Howard. They include some strong civil libertarians; they, after all, include a number whose provenance is South Africa. While one suspects most normally vote Tory, most are also likely to be 'wets', and the Tories know it. As Sir Bernard Ingham said of the appointment of Sir Richard Scott to enquire into the sale of arms to Iraq, they have 'dredged up the wettest, most liberal judge they could find' (*The Times*, 10 February 1996). Even the two most recent Chairs of the Law Commission—Mr Justice Brooke and Mrs Justice Arden—had been labelled by the press as 'liberals', while one former Commissioner—now Mrs Justice Hale—has been labelled by the right-wing press as a 'feminist' opposed to marriage.[26] The world has, indeed, changed.

However, one last point should be made. The judges operate in a different constitutional atmosphere. One of the results of consensus politics was that primacy appeared to lie with the Civil Service. The Permanent Secretaries appeared all powerful. The arrival of Mrs Thatcher in 1979 meant the arrival of a Prime Minister who believed that the Civil Service was 'part of the problem'. After twelve years of battering by Mrs Thatcher, the Civil Service has had an easier ride with Mr Major, although the policy of contracting out services and contracting the Civil Service has combined to sap power and morale from the Executive

[26] She was cited in *This Week* (4 November 1995) as saying: '[w]e should be considering whether the legal institution of marriage continues to serve any useful purpose'. Lord Mackay was said to be 'a thoroughly decent man fallen among trendies'.

branch. Parliament too has changed. While for the last seventeen years the Labour Party has been largely irrelevant, the Conservative Party has moved from being represented in the Commons by the old landed and professional classes to being composed of a much more Poujadiste grouping. Poorly paid by professional standards, and with a lifestyle many regard as unattractive, it is often assumed that the quality of MPs has dropped rapidly. It is scarcely surprising that the ever-expanding judiciary should appear increasingly significant as the power and size of the Civil Service has declined,[27] and the nature of the Conservative Party has been transformed from an establishment base to a bourgeois one, and the Labour Party moved from being an ineffective opposition to one which appeared anxious not to reveal its policies. The transformation was underlined when one newspaper reported that Tory MPs were offended by the sight of Lord Justice Scott, having finished his Report on arms sales to Iraq, riding to hounds in the hunting pink.[28] It is all a long way from Sir Winston Churchill's justification of higher judicial salaries in the 1950s by observing that 'one of Her Majesty's judges' had been observed 'waiting at an omnibus stop' (Stevens, 1993, 128).

III WHAT HAVE THE JUDGES DONE?

And where are these modern judges chiefly in disagreement with the Government?

(a) The Current Conservative Penal Policy

The public hears mainly about judicial conflicts with Government over penal policy. In particular, the judges are unhappy about the constant changes in penal policy reflected in the numerous Criminal Justice Acts since 1979 (*The Economist*, 11 November 1995, 29). These changes have allowed the Home Secretary effectively to extend the terms of imprisonment imposed by judges by deciding when prisoners should be released, then to have a fixed tariff for certain crimes (mandatory sentences), thus taking away judicial discretion allowing judges to make the sentence fit the crime. Finally, in the April 1996 White Paper, the Home Secretary appeared to have endorsed a 'two strikes and you're out' principle, described by Lord Taylor as a 'bonanza for prison architects' (*The Times*, 26 March 1996). This appears to be an adaptation of the Californian

[27] The Civil Service numbers fell from 735,400 in 1979 to 499,000 in 1996.

[28] 'Who do these guys think they are? Judges have made themselves darlings of the left by repeatedly challenging the Government, but are they really fit to play politics?', *Independent*, 17 April 1996.

system of 'three strikes and you're out' which has led to the theft of a piece of pizza from someone eating it (being the third crime of violence) resulting in life imprisonment, presumably for theft rather than lack of culinary discrimination.[29]

The judicial establishment, led by the Lord Chief Justice, felt irritated by policies which not merely took away the traditional powers of the judiciary, but endorsed the naïve belief that punishment rather than detection was the solution to the crime problem (*New Law Journal*, 1995, 1529). In May 1996, Lord Taylor resigned through ill-health, but as he did, he initiated a debate in the House of Lords where support for his view was overwhelming and that for Mr Howard sparse.[30] Even Ferdinand Mount, head of Mrs Thatcher's Think Tank from 1982 to 1984, now concedes that the Tory Right is motivated by an enthusiasm for Gingrich's *Contract with America* (Mount, 1996, 31) rather than developing independent policies. The fact that 'three strikes and you're out' appears to have led to injustice rather than a decline in crime in California is of little interest to the Conservative Right or to Mr Mawhinney, the Chairman of the Party, in the lead-up to the next election. (They should bear in mind Woody Allen's observation that 'the only contribution California has made to civilisation is right turn on red'.) The cry has also lapped over into prison policy, where spartan conditions for the IRA and long-term prisoners are matched by demand for boot-camps for the young. The North American appeal of such measures is evidenced by the looming Dole–Clinton Presidential Campaign. The No-Frills in Prison Act 1996 has just passed the House and Senate. Section 2 demands 'the elimination of luxurious prison conditions'. Under it, in-cell coffee pots and TV will go, as will prison weight-rooms, computers, and 'earned good-time credit'.[31] It should come as no surprise that Mr Howard is now echoing this American innovation, as well as in his demands for curfews for youths (*The Economist*, 8 June 1996).

(b) The Common Law

While earlier I referred to the more creative approach to the common law, nothing better illustrates its vigour than two public lectures delivered by Lord Bingham and Lord Hoffman in the spring of 1996, calling on

[29] 'Judges claim Howard is on the Wrong Side of the Law', *The Times*, 4 April 1996; 'Repeat of serious crime will carry automatic life sentence': *ibid.*

[30] H.L. Debs., 23 May 1996, vol. 572, cols. 1025–76. See also Lord Taylor, 'Howard's Production Line Justice', *The Times*, 23 May 1996. On the debate, see P. W. Davies, 'Howard Punished in each Sentence', *The Independent*, 24 May 1996; and 'Lord Taylor denounces Howard Reforms', *ibid.*

[31] 'Jail's No Frills Reality Enlightens a Judge', *International Herald Tribune*, 3 April 1996.

the courts to develop a right of privacy if Parliament did not do so.[32] Viscount Jowitt must be resting uneasily and such discomfort is shared by Lord Irvine.[33] Within the traditional areas of the common law, the appeal courts now accept a clear responsibility to develop the law. Equally dramatic is the change in statutory interpretation. The major innovation was *Pepper* v. *Hart* (1993) where the House of Lords joined the US Supreme Court in turning to legislative debates to determine the 'true meaning' of statutory interpretation. In his dissent, Lord Mackay warned of the dangers, namely that nearly all cases would fall under the allowable triggers suggested by counsel. Lord Mackay feared the policy concerns of Mr Justice Frankfurter, who, forty years ago, complained: '[w]e refer to statutes now only when legislative material is not clear'. While Lord Browne-Wilkinson said that to resort to such material was justified only when the statute was unclear, judges are now turning to such material to decide whether the statute is unclear. Like it or not, judicial power was dramatically extended.[34]

(c) Administrative Law

In terms of judicial expansion, however, the most obvious and public change has been the expansion of judicial review to provide an extensive power for the courts to intervene in procedural due process over a wide range of public and quasi-public matters, and, by subtle use of the so-called *Wednesbury* doctrine, to provide a hint of substantive due process.[35] There is little doubt that, from the public's point of view, judicial review has helped remedy a wide range of injustices. Despite press comment, however, it has always existed—Victorian judges actively used it, although for much of the twentieth century it was quiescent. Again, despite press comment, decisions under it by no means always go against the Crown. Its growth has, however, had profound political implications. The most public manifestation of this has been the Civil Service publication *The Judge Over Your Shoulder*, but almost every Government department has felt the direct impact of these developments.[36] Once again, the Home Secretary has borne the brunt of this

[32] For a questioning of the Constitutional appropriateness of this, see 'Sitting in Judgment' (editorial), *Financial Times*, 24 May 1996.

[33] 'The Judiciary: Public Controversy', H.L. Debs. (5th Ser.), vol. 572, col. 1257.

[34] See Kenny Mullan, 'The Impact of *Pepper* v. *Hart*', paper for colloquium on the House of Lords, University of Ulster, May 1995.

[35] The present state of the law is most elegantly described in de Smith, Woolf, and Jowell (1995), *passim*.

[36] e.g., the Home Secretary was criticized for changing the 'tariff' for murderers, 'Court Deals New Blow to Howard', *Guardian*, 11 November 1995; the Trade and Industry Minister for withholding documents in the Ordtec case, 'Ministers Criticised in Iraq Arms Case', *The Times*, 8 November 1995.

assault—where he found his efforts to reform sentencing,[37] the criminal compensation programme,[38] barring the Moonie leader,[39] and attempting to deport a Saudi dissident thwarted by the judges.[40] John Major has had a speech to Scotland banned from television by Lord Abernathy, and the Foreign Secretary was forced to restructure the foreign aid programme after the judges found he had taken into account inappropriate criteria in the *Pergau Dam* case (1995). Moreover, even where not willing to strike down actions, in matters ranging from Gays in the Military to the privatization of the Railways (*Guardian*, 25 November 1995) and housing for asylum-seekers,[41] judges have not hesitated to rattle sabres.

It is these cases that have led the press to take delight in both highlighting—and, one suspects, fuelling—the split between judiciary and government. The Beaverbrook press has claimed there is a 'sickness sweeping through the senior judiciary—galloping arrogance' (*Daily Express*, 4 November 1995) and, singling out Mr Justice Dyson, noting that '[w]hile European Human Rights Judges, some from countries which once sent political prisoners to Siberia, are venting their spleen on Britain, legal weevils here at home are practising their own brand of mischief' (*Sunday Express*, 1 October 1995). The Rothermere press joined in: '[n]ow it seems that any judge can take it on himself to overrule a minister, even though Parliament might approve the minister's action. This is to arrogate power to themselves in a manner that makes a mockery of Parliament'. The paper went on to accuse the judges of giving the impression that they were 'acting on a political agenda of their own' (*Daily Mail*, 2 November 1995). The *Independent* ensured balance: '[t]he Long Arm of the Law: government clashes with the judiciary are mounting—and they won't stop under Labour' (*Independent on Sunday*, 5 November 1995). Such a belief made it possible for *The Times*, when Lord Taylor was forced to resign through ill-health, to demand a Chief Justice who could 'steer his profession away from the sound of gunfire'.[42]

---

[37] See also the excitement when the appeal courts refused to allow him to extend the sentence of the child murderers of James Bulger. 'Howard Acted Unlawfully over Bulger Sentences' and 'Ruling Further Weakens Minister's Powers over Judiciary', *The Times*, 3 May 1996; 'Howard Furious at Bulger Ruling', *Independent*, 3 May 1996; 'Mr Howard is Playing with Fire' (editorial), *ibid*.

[38] *R. v. Secretary of State for the Home Department, ex parte Fire Brigades Union* (1995). See also Barendt, 1995.

[39] 'Judicial Moonshine: Howard was right to refuse Moon entry to Britain', *The Times*, 3 November 1995.

[40] 'Judge tells Howard to Reconsider Masari Case', *The Independent*, 6 March 1994.

[41] 'Judge "Reluctantly" Denies Housing for Asylum Seekers', *The Times*, 19 April 1996; 'Judge Voices Concern at Asylum Benefits Cost', *Guardian*, 27 March 1996.

[42] 'Balance in Justice' (leader), *The Times*, 4 May 1996.

(d) EU Law

In terms of encouraging judicial activism, the 1972 legislation implementing Britain's adherence to what is now the European Union has been highly significant. Among Eurosceptics, much hostility in the United Kingdom has been directed at the European Court, most recently by the White Paper before the Intergovernmental Conference in Turin.[43] In another paper before Cabinet, Michael Howard has argued that the European Court of Justice has been 'increasing its competence and adopting its own political agenda'. Relying on a paper by Sir Patrick Neill QC, he adopted the words that 'a court with a mission is a menace. A supreme court with a mission is a disaster.' The Howard solution was to forbid the English courts from enforcing Community legislation. All such cases would then presumably have to go to Luxembourg.[44]

It is arguable that the English courts have been more enthusiastic Europeans than the courts in other countries. Lord Denning set the tone when he allowed individual parties to sue in English courts for violation of EU competition law as embodied in Articles 85 and 86 of the Treaty of Rome (*Garden Cottage Foods* v. *Milk Marketing Board*, 1984). Such a start made it more natural for English courts to suspend an English statute while the European courts tested an issue—the *Factortame* case (1991, 1992), a decision which the *Daily Mail* reported under the headline 'Brussels rules the waves'.[45] By 1994, when the House of Lords, without referring the matter to EU courts, held that British legislation relating to part-time employees violated European directives and therefore was unenforceable (*R.* v. *Secretary of State for Employment*, ex parte *Equal Opportunities Commission*, 1995), *The Times* concluded that 'Britain may now have, for the first time in its history, a constitutional court'.[46] That power encouraged some sixty Tory MPs, in the Spring of 1996, to introduce legislation to prevent the European Court from holding UK statutes unconstitutional.

(e) Civil Liberties

This suspicion of Europhilia on the part of English judges is further fuelled by the changing attitude to the European Convention on Human Rights. The Convention was developed by the civil law countries of

---

[43] 'Britain Urges Cut in Power of Euro Court', *The Times*, 13 March 1996.
[44] 'Howard Splits Cabinet on Europe', *Independent*, 18 May 1996.
[45] Sir Thomas Bingham, 'Anglo-American Reflections', First Pilgrim Fathers' Lecture, Plymouth Law Society, 29 October 1994.
[46] *The Times*, 5 March 1994. It reported that the House of Lords had 'struck down' a British Statute for being 'unconstitutional'.

Western Europe in the years after the Second World War. The reaction of Attlee's Labour administration was fascinating. Lord Goddard and the other judges were satisfied that the common law was the perfect protector of civil rights. Certainly the Labour cabinet in the 1940s was appalled by the European notion that there be a Convention on Human Rights. Sir Stafford Cripps, Chancellor of the Exchequer, opposed it because it would provide protection inconsistent with 'powers of economic control which are essential for the operation of a planned economy'. Lord Jowitt showed his general distrust of foreigners:

We are not prepared to encourage our European friends to jeopardise our whole system of law, which we have laboriously built up over the centuries, in favour of some half-baked scheme to be administered by some unknown court. . . . It completely passes the wit of man to guess what results would be arrived at by a tribunal . . . drawn from various European States possessing completely different systems of law. . . . Any student of our legal institutions . . . must recoil from this document with a feeling of horror' [Lester, 1986, 46–72].

Yet the United Kingdom did adhere to the Convention in 1951 and the Commission and Court began work in 1952. Britain, after the Wilson administration in the 1960s allowed individuals to appeal, soon became its chief customer. While Lord Denning had claimed of civil liberties in England, '[w]e have not needed them to be written down in this country. The judges have been able to protect them by their decisions',[47] such enthusiasm was not shared by the new court. From birching and IRA detainees to freedom of the press and the right of journalists to protect their sources,[48] Britain not only became the Court's best customer—partly because, while adhering, the United Kingdom had not incorporated—but it lost most of the cases that were taken to the Court.

While indirectly the Convention influenced English law,[49] each appeal had to go to Strasbourg. It is not an effective system, and leading judges, led by Lord Taylor and Lord Bingham, lobbied for its incorporation into English law.[50] Finally, in 1995, Lord Lester, a frequent advocate before the Court, introduced the Human Rights Bill to effect that change. It was supported in the Lords by no fewer than eight judicial peers. While, in a watered-down form, the Bill passed the Lords, it is unlikely to be taken up

[47] H.L. Debs. (5th Ser.), vol. 224, col. 1195 (6 July 1960). Lord Simon of Glaisdale justified higher judicial pensions because 'the people owe . . . to the judiciary something they value more highly than their material property, and that is their civil liberties': H.C. Debs. (5th Ser.), vol. 525, col. 1061 (23 March 1954).

[48] Human Rights Law Report, *The Times*, 28 March 1996 (*Goodwin* v. *United Kingdom*).

[49] Ackner, Browne-Wilkinson, Scarman, Lloyd, Simon, Slynn, Taylor, and Woolf. Although how much real impact the Convention has had on UK law has been questioned (McCrudden and Chambers, 1994, 575).

[50] Not all judges think the European Convention should be the basis of an English Bill of Rights, e.g. Sir Stephen Sedley, 'Charter 88: Wrongs and Rights' in *Citizenship* (1991).

in the Commons. The Government continues to fear a weakening of parliamentary Sovereignty by giving such direct control over civil rights to the judges, since, in effect, their decision might well involve holding UK legislation unconstitutional (Lester, 1995, 198). Ironically, Sir Ti-liang Yang, Chief Justice of Hong Kong, unwisely and confidentially made an identical argument to the Beijing Government, in suggesting that China should eviscerate Hong Kong's British-imposed Bill of Rights because the Bill of Rights allowed the Courts to strike down legislation and that such conflicts led to 'chaos'.[51] In the United Kingdom, meanwhile, Government continued to fear Commission and Court in Strasbourg—and in the spring of 1996 it was reported that Lord Mackay was flying to Strasbourg to remonstrate with the Human Rights judges about their expansive tendencies.[52]

(f) The Final Straw

It was almost inevitable that judges would push the extra mile and say that judges were in fact like the Supreme Court of the United States, left with some responsibility for fundamental laws which, *de facto*, could limit the powers of Parliament. In forty-five years the Jowitt–Simonds position had been stood on its head.

This expansive thesis was advanced in two recent speeches. Lord Woolf, in his Mann Lecture, likening the current scene to the Warren Court, said simply, '[i]t is one of the strengths of the common law that it enables the courts to vary the extent of their intervention to reflect current needs, and by this means it helps to maintain the delicate balance of a democratic society'.[53] He, however, went further and argued that Parliament could not abolish judicial review:

if Parliament did the unthinkable, then I would say that the courts would also be required to act in a manner which would be without precedent. Some judges

---

[51] 'Chief's Warning over HK Bill', *Financial Times*, 19 November 1995. Martin Lee QC, Leader of the Democratic Party, noted 'public perception of the Independence of the Judiciary has been Affected'. *ibid.*

[52] 'Mackay Seeks Curb on European Court', *The Times*, 9 April 1996.

[53] 'Our Parliamentary democracy is based on the rule of law. One of the twin principles upon which the rule of law depends is the supremacy of Parliament in its legislative capacity. The other principle is that the courts are the final arbiters as to the interpretation and application of the law. As both Parliament and the courts derive their authority from the rule of law so both are subject to it and cannot act in [a] manner which involves its repudiation . . . The courts will readily accept legislation which controls how it exercises its jurisdiction or which confers or modifies its existing statutory jurisdiction. I, however, see a distinction between such legislative action and that which seeks to undermine in a fundamental way the rule of law on which our unwritten constitution depends by removing or partially impairing the entire reviewing role of the High Court on judicial review, a role which in its origin is as ancient as the common law, pre-dates our present form of parliamentary democracy and the Bill of Rights' (Lord Woolf, 1995, 58).

might choose to do so by saying that it was an irrebuttable presumption that Parliament could never intend such a result. I myself would consider there were advantages in making it clear that ultimately there are even limits on the supremacy of Parliament which it is the courts' inalienable responsibility to identify and uphold. They are limits of the most modest dimensions which I believe any democrat would accept [Woolf, 1995, 58].

If we couple this remarkable statement with Lord Browne-Wilkinson's comments about the need for the judges to control their own operations[54] and the apparent direction of human rights in the United Kingdom, the strength of the current mood of the judges can be sensed in reaching back towards a Blackstonian role for the common law.[55] Lord Woolf himself shook off some of the protective colouration that English judges had traditionally adopted. In discussing those cases where English law is voided because it conflicts with Community law, he noted: '[t]his can be explained by saying it was not Parliament's intention when passing the legislation in question to interfere with Community law . . . the fairytale is harmless, though in other jurisdictions the existence of a written constitution would be likely to make a more direct approach possible.' (Woolf, 1995, 67)

The theme was perhaps most perceptively picked up by a High Court judge, Sir John Laws:

The true distinction between judicial and elective power cannot be arrived at by a merely factual account of what the judges do or what governments or Parliament . . . do. The settlement is dynamic because, as our long history shows, it can change. . . . As a matter of fundamental principle, it is my opinion that the survival and flowering of a democracy . . . requires that those who exercise democratic, political power must have limits set to what they may do: limits which they are not allowed to overstep . . . the doctrine of Parliamentary sovereignty cannot be vouched by Parliamentary legislation; a higher-order law confers it and must limit it.[56]

On the basis of these arguments, Sir John moved on to propound his theory of fundamental laws. Moreover, he could call up academic support in favour of this position. While even the Lord Chancellor had endorsed Ronald Dworkin's argument that, in expanding the common law, judges were doing no more than relying on the fundamental princi-

[54] The judges, until the 19th century reforms, did control their own courts. The logic of the utilitarian reforms was that the operation of the courts should be placed under the reformed Civil Service. Lord Hatherley's Judicature Commission suggested that there be a Ministry of Justice to perform this task. Such a solution was unacceptable to the judges, who lobbied for the alternative solution—hence the Lord Chancellor's Office.

[55] Sir Nicolas Browne-Wilkinson, 'The Infiltration of a Bill of Rights' (1992, 405). See also Sir Stephen Sedley, 'Human Rights: A Twenty First Century Agenda' (1995, 386).

[56] Sir John Laws, 'Law and Democracy' (1995, 80–95) and 'The Constitution: Power and Principle' (Mishcon Lecture, 1996). See also Sedley (1995, 386).

ples on which the common law were based, that theory, when pushed into the public law arena, seemed more threatening to the traditionalists. What Dworkin appeared to be arguing was that any acceptable theory of a democratic model required protection of rights to balance the majoritarian impulse. These fundamental rights are not subject to the will of the majority. It reflects the long-running argument in the United States about the justification, in democratic terms, of a Bill of Rights and an unelected federal judiciary. In this country it has attracted support from the Institute for Public Policy Research and organizations like Charter 88, which normally have a more grass-roots approach. How far judges were influenced by this is not clear,[57] but they were advancing arguments novel to the English common law.

IV WHITHER THE CONSTITUTION?

(a) The Formalist Tradition[58]

The Woolf–Laws approach is not merely alien to the Jowitt–Simonds tradition, it flies in the face of three centuries of the English democratic tradition. That tradition, of course, was slow to evolve and not settled until the nineteenth century. It is important to emphasize the classical liberal element in this evolution, because the Liberal and then the Labour parties have been the natural successors of the Utilitarians, who were the force behind the nineteenth-century transformation. Supporters of both parties have, on the one hand, sought to emphasize judicial restraint and, on the other, the formalistic approach to language. The Codification Movement was a central utilitarian tenet. It was integral to the rise of democracy, as were the Field Codes in the United States, while in England it was highlighted by the Criminal Codifications in 1861 and the Sales of Goods Act in 1893. It had a more profound effect in British colonies and parts of the United States.

The judicial-restraint aspect of utilitarianism had, however, at least two other aspects. First, after Halsbury's forays into appointing judges with links to the Conservative Party in the 1890s and the first few years of this century, successive Liberal Lord Chancellors sought to make apolitical appointments. While Campbell-Bannerman's Lord Chancellor, Loreburn, appointed appeal judges because of their politics, the High Court bench became less political, and this approach was confirmed after the appointment of Haldane as Lord Chancellor in 1912. Secondly,

[57] Certainly this thinking has influenced others. See IPPR, 1991, 5–6.
[58] See Lord Steyn, 'Does Legal Formalism Hold Sway in England?', 1996 Presidential Lecture, The Bentham Club, 1996 (to be published in *Current Legal Problems*).

the logical corollary of the Home Secretary, Winston Churchill's, view that judges found it difficult to be impartial where class interests were at stake, was Lloyd-George's exclusion of the judiciary from the National Insurance scheme he was building. In turn, those law lords who were Liberals gradually took the courts away from the supervision of political and administrative issues. It was a decoupling process that emphasized intellectual and political formalism.

This Liberal tradition of formalism[59] and a minimalist role for the judiciary was carried through from the Liberal party to Labour, particularly by Haldane who, having been the Liberal Lord Chancellor from 1912 to 1915, became Labour's Lord Chancellor in 1923, and Jowitt, a Liberal who served McDonald as Attorney-General and, having been defeated as a National Liberal in 1931, survived to be Attlee's Lord Chancellor between 1945 and 1951. The same Radical–Liberal–Labour tradition could be seen in Lord Gardiner's agenda. He saw no creative role for appeal courts, and therefore advocated the abolition of the House of Lords. Even his advocacy of the Law Commission was premised on the assumption that 'lawyers' law' was unreformable by the courts and needed regular revision. A high priority was the remarkable nineteenth-century utilitarian goal, namely that contract law should be codified—a task one of Labour's stalwarts and an early Law Commissioner, Professor L. C. B. Gower, was set.

As academic law became more important, however, Labour academics added their views to the political assumptions. Sir Otto Kahn-Freund and Lord Wedderburn argued the case for keeping the courts out of labour law. Professor John Griffith provided the intellectual base for the formalistic approach to the common law. The law-is-the-law approach was essential, because otherwise judicial attitudes, predispositions, and prejudices took over and judges had bad attitudes: '[t]hese judges have by their education and training and the pursuit of their profession as barristers, acquired a strikingly homogeneous collection of attitudes, beliefs and principles, which to them represent the public interest' (Hartley and Griffith, 1981, 181). In short, judges were inevitably 'conservative and illiberal' (Griffith, 1991, 275). Old Labour's position was clear.

While Labour saw the judges as unsuitable for decision-making because of their political views, and therefore sought to have them constrained by the formalist approach to the common law, the Conservative attitude was to be more flexible towards judicial creativity, providing the judicial role did not conflict with the Diceyan concept of parliamentary sovereignty. It was Halsbury, Conservative Lord Chancellor between

[59] The formalistic approach to statutes had been strengthened by the establishment of the Parliamentary Counsel's office in 1869.

1886 and 1892 and 1895 and 1905, who was horrified to discover that the Australian Constitution allowed statutes to be declared unconstitutional: '[t]hat is a novelty to me. I thought an Act of Parliament was an Act of Parliament and you cannot go beyond it. . . . I do not know what an unconstitutional act means' (*Webb* v. *Outrim*, 1907). Dicey's icon of parliamentary sovereignty was the apparent intellectual base for the modern Conservative Party.

Lord Birkenhead consolidated the Conservative position. Appeal judges were 'the handmaidens of the legislature'. That might be thought the role model for his successors from Dilhorne to Mackay. When one encounters, therefore, the Woolf and Laws approach, with an appeal to fundamental law, there is a clash with both the Labour and Conservative traditions, and one can see this by looking at the speeches of the Labour Chancellor in waiting—Lord Irvine—as well as those of Lord Mackay.

Lord Mackay has set his face against a Bill of Rights—along with other members of the Conservative administration—on the ground that it would undermine parliamentary sovereignty. While Mackay has been relatively calm about the judges' EU decisions which he has argued are only one British statute read in the context of another British statute, he is hostile to the Woolf thesis that Parliament is constrained by fundamental laws. Perhaps not surprisingly, however, it is Lord Irvine who has sounded the most serious warning notes. He has recently reminded judges that judicial review is subject to 'the democratic imperative' and that 'courts are, in relative terms, ill-equipped to take decisions in place of the designated authority'. 'An interventionist approach to judicial review for error of law may, in part, undermine the *raison d'être* of the system of specialist administrative tribunals, which are intended by Parliament in most cases to replace, and not merely to supplement, the decision-making powers of the court.'[60]

With respect to the central government, the Irvine position is even firmer: '[t]he courts may not decide either on the validity or desirability of legislation. . . . The legislative supremacy of Parliament is not merely a legal concept, a principle of the common law, recognised by the decision of the courts. . . . It is Professor Hart's "ultimate rule of recognition"'

---

[60] Lord Irvine of Lairg (1996, 59). Recently, however, there appears to have been some rapprochement between Lord Irvine and Laws J. See especially Lord Irvine's introduction to Laws J's' 1996 Mishcon Lecture. In his introduction, Lord Irvine ascribes the disagreement partly at least to his training in Moral Philosophy at Glasgow with its Kantian flavour and Sir John Laws' classical training as an Aristotelean. Irvine argues the need for 'a fuller communitarian critique of the classic liberal notion of the autonomous moral agent, on the basis that the individual can only be fully comprehended within the context of communities'. Irvine clearly favours the European Convention on Human Rights, passed by Parliament, over an independent Bill of Rights with judges as arbiters of those rights. It may perhaps be asked why judges will not treat the former as a species of the latter.

The Human Face of Law

(Irvine, 1996, 61–2). 'The idea that an Act of Parliament could be held invalid by the judges became obsolete when the supremacy of Parliament was finally established by the Revolution of 1688.'[61] Lord Irvine has therefore disassociated himself from Mr Justice Laws' views that, where fundamental human rights are involved, the *Wednesbury* test may be weakened (Irvine, 1996, 64–6). He is clearly uncomfortable with the *Pergau Dam* case (1995):

The soundness of a development in the context of an overseas aid statute requires evaluation and that should be for the Secretary of State not the court. ... The courts should take care to abstain, under the mantle of construction, from elevating what is, in truth, a mere relevant consideration into a or the purpose of a statutory provision, thus curbing a valuable and legitimate facet of administrative autonomy.[62]

Lord Irvine has, however, conceded that under Community law there is 'a species of fundamental law' and he attributes *Pepper* v. *Hart* to the 'spillover effect' of EU law. With respect to Woolf and Laws, with whom Lord Irvine associated Mr Justice Sedley and Sir Robin (now Lord) Cooke, President of the New Zealand Court of Appeal, Lord Irvine said:

Of these suggestions four things must be said. First, they are contrary to the established laws and constitution of the United Kingdom and have been since 1688. Second, many would regard as inconceivable, on the part of any Parliament which we can presently contemplate, any assault on the basic tenets of democracy which might call for the invocation of the judicial power claimed. ... I have to wonder whether it is not extra-judicial romanticism to believe that judicial decision could hold back what would, in substance, be a revolution. ...

Third, the danger with any extra-judicial claim of right to review the validity of any Act of Parliament is that to many it smacks of judicial supremacism. The role and significance of the judiciary in our society will be hugely enhanced if the European Convention on Human Rights is incorporated by Parliament into our law. ... The traditional objection to incorporation has been that it would confer on unelected judges powers which naturally belong to Parliament. That objection, entertained by many across the political spectrum, can only be strengthened by fears of judicial supremacism.

Fourth, it has to be made plain that those judges who lay claim to a judicial power to negate Parliamentary decisions, contrary to the established law and uses of our country, make an exorbitant claim ... it is our constitutional imperative of judicial self-restraint which must inform decision making in public law.[63]

[61] 'The Judiciary: Public Controversy', Lord Irvine, H.L. Debs. (5th Ser.), vol. 572, col. 1255.
[62] Lord Irvine, 'Judges and Decision-Makers', 69. On this see reaction by David Pannick QC, 'Why Judges Cannot Avoid Politics', *The Times*, 7 November 1995.
[63] Irvine, 'Judges and Decision Makers', 76–8. See 'Judges' Claims Criticised by Labour Law Chief', *Independent*, 17 October 1995; 'Labour Law Chief Attacks Judges' Supremacy Claim', *The Times*, 26 October 1995. 'I regard as equally unwise a number of recent extra-

With Lord Bingham now as Lord Chief Justice,[64] his attitude to parliamentary sovereignty may be reassuring to both Labour and Conservative. At the 1994 Pilgrim Fathers' Lecture in Plymouth, he said: '[i]f Parliament were clearly and unambiguously to enact, however, improbably, that a defendant convicted of a prescribed crime should suffer mutilation, or branding, or exposure in a public pillory, there would be very little a judge could do about it—except resign.' (Bingham, 1994) Moreover, Conservatives at least can take heart from another stance of the new Chief, suggesting caution about direct attacks on the Home Secretary for his penal policy. Bingham comes from the more intellectual wing of the Bar and appears sceptical about the robust Taylor views, based on the enthusiasm of the Circuiteer. The Bingham view is that, while the Howard proposals are undesirable, they fall within the legitimate purview of the legislature—and that judicial observations should therefore be at least somewhat muted. As he put it, while he shared the concerns about Howard's policy for mandatory sentencing and reducing judicial discretion, he did not share the concerns about the constitutional issues. 'As Parliament can prescribe a maximum penalty without infringing the constitutional independence of the judges, so it can prescribe a minimum.'[65]

In the long term, then, just as it will be necessary to welcome judicial activism where appropriate, it will be necessary to accept judicial restraint where appropriate, and the public arguments are beginning to develop. While Lord Goff has said of the role of politics and the role of judges, 'although I am well aware of the existence of the boundary, I am never quite sure where to find it', Lord Mustill said, in the *Firemans Case*,[66] the attacks on the Home Secretary's powers 'push to the very boundaries ... the distinction between court and parliament established ... in 1688'. In addition to his constitutional arguments, Lord Mustill has been gradually spelling out an articulate and sophisticated view of judicial restraint. In *South Yorkshire Transport* (1993) he set out to ensure

judicial statements by distinguished judges that in exceptional cases the courts may be entitled to hold invalid statutes duly passed by Parliament. This causes ordinary people not only to believe that judges may have got over and above themselves but that perhaps they are exercising a political function in judicial review cases instead of simply upholding the rule of law'; Lord Irvine, 'The Judiciary: Public Controversy', H.L. Debs. (5th Ser.), vol. 572, col. 1255.

[64] 'Bingham to Succeed Taylor as Lord Chief Justice', *Independent*, 17 May 1996; 'Shake-up in Top Law Jobs Offers Prospect of Radical Pairing', *The Times*, 17 May 1996.

[65] 'Bingham Finds No Fault with Minimum Prison Sentences', *The Times*, 27 February 1996. See also 'The Protection Paper' (leader), *The Times*, 4 April 1996.

[66] See also Lord Keith, who thought that to grant relief would 'represent an unwarrantable intrusion by the court into the political field and a usurpation of the function of parliament'. *R.* v. *Secretary of State for the Home Department, ex parte Fire Brigades Union* (1995, 513).

that *Wednesbury* was not used as covert substantive due process. He dissented in *R.* v. *Brown* (1994), believing that it was not the role of the courts to invent a new crime to cover consenting adults indulging in sado-masochistic practices. In *White* v. *Jones* (1995) he took the cautious approach, justifying his refusal to hold a dilatory solicitor liable to a disappointed potential legatee, with an elegant blend of policy reasoning and scepticism about the extension of *Hedley Byrne* v. *Heller.*

In extrajudicial writing he has distinguished 'liberal' and 'conservative' judicial work and noted, ascerbically, 'this banality of discourse is encouraged by some judges who long to talk to the press and to appear on television'.[67] He has doubted whether judicial filling of gaps in the law 'is constitutionally desirable and whether the judges have the right qualifications to perform the task'. After labelling judicial styles classical, neo-classical, and romantic, he has argued the pendulum theory of judicial creativity and restraint:

If judicial law-making has come to seem too conventional, so that the growth of the law is stunted, a more free approach to the exploitation of legal materials becomes tolerated and even encouraged. But if this is seen as going too far, with judicial creativity too wild and unpredictable, informed opinion creates a force in the opposite direction, tending to impel judicial methods back towards the norm. The result is a slow but repeated oscillation of judicial methods [Mustill, 1996].

(b) The Public Debate

There is thus not one clash between the judges and the politicians, but a series of clashes. On the one hand, while it is fair to generalize about the views of the leading judges, as Mr Justice Holmes said, 'to generalise is to omit'. In certain constitutional areas, the new Lord Chief Justice will urge caution. In a more general way, Lord Mustill is articulating what is essential as judges move more into the centre of the political arena, namely a generalized rationalization of judicial restraint. The judges being creative in traditional common law areas may well be commended; it may well be 'constitutional' for judges to develop a right to privacy;[68] judicial review is vital to ensure fairness in society now that it seems that Parliament is largely ineffective in controlling executive discretion in individual cases; decisions on the EU and its form of supremacy have been handed to the judiciary by Parliament; and the enforcement of the

---

[67] It is said that Lord Mustill is now unwilling to take part in legislative debates in the House of Lords.

[68] The power of the courts to do this has now been mooted by Lords Bingham and Hoffman, but doubted by Lord Irvine. 'The Judiciary: Public Controversy', H.L. Debs. (5th Ser.), vol. 572, col. 1259. Lord Wilberforce, however, thought 'privacy is one of those areas where it may be appropriate for the judge to take a hand': *ibid.,* col. 1267.

European Convention, if not a Bill of Rights, may well be added to its responsibilities. At the same time, direct attacks on the government policies involving sentences are likely to justify complaints that the judges have moved over the line from the judicial to the political, if judges claim some constitutional prerogative for such attacks. Judicial claims to be guardians of fundamental laws are likely to be met with understandable hostility as a breach of the traditions of parliamentary supremacy.

The Government is surely not without fault. Andrew Le Seuer has recently argued that the Conservative Government—and particularly the Home Secretary—has gone out of its way to provoke the judicial-review dispute: '[t]he debate itself is a part of a government strategy for coping with judicial review.' He argues that some government departments have been ignoring their own legal advice in fighting judicial-review cases, because it puts the Conservative Government in the position of arguing the policies it knows will appeal to Archie Bunker and Essex Man, while the judges look wet and subversive (Le Seuer, 1996, 8, 10). Certainly the Home Secretary and even the Prime Minister have said things about judges which might be thought to violate *Erskine May's* injunction against 'reflections on a judge's character or motives' or 'language disrespectful' of the judiciary. The Home Secretary was heard to say of Dyson J: '[t]he last time this particular judge decided against me, which was in a case which would have led to the release of a large number of immigrants, the Court of Appeal decided unanimously that he was wrong.'[69] Not very shocking; but deviating from the traditional norm, particularly as leading counsel for the Government had already advised against an appeal.[70]

The temptations are clear. In defence of the judges, Ferdinand Mount argues that 'the Renaissance of judicial review is a healthy reaction, not a gratuitous interference. The judges have moved in to remedy the deficiencies of an over-mighty, over-whipped, single chamber parliament' (Mount, 1996, 31). *The Economist* has claimed that the growth of judicial review has had 'less to do with a new generation of supposedly activist judges eager to expand their power than with the vastly expanded reach of Government itself' (*The Economist*, 1995, 22). At the same time, the main disputes over judicial review and Michael Howard's penal policy may have put the judges in a political position from which it will be difficult for them to extricate themselves—at least in a way that allows judicial independence and the separation of powers to grow intelligently.

Writing of the two most important cases in 1994, *Pergau Dam* and the *Criminal Injuries Board*, Alan Watkins said: '[p]rogressive persons

[69] 'Today', BBC Radio 4, 29 September 1995.
[70] See also Leader, 'Judge Over Your Shoulder: Modern Courts and the Modern Politician', *The Times*, 17 October 1995.

approve the courts' judgments because they disapprove of the two ministers' actions and of the Government generally. But what would Mr
Robin Cook say if the courts prevented him, as Foreign Secretary, from
donating money to what a Labour Cabinet considered a worthy cause?'
(*Independent on Sunday*, 13 November 1994) Others pointed out that
whatever pleasure Labour was taking in the judges' activities in judicial
review, they had not enjoyed the work of judges in *Laker* (1977) and the
Grammar School (1977) cases. And the problem was put in a slightly different way by Andrew Marr in his *Ruling Britannia*:

Senior judges have enjoyed the popularity and power which judicial review and
the rise of European law has given them; talking privately one senses that they are
fully aware of their upward mobility in the British system. But it is not so long
since the judiciary's name was mud after the Guildford Four and Birmingham Six
miscarriages of justice. In future, where they seem out of touch, or silly, they will
find themselves pilloried and criticised, by politicians as well as the media, more
openly and harshly than they are accustomed to. In the fluid, ever-changing
'marketplace of authority', where the judiciary is hawking its judgments so happily, no authority is sacrosanct or forever, it has to be earned, and earned again,
day after day, instance after instance. The more the judges overturn or challenge
the deeds of elected politicians, the more they themselves will come to be judged
in a similar way. [Marr, 1995, 289–90]

One can see what Marr means. The *Spectator* unleashed Boris
Johnson, the scourge of Brussels, in June 1995. Beginning with quotes
from a Cabinet Minister that the judges 'are socially corrupt', he
recorded the resentment among politicians that Nolan and Scott were
'now sitting in assize over the ministers and the entire political establishment'. Sir Ivan Lawrence QC MP, Tory backbencher and powerful
Chair of the Home Affairs Committee, was the authority for the remark
that

we've opened up a whole field and made it impossible for the Government to
make any decision without being challenged. . . . The alleged disaster in question
is the process of judicial review, which is demonstrably transforming the British
Constitution. . . . What is the point of being Her Majesty's Secretary of State for
Home Affairs, must be asking himself, if he cannot decide whether or not
Mohammed Fayed deserves a passport.

Not only did Johnson take issue with the Woolf thesis, but pointed at
Mr Justice Sedley, who had hailed 'a new culture of judicial assertiveness
to compensate for and in places repair the dysfunction of the democratic
process', as a former Marxist.[71]

---

[71] Sedley J had not endeared himself to ministers by describing the Government's consultation paper on night flights at Heathrow as 'devious and deeply unattractive' and 'a far-
rago of equivocation'. 'Air Transport 2: Noisy Flights', *Economist*, 11 November 1995, 37.

Johnson explained the change of attitude, and willingness to court 'the public opportunism that attaches to those who espouse one side of the political debate or the other' to what one QC allegedly described as 'a change in the balance of the legislature and the quality of the judiciary'. These very able barristers, who no longer bothered with becoming MPs,

having been raised to the bench, and having made their pile as barristers . . . are trying to have their cake and eat it. They rejoice in the fancy new grounds for judicial review being imported from Europe . . . and . . . some of them relish the chance to engage in the political process. For these judges are no longer snaggle-toothed Wykehamists who think Gazza is a pop star. A new generation is coming up, and what especially enrages the Government is that their judgments tend to go in a liberal direction: if they are frustrated politicians, they sometimes seem to be frustrated Labour politicians. [Johnson, 1995, 8]

A few days later, Lord Taylor responded to the allegations in his Mansion House speech:[72]

In respect of Judicial Review, however, recent public and press criticism of the judiciary has moved beyond comment on the decisions reached and focuses increasingly on the legitimacy of the judges taking such decisions at all. If a judge strikes down the decision of a Minster, if a judge is appointed by the Government to investigate a matter of public concern, reports or is thought to be going to report adversely about individuals or groups within his terms of reference, cries are raised that he has got above himself. Phrases like 'power hungry' and 'frustrated politicians' are entering the commentators' lexicon. The suggestion seems to be that the senior judiciary have decided to mount a bloodless coup and to seize the commanding heights of the constitution.

. . . I have to assure you nothing could be further from the truth. The judges have no such ambition.

Three months later, Michael Howard gave his rabble-rousing speech at the Conservative Party Conference in October. Lord Chief Justice Taylor at once responded with a vigorous rebuttal. Hugo Young argued that Taylor should not have done it, but was driven to it by Howard's decision to 'take discretion from the judges and hand it over, incrementally year on year, to the party conference. . . . Since the Labour Party is terrified to do so, the LCJ steps forward as defender of the public interest.' Young went on, however, to castigate Lord Irvine who was 'to the civil law judges, what Michael Howard is, brutishly, to the criminal law judges. . . . He seems to be getting ready for office by waving the judges off his future turf. . . . What the judges, and the country will have to get used to is a more adversarial relationship between them and politicians, whoever is in power'.[73] With the Government anxious to evade part of

[72] Lord Taylor, speech, 'Lord Mayor's Dinner to H.M. Judges', 5 July 1995.
[73] Hugo Young, 'When Judges put Ministers in the Dock', *Guardian*, 17 October 1995.

the Nolan Report and individual ministers working to rubbish the Scott Report, the newspapers had a field day: 'Judges vs. the Government' was a typical example.[74]

In its news reporting *The Times* sensationalized the dispute, with one anonymous civil servant reported as saying that ministers were 'gunning for judges' since they were 'seen as the last bastion of the liberal establishment'. A judge was alleged to have said the Government was running 'a hate campaign . . . to pour poison on the views of the judiciary'. A Conservative MP saw Mr Justice Sedley's finding of a procedural flaw banning the visit of the Rev. Moon as a 'further example of the contempt with which some members of the judiciary seem to treat the views both of this House and the general public'. Mr Howard's deputy, Ann Widdecombe, was 'quite worried about the pronouncements of some of the judges who appear to think that there is a policy role to be adopted by some of the judiciary'.[75]

Lord Hailsham, the former Chancellor, opined: 'I think there is a danger at the moment of the judiciary entering into the field of the executive, but vice versa there are signs of the executive encroaching on the judiciary. They should both mind their steps.' Behind the scenes, however, one Minister expressed delight about Michael Howard's sentencing proposals: '[t]he judges will hate it. It'll be great. We're going to take them on. . . . It will be us against the judges and I have no doubt who the public will back.' Lord Lester, a Liberal Democrat, described the Tory attacks as 'ignorant, insolent and trumped up' and, sounding almost like Lord Goddard added: 'we have some of the finest judges in the world and for ministers to suggest they are partisan is a gross defamation' (Lightfoot and Prescott, 1995).

The next public embarrassment came from the Government when the Party Chairman, Brian Mawhinney, leaked one of the Lord Chancellor's Cabinet Briefing Papers to the political editor of the *Daily Telegraph*, who was led to believe that the document was about to be delivered as a speech by Lord Mackay. The document appeared to be a warning to the judges to toe the line. The flap led to a formal press release from the Lord

[74] 'It used to be easy to caricature the judges. They were reactionaries, they were Establishment, they never doubted the evidence of the police, they were so out of touch they didn't know who The Beatles were, and come hell or high water they would back a Conservative government. . . . In Britain, governments have been winning a smaller share of the electorate, and party loyalties have been weakening steadily for 30 years or more. Assuming people want somebody they can look up to and trust, there is a vacuum that judges have been able to step into.

The British judiciary has enhanced its capacity to do this by seeking to change, in the space of a few short years, virtually every negative element of the traditional judicial stereotype': Stephen Ward, *Independent*, 3 November 1993.

[75] Liz Lightfoot and Michael Prescott, 'Too Big for Their Wigs?', *Sunday Times*, 5 November 1995.

Chancellor saying 'I would never warn the judiciary not to overstep their powers by using judicial review to challenge ministerial decisions.' The situation had not been helped, however, by Sir Ivan Lawrence, announcing that 'we shall statutorily have to restrict judicial review.'[76]

So it went on. Lord Justice Rose predicted that tougher sentencing policies would lead to more murder—what incentive does the rapist have to leave his victim alive?[77] Lord Donaldson, the former Master of the Rolls, was outspoken in his attacks on the Government's sentencing policy.[78] The *Sunday Times*, the most inflammatory newspaper in the Murdoch group, said it all in an editorial entitled 'Howard Must Win':[79]

John Major and his ministers are at loggerheads with the judiciary as never before. . . . Mr Howard is viewed by many judges as an ambitious, right-wing populist who shamelessly plays on people's instincts on law and order. Tory MPs who support his stand regard most judges as privileged occupants of an ivory tower who have long forgotten whatever they knew of life outside their comfortable security perimeter. . . . Judges would be foolish to assume too high a degree of public respect. . . . Much rests on the outcome of Howard v. the Judges. This time, as Labour leaders recognise, it is in the public interest that Mr Howard wins.

(d) Where Will the Story End?

As Harold Wilson taught us, a week is a long time in politics. But we know that there has to be an election by the spring of 1997 and, presumably, there will be a Labour win, although we have seen the pollsters wrong before. Presumably, however, Lord Irvine will soon be Lord Chancellor and, since he is more conservative than Lord Mackay, particularly on professional matters, there is likely to be less friction with the judges. Lord Irvine will presumably be anxious to emphasize the role of Lord Chancellor as head of the judiciary (and protector of the judges and the legal system), rather than his role as politician and member of the executive. Similarly, as Lord Bingham moves over to be Chief Justice, one can expect fewer public conflicts over penal policy and a dampening down of hints of judicial resort to fundamental law.

It will not be all plain sailing, however. Lord Irvine, if he does become Lord Chancellor, while he will be even less sympathetic than

[76] 'Judges Warned to Keep in Line', *Daily Telegraph*, 7 December 1995; LCO, Press Notice, 7 December 1995 ('Lord Chancellor Corrects Erroneous *Daily Telegraph* Article'); 'Lest Ye Be Judged', leader, *The Times*, 8 December 1995; 'Major Urged to End Cabinet Feud', *Sunday Times*, 10 December 1995; 'The Indignity of It', *Economist*, 16 December 1995.
[77] 'Tougher Jail Terms "Mean More Murder"', *The Times*, 1 February 1996.
[78] e.g. 'Howard's Proposals "Depress Judges"', *Independent*, 8 April 1996.
[79] 'Howard Must Win' (leader), *Sunday Times*, 10 March 1996.

Lord Mackay towards notions of fundamental law, will also be less enthused about some of the developments in judicial review. Nor are members of the Labour Cabinet likely to feel any better about having judges intervening in what the judges may regard as a procedural matter, but the politicians are likely to think of as a substantive one. Lord Irvine will not welcome comments that the judges are helping to restore a balance in democracy.[80] At the same time, Labour will find it difficult to curb judicial review by statute,[81] as demanded by Tory backbenchers. Equally, because of the party's formal commitment to the EU, it will presumably be committed to continuing the power of the European Court in Luxembourg and, if Parliament incorporates the European Convention on Human Rights, those of the European Commission and Court of Human Rights in Strasbourg.

This latter move will presumably go through, but, as even Lord Irvine realizes, it will give greater powers and status to the judges. In fact, the new administration is likely to be pulled in various different directions. In the end, the incorporation of the European Convention on Human Rights may be opposed by some Labour backbenchers, as well as most Conservatives, since it will involve a significant transfer of parliamentary sovereignty to the court[82]—in short it will make the House of Commons less important. (We should not minimize the constitutional significance of constantly reducing the power of the Lower House, especially as the Lords increasingly appears as a grand quango.) At the same time, Lord Irvine has said the courts will handle any constitutional issues raised by devolution to Scotland (*The Times*, 10 February 1996)—another potential clash for law and politics. On the other side, however, Labour penal policy is likely to be more in the direction of detection than punishment—although even that is far from certain.[83] Nevertheless, Lord Irvine has made it clear that, while Mr Howard gives every indication of

playing politics with the administration of Justice, . . . if Parliament were to legislate for these proposals it would be neither unconstitutional nor prejudicial to

[80] 'I regard as unwise observations off the bench by eminent judges that the courts have reacted to the increase in the powers claimed by government by being more active themselves, and adding for good measure that this has become all the more important at a time of one-party government. It suggests to ordinary people a judicial invasion of the legislature's turf': 'The Judiciary: Public Controversy', H.L. Debs. (5th ser.), vol. 572, col. 1255.

[81] Lord Irvine has made a commitment not to: *ibid.*, col. 1256.

[82] Lord Wilberforce recently put it dramatically: 'we have to face up to the fact that if we bring the European Convention on Human Rights or any Bill of Rights into operation, that will extend the power of judges and not restrain it because judges will be called upon to give interpretations to all sorts of vague expressions which are inevitably used in Bills of Rights, and which are found in the European Convention and which are really policy decisions': *ibid.*, col. 1267.

[83] 'Crime and Punishment', *Economist*, 8 June 1996, suggesting that Labour is terrified of appearing soft on crime.

the independence of the judiciary. Parliament is free to fix both minimum and maximum sentences. To claim that judicial independence is as a result threatened is to confuse.[84]

The judges may find the new administration as tough as the old.

The judges, however, will need to do some clear thinking and to work out strategies. The new Government may well want to take the advice of *The Economist* (1995): '[t]he best answer to current rows is a proper separation of powers in Britain.' The Lib–Lab think tank, the Institute for Public Policy Research, has already produced a version of a written constitution which deconstructs the office of Lord Chancellor and establishes the judges as closer to the American system of a co-equal branch of government (IPPR, 1991). Certainly, the politicians will have to think carefully how the inevitably increasingly powerful judges should be appointed and treated.

Whether the judges are capable of taking a strategic position is open to doubt. Lord Browne-Wilkinson has already put the case for the court system to be run by the judiciary, subject only to funds voted by Parliament (Browne-Wilkinson, 1988). This, in principle, would be similar to the situation in the United States where, for instance, this spring, Congress has been questioning the federal judges on why they spend so much on judicial conferences ('boondoggles' says Senator Grassly, Republican of Iowa). Meanwhile Senator Cohen, Republican of Maine, has called for a moratorium on building new courthouses and Senator John McCain, Republican of Arizona, has called for an Inspector-General position within the Administrative Office of the Federal Courts. Gilbert Merritt, Chief Judge of the Sixth Circuit, is concerned about the 'very intense scrutiny' in Congress and 'the generally negative attitude' towards the judiciary on Capitol Hill that borders on name-calling. It all sounds faintly familiar. Fortunately, the Chair of the Judicial Budget Committee is the talented and politically astute Richard Arnold, Chief Judge of the Eighth Circuit, who hides his prep-school provenance under an Arkansas accent. He purports to enjoy questions from Members of Congress: '[t]here's always been an inherent tension among the three branches of government. It is part of the constitutional plan. . . . And there's certainly nothing wrong with them questioning how we spend our money. That's part of their duty' (*ABA Journal*, 1996, 24). Is Lord Browne-Wilkinson's Oxford background ready for this?

If a clearer separation were to occur, *The Economist* (1995) would argue that the judges should be more vigorous, not less, in judicial review, and a great deal more civil-libertarian in dealing with a Bill of Rights. Again, however, the cost would be high. *The Economist* shares the

---

[84] 'The Judiciary: Public Controversy', H.L. Debs. (5th Ser.), vol. 572, col. 1256.

view that there would have to be an end of law lords sitting in the House of Lords. As *The Economist* puts it 'if the judiciary is to act as an effective check on overweening government, it should be untainted by direct involvement with either the legislature or the executive'. Equally, however, Lord Bingham must be right in constitutional terms when he says:

However, ill-conceived his ideas—similar measures have had little impact on the United States—Mr Howard has a perfect right to propose them. Sentencing policy is not the preserve of the judiciary, but a legitimate matter for public debate. Judges should be heard on the subject; but they should be only one voice among many.

As the judges expand in some political areas they need to retrench in others. The time may well have come, for instance, for the judiciary to decide that it will no longer undertake political enquiries. What Sir Richard Scott's enquiry suggests is that such matters, whatever the dangers, are best left to Parliamentary Select Committees, which should be given broader subpoena powers. Where judges may still perform a useful public service would be in disasters or factually complex enquiries like Aberfan or BCCI. Deciding wage claims or getting governments out of tricky political situations should not be the responsibility of the judicial branch. As Lord Simon said recently: 'every time that a judge is called upon to conduct such an inquiry, he is embroiled in a controversial issue and his detachment may be compromised. Indeed, the reputation for detachment of the judiciary as a whole may be compromised.'[85]

If a greater separation of powers is actually to take place, there will have to be a more open arrangement for choosing judges. While judges have been much more willing to think the unthinkable, and to take more power, through judicial review, or demand more power, by urging the implementation of the European Convention on Human Rights, they have, led by Lord Mackay, steadfastly resisted all changes—such as those suggested by Justice (1993)—that the judiciary be chosen in a more open manner. Moreover, it may be that the judiciary will have to reconcile itself, if not to a political element in its choice, at least to a more political selection process. Until well into this century the choice of law lords was assumed to be a political one, whether it was the Scottish Liberal Lord Shaw or the Irish Conservative Lord Atkinson. Yet it is arguable that many of the more successful appointments, during the generally barren judicial years, were of those with some political experience, such as Lords Somervell, Reid, and Dilhorne. It would not be so ahistorical to move back in that direction. Lord Kilmuir said he would take into account service in the House of Commons in making judicial appointments. It was a promise that was not fulfilled, and the accepted view in

---

[85] 'The Judiciary: Public Controversy', H.L. Febs. (5th Ser.), vol. 572, col. 1282.

the profession is that such failure was desirable. Perhaps the professional view is, however, wrong. Many believe that Denning's Report on Profumo and Scott's on Arms to Iraq would have been more persuasive if those judges had had more experience of government and politics. It is not a view that can be dismissed out of hand.

Politically, too, it may be necessary to make a token gesture to those from whom power is being taken. Just as it might help if the judges were more politically experienced, the more powerful the judges become the more the public and politicians will be interested in their political views. When Israel was established in 1948, with essentially a British judicial system, the Constitution provided that the judiciary should be chosen by an apolitical Judicial Commission. As the Supreme Court of Israel has moved, however, further into the centre of political controversy, taking on such matters as the exiling of political dissidents to Lebanon, the Knesset demanded representation on the Commission. In South Africa, Nelson Mandela had argued that the President should choose the Constitutional Court. The Constitutional Convention rejected that, so that its members are now chosen by the President, but then are subject to review by the Senate. (This is a system confirmed by the recent Constitutional Convention.) For a court that has already outlawed capital and corporal punishment, such a review system, coupled with hearings, may be singularly appropriate. Certainly the German Constitution Court provides similar safeguards, with half its members chosen by the Bundestag and half by the *Länder*. As the Court in Karlsruhe, however, has moved to address such issues as the right to send German troops to Bosnia, has struck down mandatory crucifixes in Bavarian schools, and has just been faced with the relationship of the Basic Law to the new anti-immigration law, the political involvement in the choice of judges may be strengthened still further.

If the judges—or others—were to press for a clearer and cleaner separation of powers in Britain, some similar system of checks and balances would be needed. While the English judicial mind is understandably horrified by the US Senate judicial hearings on Robert Bork or Clarence Thomas, they are an important part of giving democratic legitimacy to unelected judges, who go on to give decisions which the public understandably regards as political. Moreover, in the day-to-day work of the Senate Judiciary Committee, such investigations play an important role in asking questions about judgment[86]—for instance, should Mr Justice Breyer have remained a member of Lloyd's while he sat as a judge of the First Circuit—or can a judge who belongs to a club that

[86] A Bipartisan Commission under Lloyd Cutler is currently examining methods of streamlining appointments to the Federal bench: *International Herald Tribune*, 17 May 1996.

discriminates against women be appointed to the federal bench, which is responsible for enforcing equal protection and sex-discrimination legislation. At the time of the promotion of Mr Justice Morris Arnold, brother of the Chief Judge, to the Eighth Circuit Appeals Court, Senator Joseph Biden, Democrat of Maryland, and the Chair of the Judiciary Committee, required Judge Arnold—whose Arkansas accent hides not merely a prep school background, but a Yale College one as well—to resign from the Athenaeum in London.[87] That may be a portent of the future if English judges really are to implement (and strengthen) Article XIV of the European Convention—although a Conservative MP has recently opined that in England the commitment one makes to the Committee of the Athenaeum may take precedence over any judicial enforcement of the European Convention.

The time has come for the judges to be outspoken about what they see as their role. It is time too for the politicians to admit that the country needs help to establish individual rights—question time and even the expansion of parliamentary committees leaves a great deal to be desired in terms of effective control. It is irrelevant to praise or attack judges unless their role is clarified and articulated. It is time too for academic lawyers to move away from a formal analysis of the independence of the judiciary and to develop a more effective rationalization for the role of the judiciary in a democracy. It is here that the future of socio-legal studies is so vital; the Oxford Centre could provide the leadership that is vitally needed. Such a development should bring with it sophisticated analyses of both judicial activism and judicial restraint, and might even justify a reconstructed constitutional role for the judicial branch.

REFERENCES

BOOKS, ARTICLES, ETC.

ABEL-SMITH, BRIAN, and STEVENS, ROBERT (1967), *Lawyers and the Courts: A Sociological Study of the English Legal System 1750–1965* (Heinemann, London).
—— and —— (1968), *In Search of Justice: Society and the Legal System* (Penguin Press, London)
AMERICAN BAR ASSOCIATION JOURNAL (1996), 'Court Spending Under Review', February, 24.
BARENDT, ERIC (1995), 'Constitutional Law and the Criminal Injuries Compensation Scheme' [1995] *Public Law*, 357.

---

[87] For the European Convention on Human Rights view of sexual (and other discrimination) see Art. XIV. Discussed by Fenwick (1994, 68 ff.).

—— (1995), 'Separation of Powers and Constitutional Government' [1995] *Public Law* 599.

BINGHAM, SIR THOMAS (1994), 'Anglo-American Reflections', First Pilgrim Fathers Lecture, Plymouth Law Society, 29 October.

BROWNE-WILKINSON, SIR NICOLAS (1988), 'The Independence of the Judiciary in the 1980s' [1988] *Public Law* 44.

—— (1992), 'The Infiltration of a Bill of Rights' [1992] *Public Law* 405.

CARTWRIGHT, T. J. (1975), *Royal Commissions and Departmental Committees in Britain* (Hodder and Stoughton, London).

DE SMITH, S. A., WOOLF, LORD, and JOWELL, J. (1995), *De Smith's Judicial Review of Administrative Action* (5th edn. (Lord Woolf and Jeffrey Jowell), Sweet and Maxwell, London).

FAIRLIE, HENRY (1963), *The Establishment*.

FENWICK, HELEN (1994), *Civil Liberties* (Cavendish, London).

GRIFFITH, J. A. G. (1991), *The Politics of the Judiciary* (4th edn., Fontana, London).)

HARTLEY, T. C., and GRIFFITH, J. A. G. (1981), *Government and Law* (2nd edn., Weidenfeld and Nicolson, London).

IPPR, (1991), *The Constitution of the United Kingdom* (Institute for Public Policy Research, London).

IRVINE OF LAIRG, LORD (1996), 'Judges and Decision Makers: The Theory and Practice of *Wednesbury* Review' [1996] *Public Law* 59–78.

JENKINS, SIMON (1995), *Accountable to None: The Tory Nationalisation of Britain* (Hamish Hamilton, London).

JONES, P. A. (1966), 'Rival Law Reformers', 110 *Solicitors' Journal* 733.

JOWITT, LORD (1948), 206 *Law Times* 318.

JUSTICE (1993), *The Judiciary in England and Wales* (Justice, London).

KERRY, SIR MICHAEL (1983), 'Administrative Law and the Administrators', *Management in Government* vol. 3.

LAWS, SIR JOHN (1995), 'Law and Democracy' [1995] *Public Law* 72–93.

—— (1996), 'The Constitution: Power and Principle', Mishcon Lecture (to be published in *Public Law*).

LE SUEUR, ANDREW (1996), 'The Judicial Review Debate: From Partnership to Friction', *Government and Opposition* vol. 31.

LESTER, ANTHONY (1986), 'Fundamental Rights: The United Kingdom Isolated?' [1986] *Public Law* 46–72.

—— (1995), 'The Mouse That Roared: The Human Rights Bill, 1995' [1995] *Public Law* 198.

MACKAY, LORD (1987), 'Can Judges Change the Law?', *Proceedings of the British Academy* vol. 73, 285.

MARR, ANDREW (1995), *Ruling Britannia* (Penguin Press, London).

MCCRUDDEN, J. C., and CHAMBERS, G. (eds.) (1994), *Individual Rights and the Law in Britain* (Clarendon Press, Oxford).

MOUNT, FERDINAND (1996), 'From Major to Maurras', *Prospect*, March, 31.

MULLAN, KENNY (1995), 'The Impact of *Pepper -v- Hart*', paper for colloquium on the House of Lords, University of Ulster, May.

MUSTILL, LORD (1996), 'What Do Judges Do?' [1995–6] *Sartryck ur Juridisk Tidskrift*, Nr 3, 622.

NEW LAW JOURNAL (1995), 'The Dangerous Criminals Act, 1996', 20 October, 1529.

REID, LORD (1968), 'Law and the Reasonable Man', *Proceedings of the British Academy* 193.

RISKE, HENRY J. (1996), 'A Duffel Bag of Controversy for Judge', *American Bar Association Journal*, May.

SEDLEY, SIR STEPHEN (1991), 'Charter 88: Wrongs and Rights', *Citizenship*.

—— (1994), 'The Sound of Silence: Constitutional Law Without a Constitution', 110 *Law Quarterly Review* 270.

—— (1995), 'Human Rights: A Twenty First Century Agenda' [1995] *Public Law* 386.

STEVENS, ROBERT (1983), *Law and Politics: The House of Lords as a Judicial Body 1800–1976* (Weidenfeld and Nicolson, London).

—— (1993), *The Independence of the Judiciary: The View from the Lord Chancellor's Office* (Clarendon Press, Oxford).

—— (1994), 'On Being Nicer to James and the Children', *New Law Journal*, November 25, 1620.

—— and YAMEY, BASIL (1965), *The Restrictive Practices Court: A Study of the Judicial Process and Economic Policy* (Weidenfeld and Nicolson, London).

STEYN, LORD (1996), 'Does Legal Formalism Hold Sway in England?', Presidential Lecture, The Bentham Club (to be published in *Current Legal Problems*).

TAYLOR, LORD (1995), 'Lord Mayor's Dinner to H.M. Judges', speech, July 5.

WILSON, HAROLD (1994), 'The County Court Judge in Limbo', *New Law Journal*, October 21.

WOOLF, LORD (1995), 'Droit Public—English Style' [1995] *Public Law* 57.

NEWSPAPER AND OTHER ARTICLES

The Economist:

'Air Transport 2: Noisy Flights', 11 November 1995.
'The Failure of the Criminal Justice Act', 11 November 1995, 29.
'Politicians v. Judges', 16 December 1995, 22.
'The indignity of it', 16 December 1995.
'Crime and Punishment', 8 June 1996.
'Crime in America', 8 June 1996.

The Guardian:

Hugo Young, 'When Judges put Ministers in the Dock', 17 October 1995.
'Court Deals new Blow to Howard', 11 November 1995.
'Legal Threat to Rail Sell-off', 25 November 1995.
'Judge Voices Concern at Asylum Benefits Cost', 27 March 1996.

The Independent:

Stephen Ward, 3 November 1993.
'Judge tells Howard to Reconsider Masari Case', 6 March 1994.
'Judges' Claims Criticised by Labour Law Chief', 17 October 1995.

'Howard's Proposals "Depress Judges"', 8 April 1996.
'Judges Told to Dispel "Aloof" Image', 16 April 1996.
'Who do These Guys Think They Are? Judges have made Themselves Darlings of the Left by Repeatedly Challenging the Government, But are They Really Fit to Play Politics?' 17 April 1996.
'Howard Furious at Bulger Ruling', 3 May 1996.
'Mr Howard is Playing with Fire' (editorial), 3 May 1996.
'Bingham to Succeed Taylor as Lord Chief Justice', 17 May 1996.
'Howard splits Cabinet on Europe', 18 May 1996.
'Lord Taylor Denounces Howard Reforms', 24 May 1996.
P. W. Davies, 'Howard Punished in Each Sentence', 24 May 1996.

The Independent on Sunday:

13 November 1994.
5 November 1995.
31 March 1996.

International Herald Tribune:

'Amid Political Flak, Judge in Drug Case Reverses View', 3 April 1996.
'Jail's no Frills Reality Enlightens a Judge', 3 April 1996.
'Clinton Chides Foes Over Judge' 4 April 1996.
17 May 1996.

The Sunday Times:

Liz Lightfoot and Michael Prescott, 'Too Big for their Wigs?', 5 November 1995.
'Major Urged to End Cabinet Feud', 10 December 1995.
'Howard Must Win' (leader), 10 March 1996.
Comment, 10 March 1996.
'Gentlemen of the Jury Find Harman "The Terrible" Guilty', 12 May 1996.

The Times:

5 March 1994.
Leader, 'Judge over Your Shoulder: Modern Courts and the Modern Politician', 17 October 1995.
'Labour Law Chief Attacks Judges' Supremacy Claim', 26 October 1995.
'Judicial Moonshine: Howard was Right to Refuse Moon Entry to Britain', 3 November 1995.
'Mackay Seeks Curb on European Court', 9 April 1996.
David Pannick QC, 'Why Judges Cannot Avoid Politics', 7 November 1995.
'Ministers Criticised in Iraq Arms Case', 8 November 1995.
'Lest Ye Be Judged', Leader, 8 December 1995.
'Tougher Jail Terms "mean more murder"', 1 February 1996.
10 February 1996.
'Bingham Finds no Fault with Minimum Prison Sentences', 27 February 1996.
'Britain Urges Cut in Power of Euro Court', 13 March 1996.
26 March 1996.
'The Protection Paper' (leader), 4 April 1996.

'Judges Claim Howard is on the Wrong Side of the Law', 4 April 1996.
'Repeat of Serious Crime will Carry Automatic Life Sentence', 4 April 1996.
'Judge "Reluctantly" Denies Housing for Asylum Seekers', 19 April 1996.
'Howard Acted Unlawfully over Bulger Sentences' 3 May 1996.
'Ill Health Forces Chief Justice to Retire Early', 3 May 1996.
'Ruling Further Weakens Minister's Powers over Judiciary', 3 May 1996.
'Balance in Justice' (leader), 4 May 1996.
'Shake-up in Top Law Jobs Offers Prospect of Radical Pairing', 17 May 1996.
Lord Taylor, 'Howard's Production Line Justice', 23 May 1996.
'Judging Judges: Bingham and Woolf Should be Welcomed, But Act Warily' (leader), 25 May 1996.
Simon Jenkins, 'The Minister and Judge', 25 May 1996.

Others:

Boris Johnson, 'The Long Arm of the Law', *Spectator*, 17 June 1995.
Sunday Express, 1 October 1995.
Daily Mail, 2 November 1995.
Daily Express, 4 November 1995.
This Week, 4 November 1995.
'Chief's Warning over HK Bill', *Financial Times*, 19 November 1995.
'Judges Warned to Keep in Line', *Daily Telegraph*, 7 December 1995.
LCO Press Notice, 7 December 1995 ('Lord Chancellor Corrects Erroneous *Daily Telegraph* Article').
'Sitting in Judgment' (editorial), *Financial Times*, 24 May 1996.
The Observer, 26 May 1996.

CASES

Anisminic Limited v. *Foreign Compensation Commission* [1969] 2 AC 147.
Candler v. *Crane Christmas* [1951] 2 KB 164 (CA).
Dorset Yacht v. *Home Office* [1970] AC 1004.
Earl Fitzwilliam's Wentworth Estates Co. v. *Minister of Housing and Local Government* [1952] AC 362.
Franklin v. *Minister of Town and Country Planning* [1948] AC 87.
Garden Cottage Foods v. *Milk Marketing Board* [1984] 1 AC 130.
Goodwin v. *United Kingdom*, Human Rights Law Report, *The Times*, 28 March 1996.
Hedley Byrne v. *Heller* [1964] AC 465.
Jacobs v. *LCC* [1950] AC 361.
Laker Airways v. *Department of Trade* [1977] QB 643 (1976).
Morrison v. *Olsen*, 487 US 654 (1988).
Pepper v. *Hart* [1993] AC 593.
R v. *Brown* [1994] 1 AC 212.
R v. *Monopolies and Mergers Commission*, ex parte *South Yorkshire Transport* [1993] 1 WLR 23 (HL).

R v. *Secretary of State for Employment,* ex parte *Equal Opportunities Commission* [1995] 1 AC 1.

R v. *Secretary of State for Foreign and Commonwealth Affairs,* ex parte *World Development Movement Limited* [1995] 1 WLR 386, (DC) (The *Pergau Dam* case).

R v. *Secretary of State for the Home Department,* ex parte *Fire Brigades Union* [1995] 2 AC 513.

R v. *Secretary of State for Transport,* ex parte *Factortame,* [1991] 1 AC 604 and [1992] AC 85.

Ridge v. *Baldwin* [1964] AC 40.

Secretary of State for Education and Sciences v. *Thameside Metropolitan Borough* [1977] AC 1014 (CA and HL).

Smith v. *East Elloe RDC* [1956] AC 736.

Webb v. *Outrim* [1907] AC 81.

White v. *Jones* [1995] 2 AC 207.

Youngstown Sheet & Tube Co. v. *Sawyer* 343 US 579 (1952).

Index